Mastering Roblox Coding

The unofficial guide to leveling up your Roblox scripting skills
and building games using Luau programming

Mark Kiepe

BIRMINGHAM—MUMBAI

Mastering Roblox Coding

Group Product Manager: Rohit Rajkumar

Publishing Product Manager: Ashitosh Gupta

Senior Editor: Aamir Ahmed

Senior Content Development Editor: Rakhi Patel

Technical Editor: Shubham Sharma

Copy Editor: Safis Editing

Project Coordinator: Sonam Pandey

Proofreader: Safis Editing

Indexer: Subalakshmi Govindhan

Production Designer: Shankar Kalbhor

Marketing Coordinator: Elizabeth Varghese

First published: August 2022

Production reference: 1290722

Published by Packt Publishing Ltd.
Livery Place
35 Livery Street
Birmingham
B3 2PB, UK.

ISBN 978-1-80181-404-1

www.packt.com

Contributors

About the author

Mark Kiepe is an experienced Roblox Programmer and Game Designer with over six years of experience. He has contributed to several successful Roblox games. Besides these achievements, he is also the Co-Owner of a Roblox Game Studio called Sarcastic Studios, with games such as Pet Store Tycoon and Dream Island. Mark has contributed to more than 150 million play sessions across all games at the time of writing.

Mark started as a self-taught programmer on Roblox. What he learned on Roblox helped him in college. He currently attends a University of Applied Sciences in The Netherlands, where he studies Software Development.

I want to thank my parents and brother for their continuous support while writing this book. I am incredibly grateful for the amount of motivation they have given me.

Thanks to everyone at Packt for helping me write this book. It means the world to me.

I want to give a special thanks to Aamir and Rakhi. I have learned so much about writing through your feedback that I would have never accomplished without them.

I would also like to thank Vaideeshwari for giving me the opportunity to write this book.

About the reviewers

Arnav is a UGC Event Organizer working alongside DevRel for Roblox. He has hosted numerous events on the platform and is also an experienced developer. He has over 350 million contributed visits. He is known by his Roblox username "AceDevArnav" and is also the owner of Ace Developing Studios , which is one of the rising studios on Roblox with its upcoming games and UGC items.

Mir Ali was born in Karnataka, India on June 4, 1983. He studied in Dubai, UAE. He learned programming from the 6th Grade, starting with Q Basics, and then learning C and C++. He found these boring, as there was no way to visualize the results, and nothing made sense to him back then, except for a few ways of using IF statements, and a calculator that he made himself. He also couldn't quite figure out what the lines of code were, when they started, or what OOP was. He therefore called it quits on programming and took a journey into building Gaming PC and servers. He then did his Cisco certification and went deeper to configure ATM relays and protocols, and calculate IP addresses for big companies.

Years passed by, and he became a father. One day his son came to him and asked, "Father, what is LUA, and how do you make an obby with rotating parts?" Mir Ali saw hope in his son's eyes, and got up, opened Roblox, and started teaching him. He taught his son IF conditions and operators, which were easy until he reached a syntax ":", which was from OOP. This was when lightning struck him, and everything made sense. He taught his son a full library of LUA, including Bitwise operations, and made his own Physics and network library from scratch. Now, instead of his son, Mir Ali teaches corporate giants such as Accenture, Vodafone, Microsoft, and Walmart, to name but a few. He teaches the procedural generation of buildings and environments with complex floors, and ways to enter them. He also teaches Deep math and trigonometry, such as how to make your own Math library. Last but not least, Mir Ali teaches M.L and A.I.

To my children, Arafath, Ishan, Hasanath, and Saleyhath, who motivated me.

Table of Contents

2

Writing Better Code

3

Event-Based Programming

Part 2: Programming Advanced Systems

4

Securing Your Game

5

Optimizing Your Game

6

Creating User Interfaces for All Devices

7

Listening to User Input

8

Building Data Stores

9

Monetizing Your Game

Part 3: Creating Your Own Simulator Game

10

Creating Your Own Simulator Game

Preface

Roblox is a platform with over 47 million **daily active users** (**DAU**). Everyone can play and create games or experiences, as Roblox likes to call them, for free. Experiences on Roblox are all made by other users. This means that you are playing experiences made by other gamers! Anyone can start creating on Roblox for free even if you have no experience. Roblox provides an easy-to-use game engine that allows you to create and publish a simple game in less than five minutes for you and your friends to hang out. All the technical aspects of hosting your game and allowing others to join your experience are handled by Roblox for free as well. In addition, players can purchase items in your experience. When they do this, Roblox gives you a percentage of this sale. And the best part is that you can get paid real-life money when many users buy your in-game items.

Who this book is for

Roblox players, beginner programmers, and those that are able to program in different programming languages who wish to learn how to program games in Roblox. You will take your programming skills to the next level with advanced concepts simply and effectively. Besides programming, you will learn how to use Roblox Studio to the fullest. Basic knowledge of Roblox is recommended before starting with this book. A short refresher is provided for those who have not used Roblox for some time.

What this book covers

Chapter 1, Getting Up to Speed with Roblox and Luau Basics, will take a look at Roblox and Roblox Studio. We will start by creating a few simple scripts that explain the fundamentals of programming in Roblox Luau.

Chapter 2, Writing Better Code, will take the knowledge of chapter one to the next level. We will start reducing duplicate code using functions, tables, loops, and modules.

Chapter 3, Event-Based Programming, will explain how to program based on events. This greatly reduces the amount of unnecessary loops. Besides this, we can base certain actions on changes happening to our game.

Chapter 4, Securing Your Game, will cover the Server-Client model. We will learn what both are and how to let them communicate with each other while making sure all of this happens securely.

Chapter 5, Optimizing Your Game, will explain the fundamentals of optimizing your game. You will learn about StreamingEnabled, animations, and Tweens.

Chapter 6, Creating User Interfaces for all Devices, will teach you everything about **graphical user interfaces (GUIs)**. In addition, you will know how to ensure they scale properly on phones, tablets, desktops, and even consoles.

Chapter 7, Listening to User Input, will teach you how to listen to user input when players try to interact with your game. You will learn how to listen to input from phones, tablets, desktops, and even consoles.

Chapter 8, Building Data Stores, will explain how to make player progress save even when players decide to rejoin your game at a later moment. You will learn many ways to ensure your data stores are safe.

Chapter 9, Monetizing Your Game, will explain how to start monetizing your game. You will learn how to implement and sell game passes, developer products, premium benefits, and third-party sales.

Chapter 10, Creating Your Own Simulator Game, concludes the book by combining many of the previously mentioned systems into one game. You will get tips on how to solve problems that you might face while programming a game.

To get the most out of this book

You will need to have an active Roblox account and have the Roblox Player and Roblox Studio installed on your computer. All code examples in this book have been tested on a Roblox version from July 2022 using Windows 11. However, they should work in future releases of Roblox too.

Software/hardware covered in the book	Operating system requirements
Roblox Player	Windows 7 and higher.
	Mac 10.10 and higher.
	iOS 9 and higher.
	Android 5.0 and higher.
Roblox Studio	Windows 7 and higher.
	Mac 10.11 and higher.
Microsoft Xbox Controller	

It is recommended to own a Microsoft Xbox controller or an Xbox One and newer to test user input in Chapter 7, Listening to User Input

If you are using the digital version of this book, we advise you to type the code yourself or access the code from the book's GitHub repository (a link is available in the next section). Doing so will help you avoid any potential errors related to the copying and pasting of code.

Download the example code files

You can download the example code files for this book from GitHub at `https://github.com/PacktPublishing/Mastering-Roblox-Coding`. If there's an update to the code, it will be updated in the GitHub repository.

We also have other code bundles from our rich catalog of books and videos available at `https://github.com/PacktPublishing/`. Check them out!

Code in Action

The Code in Action videos for this book can be viewed at `https://bit.ly/3OEocEy`.

Download the color images

We also provide a PDF file that has color images of the screenshots and diagrams used in this book. You can download it here: `https://packt.link/2Zmph`.

Conventions used

There are a number of text conventions used throughout this book.

`Code in text`: Indicates code words in text, database table names, folder names, filenames, file extensions, pathnames, dummy URLs, user input, and Twitter handles. Here is an example: "Mount the downloaded `WebStorm-10*.dmg` disk image file as another disk in your system."

A block of code is set as follows:

```
function add(x, y)
     print(x + y)
end

add(5, 5)
```

When we wish to draw your attention to a particular part of a code block, the relevant lines or items are set in bold:

```
{
     ["class"] = "H1",
     ["id"] = 12345,
     ["name"] = "Lauren",
     ["times late"] = 0
}
```

Bold: Indicates a new term, an important word, or words that you see onscreen. For instance, words in menus or dialog boxes appear in **bold**. Here is an example: "In the **Output** frame, you can see the sum of the numbers we provided as arguments."

> **Tips or important notes**
> Appear like this.

Get in touch

Feedback from our readers is always welcome.

General feedback: If you have questions about any aspect of this book, email us at customercare@ packtpub.com and mention the book title in the subject of your message.

Errata: Although we have taken every care to ensure the accuracy of our content, mistakes do happen. If you have found a mistake in this book, we would be grateful if you would report this to us. Please visit www.packtpub.com/support/errata and fill in the form.

Piracy: If you come across any illegal copies of our works in any form on the internet, we would be grateful if you would provide us with the location address or website name. Please contact us at copyright@packt.com with a link to the material.

If you are interested in becoming an author: If there is a topic that you have expertise in and you are interested in either writing or contributing to a book, please visit authors.packtpub.com.

Share Your Thoughts

Once you've read *Mastering Roblox Coding*, we'd love to hear your thoughts! Scan the QR code below to go straight to the Amazon review page for this book and share your feedback.

https://packt.link/r/180181404X

Your review is important to us and the tech community and will help us make sure we're delivering excellent quality content.

Part 1: Start Programming with Roblox

This part of the book will focus on the basics of Roblox development. It is highly recommended to have a basic knowledge of Roblox and Roblox Studio. However, everything is explained from the ground up using best practices that will help you throughout the rest of the book. This is still addressed as it is a must-have for the rest of the book.

This section comprises the following chapters:

- *Chapter 1, Getting Up to Speed with Roblox and Luau Basics*
- *Chapter 2, Writing Better Code*
- *Chapter 3, Event-Based Programming*

1

Getting Up to Speed with Roblox and Luau Basics

In this chapter, we will start by looking at what Roblox is. Once we know this, we will learn about Roblox's programming language. Then, we will proceed to understand the basics of this programming language, such as the data types and variables. We will learn how to perform unique operations on each of these data types, such as math operations. Once we know this, we can slowly increase the complexity of our scripts. We will then use conditionals to take our scripts to another level. Conditionals allow us to change the behavior of our code depending on data. Finally, we will learn all about scopes. We will learn what they are and why it is crucial to keep them in mind while coding.

The following topics are covered in this chapter:

- Understanding Roblox and Luau
- Understanding and using data types in Luau
- Introducing variables
- Using conditionals
- Understanding scopes
- Exercises

By the end of this chapter, you will have learned how to make scripts in Roblox. In addition, you will know how to make simple systems in your experience.

Technical requirements

To start programming with Luau, you need access to a device with internet access. This can either be a Windows or a Mac device.

You need to download the following software:

- Roblox Player
- Roblox Studio

To install Roblox Player and Roblox Studio, please follow the steps in the following article:

`https://en.help.roblox.com/hc/en-us/articles/204473560`

All the code examples for this book can be found on GitHub at `https://github.com/PacktPublishing/Mastering-Roblox-Coding`.

The CiA video for this chapter can be found at `https://bit.ly/3ORIwT7`.

Understanding Roblox and Luau

In this section, we will start by looking at what Roblox is and what makes it unique. Then, once we understand the fundamentals of Roblox, we will learn about the programming language that Roblox uses for its games.

Roblox is a really popular platform for children around the world. This is because they can play almost anything they want. With over 24 million different experiences, as Roblox likes to call their games, you can be almost anything. You can become a pirate, be the king of a castle, escape prison, or stop players from escaping. The possibilities are endless. And the best part is that it is completely free to play. According to Roblox, in September 2021, 47 million unique users played Roblox daily. Once you have created your account in a few clicks, you are ready to join an almost unlimited and constantly increasing supply of experiences.

Creating an account

To make an account on Roblox, visit this link:

`https://www.roblox.com/signup`

Roblox is unique because other players make all these experiences that you can join. Anyone that creates a Roblox account can create a game. Besides Roblox Player, which allows you to join experiences, there is an additional application called Roblox Studio. With it, you can create your very own experiences.

At the time of writing this book, there are over 9.5 million developers on the platform. These developers can unleash their creativity and make anything they want. Roblox also takes care of all the complex and technical tasks involved in hosting and maintaining games. All you have to focus on is creating the game. Roblox takes care of the rest. The platform ensures that your game shows up for your friends, and makes sure that you and your friends can join the game. They make sure that you can report people who misbehave and bans them from the platform. These systems, among many more, are provided by Roblox. If you make games using other game engines, these systems all have to be made and operated by you. This is pricey and very time-consuming.

However, this is not even the best thing that Roblox has to offer. You are also able to monetize the experiences! Roblox has a virtual currency called **Robux**. Players can purchase this with real-life money. When they convert their money into Robux, they can use it throughout the entire site to buy different things. This varies from purchasing clothing for your avatar to purchasing in-game perks for any game you like. When someone purchases something in your game, you get 70% of the sale. You can convert this earned Robux currency back to real-life money. This is called the **Developer Exchange** program. Some developers on the platform make over 1 million USD yearly!

Most of the time, these developers do not work alone. There is usually an entire team of developers that work on a game. These developers have different roles. The most common developers on a team are programmers and builders. However, other developer roles can be added if teams start to grow. In addition, other developer roles exist, such as animators, modelers, UI designers, music composers, and possibly even more. As previously stated, this book is about the programming aspect of Roblox. So, let us learn more about the programming language that is used to code Roblox experiences.

Introducing Luau

Roblox uses a programming language named **Luau**. Luau is an easy-to-learn yet powerful programming language. Luau is a heavily modified version of the programming language called Lua.

Because Roblox Luau has a relatively low learning curve compared to other programming languages, it is an ideal programming language to start with, especially for younger developers or aspiring developers. Even if you have no interest in creating experiences on Roblox, this is still a great starting point. In general, programming in any language teaches you how to think logically. This is useful even when you are not programming. By the end of this book, you will be able to analyze coding problems, split them into smaller tasks, and overcome them.

If you are hoping to program in other languages in the future, this is an excellent place to start. You might argue that if you know how to program in one programming language, you can program in all of them. This is because programming is basically instructing a computer on what to do. When nothing is specified, the computer does nothing. The only real difference between most programming languages is **syntax**. The syntax is basically what words you type in your script. Most programming languages use the same words. However, the syntax may differ.

Becoming a master in Roblox game development gives you a head start when programming in other languages. Regardless, before switching to another language, you first have to master Luau. It takes a lot of practice to understand everything in this programming language fully. This will most certainly be very stressful and confusing. Therefore, this book slowly progresses in complexity. A basic understanding of Roblox is highly recommended.

Roblox is a unique platform where people can play millions of experiences for free. The amazing thing about these experiences is that other users on the platform make them. There are a lot of different roles that you can have as a developer on the platform. You can be a modeler, animator, graphics artist, and even a programmer.

In the next section, we make our very first Luau script.

Understanding and using data types in Luau

In this section, we will learn everything about data types in the Luau programming language. Let us start with the absolute basics. Programming is all about data. This data can be anything:

- The player's in-game money
- The spot the player is in during a race
- The number of criminals that they have arrested, or anything else

All of the mentioned examples are numbers. The in-game money can be 100, the race position can be 1, and the number of criminals arrested can be 3. In programming languages, we have numbers too. **Numbers** are our first data type.

Internal usage of the number data type

Sometimes, a difference between **numbers** and **integers** is made in the documentation. In Luau, integers are a part of the number data type. Internally, Luau changes between doubles, floats, and integers. If the documentation specifies an integer, you can expect the number to be stored as an integer internally. When a number is documented, it is internally stored as `float` or `long`. Do not worry if this does not make sense. This knowledge is not required in Luau.

We can have more than just numbers. We can also have sentences. Examples of sentences can be the player's username, a roleplay name, or a chat message. These sentences are called **strings** in programming. Strings are our second data type.

You might have heard of our third data type, a **Boolean**. A Boolean is `true` or `false`. People often say programming is about ones and zeros, and true or false. There are no other possibilities for Booleans.

In the following sections, we will learn about all the things that we can do with these three data types. We will start by making a script to test out these data types.

Creating a script

Well, great to know about these three data types, but what can we do with them? Let us start Roblox Studio and follow these steps:

1. First, create a new baseplate. Because the book assumes basic knowledge of Roblox and Roblox Studio, this is not explained.
2. Once created, open **Explorer**. It should be visible by default. Search for something named **ServerScriptService**. You can see this in *Figure 1.1*.

3. Right-click on **ServerScriptService**, select **Insert Object**, and add a new script. Make sure you did not accidentally make a `LocalScript` instance. The difference is explained later in the book. Once added, the **Explorer** window should look like this:

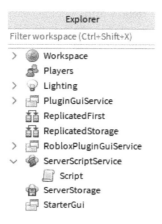

Figure 1.1 – Your created script

4. Double-click on the script you just created and you should see the following code in the script:

```
print("Hello world!")
```

Now we know how to create a new script. In the next section, we will run this script and see its output. Besides that, we dive deeper into what this piece of code means.

Hello, world!

In Roblox, all scripts start when the game begins. We can start the game by pressing the **Play** button in Roblox Studio. Once pressed, you will see your character appear in a running game. The game still looks empty, as if nothing has happened. There are no scripts in a baseplate game by default, and the one we just added does not do much. However, it definitely does something. It just cannot be seen by a regular player. We have to open the **Output** frame to see this. To open the **Output** frame, click on the **Output** button under the **View** section, as shown here:

Figure 1.2 – Opening the Output frame

> **Shortcut**
> Instead of pressing the **Play** button, you can press the *F5* key on your keyboard.

Once we open the **Output** frame, we see **Hello world!**. Looking back at the script we created, we see the **Hello world!** part. However, one part is missing in **Output**; this is the print () part. That is because print () is a function in Luau. Functions are explained later in this book. For now, remember that print () prints the text that we passed to it in **Output**.

We should zoom in on the **Hello world!** part of the script. We previously learned that programming languages have sentences. They are called **strings**. **"Hello world!"** is a sentence; therefore, it is a string. We can see that this is a string because it is surrounded by quotation marks ("). Roblox Studio also recognizes this as a string and gives it a particular color in your script.

Strings can be anything; go ahead, change the **Hello world!** part to something else, your name, for instance. Your script could look like this:

```
print("James")
```

If we run the script that you just edited and open **Output**, you should see your name appear.

We now know what **Hello world!** means and what the print () function does. Consider the print () function as your trusted friend that will keep you informed on what your script is doing. This will help us to understand what is going on and come up with solutions for possible errors. In the following section, we will look at printing numbers.

Numbers

There are more data types than just strings. You can print all of these data types. Let us start with numbers. Change your name to any number, for instance, the number eight. Your code might look like this:

```
print("8")
```

If we run the game and open the **Output** frame, we can see that the number you chose was printed instead of your name. Did you notice how the number is the same color as the string in the Roblox Script Editor? As mentioned before, something that defines a string is quotation marks. The quotation marks are still there in the preceding code, but the correct number was printed. This is because the programming language still sees your number as a string. This is possible because numbers can be stored in strings too.

If we want to make sure our number is recognized as an actual number, we have to remove the quotation marks around the number. So, for example, your code could look like this now:

```
print(8)
```

Notice how the color of the number changed in the Script Editor?

In this section, we learned how to print numbers and how to differentiate numbers from strings in our code. In the following section, we dive deeper into the unique things we can do with numbers, such as math operations.

Math operations

If we run the code, we see the same line in **Output**. So, why bother making it a number instead of using strings? We previously mentioned that they are different data types. Different data types also serve different purposes. Numbers can do things that strings cannot do. Let us take a look at it from an easy perspective. In school, you used numbers during math. What did you use numbers for? Most likely to calculate things. You were adding, subtracting, dividing, multiplying, and whatnot. These are all things that you can do with numbers, whereas you probably had to write many sentences in English class. The chance is meager that you used multiplication on sentences.

Now that we have a number in our script, let us do some math. We start by adding the number three to the already present number eight. We do this by using the + operator. Try doing this for yourself. The script should look something like this:

```
print(8 + 3)
```

If we run the script, it should say 11 in **Output**. Congratulations, you have now made your first math operation in a programming language. However, we can do many more math operations. Try subtracting (-), multiplication (*), and dividing (/).

> **Tip**
> You can add multiple print statements below each other to create a larger script that performs multiple math operations at once.

Your code should look something along these lines:

```
print(8 + 3)
print(8 - 3)
print(8 * 3)
print(8 / 3)
```

We have two more math operations that you can do on numbers: exponentiation (^) and the modulus (%). For exponentiation, you can do something like this:

```
print(8 ^ 3)
```

The result of this operation would be 512. What happens when using this operator is that the number before the caret (^) gets taken. The number gets multiplied against itself as many times as stated behind the exponentiation operator. To make this easier, the operation 8 ^ 3 translates to 8 * 8 * 8. If we switched the numbers and made the operation 3 ^ 8, the operation would be translated to 3 * 3 * 3 * 3 * 3 * 3 * 3 * 3.

The last operator is the modulus. This operator is commonly forgotten, especially in Roblox programming. The modulus operator (%) looks like a percentage; however, it is absolutely not a percentage. Do not let it fool you. The modulus operator takes the number behind the % and multiplies itself as many times as it fits into the number before the operator. Once it reaches its limit, it subtracts its total multiplication from the first number and gives back the difference. This operator is not easy to understand.

To visualize it, we take the operation 8 % 3. The number three fits twice into the number eight, because three times two is six, and six is lower than eight. If we multiplied it once more, we would do it three times, resulting in nine. Nine does not fit in eight. Then, we subtract six from eight. What is left is two. The operation 8 % 3 would return two. This is probably the most confusing operator so far. It is confusing because it is never taught during math in school.

> **Tip**
> You can try to make a few operations in your script to test this operator yourself.

We learned how to program math operations. In the next section, we will learn how to combine these math operations in one statement.

Combining math operations

Something that the modulus operator can do is combine different operators in one statement. We can do this too. Execute the following code:

```
print(8 + 3 * 2)
```

Notice how the result of this execution is 14? During math, you probably learned about the order of operations. The order of operation tells you in which order you have to execute each operation. In programming languages, we do the same. Luckily, it is the same order of execution taught in school. You probably heard of PEMDAS to help you remember this order. **PEMDAS** stands for Parentheses ((and)), Exponents (^), Multiplication (*), Division (/), Addition (+), and Subtraction (-).

In the previous code example, the three times two is executed first. If we wish to execute 8 + 3 first, we can surround it with parentheses. Your code would look like this:

```
print((8 + 3) * 2)
```

The outcome of this math operation changed from 14 to 22. Do you see that there are two opening parentheses directly behind `print`? Having multiple parentheses is allowed because the programming language understands that the first closing parenthesis, which is the one behind the three, is the closing one for the last opening parenthesis.

We learned that we could do math operations with the number data type in the previous two sections. Previously, we learned about multiple data types. The following section explores the unique things that we can do with strings.

String concatenation

Now that we know how to use numbers, we can look at some of the cool things that you can do with strings. We cannot do math with strings, but we can combine them. When combining strings, we use an operator called **concat**, short for **concatenate**. This operator is two dots directly after each other (..). Let us try to concatenate two strings in a `print` function.

First, we need two strings. As shown in the following code snippet, this is done by enclosing the message with quotation marks ("). Then, you can choose the sentence that you wish to insert into your string yourself. For this example, two strings that say "Hello" and "Laura" are combined:

```
print("Hello " .. "Laura ")
```

Hello Laura appears as one string in **Output** when you start your game. This operator is the only thing that you must use to concatenate two strings into one. Now, try to concatenate three strings into one by using what we just learned. As you might have guessed, it looks like this:

```
print("Hello " .. "Laura " .. "! ")
```

Now we know how to concatenate different strings into one. The following section teaches you about another unique thing with strings: escape characters.

Escape characters

If you want to display a string on the next line, we can add another print. Most of the time, this is not the ideal solution. There is a simple alternative for this. It is called a **new line escape character**. The name sounds more complicated than it is. This new line escape character looks like this: \n. In the same script, suppose that we want to greet someone and tell them it is Monday on a new line. Your code should look something like this:

```
print("Hello Peter!\nToday is Monday! ")
```

If you run this script, **Hello Peter!** appears on the first line, and **Today is Monday!** appears on the second one.

Another practical escape character is for a horizontal tab. This escape character mimics the same thing that happens when you press the *Tab* button on your keyboard in your preferred text editor. This **horizontal tab escape character** looks like this: \t. This escape character comes in handy when creating lists. For example, printing a shopping list can look something like this:

```
print("Shopping List:\n\t- Bread,\n\t- Butter,\n\t- Milk.")
```

> **Tip**
> Try to play around and create a few strings yourself. Practicing with strings is the best way to ensure you know how to use them.

We now know how to use the **new line escape character** and the **horizontal tab escape character**. Previously, we also learned how to concatenate two strings into one, and before that, we learned about the unique things that we can do with numbers. But what if we wanted to combine both data types into one print statement? The following section teaches you how to do this.

Casting data types

What if we tried to combine a string and a number in the same print statement? For example, we have a string that contains the number four and the number five. If we want to concatenate them, our script looks like this:

```
print("4" .. 5)
```

For some reason, this statement prints 45 in **Output**. Behind the screen, the system sees a string trying to concatenate with a number. We know that strings can contain numbers. The system knows it too. So, Luau helps you out and turns the number 5 from your statement into a string that contains the number 5. Then, the two strings merge into one. As a result, we get an output of 45.

Instead of letting the programming language figure out how to solve this issue, we can specify that we want to do it this way. We can use more functions besides the print() function. One of them is tostring(). This function turns any data given between the parentheses into a string:

```
print("4" .. tostring(5))
```

If we change the operator from a concatenation (..) into an addition (+), do we get an error?

```
print("4" + 5)
```

This code gives an error. This error occurs because you used an operator used for numbers on a string. But did we not use an operator used for strings on a number too? Yes, however, we know that strings can contain any character, including non-numbers. Therefore, Luau cannot change a string into a number unless we specifically tell it to do so.

We can tell Luau to change a string into a number using the `tonumber()` function. For example, if we put the string that contains the number four into this function, our operation should work:

```
print(tonumber("4") + 5)
```

As expected, the result of this operation is 9 and not 45. However, what if we wanted to use the same string and number and get the result 45, while having both pieces of data as numbers and not strings? We can combine the `tonumber()` and `tostring()` functions to achieve this:

```
print(tonumber("4" .. tostring(5)))
```

One disclaimer when using the `tonumber()` function: this function does not always work. For example, if your string contains anything other than numbers, this function returns something called `nil`. Nil means nothing. If you are not careful and your function returns `nil`, and your script does not expect this, an error occurs. Try it for yourself:

```
print(tonumber("a5")) -- This will return nil.
print(tonumber("a5") + 6) -- This will give an error.
```

Now we know how to cast strings into numbers and the other way around. We also learned how to combine numbers and strings in one statement. In the next section, we look at Booleans, our final data type.

Booleans

Last but not least, we can also print Booleans. Printing Booleans is not very difficult on its own. However, there are some operations for Booleans as well. For now, let us start with printing `true` and `false`. Your script should look something like this:

```
print(true)
print(false)
```

When printing Booleans, there are no quotation marks (`"`) required. The reason for this is because Booleans are not strings. Instead, they are a unique data type. In the next section, we look at logical operators.

Logical operators

Similar to the other data types, there are some operators that we can use to create operations with Booleans. These are the and (`and`) and the or (`or`) operators. There are no special characters for these operators; they are just text. However, these operators do have a particular name. They are called **logical operators**.

Let us start with the and operator. To keep it simple, let us use a real-life example of asking your parents for permission to purchase a new game. The answers your parents give are Booleans, yes (`true`) or no (`false`). Because we are talking about the and operator, you need both your parents to agree on purchasing a new video game.

If both of your parents allow you to purchase the video game, you have two `true` Booleans. Our expected result is `true` if we put this into our `print` script:

```
print(true and true)
```

Roblox Studio might warn you when you enter this script because it already knows that the result is always `true`. Therefore, the statement is redundant. However, to help you understand these operations, you can ignore the warning and execute the script.

Now, one of your parents says no. Make a script where one of the Booleans is `false`, and execute it. Your script can look like this:

```
print(true and false)
print(false and true)
```

Both of these statements return `false`. As mentioned before, we are using the and operator. Using this means both parents in our scenario have to agree. If either does not agree, the deal is off.

As you might have guessed, when both your parents do not agree, and both Booleans are `false`, the statement always returns `false`. However, for the sake of understanding, you should try the script regardless. Your script can look something like this:

```
print(false and false)
```

Besides the and operator, Booleans also have the or (`or`) operator. For the or operator, we use a different example. Imagine you are selling something online. You only need one buyer that wants to pay the price you have set. In the best-case scenario, both customers are interested in purchasing your item. Your script looks something like this:

```
print(true or true)
```

The result of this is `true`. The only problem is picking which person you sell your product to. This problem, however, is not something you have to solve through coding.

Now, only one person agrees. So, the code looks like this:

```
print(true or false)
print(false or true)
```

Unlike with the and operator, these both return true. When selling an item, you do not need multiple sellers. One is enough to sell your item to. However, both would be false when there are no sellers at all. The sale cannot go through. Your code looks like this:

```
print(false or false)
```

We have now seen the logical operators that we can use on Booleans. It might seem pointless, but we will see why this is important in the *Using conditionals* section.

In this section, we learned all about data types. We learned about three different data types: numbers, strings, and Booleans. We learned how to print them to **Output** and about the special operations that we can do on them. We learned how to do math operations on numbers, how to combine strings, and how to use logical operators on Booleans. In the next section, we take these data types to the next level by using variables.

Introducing and using variables

Now that we know about the essentials of programming and data, we can start using this data to start doing things. In this section, we will learn about **variables**. We will learn what they are, what they are helpful for, how to update them, and how to improve the quality and readability of our code by using variables. Variables are all about temporarily storing your data somewhere. In Luau, the variables for all data types look the same.

To create a variable, follow these steps:

1. First, you define a variable by putting local into your script.
2. Then, you put the name of your variable. The name of the variable can be anything. Try to make your variable names as logical as possible, as it helps when the size of your script starts to increase.
3. Once your name is defined, you put an equal sign (=).
4. Finally, you can specify the data that you wish to store in this variable. You can see an example of a variable structure in the following code:

    ```
    local your_name_here = your data
    ```

You can consider variables as temporary boxes that store any data that you specify behind the equal sign (=) under a specific name. Now, if we want to store a name, for instance, Emma, in a variable, it looks like this:

```
local name = "Emma"
```

We learned that the quotation marks (") around a sentence define a string. You can see this is the case for the preceding example, which means we just stored a string in a variable that is named name.

Now that we know how to make a variable, let us continue to learn about some of the best practices when creating a variable in the following sections.

Lower and upper camel case

Variables can be named anything. However, it is custom to start your variable name with a lowercase letter. If your variable name consists of multiple words, the first letter of the first word is a lowercase character, and the first letter of each word after that should be a capital letter. There is no practical reason for this, and it is just for the readability of your code. Here are some examples of correct variable names:

```
local firstName = "Emma"
local randomNumbers = 125
local isThePlayerAFK = false
```

This way of naming variables has a name. It is called **lowerCamelCase**. This method of naming variables is not unique to Roblox or Luau. Many tech companies around the world use it. It is a good habit to teach yourself to do this from the start.

Besides the lower camel case, another "camel case" is good to know. This other camel case is **UpperCamelCase**. The first character is capitalized with this naming method instead of using a lowercase character. You primarily use the upper camel case method when naming scripts.

We now know how to name our variables correctly. In the next section, we will learn how to update the value of our variables.

Updating variables

Besides storing data, what can we do with it? Everything that you can do with the data you learned about. The only difference is that you can now use the variable's name instead of direct data, as shown here:

```
local firstName = "Alexander"
print(firstName)
```

> **Order of execution**
>
> Notice how we defined the variable before the print? The reason for this order is that the system reads the script line by line when the script gets executed. When it arrives at the line of the variable, it puts the variable into your computer's memory. If it gets to the print first, it tries to find the firstName variable in your memory. If the variable does not exist, it cannot be printed and gives an error. It is custom to put all of your variables at the top of the script to prevent this from happening.

The same output appears when you insert the string directly into the print function. However, when you have 10 different `print` statements that would all print **Alexander** and you wish to change Alexander to William, you only have to change it in one spot. The variable's value is the only thing that has to be changed for all prints to be automatically updated.

Let us take a better example. We have a number that starts at zero. We updated it five times. Each time we update the number, the number gets printed. We only use one variable for the number that we have. Your code can look something like this:

> **Disclaimer**
>
> The code you are about to see is imperfect, and we will improve it later. Methods for removing duplicate code are taught in *Chapter 2, Writing Better Code.*

```
local currentNumber = 0

print(currentNumber)
currentNumber = currentNumber + 1
print(currentNumber)
currentNumber = currentNumber + 1
print(currentNumber)
currentNumber = currentNumber + 1
print(currentNumber)
currentNumber = currentNumber + 1
print(currentNumber)
currentNumber = currentNumber + 1
print(currentNumber)
```

Let us take a look at the preceding code. First, we see a `currentNumber` variable that starts at 0. The first `print ()` puts the variable, with the value 0, in the **Output** frame. Then, it does something that we have not seen before. It takes the variable's name, puts an equal sign (=) behind it, states its name again, and does a math operation that adds one.

We start with what we know. We know how math operations work, and we know how variables work. `currentNumber + 1` is a math operation with a variable. We can assume that this works the same way as any other math operation. It takes a look at the variable's value, which is 0 for our current scenario, and then adds 1 to it. The result of this math operation would be 1. What Luau does behind the screen is change the line that we are executing to this:

```
currentNumber = 1
```

Hopefully, the statement that we have right now looks a bit familiar. It is not an exact match. However, you might recognize it from how we create variables. The only thing missing from creating a variable and our current code is the `local` part. We know that the `local` part is used when creating a variable. What if the statement that we have right now updates an existing variable to a new value? It would make sense. Just translate our current statement to something you can say out loud: "Current Number Equals One." The `currentNumber` variable now has the value of one.

Hopefully, analyzing the code helps you realize what to do when you do not understand the code that you just read. First, try to look for the parts that you understand and figure out the rest from there.

Now we know how to update the value of a variable. In the next section, we learn about a **best practice** when updating variables.

Removing magic numbers

Now that we understand the script from the previous section, we know how to make variables and update them. But, as we said previously, the code is not ideal. Previously, we had an example where we incremented the number by 1. However, what if for our current example we do not want to increment a variable by 1 but by 2? We have to change our code in so many places. We could have prevented this by making a second variable that would determine the amount by which we would increment our variable. An improved version of the code would look something like this:

```
local currentNumber = 0
local incrementValue = 2

print(currentNumber)
currentNumber = currentNumber + incrementValue
print(currentNumber)
currentNumber = currentNumber + incrementValue
print(currentNumber)
currentNumber = currentNumber + incrementValue
print(currentNumber)
currentNumber = currentNumber + incrementValue
print(currentNumber)
currentNumber = currentNumber + incrementValue
print(currentNumber)
```

This code does what we initially wanted to do. Now, if we want to change our increment value from 2 to 3, there is only one spot we have to change it in. Using a variable makes it much easier to maintain for the future. Besides that, the code is a lot more readable as well. Before, there was just a number in your code; we had no idea what the purpose of this number was.

The number we just removed from our script has a name in programming. It is called a **magic number**. Magic numbers are pieces of data used multiple times in your script and do not explain what they do or what their purpose is, just like the example we just had. To prevent the usage of magic numbers, we can introduce a variable. Using magic numbers when programming is considered a **code smell** and should be avoided.

There is an even shorter way of writing this code. Notice how you were writing the current number variable multiple times per line? We do this because we have to define the variable that we are updating and also to get the current value of this variable. We can change the equals sign (=) to an operator that assigns and adds (+=) as follows:

```
local currentNumber = 0
local incrementValue = 2

print(currentNumber)
currentNumber += incrementValue
print(currentNumber)
currentNumber += incrementValue
print(currentNumber)
currentNumber += incrementValue
print(currentNumber)
currentNumber += incrementValue
print(currentNumber)
currentNumber += incrementValue
print(currentNumber)
```

Our code works the same, and the only difference is that we no longer have to write the variable's name twice; we used it twice per line. Currently, we are using an operator that assigns and adds (+=); however, there are other operators like this for different math operations. For example, we also have one for assigning and subtracting (-=), assigning and multiplying (*=), and assigning and dividing (/=). Try using these new operators in a script similar to the one previously.

We just learned about a best practice to make our code more efficient while removing our magic number code smell. However, there is another best practice we can use to improve the readability of our code. The following section explains how to use constants in Luau.

Introducing constants

So far, we have made an immaculate script. However, we can do one more thing to improve the readability of this script. Most programming languages have something called **constants**. Constants are a special type of variable. The value of these variables is set once and can never be changed while running the script.

Previously, we said that the final thing was to optimize the script's readability. This is only for readability purposes because Luau does not have constants. However, constants have a unique method of naming. You learned to name variables by using the lower camel case method. For constants, you have to write the full name of the variable in capitals. When the name of your constant consists of multiple words, an underscore (_) is added to separate the different words; this is something we can do in Luau. This way, other programmers know that this variable never changes, even though it is technically possible.

In the example we used, we can find a candidate for a constant. The currentNumber variable gets constantly updated with a new value. This variable is not a candidate to become a constant. On the other hand, our other variable is an excellent candidate to become a constant. The variable only defines the amount that the currentNumber variable is incremented by. If we turn this variable into a constant, our script looks like this:

```
local INCREMENT_VALUE = 2
local currentNumber = 0

print(currentNumber)
currentNumber += INCREMENT_VALUE
print(currentNumber)
currentNumber += INCREMENT_VALUE
print(currentNumber)
currentNumber += INCREMENT_VALUE
print(currentNumber)
currentNumber += INCREMENT_VALUE
print(currentNumber)
currentNumber += INCREMENT_VALUE
print(currentNumber)
```

If our script had been a bit different, our constant might have changed back to a standard variable. If, halfway through the script, we wished to change our increment value from two to three, it would have to be a variable again. As you can see, introducing a constant depends on what you wish to achieve with your script, and you have to look into the future as well. Do you wish to allow your script to be modified so this might be possible in the future? If so, it might be a good idea to keep it as a variable.

As you can see, when and when not to introduce a constant is a vague area. It is perfectly fine if you wish to never use constants in Luau. After all, Luau does not even have the implementation of a constant, and it is just about readability.

> **Tip**
> When in doubt about introducing a constant, do not do so. In Luau, it is better to keep a standard variable than to have an incorrectly implemented constant. This book, however, uses constants when required from now on.

Now that we know how to use variables and constants, we are ready to take our coding skills to an even higher level. The next section teaches us how to make our code perform different actions depending on our data.

Using conditionals

In this section, we will level up our code and learn everything about **conditionals**. Conditionals allow us to perform different actions depending on the provided data. These different actions can be anything. We are allowed to program these actions ourselves. Here is an example script that prints something based on the player's position during a race:

```
local playerPosition = 1

if playerPosition == 1 then
    print("You are in the first place!")
end
```

The following text is printed in the **Output** frame when running this script: "**You are in the first place!**" However, when we change the value of the `playerPosition` variable to any other number, nothing appears in **Output**. The reason nothing appears is because of our `if` statement. To clear up any possible confusion, an `if` statement is a conditional.

Everything you place between the `if` and the `then` part gives a Boolean. Everything between `then` and `end` is executed when this Boolean gives `true`. If this is not the case, the code continues after the `end` statement.

Two things were just said to explain the `if` statement. We test to see whether this is correct in the following two sections.

Relational operators

We first said that everything between the `if` and the `then` statements has to return a `true` Boolean. We can confirm this by making a print statement. Execute the following code:

```
local playerPosition = 1
print(playerPosition == 1)
```

Notice how the result of this script prints `true` in **Output**? Now, if we change the value of our variable to two and execute the script, the result is `false`. It is `false` because we use the equal to (`==`) operator, a **relational operator**. When using a relational operator, the outcome is always a Boolean.

Equal to (==) is not the only relational operator that we have. The following is a list of all the relational operators that we have in Luau:

Operator	Name	Description
==	Equal to	The data on both sides of this operator has to match exactly. Example: 5 == 5 returns true, 5 == 6 returns false.
>=	Greater than or equal to	The number on the left side must be greater or equal to the number on the right side. Example: 10 >= 5 returns true, 4 >= 5 returns false.
<=	Smaller than or equal to	The number on the left side must be smaller or equal to the number on the right side. Example: 4 <= 5 returns true, 10 >= 5 returns false.
>	Greater than	The number on the left side must be greater than the number on the right side. Example: 5 > 4 returns true, 5 > 5 returns false.
<	Smaller than	The number on the left side must be smaller than the number on the right side. Example: 4 < 5 returns true, 5 < 5 returns false.
~=	Not equal to	Data on both sides of this operator cannot match. Example: 5 ~= 128 returns true, 128 ~= 128 returns false.

Table 1.1 – Relational operators explained

Now that we know how to make a simple if statement, we can increase the complexity by adding an else statement in our conditional. The next section explains how to do this.

if-else conditionals

The second thing that we said was that if the result of this relational operator comes back false, everything between then and end is skipped, and the script continues behind end. We can test this as well. We can put another print behind end and test whether it is executed, even when the result is false. Execute the following code:

```
local playerPosition = 1

if playerPosition == 1 then
    print("You are in the first place!")
end
print("Script completed.")
```

When we have our variable set to 1, both prints appear in **Output**. However, if we change the value of our variable to 2, only **Script completed.** ends up in the console.

Let us change our program. If a racer is in the top three, their position must be printed. If the racer is not in the top three, a motivational text is printed to support them. Let us try to implement this:

```
local playerPosition = 1
if playerPosition <= 3 then
    print("Well done! You are in spot " .. playerPosition
    .. "!")
end
print("You are not in the top three yet! Keep going!")
```

This code works, sort of. When we are in the fourth spot, the motivating text is printed. However, both messages are printed when we are in the top three. We can prevent this by making two if statements below each other. So, your code would look like this:

```
local playerPosition = 1

if playerPosition <= 3 then
    print("Well done! You are in spot ".. playerPosition ..
    "!")
end
if playerPosition > 3 then
    print("You are not in the top three yet! Keep going!")
end
```

This code works. It does what we want. However, there is a better way to do this. We also have an else option. Remember when we said that the code continues after end? There is an exception. If we add else before end, this part is executed first. When the code is false, the else section is always executed. Visualized, an if-else statement looks like this:

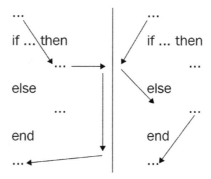

Figure 1.3 – An if-else statement visualized

Now that we know how an `else` statement works, let us **refactor** our code to use this instead. Refactoring code is changing how it looks while keeping the same functionality. Our refactored code looks like this:

```
local playerPosition = 1
if playerPosition <= 3 then
    print("Well done! You are in spot " .. playerPosition
    .. "!")
else
    print("You are not in the top three yet! Keep going!")
end
```

We have learned how to use the `else` statement. In the next section, we will learn about another statement that we can use in conditionals. This other statement is `elseif`.

Using elseif

This code looks a lot better. If we want another message for the players in spots four and five, this is possible. After all, they are almost there. We face another issue. We cannot add another `if` statement in an already existing `if` statement. Or can we? Let us take a look at this code:

```
local playerPosition = 1

if playerPosition <= 5 then
    if playerPosition <= 3 then
        print("Well done! You are in spot "..
        playerPosition .. "!")
    else
        print("You are almost there!")
    end
else
    print("You are not in the top three yet! Keep going!")
end
```

This code does exactly what we want. However, it looks confusing. Our first `if` statement checks whether the player's position is below five. Then, it checks whether the position is below three. Right, we already had this. There are just two `if` statements to get this now. Then, we get to the first `else` statement. The number has to be either four or five to even get here. Then, we reach our final `else`. This final `else` is where all the numbers larger than five end up. As you can see, the system works. It just requires a bit more time to understand what is going on.

There is a better alternative. We already know about `if` and `else`. There is a combination of this, `elseif`. An `elseif` statement could be placed after `if` and before `else`. Because `elseif` is also `if`, we can add another expression.

> **Tip**
> The expression is the part between `if`/ `elseif` and `then`.

Our code with `elseif` would look like this:

```
local playerPosition = 1

if playerPosition <= 3 then
    print("Well done! You are in spot " .. playerPosition
      .. "!")
elseif playerPosition <= 5 then
    print("You are almost there!")
else
    print("You are not in the top three yet! Keep going!")
end
```

This looks much better! At a simple glance, you can see exactly what this code does.

Before we came up with the solution to use an `elseif` statement, we tried using a **nested if statement**. In the following section, we take a deeper dive into these nested `if` statements.

Nested if statements

There is still a slight issue with our code. What if you accidentally change the player's position to zero? Or a negative number? As of right now, the system cannot handle this.

First, we must determine how many players there can be in a race to fix this problem. Let us say a race has a minimum of 1 player and a maximum of 8 players. This means that the player position has to be between those numbers. These numbers can be variables. As a matter of fact, they can even be constants. The minimum and the maximum number of players never change while the script runs.

Besides the new constants, there are multiple ways of implementing this feature. Here are two correct methods of implementing constants:

```
local MINIMUM_PLAYERS = 1
local MAXIMUM_PLAYERS = 8
local playerPosition = 1
```

```
-- Checking player's position
if playerPosition >= MINIMUM_PLAYERS and playerPosition <= 3
then
    print("Well done! You are in spot " .. playerPosition
    .. "!")

elseif playerPosition >= MINIMUM_PLAYERS and playerPosition <=
5 then
    print("You are almost there!")

elseif playerPosition >= MINIMUM_PLAYERS and playerPosition <=
MAXIMUM_PLAYERS then
    print("You are not in the top three yet! Keep going!")

else
    warn("Incorrect player position [" .. playerPosition ..
    "]!")

end
```

Let us take a look at this code. The first thing that we notice is the text behind - -. This is something that has not been mentioned yet. By using - -, you can make comments in your code. These comments do not get executed, but they help other developers when reading your code.

The second new thing is the warn() function used in the else statement. The warn() function is almost identical to the print() function. The only difference is that the color in **Output** turns orange. This is because you use this method to warn, as the name implies. When you see a warning in your **Output**, usually someone did something that the system prevented, such as having a wrong playerPosition in our case.

Something else that we have not seen before is the and operator in an if statement. When we learned that the true and true expression gives true, it probably did not feel like something substantial. However, we have the same thing in our if statement right now. So, it is essential to understand.

> **Tip**
>
> If you have forgotten how the and or the or operator works, it might be wise to reread the *Logical operators* section in this chapter.

The only thing that could be improved is the expression, which checks whether the position is higher than the minimum multiple times. Therefore, in this scenario, it is not an ideal solution. We can change this by having an `if` statement inside another one. Your code would look like this:

```
local MINIMUM_PLAYERS = 1
local MAXIMUM_PLAYERS = 8
local playerPosition = 1


-- Checking if the player's position is a valid number
if playerPosition >= MINIMUM_PLAYERS and playerPosition <=
MAXIMUM_PLAYERS then
    -- Getting correct message based on player's position
    if playerPosition <= 3 then
        print("Well done! You are in spot "..
        playerPosition .. "!")
    elseif playerPosition <= 5 then
        print("You are almost there!")
    else
        print("You are not in the top three yet! Keep
        going!")
    end
else
    -- The position of the player is not valid
    warn("Incorrect player position [" .. playerPosition ..
    "]!")
end
```

This example uses an `if` statement within an `if` statement. `if` statements within `if` statements are perfectly allowed. There is even a name for this. The `if` statement within the other statement is called a **nested if statement**. It is good practice not to have more than three `if` statements within each other. Later in the book, we will learn ways to reduce the amount of nested `if` statements, such as by using functions and loops. You can find this information in *Chapter 2, Writing Better Code*.

We now know how to use conditionals in our code properly. We can use `if`, `elseif`, and `else` statements. If you practiced yourself, you might have run into issues where certain variables were not accessible throughout your entire script. These variables were not accessible because of **scopes**. In the next section, we take a look at what these scopes are.

Understanding scopes

In this section, we will learn what **scopes** are and why you have to keep them in mind when coding. First, we will start by looking at how a new scope is made. Scopes are something you have already worked with; you just did not realize it. Every time we had an `if` statement, did you notice how the code before the end was spaced to the right? The reason for this spacing is because this section is a new scope. A quick note: spacing your code to the right does not create a new scope.

But what can we do with scopes? Scopes are not necessarily something that you can use but rather something you have to keep in mind. We have already seen a new scope being created when using an `if` statement. There are a lot more situations where scopes are created. The following code is something you can do for the sole purpose of creating a scope:

```
do
    print("New Scope")
end
```

When a scope starts, it executes the code within it. If there is another scope within an already existing scope, all of the data from the scope above is for the scope below. If there is data in a scope that the current scope is not in, you cannot access that data.

Scopes accessing certain data sounds really confusing. Here is an example that demonstrates it:

```
local outsideScopeData = "this is accessible everywhere"

do
    -- New Scope
    print(outsideScopeData)

    -- New data in this scope
    local insideScopeData = "This data is accessible in
    this scope."

    -- Printing in scope data
    print(insideScopeData)
end

-- Printing data outside of the scope
```

```
print(outsideScopeData)
print(insideScopeData) - This data does not exist
```

Our first variable is not inside of a scope. Therefore, the scope it is in is called the **global scope**. This section of your code is accessible everywhere in your code.

Next, we start our first scope. To test whether we can access the variable from the global scope, we have a `print` statement that prints the `outsideScopeData` variable. We can access this variable because your new scope is inside the global scope. Because our new scope is inside the global scope, all of the data that the global scope has, our new scope has as well.

Then, we create a new variable inside of our new scope. This data does not exist in the global scope. Inside our new scope, we print this new data using the `print()` function. We can do this because this data is inside the current scope and thus exists.

Our scope comes to an end. We can see this because of the `end` line. After this, we are back in the global scope. First, we try to print `outsideScopeData`. We can do this because this variable exists in the global scope. Then, we try to print a variable created inside a scope. However, printing this variable does not work. Printing this does not work because our current scope, the global scope, does not exist inside the scope where this variable has been made. Therefore, we cannot access the data from here.

What if we wanted to make the variable inside the scope and still print it inside the global scope? We can make a variable with no data inside the global scope. Then, we can set this empty variable to our desired value inside the new scope. This works because the variable is made in the global scope and set inside another scope. You can see this in practice in the following code snippet:

```
local outsideScopeData = "this is accessible everywhere"
local dataSetInScope

do
    -- New Scope
    print(outsideScopeData)

    -- Setting data in this scope
    dataSetInScope = "This data is accessible in this
    scope."

    -- Printing in scope data
    print(dataSetInScope)
```

```
end

-- Printing data outside of the scope
print(outsideScopeData)
print(dataSetInScope)
```

As you can see, we have created a variable missing the = your_data part of a variable. If we do this, Luau automatically turns this into a nil variable. We could have done this ourselves as well. Our variable would have looked like this:

```
local dataSetInScope = nil
```

Then, inside the scope, we set the variable with new data. Because the variable exists in the global scope, the data is not thrown away when the scope ends. This is why we can print the correct result in the last line of this script.

Now that we know how scopes work, we have finished everything that the first chapter offers. In the following section, we put into practice the learned information.

Exercise 1.1 – Changing properties on a part

For this exercise, we use something we have not explained before. Therefore, this exercise starts with a short introduction to what is required. Please note that both this new information and all of the information explained before are required for these exercises. Therefore, it is highly recommended to do the exercise once you understand everything explained before.

In your **Explorer** menu in Roblox Studio, the same menu that you make scripts in, find something called the Workspace. Inside the Workspace, you can find everything that your players can see in-game. This includes the part that your avatar spawns on. This part is called the baseplate.

If you open the **Properties** frame and click on the baseplate, you can see that this **instance** exists by combining a lot of data. In *Figure 1.4*, you can see the **Properties** frame. One of the things that you can see is the name of the part. For the baseplate, this is set to **Baseplate**. However, a name is just a string. There are other properties, such as **Anchored**. This property determines whether the part is locked in its location or whether it is moveable in the game. There is a checkbox next to this property. This checkbox can be on or off. Sounds familiar? This is basically a Boolean.

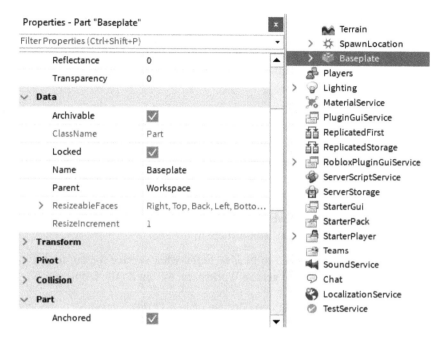

Figure 1.4 – Baseplate properties

Then, there are also numbers. For instance, the **Transparency** property is a number between 0 and 1. This determines the visibility of the part. Finally, some properties have multiple numbers separated by a comma. These are special data types that we have not yet seen. For now, there are two of these new data types that you can find on a part: **Color3** and **Vector3**. A Color3 data type determines the color and a Vector3 data type determines the 3D size. This can be a position, size, rotation, and a lot more.

Both of these data types contain the number data type. That is why you see three numbers separated by a comma in these locations. For example, to make a new color, you use the following code:

```
Color3.fromRGB(0, 0, 0) -- Black Color
Color3.fromRGB(255, 255, 255) -- White Color
```

RGB, which stands for **Red**, **Green**, and **Blue**, is three numbers that each range from 0 to 255. Therefore, a combination of three of these numbers makes a color.

We also mentioned Vector3 data types, and you can make these using the following code:

```
Vector3.new(25, 25, 25)
Vector3.new(100, 25, 50)
```

A `Vector3` data type also contains three different numbers. These resemble the *x*, *y*, and *z* axes. The *x* and the *z* axes determine the width, and the *y* axis determines the height. In our first example, we made a `Vector3` data type with a width of 25, a length of 25, and a height of 25. This is basically a cube.

> **Tip**
>
> By using the **Properties** window, you can manually change the values of each property. Try playing around with some of the properties that we mentioned before. This gives you a better understanding of how they work, especially the new data types.
>
> You need to start the game for some properties to go into effect.

Now that we know how these properties work, we can change them using a script. Before we can do this, we need to tell the script somehow which part we are trying to change. We need a reference for this. This reference directly points to a part somewhere in the game.

Before we can make a reference, we need to be able to tell what **service** we can find it in. For the baseplate, this is in the Workspace. So, to get the Workspace, we can do the following:

```
local workspaceService = game:GetService("Workspace")
```

However, because the Workspace is used a lot, there is a shorter way to reference it. We can simply use the `workspace` keyword to get a reference without having to use the `:GetService()` function, as shown here:

```
local workspaceService = workspace
```

Now that we know how to reference the Workspace, we can look through all of its **children**. In programming, children are instances inside of another instance. The parent is the instance that the current instance is inside of. This parent is a property that we can see within the **Properties** frame. If we open the properties, select **Baseplate**, and look for a property called **Parent**, we can see that the parent of this instance is the Workspace. This makes sense because, when we opened the Workspace, one of the first children we saw was the **Baseplate** part. To finish the reference toward the baseplate, our reference would look like this:

```
local baseplate = workspace.Baseplate
```

Now that we have the reference to our part, we can change properties. Changing properties is similar to updating a variable. First, you put what you want to change. This is our reference and the name of the property. Then, we put an equal to (=) and the new value. For example, if we want to change the reflectance of our part, our code looks like this:

```
local baseplate = workspace.Baseplate

baseplate.Reflectance = 1
```

Exercise:

1. Open a new baseplate in Roblox Studio.

   Create a new script in **ServerScriptService**.

2. Create a new variable named `baseplate` to reference the baseplate.

3. Print the name of the baseplate using the following:

   - The `baseplate` variable
   - The **Name** property of the baseplate
   - The `print()` function

   Execute the script and confirm that **Baseplate** shows up in the **Output** frame.

4. In your script, change the **Name** property of the baseplate to something else.

   Execute the script and ensure that your new name appears in the **Output** frame.

5. Change your `print()` statement, so that it prints the following:

   The name of the baseplate is: 'name of your baseplate here'

6. Execute the script by using the following:

   - The `baseplate` variable
   - The **Name** property of the baseplate
   - String concatenation

   Confirm that the correct string shows up in the **Output** frame.

7. Change the **CanCollide** property of the baseplate to `false`.

   Execute the script and confirm that your avatar falls through the baseplate.

8. Change the **Color** property of the baseplate to a new RGB color with the RGB code: Red: `51`, Green: `88`: Blue: `130` (Storm Blue).

   Execute the script and confirm that the baseplate has another color.

9. Create a variable named `terrain` that references the **Terrain** object in the Workspace.

10. Change the **Parent** property of the baseplate to reference the **Terrain** object by using the following:

    - The variable named `baseplate`
    - The variable named `terrain`
    - The property of the baseplate with the name **Parent**

Tip for 10: The **Parent** property does not have a value as a data type but as a reference. The current reference is to the Workspace parent. Set the value of this property to reference **Terrain**.

An example answer to this exercise can be found on the GitHub page for this book: `https://github.com/PacktPublishing/Mastering-Roblox-Coding/tree/main/Exercises`.

We combined the knowledge that we learned about programming with this exercise to make a visual change in our game. In the next exercise, we will make another system.

Exercise 1.2 – Police system part I

This exercise creates a simple police system that calculates a ticket price based on input.

System description

The police want a system where they can set a variable for the speed that a driver was going at, and a variable where they can set whether the driver had a license with them. There should be variables that determine the height of the ticket for each crime. There should also be two variables that state the maximum speed the driver is allowed to go and whether it is required for them to have a license. Combining this data should give one ticket price even if multiple crimes were committed. If there were no crimes committed, the ticket price would be 0. The ticket price should be displayed in **Output** with the following text: **Ticket Price: 0**. The number depends on the height of the ticket.

Try to conclude what variables you need based on the system description. Again, analyzing a problem helps you to create a correct system.

Based on the system description, we can conclude the following facts:

- There should be two variables that the police can set. These variables are for the speed (`speed`) and whether the driver had a license (`hasLicense`) with them.
- There should be two variables (constants?) that determine the ticket price for each crime.
- There should be two variables (constants?) that determine the maximum allowed speed and whether it is required to have a driver's license.
- There should be a variable that holds the height of the ticket (`ticketPrice`).

Now that we know this, let us start programming our system. Follow these steps:

1. Open a new baseplate in Roblox Studio.
2. Create a new script in **ServerScriptService**.
3. Create the variables we concluded from the system description.
4. Create an `if` statement that checks whether the driver was going over the speed limit and applies the following:

    - If the driver was going over and not at the speed limit, increase the ticket price
    - If the driver was not going over the speed limit, do nothing

5. Create an `if` statement that checks whether the driver was violating the driving license rule and applies the following:

    -   If it is required to have a driver's license and the driver has a driver's license, nothing happens

    -   If it is required to have a driver's license and the driver does not have a driver's license, increase the ticket price

    -   If it is not required to have a driver's license and the driver has a driver's license, do nothing

    -   If it is not required to have a driver's license and the driver does not have a driver's license, do nothing

6. Use the `print()` function to print the correct sentence. Refer to the software description for the required sentence.

Execute your script and confirm that it works as described in the software description. Try to fix any errors that could show up in the **Output** frame. An example answer to this exercise can be found on the GitHub page for this book:

`https://github.com/PacktPublishing/Mastering-Roblox-Coding/tree/main/Exercises`

Exercise 1.3 – Understanding a script

In this exercise, we will insert a script into our game to understand what it does. This script will be given to you in this exercise. It is recommended that you look at this script and recreate it. Try not to copy and paste the script from the GitHub page for this book, as you will learn less by doing this.

Follow these steps:

1. Open a new baseplate in Roblox Studio.

2. Create a new script in **ServerScriptService**.

3. Inside the previously made script, insert the following code:

```
local spawnLocation = workspace.SpawnLocation

if
    spawnLocation.Position.X == 0
    and
    spawnLocation.Position.Z == 0
then
    print("Spawn is in the center!")
```

```
else
    print("Spawn is not in the center.")
end
```

4. Start playing the game. If you do not move SpawnLocation, a **Spawn is in the center!** message should appear.

5. Next, move SpawnLocation by using the **Move** tool in the **Home** section. Did the message change?

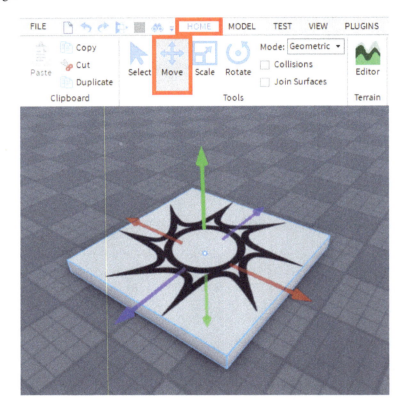

Figure 1.5 – Moving SpawnLocation

6. What happens when you place SpawnLocation in the center and change the height? Why does this happen?

The code used in this exercise can be found on the GitHub page for this book: https://github.com/PacktPublishing/Mastering-Roblox-Coding/tree/main/Exercises.

Summary

Roblox is a unique platform where people can play millions of games for free. The amazing thing about these experiences, as Roblox likes to call their games, is that other users make them on the platform. There are a lot of different roles that you can have as a developer on the platform. You can be a modeler, animator, graphics artist, and even a programmer.

Programmers on Roblox use a language called Luau. Programming is all about manipulating data to change something in the game. There are different data types in programming. The most common and essential data types are strings, numbers, and Booleans. These basic data types can make completely new data types, such as `Color3` and `Vector3`. We learned how to use these data types and what purpose each has. We learned about how to do math operations on numbers, string concatenation, and relational operators using Booleans.

This data can be stored in variables. We learned how to update these variables. We saw that these variables are very similar to properties on instances such as parts. We learned that these properties are what make an instance unique. You can change these properties, and something changes. For example, if you change the color of a part using the `Color3` data type, you will see the color of the part change.

Because not all data is the same, we can take different actions depending on the data provided. For this, we have conditionals. We saw how conditionals go hand-in-hand with Booleans. We learned that conditionals have something called expressions to determine whether certain data is what we are looking for. If this is the case, a particular scope gets executed. If this is not the case, we can choose to do nothing or execute another scope of code by using the `elseif` and `else` statements.

We learned that these scopes have all the data that all the scopes above them have. Furthermore, we saw how each scope can also make its own data. The scopes above it do not know about it. Only the scope itself and the nested scopes know about it.

In the first exercise, we also learned how to make visual changes in our game. We learned how references to instances in the game work and how to change the properties on these instances. Besides this, we also learned how to create a system based on a given system description.

In the next chapter, we will start improving the quality of our code. We will learn ways to minimize duplicate code and make more advanced systems using functions, tables, loops, and modules.

2
Writing Better Code

This chapter is all about using what we learned in the previous chapter and taking it to the next level. In this chapter, we will start by looking at functions. We will learn how and when to use them. Functions allow us to reduce the amount of duplicate code in our scripts. Once we have gained an understanding of this, we will then continue by looking at tables. Tables allow us to store a lot of data in just one variable. Once we have understood tables, we will start using loops. We will learn about all the different loops that Luau has. Besides that, we will use these loops in the tables that we make. Toward the end of the chapter, we will also explain modules. Modules allow us to write less duplicate code spread over multiple scripts.

In this chapter, we will cover the following topics:

- Using functions
- Storing data types in tables
- Programming loops
- Using modules
- Exercises

By the end of this chapter, you will have learned about the fundamentals of programming in Luau. You will understand and learn more about functions, tables, loops, and modules and know why and when to use them. In addition, you will also know the best practices when using them.

Technical requirements

To start programming with Luau, you need access to a device with internet access. This can either be a Windows device or a Mac device. Additionally, you need to download the following software:

- Roblox Player
- Roblox Studio

All the code examples for this chapter can be found on GitHub at `https://github.com/PacktPublishing/Mastering-Roblox-Coding`.

The CiA video for this chapter can be found at `https://bit.ly/3oxUMx7`.

Using functions

In this section, we will start using something called functions. Let us start by finding out when to use functions. In *Chapter 1*, *Getting Up to Speed with Roblox and Luau Basics*, we saw the following code:

```
local MINIMUM_PLAYERS = 1
local MAXIMUM_PLAYERS = 8

local playerPosition = 1

-- Checking if the player's position is a valid number
if playerPosition >= MINIMUM_PLAYERS and playerPosition <=
MAXIMUM_PLAYERS then

    -- Getting correct message based on player›s position
    if playerPosition <= 3 then
        print("Well done! You are in spot " .. playerPosition
        .. "!")
    elseif playerPosition <= 5 then
        print("You are almost there!")
    else
        print("You are not in the top three yet! Keep going!")
    end

else
    -- The position of the player is not valid
    warn("Incorrect player position [" .. playerPosition ..
    "]!")
end
```

The preceding code determines what message the user sees based on their position.

Now, let us say that, once this code runs, we want to change the position from first place to fourth place. Then, we want to get a new and different message based on their new position.

We can easily do this. In the preceding code example, below the last end, we can change the variable for the player position and copy and paste the entire if statement. Easy, everything works. Now, we want to change the player position again. We repeat the same process repeatedly until your script is 10,000 lines with the same if statement. Then, we realize that instead of having the same message for numbers four and five, we want to give them different messages. So, we have to change our if statement a few hundred times. That is going to be a lot of work.

In the following sections, we will learn how to solve this problem using functions. First, we will see examples of how functions are used and everything we can do with them.

Making a function

In this section, we will learn what a function is and what we need to do to make them. Functions contain code that we can reuse as many times as we want in the script. Therefore, we do not have to use the same code repeatedly. Instead, we call the function for it. First, let us make a function. The following code snippet shows you what a function looks like:

```
function printSomething()
    print("This was printed in a function!")
end
```

Let us analyze this function. A function starts with the function keyword. Then, we provide the name of our function. For functions, we also use the lower camel case naming method. After the name, we add parentheses, (). Similar to if statements and do statements, a new scope is made. For if statements, this scope is only executed if the result of the expression is true. Functions do not have expressions.

So, if we do not have expressions, how does the system know this code must be executed? Right now, if we run our script, nothing shows up in the console. That is because we never told the function to execute. The previous scripts we made were executed in the order of the lines. Functions only get executed when they are told to be. You can execute a function by putting its name followed by parentheses, as follows:

```
function printSomething()
    print("This was printed in a function!")
end


printSomething()
```

Now our code gets executed. Well done! We learned how to make our first function. In the next section, we will learn how to make our functions a bit more complex by using parameters and arguments in functions.

> **Tip**
>
> For readability reasons, a function might only have one purpose.
>
> If a function is responsible for doing multiple things, the function should be split up into separate functions that call each other.

Parameters and arguments

In this section, we will start using parameters and arguments. But first, let us look at the racing example again. The entire `if` statement could be a function. This way, we prevent the previously described problem where we would have to copy and paste the entire `if` statement repeatedly:

```lua
local MINIMUM_PLAYERS = 1
local MAXIMUM_PLAYERS = 8
local playerPosition = 1

function givePositionFeedback()
    -- Checking if the player›s position is a valid number
    if playerPosition >= MINIMUM_PLAYERS and playerPosition <=
    MAXIMUM_PLAYERS then
        -- Getting correct message based on player›s position
        if playerPosition <= 3 then
            print("Well done! You are in spot "
            .. playerPosition .. "!")
        elseif playerPosition <= 5 then
            print("You are almost there!")
        else
            print("You are not in the top three yet! Keep
            going!")
        end
    else
        -- The position of the player is not valid
        warn("Incorrect player position [" .. playerPosition
        .. "]!")
    end
end

givePositionFeedback()
```

```
playerPosition = math.random(1, 8)
givePositionFeedback()
```

Let us take a look at the preceding code. We get two different results in the **Output** frame when we run the code even though we only use the `if` statement once. This is because we made a function and called it twice. Other than that, the code is not very different. However, we have not seen the `math.random(1, 8)` part. Luau has a few built-in math functions that we can use. One of them is `math.random()`. What this does is that it takes a random number from between the two numbers you provided. In our case, we provided numbers one and eight. Therefore, the result of this function will be a number between those two values.

Now that we are talking about it, `math.random()` is a function. We call this function in a similar way to how we call our other functions. We say the name of the function and add parentheses at the end. However, for the `math.random()` function, we can give the function data inside the parentheses. On second thought, we have also seen this with the `print()` and `warn()` functions.

We can do this in our function, too. The data that we give inside of the parentheses is called **arguments**. When we receive this data inside our function, this same data is now stored in **parameters**.

Let us modify our current code so that `playerPosition` is no longer a global variable but a parameter:

```
Local MINIMUM_PLAYERS = 1
local MAXIMUM_PLAYERS = 8

function givePositionFeedback(playerPosition)
    -- Checking if the player's position is a valid number
    if playerPosition >= MINIMUM_PLAYERS and playerPosition <=
    MAXIMUM_PLAYERS then

        -- Getting correct message based on player's position
        if playerPosition <= 3 then
            print("Well done! You are in spot "
            .. playerPosition .. "!")
        elseif playerPosition <= 5 then
            print("You are almost there!")
        else
            print("You are not in the top three yet! Keep
            going!")
        end
```

```
        else
            -- The position of the player is not valid
            warn("Incorrect player position [" .. playerPosition
            .. "]!")
        end
    end

givePositionFeedback(math.random(1, 8))
givePositionFeedback(math.random(1, 8))
```

> **Tip**
> As a general rule, we keep the length of our function below 25 lines. This is to improve the
> readability of our code.

In the preceding code, we still see `playerPosition`; the only difference is that it is no longer a
global variable. This is because it is a **parameter** now. The value of this parameter is defined when
we call the function at the bottom of the script. Here, we use the `math.random()` method as an
argument. This argument is going to be a value between one and eight. Our script can work with this.

We just saw how to give our function a parameter. But what if we wanted our function to have multiple
parameters? In the next section, we will see how to give our function multiple parameters.

Multiple parameters

In this section, we will see that functions can have multiple parameters. We have seen this happen in
the `math.random()` function. Parameters and arguments are separated using commas (,).

Let us make a simple calculator script by using functions and parameters. First, we will make a simple
add function. This function is going to have two parameters. These parameters are going to be the
numbers that it counts. For now, we will call these numbers x and y:

```
function add(x, y)
    print(x + y)
end

add(5, 5)
```

Here, we used two parameters. In the **Output** frame, you can see the sum of the numbers we provided
as arguments.

But what if we accidentally give another argument when calling the function? In that case, our functions need two parameters: x and y. However, it gets three. Let us see what happens when we try to do the following:

```
function add(x, y)
    print(x)
    print(y)
end


add(1, 2, 3)
```

When we run the code, numbers 1 and 2 get printed, and number 3 gets ignored. This makes sense because we did not make a print for this argument. We can conclude that we can send as many arguments as we want to a function even if we do not use them without getting errors. Even though this is possible, you should not do it. Sending useless data to a function is a bad practice and creates extra work for no reason.

However, what happens when our function needs two parameters and only gets one? Take a look at the following code:

```
function add(x, y)
    print(x, y)
end


add(1)
```

Number 1 gets printed correctly. However, for the y parameter, nil is printed. We have seen nil before. In Luau, nil means nothing. For example, if we try to do a math operation with nil, we get an error. Of course, we do not want to create errors. In the next section, we will learn a method to ensure there are no parameters with the nil value.

Default parameter values

Sometimes, your function relies on having your parameters set. When parameters are not set, we can give them a default value. We can do this by using two things that we learned about earlier. In this section, we will learn how to make default parameter values by using if statements and setting new values to variables.

Let us take a look at the updated code:

```
function add(x, y)
    -- Default values for your parameters
```

```
        if x == nil then
            x = 0
        end
        if y == nil then
            y = 0
        end


        -- Function logic
        print(x)
        print(y)
    end


    add(1)
```

Now if we run our script, instead of `nil` being printed, the **Output** frame shows the default value, 0. Our `if` statement checks whether the parameter is not `nil`, and if it is, we change the parameter's value to 0.

Because we do not specify that our parameter has to be a number either, we can bypass this `if` statement and still crash the code. Suppose we give a string instead of a number, our `if` statement would miss the wrong parameter. Luckily, we have something to get the name of the data type. The method to get this name is called `typeof()`. Let us improve our default data:

```
function add(x, y)
    -- Default values for your parameters
    if x == nil or typeof(x) ~= "number" then
        x = 0
    end
    if y == nil or typeof(y) ~= "number" then
        y = 0
    end


    -- Function logic
    print(x)
    print(y)
end


add(1, "2")
```

Now that we use the `typeof()` function, we can check whether the data type provided in the parameters is a number and not another data type such as a string. Our parameters are now fully protected from not having a set or having a wrong data type as a value.

These default parameters are a lot of work to implement. Therefore, it is custom to only implement these default parameter values when using your parameter as an **Optional Parameter**. An optional parameter is something that is not necessarily required for your function.

Another use case for default parameter values is when multiple developers use your function, and you are unsure how they will use it. We will talk more about this use case in the *Using modules* section.

> **Note**
>
> Sometimes, you can make an error somewhere in your script, and you do not get an error because you use default parameter values. In those scenarios, it might be challenging to find what is wrong with your script. After all, your default values are to prevent errors. However, you can tackle this by adding a warning message (`warn()`) when a default value is being used, as discussed in the *Nested If statements* section of *Chapter 1, Getting Up to Speed with Roblox and Luau Basics*.

Now that we understand how to make parameters and arguments, we can move on to the next cool thing we can do with functions: **return types**. In the following section, we will learn how to make our function return data.

Returning functions

In this section, we will start improving our calculator by adding **return types** to our functions. Let us continue developing our calculator. We already have an `add()` function. Let us make one that subtracts numbers. It looks pretty similar to the `add()` function. See the following code snippet:

```
function add(x, y)
    print(x + y)
end

function subtract(x, y)
    print(x - y)
end

add(5, 5)
subtract(10, 5)
```

Our code works, but we can do nothing with the generated data. What if we, first, use the add()
function, and then subtract something from the number we just calculated the sum of? Somehow,
we need the result of our previous operation. We can create a global variable that stores the result of
the previous operation.

Creating a global variable for this is a **Bad Practice**. We try to avoid using global variables as much
as possible. Usually, there is a much better alternative available. Functions can give back a result. We
have already seen this happen with the math.random() function. We used this function as an
argument. We were able to do this because this function returns a new number. Instead of printing
the number, let us make the function return the result of the operation. To do this, we can use the
return statement, as follows:

```
function add(x, y)
    return x + y
end

function subtract(x, y)
    return x - y
end

local sum = add(5, 5)
local difference = subtract(10, 5)
```

Using the return statement, we can use this method as an argument or store it in a variable, as
shown in the preceding code. Now that we know how this works, we can make the previously described
system. First, we can use the add() function, followed by the subtract() function that uses the
result of the add() function. Our system looks like this:

```
function add(x, y)
    return x + y
end

function subtract(x, y)
    return x - y
end

local result = subtract(add(5, 5), 5)
print(result)
```

Now that we understand how to use return values, let us try to return multiple values from our functions. In the next section, we will see how to do this.

Multiple return values

Functions returning more than one value are not often seen, but they can be useful. For example, if we wanted to make a function that adds and subtracts and gives back both values using one function, we could do that. It looks like the following:

```
function add(x, y)
    return x + y
end

function subtract(x, y)
    return x - y
end

function addAndSubstract(x, y)
    return add(x, y), subtract(x, y)
end

local sum, difference = addAndSubstract(10, 5)
```

We added a new function, but there is nothing special about it. It is a normal function with two parameters. What is noteworthy, however, is that the return calls two functions: the add() function and the subtract() function. A comma separates the call of these functions (,). This separation with commas is something we saw when we added multiple arguments and parameters, too.

Nevertheless, how do we store both return values in a variable? Well, we do not. However, we can make two variables for each value. We have done this before. The only difference is a small shortcut when making these variables, which you can see in the preceding code example. Once again, we use the comma to have multiple variables in one line.

First, we use the local part that defines a new variable. Then, we have the variable's name as we are used to. The only difference is that we have multiple variables separated by commas instead of one variable name. Once we have defined all our variable names, we place the equals (=) sign, as we are used to. Then, we set the value of the variable.

We did this in the preceding example, too. The only thing that might look confusing is that we only set one variable. It might look like we are doing that, but we are not. Indeed, we call one function, but because this function returns not one but two values, two variables get set.

Instead of having a function that returns two values, we could have just called both functions while defining our variable. It would have looked like this:

```
function add(x, y)
    return x + y
end

function subtract(x, y)
    return x - y
end

local sum, difference = add(10, 5), subtract(10, 5)
```

You would probably end up using the second option more often than making a function with two return values. However, in some scenarios, there is a real advantage to having multiple return values. We will see some of these advantages throughout the book, such as in *Chapter 3, Event-Based Programming*.

Either way, it is good to understand how multiple return values work in the case of a scenario where you work with a function that has it.

Now that we know all about return values, let us look at something else we can do with functions. Similar to `if` statements, we can nest functions, too. In the next section, we see how to nest functions.

Nested functions

In the previous sections, we learned a lot about functions. Nevertheless, did you know that a function is a variable? In this section, we will learn how to use this knowledge to make nested functions.

Previously, we defined functions using `function functionName()`. However, behind the scenes, Luau changes your function to a variable. Therefore, you can also make a function like this:

```
local printSomething = function(whatToPrint)
    print(whatToPrint)
end

printSomething("Hello World!")
```

If we write our function like this, we can give this variable to a function as an argument. Then, we can execute a parameter because it is a function.

You do not see this happen very often. However, because functions are technically a variable, can we have functions inside of functions? Yes, that is possible. Functions within functions are called **Nested Functions**.

But why would we use nested functions? Can we not just use two separate functions? Yes, you can use two separate functions. The only reason to use a nested function is to avoid making a new global function with the same parameters. There is one condition, though; you need to ensure the function you make as a nested function will never be required by another function. So, to prevent duplicate code, it makes no sense to have two nested functions that do the same thing.

Let us take a look at our calculator example again. Our calculator always needs to calculate the sum and the difference. In this case, we can turn our add and subtract functions into a nested function inside the `addAndSubtract()` function. It looks like this:

```
function addAndSubstract(x, y)
    -- Nested add function
    local function add()
        return x + y
    end

    -- Nested subtract function
    local function subtract()
        return x - y
    end

    -- Returning result
    return add(), subtract()
end

local sum, difference = addAndSubstract(10, 5)
```

Now that we turned our `add()` and `subtract()` functions into a nested function, we no longer need to give these functions parameters. Instead, we can simply get the parameter values from the `addAndSubtract()` function that is higher in the scope.

In a real calculator system, you would never see this. It might seem efficient to have the same function for all your operations and use the returned variable you want, but the opposite is true. Why perform math operations knowing you are not going to use the data?

> **Tip**
>
> Most of the time, it is good to avoid nested functions. Although, there are a few exceptions. In *Chapter 3, Event-Based Programming*, we will see some useful use cases for nested functions.

Now that we know all about functions, there is only one thing left for us to cover: best practices when using functions. These best practices are covered in the next section.

Best practices when using functions

In this section, we will cover another best practice when using functions. We have already seen some of the best practices you have to keep in mind throughout the previous sections. These ensure that our functions only have one purpose and prevent us from writing functions with more than 25 lines.

Besides the best practices we have just mentioned, there is another one. Now that we know how to use functions, we are no longer supposed to write our code outside of functions. One exception is the global variable. However, try to replace global variables with parameters as much as possible.

These functions still have to be called at some point. Make a setup() function that includes these calls when this is required. This way, you only have one function call at the bottom of your script.

Our calculator system should look like the following when using a setup function:

```
function setup()
    local sum = add(5, 5)
    local difference = subtract(10, 5)
    print(sum)
    print(difference)
end



function add(x, y)
    return x + y
end

function subtract(x, y)
    return x - y
end



setup()
```

Now that we understand these best practices, we have learned everything we need to know about functions.

In the previous sections, we learned how to make a function. Additionally, we learned about parameters and arguments in functions. They allow us to provide specific functions with specific data without using a global variable. Besides that, we have also seen how to give a function a return value. This allows us to use the outcome of a function for something else. Finally, we learned that functions are variables. Because of this, we were able to nest functions.

In the next section, we will introduce something new related to variables. The following section is all about tables.

Storing data types in tables

In this section, we will learn all about tables. We will learn what they are and what they are helpful for. To explain tables, we will take the example of a school system that stores data from its students.

You are probably aware that schools have data on their students. This data varies from your name, your class, and your test results.

Currently, we know of a way to store data. We can do that by using variables. So, let us make a school system that stores data.

For now, let us first focus on the variables:

```
local STUDENT_NAME_1 = "William"
local STUDENT_NAME_2 = "Sophie"
```

Currently, we have two variables for the first two students. An average class has about 20 students. Therefore, we would need 20 different variables for the first class alone. Now imagine this for an entire school. Having this many variables is very unorganized.

In the following sections, we will learn how to organize this data better by using tables.

Storing data in a table

There is a solution. Usually, when you start counting, as demonstrated in the preceding example, there is a better alternative to your variable names. This alternative uses a table; tables are a list of data. There is no size limit on this list.

We can use this table to store the names of our students. For example, our table could look like this:

```
local students = {"William", "Sophie"}
```

If we take a good look at the preceding code, we can see that it is not very different from something we saw earlier. Remember, in the *Multiple return values* section, we made a function that returned multiple values? Here, we had multiple variables on the same line. It looked something like this:

```
local student1, student2 = "William", "Sophie"
```

As you can see, it is almost identical. The primary difference is that the array only defines one variable (students), whereas the other example defines two variables (student1 and student2). Another difference, which is even smaller, is after the equals (=) sign. We have two strings separated by a comma (,). However, for the table, we have our values surrounded by curly brackets ({ and }).

If we want to add another student's name to the table, we can simply place another comma (,) and place a new string behind it. We do not have to create another variable name as it is all stored in the students table.

Something unique about these tables is that you can place any data type in the same table. That means we can save data with different data types in the same table. Here is an example of a table that stores information about a student:

```
local studentInfo = {"James", 10284281, "5'9", true}
```

The preceding code is from a non-existing student. The first data in the table is the first name of the student as a string, followed by the student ID, which is a number. The school is also aware of the student's height, which is stored as a string. Finally, we have a Boolean that determines whether the student is an active student or not.

In this section, we learned how to make a table. Besides this, we have compared a table to standard variables to see the advantages. But we already know how to read data from variables. So, how do we get the data from a table? In the next section, we will learn how to read data from a table.

Reading data from a table

When using variables, we can do whatever we want with the value by simply using the variable's name. For tables, it works differently. If we print out the students table and open the **Output** frame, we should see something interesting. The following code snippet shows you how to print a table:

```
local students = {"William", "Sophie"}
print(students)
```

In the **Output** frame, the following appears:

```
{
    [1] = "William",
    [2] = "Sophie"
}
```

At first glance, the output and the given input might look different, but we will see many similarities if we look at the output again. For starters, we see the curly brackets, and we also see the students' names. The only thing we do not see in our table is those weird numbers.

These **numbers** make more sense than you might think. They are the **indexes** of the values within the table. So, what are indexes? Let us take another look at the table. The first string in the table is `William`. Next, we see the number one in our **Output** frame, followed by the `William` string.

This index tells us your data's position within the table. You can see this index as a variable name within a table. The index in the Luau tables starts at one and keeps counting up depending on the number of items within the table.

We can use this index to specify which item we want to print within the table. We do this by specifying the name of the table followed by brackets ([and]):

```
local students = {"William", "Sophie"}
print(students[1])
```

If this index data is not interesting for what you are trying to do, and you only want to print all the values within the table, you can use a built-in function called `unpack()`:

```
local students = {"William", "Sophie"}
print(unpack(students))
```

In this section, we saw how to read data from a table. Besides that, we learned how the internal structure of a table works. Each piece of data gets a unique index. We use this index to get specific data from a table. In the following section, we will learn how to add new data to a table.

Setting data in a table

Adding a new item to an existing table is simple. There is a built-in function that has been written that does it for us. This built-in function is called `table.insert()`, and you can see it used in the following code snippet:

```
local students = {"William", "Sophie"}
table.insert(students, "Robbert")
```

The only new thing in this script is the `table.insert()` function. The name gives away what the function does. Your first argument of the `table.insert()` function is the table you wish to add your second argument into. If we print the table and look at the indexes, we see that student `Robbert` is now in index 3.

However, what if we accidentally put the wrong name into our table? Can we remove or update the data that is in a table? Yes, we can. We can use the table's name and combine it with the value index we want to change. For example, we want to change **Robbert**, index 3, to **Robert** because we made a typo. Our script looks like this:

```
local students = {"William", "Sophie", "Robbert"}
students[3] = "Robert"
```

Knowing this, would it be possible to take an index, such as index 4, and set an item here? Essentially, that is what the `table.insert()` function does. Let us try to write our custom table insert function:

```
local students = {"William", "Sophie", "Robert"}

function setup()
    customTableInsert(students, "Emily")
    print(unpack(students))
end

function customTableInsert(table, newData)
    -- Getting index info
    local currentIndex = #table
    local newIndex = currentIndex + 1

    -- Setting new data
    table[newIndex] = newData
end


setup()
```

Let us take a look at the `customTableInsert()` function we made. Our first variable is the current index of the table. We get this index by putting a hashtag (#) in front of the table's name. This hashtag is the length operator. We use this operator to get the length of the tables.

After that, we get the new index variable. The new index variable takes the current length of the table and adds one. For example, if we have three items in a table, our `currentIndex` variable would be **3**. Therefore, adding one gives us **4**. This index is not taken yet and adds a new value to our table.

If we want to remove someone from our table, we can update the index and set the value to `nil`. However, there is a much better alternative: a built-in function from Roblox. It is called `table.remove()`. The difference between setting the value to `nil` and using this function is that when you use `table.remove()`, all the indexes behind it get changed. Moving all the indexes prevents any empty indexes in your table. In comparison, setting the value to `nil` results in having an empty spot within your table. You can use the `table.remove()` function like this:

```
local students = {"William", "Sophie", "Robert"}
table.remove(students, 3)
```

In this section, we learned how to update existing data in our table. Besides that, we learned how to insert a completely new item into our table. Finally, we also learned how to remove data from our table using the `table.remove()` function.

If we understand all these things, we know the basics of tables. However, there is another cool thing we can do with tables. Currently, we work with indexes, but what if we could use strings as an index? **Dictionaries** allow us to do this. In the next section, we will take a good look at dictionaries.

Using dictionaries

Currently, we have a table with the names of our students. But what if we wanted to store much more information about each student? For instance, we want to store the first name, the student ID, the class name, and the number of times that the student was late. Our table could look like this:

```
local studentInfo = {
    "Lauren",
    12345,
    "H1",
    0
}
```

While this works, we do have a visual problem. Without reading the description of what we were going to make, you probably have no clue what any of these values mean. One solution could be to add comments before the value. However, Luau has something that can help us out here. It is called a **dictionary**.

Have you ever looked at a real-life dictionary? You look up a word, and it gives you the meaning of that word. Luau dictionaries are similar to this. Dictionaries have a key and a value that belongs to this key. This key can be a number, a string, or any other data type. You can see this key as an index of tables.

A dictionary of our student info could look like this:

```
local studentInfo = {
    name = "Lauren",
    id = 12345,
    class = "H1",
    ["times late"] = 0
}
```

At first glance, the meaning of each piece of data is instantly clear. Keep in mind that the `times late` key is written differently. It is surrounded by brackets (`[` and `]`) and quotation marks (`"`). The reason for this is because there is a space in between the words `times` and `late`. When using spaces, always put brackets and quotation marks around them.

Now, let us take a look at what happened to the indexes of our dictionary:

```
{
    ["class"] = "H1",
    ["id"] = 12345,
    ["name"] = "Lauren",
    ["times late"] = 0
}
```

As you can see, there are no numbers to identify which value belongs to which index. Our indexes are now strings. Because we are using a dictionary, we do not call them indexes but **keys**. Getting data from a dictionary looks simpler than getting data from a table:

```
local studentId = tableStudentInfo[2]
local studentId = dictionaryStudentInfo["id"]
```

Because you specify a key rather than an index between the brackets, it is instantly clear that you are getting the **id** key for this student from the dictionary without even looking at the variable's name.

In this section, we learned how to use dictionaries. Previously, we also learned how to make tables. Similar to `if` statements and functions, we can also nest tables. In fact, we can also nest tables with dictionaries. Having nested tables is called a **Multi-Dimensional** table. In the following section, we will learn all about these multi-dimensional tables.

Multi-dimensional tables

Now we have two systems: one that contains each student's information and one that contains all the names. The ideal situation would be to combine them. Right now, we have variables that contain all the names and variables that contain information about the individual students. We want one variable that contains all students and all student information.

For this, we can use **multi-dimensional** tables. So, what are multi-dimensional tables? So far, we have seen tables that contain data inside of them. However, it is possible to have tables that contain other tables. We can put our data into this second table.

This multi-dimensional table is the perfect solution for our current system. In addition, we can put a dictionary inside a table to make it even better. Let's see what our system looks like if we use a multi-dimensional table:

```
local students = {
    {
        name = "William",
        id = 1,
```

```
                class = "H1",
                ["times late"] = 0
        },
        {
                name = "Sophie",
                id = 2,
                class = "H1",
                ["times late"] = 0
        },
}
```

The previous code snippet is what our multi-dimensional school system looks like. Let us look at the table to see whether we know the indexes and keys of our data:

```
{
    [1] = {
        ["class"] = "H1",
        ["id"] = 1,
        ["name"] = "William",
        ["times late"] = 0
    },
    [2] = {
        ["class"] = "H1",
        ["id"] = 2,
        ["name"] = "Sophie",
        ["times late"] = 0
    }
}
```

Now, we can see that the dictionary gets an **index** within the table. Inside this dictionary, there are **keys** for each data.

We have seen how to combine tables and dictionaries. While doing this, we made a multi-dimensional table. Having one has some advantages. In the next section, we learn how to get rid of redundant keys in favor of indexes.

Using indexes as IDs

Because the student info dictionary gets an index, does that mean our id key is unnecessary? Yes, this is an advantage you get when having a dictionary inside a table. Because each item in a table gets an index, you can use this index as an `id` key, which makes any custom `id` key redundant. For example, our code could look like this if we remove our `id` key:

```
{
    [1] = {
        ["class"] = "H1",
        ["name"] = "William",
        ["times late"] = 0
    },
    [2] = {
        ["class"] = "H1",
        ["name"] = "Sophie",
        ["times late"] = 0
    }
}
```

We learned how to use the index of data in a table to replace any `id` keys. Now that we know about this small optimization, we can continue to the next subsection. In the next subsection, we will learn how to read data from a multi-dimensional table.

Getting data from a multi-dimensional table

Previously, we saw how to get data from a table and a dictionary. Now, we have to combine them. Technically, we are going to combine three things that we previously learned. For starters, we will combine what we learned about getting data from tables with what we learned about references. With references, we referred to an **object** somewhere in the game, for example, somewhere in **Workspace**. However, this time, we have to reference something in a table. Take a look at the following code:

```
-- Reference to something in Workspace
workspace.Baseplate

-- Reference to something in a table
tableName[1]

-- Reference to our multi-dimensional table
students[1]["class"]
```

The first line we see is how we reference something in the Workspace. References are similar to multi-dimensional tables. First, we reference the **Workspace**, followed by a reference to the **Baseplate**. The difference is that we separate our **children** using dots (.), whereas, with tables, we use indexes surrounded by brackets ([ ]). You can see how we referenced something in a one-dimensional table on the second line.

Finally, we have our reference to a multi-dimensional table. First, we state the table's name, followed by the index of the dictionary we want. Lastly, we define which key we want to reference within this dictionary.

> **Practice**
>
> Try making a multi-dimensional table and referencing a few indexes/keys.

Now that we understand how to reference data from a multi-dimensional table, it is time to learn how to update it. The following subsection explains how to do this.

Updating data in a multi-dimensional table

As you might have guessed, setting data inside a multi-dimensional table is the same as a normal table. You can refer to and set your new data as follows:

```
students[1]["Name"] = "John"
```

There is one new and noteworthy thing here. How are we supposed to add a whole new student to our table when the game is running? Well, the thought sounds more complex than the reality:

```
local students = {}

function addStudent(studentName, studentClass)
    table.insert(
        students,
        {
            name = studentName,
            class = studentClass,
            ["times late"] = 0
        }
    )
end


addStudent("Nicole", "H1")
```

We just use the `table.insert()` function. However, instead of having a data type as a second argument, this time, we set a whole table. As we learned earlier, Luau tables can contain all data types, including other tables.

> **Note**
>
> When we spoke about dictionaries, we mentioned keys being easier to read than indexes. Yet, we still use indexes for our students. While it is more challenging to read than if we chose to use the student's name as the key, this has one major issue. Keys can only exist once per dictionary. There will almost certainly be students with the same name. With indexes, this is not an issue. There can be students with the same name because they get a different index.

Now that we know everything about multi-dimensional tables, we can move on to the last tables section. Previously, we learned that tables could contain all data types. However, what about functions? In the next section, we will learn all about functions in tables.

Functions in a table

In the *Nested Functions* section of this chapter, we learned that functions are variables. Additionally, we learned that you could store anything inside tables, including functions.

Previously, we made a simple calculator. Technically, this is something we can do inside a table, too. Take a look at the following code:

```
local calculator = {
    ["Add"] = function(x, y)
        return x + y
    end,
    Subtract = function(x, y)
        return x - y
    end
}
```

If we want to use the Add() function, first, we need to reference the function. Referencing the function works in the same way as referencing standard data in a table. Once we have referenced the function, we add parentheses that include the arguments we want to give it, as we are used to. Our code would look like the following:

```
local calculator = {
    ["Add"] = function(x, y)
        return x + y
    end,
    Subtract = function(x, y)
        return x - y
    end
```

```
}

print(calculator["Add"](5, 5))
print(calculator.Subtract(10, 5))
```

Now we know how to include functions in our tables, and we know all of the fundamentals and more. So far, they are great for storing data, but we still need to reference indexes to access something. In the next section, we will learn how to use loops. Of course, loops can be used for tables, too!

Programming loops

Quite a few times, we have made systems without taking them to the fullest, primarily because we missed knowledge of loops. Loops allow us to repeat a process multiple times without having to copy and paste the same code over and over again. This section explains everything you need to know about loops.

Here is a list of the three different loops that Luau has:

Name	Purpose
while Loop	A `while` loop keeps repeating the same thing repeatedly until a condition is met. The condition is met once the expression returns `true`, similar to `if` statements. However, this condition gets checked before the code that would repeat is executed.
repeat … until	A `repeat` loop is almost identical to a `while` loop. However, there are two differences: 1. Unlike the `while` loop, the condition of the `repeat` loop gets checked after the code inside the loop gets executed. This means that the code always gets executed once. 2. `while` loops run when a condition is `true`. This is not the case for `repeat` loops; they stop when the condition is `true`.
for Loop	A `for` loop gets executed a previously set number of times regardless of the outcome. For example, the `for` loop is usually seen when looping through tables.

In the following sections, we will dive deeper into each of these loops.

while loops

The first loop we will look into is the `while` loop. As previously mentioned, a `while` loop keeps repeating the same code until a condition is met. Let us take a look at the following code:

```
function randomBoolean()
    return math.random(0, 5) == 0
```

```
end

function countTries()
    -- Counter variable
    local tries = 0

    -- While Loop
    while randomBoolean() == false do
        tries += 1
    end

    -- Prints the tries it took for the loop to end
    print("It took " .. tries .. " tries to end the loop.")
end

countTries()
```

Let us take a look at this code. The first function, randomBoolean(), is small but has multiple noteworthy items. It uses the math.random() function that is built into Roblox Luau. The math.random() function generates a random number between 0 and 5. Let us suppose this randomly generated number is 0. Then, true is returned. If not, false is returned.

Then, we have the countTries() function that includes a **while** loop. This function calls the randomBoolean() function as many times as possible until it returns true. If it returns true, the loop ends, and the print gets executed. If it returns false, we increment our tries variable by 1.

Wait, the randomBoolean() function has to return true for the loop to end? Why do we check whether it returns false then? Checking whether it returns false is not a mistake in the book! It might seem confusing at the start, so let us go over it. If the math.random() function picks 0, it returns true. If it does not, it returns false. We have false == false in our loop's condition if it returns false. As we learned in the *Using Conditionals* chapter, false == false gives true. So, our while loop continues for as long as our condition equals true.

Because we use a while loop, our condition gets executed before our tries counter gets incremented. Having our condition executed first means that our tries counter remains 0 if the first execution returns true. This is because the code inside the while loop never gets executed. After all, the condition is never true because true == false gives false.

On the other hand, if we were to use a repeat until loop, the increment of tries would always be executed. A repeat until loop executes before checking the condition, whereas the while loop checks the condition before executing what is inside of the loop. In the next section, we will learn all about the **repeat until** loop.

repeat until loops

If we change the code from the previous section and use a `repeat` loop instead of a `while` loop, our code would look like the following:

```
function randomBoolean()
    return math.random(0, 5) == 0
end

function countTries()
    -- Counter variable
    local tries = 0

    -- Repeat Until Loop
    repeat
        tries += 1
    until
    randomBoolean() == true

    -- Prints the tries it took for the loop to end
    print("It took " .. tries .. " tries to end the loop.")
end

countTries()
```

The code for the preceding **repeat until** loop looks almost identical to the version that uses a **while** loop. It makes sense; both loops serve the same purpose. The real difference is that the `tries` variable is always equal to or greater than 1. No matter how many times you run your script, this will always be the case. This is because we use the `repeat until` loop. The `repeat until` loop executes its code before checking whether the condition is `true`.

This time, we check whether the `randomBoolean()` function returns `true`. It makes sense because if the `randomBoolean()` function returns `true`, we have the `true == true` condition, and the function stops. In comparison, when the function returns `false`, the condition would be `false == true`, which is `false`, resulting in the loop going again.

> **Practice**
>
> If this is the first time you have heard of these loops, they are probably really complex. Therefore, it is highly recommended that you practice with these loops.
>
> A good exercise could be to recreate the previous **while** and **repeat until** loops without looking at the book's code. That way, you experience what each loop does.

Now that we understand how the **while** and **repeat until** loops work, we can move on to the final loop Luau has to offer.

for loops

for Loops are the most common and, therefore, the most important to understand. There is only one difference between a `for` loop and other loops. The difference is that a `for` loop gets a fixed number of loops before starting. In comparison, the `while` and `repeat` loops can technically run forever.

Let's take a look at the following code:

```
for i = 1, 10 do
    print(i)
end
```

The preceding `for` loop prints the numbers 1 to 10 individually. Let us look at i first. This letter is a variable, which means you can name it anything. Usually, programmers take the i character as it is short for **index**. However, it is usually better to give it a name that better explains your variable. For example, this variable could also be named `numberCounter`.

Then, we see an equals (=) sign, followed by 1, a comma (,), and the number 10. If you run the code, you can probably guess what it does. The number 1 is your loop's starting number; therefore, the i variable starts at one. The loop stops when the variable reaches the number 10. Every time the loop runs, the variable automatically gets incremented with one.

If we wanted to increase our variable by 2, we can add another comma (,) behind the 10 and specify what number we want to increase it by:

```
for numberCounter = 1, 10, 2 do
    print(numberCounter)
end
```

Now, we have changed our increment value to two. When we run our code, we get the following numbers in our **Output** frame: **1, 3, 5, 7,** and **9**. Then, it stops even though it never reached the limit we put it on. 9 is the smallest number that fits into 10 with our current increment value. It is good to know that the loop stops even when you are not hitting your limit explicitly.

But there is another `for` loop. This other `for` loop is mainly used to loop through tables:

```
local messages = {"Hello", "how", "are", "you"}

for i, v in pairs(messages) do
    print(i, v)
end
```

In the preceding example, we have a table with four strings. Then, we have a `for` loop that goes through them. First, we see `i` again. Once again, this variable serves as the **index** variable. However, this time, it is the current item's index in the table. Then, we have the `v` variable. This is short for **value**. This variable contains the data that matches the current index within the table.

After the variables, we have `pairs(messages)`. The `pairs()` function allows you to loop over a table and fills both the `index` and `value` variables. Once again, it is highly recommended that you find a fitting name for these variables instead. The thing with the `pairs()` function is that it is not guaranteed to give the results in the same order as our table. Not having the same order means getting the `how` string before the `Hello` string. If the order in which you are looping through the table is essential, you can use `ipairs()` instead. This function ensures `Hello` gets read before the `how` string.

However, you cannot always use the `ipairs()` function. If you are looping through a dictionary, the `ipairs()` function gives no result. Therefore, when looping over dictionaries, you should always use the `pairs()` function.

> **Tip**
> Sometimes, you are not going to use the index variable or the value variable. In those scenarios, it is custom to name it as an underscore (_) instead.

Now we know about the `for` loop, and we understand how to use all three loops in Luau. In the following sections, we will expand our knowledge of loops. In the following section, we will learn how to `Break` and `Continue` our loop.

Continuing and stopping a loop

Let us go back to the school system we had when we learned about tables. Our two-dimensional table looked like this:

```
local students = {
    {
        name = "William",
```

```
        class = "H1",
        ["times late"] = 0
    },
    {
        name = "Sophie",
        class = "H1",
        ["times late"] = 0
    },
}
```

Let us make a function that loops through `students`. Because we have a table, we can use a **for** loop. The index variable is the student's ID, and the value variable is the dictionary that contains the student info. Knowing this, we can make a `for` loop.

We can look for the key named `name` inside the student info. Then, we can make an `if` statement to see whether the name in the dictionary matches the name we are looking for. Take a look at the following code:

```
local students = {
    {name = "William", class = "H1", ["times late"] = 0},
    {name = "Sophie", class = "H1", ["times late"] = 0},
}

function findStudent(studentName)
    -- Looping through students
    for studentId, studentInfo in pairs(students) do
        print("Current Student Id: " .. studentId)

        -- Getting the name of the current student
        -- that belongs to this student id.
        local currentStudentName = studentInfo["name"]

        -- Checking if student name matches the one
        -- we are looking for
        if currentStudentName == studentName then
            print("Found!")
        else
            print("Someone else.")
```

```
            end
        end
  end


  findStudent("William")
```

This code is an excellent start! There is just one problem with the preceding code. If we find the student we are looking for, the loop continues. However, we want our function to stop when the right person is found. Luau has something for this. It is called `break`. When you run the `break` statement in a loop, the loop stops.

> **Note**
>
> If the function that contains the loop has more code than the loop, it is still executed. This is the difference between the `break` statement and the `return` statement. The `return` statement makes both the loop and the function stop.

If we add the `break` statement, our code looks like this:

```
function findStudent(studentName)
    -- Looping through students
    for studentId, studentInfo in pairs(students) do
        print("Current Student Id: " .. studentId)

        -- Getting the name of the current student
        -- that belongs to this student id.
        local currentStudentName = studentInfo["name"]

        -- Checking if student name matches the one
        -- we are looking for
        if currentStudentName == studentName then
            print("Found! Stopping loop")
            break
        else
            print("Someone else, continuing.")
            continue
        end
    end
end
```

> **Note**
> Only the function is shown in the preceding code to reduce space. Replace this new function in the full version of the code.

Now that we are using the `break` statement, the loop will stop if we find whom we are looking for. As you can see, there is also a `continue` statement in the `else` part of your condition. When the `continue` statement is executed, the loop directly restarts even if something else was below the `if` statement.

If we want to modify our function and add a warning if you are looking for a student that does not exist, we can add a `warn()` function below the loop. As previously mentioned, the `break` statement only stops the loop, not the function.

So, if we want to implement this, we have to change our `break` statement into a `return` statement, as it stops the entire function, not just the loop. Then, we can add a warning below our `for` loop that nothing was found. After all, you can only reach this point if you do not reach the `return` statement:

```
function findStudent(studentName)
    -- Looping through students
    for studentId, studentInfo in pairs(students) do
        print("Current Student Id: " .. studentId)

        -- Getting the name of the current student
        -- that belongs to this student id.
        local currentStudentName = studentInfo["name"]

        -- Checking if student name matches the one
        -- we are looking for
        if currentStudentName == studentName then
            print("Found! Stopping function")
            return
        else
            print("Someone else, continuing.")
            continue
        end
    end

    -- student was not found
```

```
        warn("Student [" .. studentName .. "] does not exist.")
end
```

The preceding code is the updated function for our new system. Try it for yourself.

This section taught us how to use the `continue` and `break` statements for loops. We have also seen a use case where we use the `return` statement instead of the `break` statement. In the following section, we will learn how to deal with large loops without making our system lag or crash.

Large oops

Sometimes, the loop you have runs forever or runs complex code many times. You will notice that your Roblox Studio stops responding if you do this. Usually, Roblox automatically stops your loop after a while, but this is not always the case.

Either way, this is not ideal. However, we have a solution. We can use the `task.wait()` function. This function pauses your current thread until the specified time is over:

```
while true do
    print("Loop is running.")
    task.wait(1)
end
```

The preceding code prints **Loop is running** every second. The `task.wait(1)` function gets the parameter of `1`. This specifies the duration it has to pause the thread. Now if we want to stop our loop for 2 seconds, we can simply change 1 to 2. If we remove the parameter altogether, the wait pauses the script for a really short time. If you want to see exactly how long this takes, you can execute the following code:

```
print(task.wait())
```

This code prints the exact duration it paused the thread for.

Now we know how to pause our thread. Additionally, we know how to prevent our desktop from lagging. Therefore, we know all the fundamentals of loops.

Previously, we learned about three different loops for Luau. The **while, repeat... until**, and **for** loops. We learned what each loop is used for. Then, we learned how to break out of the loops and restart the loop for the next interval by using the `continue` statement and the `break` statement. Finally, we also learned how to pause threads for a certain period to prevent our system from lagging when having large loops.

In the next section, we will learn about **modules**. Previously, we learned how functions prevent duplicate code in our script. Modules do the same. However, they prevent duplicate code being spread over multiple scripts instead of inside one script.

Using modules

So far, we have learned a lot about programming. First, we learned that programming is all about data. Then, we learned about many ways to optimize our code, such as using variables, conditionals, functions, tables, and even loops. All of these ensure we can write our code more efficiently without copying the same thing repeatedly.

There is one small optimization left for us to cover. The items we previously listed are all optimizations within the same script. Sometimes, we want systems to use another system. So, how do we transfer one particular script's data to another script?

In the following sections, we will learn how to use **modules**. Modules are their own "script" but can be **required** in another script. This way, things that the module knows can be used in your other script. What you just read probably sounds complex, so let us continue our student system to explain all of this in more detail.

Creating a module script

First, we need to figure out what we want to make. Let us think about the systems a school might have. For example, schools give their students grades. Grades are something we can add to our student's table. Schools giving their students grades can be a unique system. Another system might keep track of the student's presence during classes. Both systems need access to the student's table. Therefore, the system with the student's table can be a module. We will start by implementing a module.

Because modules are not scripts, we have to make a new **ModuleScript**. You can do this in the same way you make scripts. However, this time, do not select **Script** but make a `ModuleScript`. Place the **ModuleScript** in the **ServerStorage** service instead of the `ServerScriptService` service.

The default code of a module script looks like this:

```
local module = {}


return module
```

What's unique about a module is that it needs to have a table variable. The default table variable is named `module`, but you can name the variable anything. It is custom to rename your variable to the same name as your `ModuleScript`. At the end of the module, you have to return this table. Returning this variable has to be the last thing you do in your module:

```
local StudentSystem = {}

local students = {
    {
        name = "William",
```

```
            class = "H1",
            ["times late"] = 0,
            grades = {}
        },
        {
            name = "Sophie",
            class = "H1",
            ["times late"] = 0,
            grades = {}
        },
    }


function StudentSystem:GetStudentInfo(studentName)
    -- Looping through students
    for _, studentInfo in ipairs(students) do
        -- Getting the current student›s name that belongs to
        -- this student id.
        local currentStudentName = studentInfo["name"]



        -- Checking if student name matches
        if currentStudentName == studentName then
            return studentInfo
        end
    end


    -- Student was not found
    warn("Student [" .. studentName .. "] does not exist.")
end


return StudentSystem
```

We have added our student's table and our :GetStudentInfo() function. However, there is one noteworthy change in the code. This change has to do with the **naming of our function**. The table variable that we return is specified in the function's name. We do this to ensure this function can be used when another script uses this module. If we forgot this, our function would still not be accessible in another script.

Now that we know how to make a `ModuleScript`, and how to make functions that can be accessed from other scripts, we can move on to the next section. The following section explains how to **require** this module from another script.

Requiring the module from another script

Now, let us make a normal script in **ServerScriptService**. First, we need to require this module. The module is called `StudentSystem` and can be found in **ServerStorage**. We need a reference to the **ServerStorage** service, and then we need to call `require()` on the module. We can do that in the following way:

```
local ServerStorage = game:GetService("ServerStorage")
local StudentSystem = require(ServerStorage.StudentSystem)
```

> **Note**
>
> Notice how both variables start with an uppercase character instead of a lowercase character? This naming method is allowed because services and modules are excluded from the lower camel case naming method and use the upper camel case naming method.

Now, we have included the `StudentSystem` module in our script. If we want to call a function from this module, we state the variable's name, `StudentSystem`, and then add a colon (`:`) followed by the function's name and parentheses:

```
print(StudentSystem:GetStudentInfo("William"))
```

> **Extra Exercise**
>
> If you wish to practice more with modules, make a function to add a number in the student's `grades` table. Use the `table.insert()` function for this. To keep it simple, use numbers that range from 1 to 10 instead of letters like **A**.
>
> Another good exercise is to make a function that calculates the student's average grade. You can use loops to calculate the sum of grades and then divide it by the student's number of grades.
>
> Example answers to both exercises can be found on the GitHub page of this book:
>
> `https://github.com/PacktPublishing/Mastering-Roblox-Coding/tree/main/Exercises`

Now that we understand how modules work, we have finished everything the second chapter offers. In the following section, we will practice with the information we have learned.

Exercise 2.1 – simple elevator

In this exercise, we will create a simple elevator to enable us to practice more with loops. We will create a simple part that we will move upward. When players stand on this part, they will automatically go up, resulting in an elevator effect happening.

To create our elevator, follow these steps:

1. Open Roblox Studio and create a new Baseplate.

2. Create a new part in the **Workspace** named `Elevator`.

3. Create a new script in **ServerScriptService**.

4. Make a reference to the `Elevator` part in the **Workspace**.

5. Create a loop that increases the height of the part by changing the **Position** property of the part. Once the loop is done, the part should be `100` studs higher. If the original position was `{0, 0, 0}`, then the new position should be `{0, 100, 0}`. The position should increase every second.

   Tip for 5: If you cannot figure out which loop to use, read the *Programming loops* section again. Our elevator should increase its height by `100` studs which is a previously set amount.

Play the game and check whether the **Elevator** part goes up correctly. Make sure the part does not go up endlessly. If this is the case, you might have chosen the wrong loop. If the **Output** frame displays any errors, try to fix them. An example answer to this exercise can be found on the GitHub page for this book:

`https://github.com/PacktPublishing/Mastering-Roblox-Coding/tree/main/Exercises`

Exercise 2.2 – converting loops

In this exercise, we will convert a functioning `while` loop into a `repeat` loop. Both loops are very similar. In the *Programming loops* section, we explained the difference between both. Take a look at the following code snippet:

```
local spawnLocation = workspace.SpawnLocation

while true do
    spawnLocation.Orientation += Vector3.new(0, 1, 0)
    task.wait()
end
```

This code snippet rotates **SpawnLocation** in the **Workspace**. Feel free to run this script before you convert it.

Exercise:

- Convert the preceding code snippet into a `repeat` loop.

- What is different about the condition of the `repeat` loop compared to the `while` loop, and why?

Play the game and make sure the spawn location rotates. If the **Output** frame displays any errors, try to fix them. An example answer to this exercise can be found on the GitHub page for this book:

```
https://github.com/PacktPublishing/Mastering-Roblox-Coding/tree/
main/Exercises
```

Exercise 2.3 – Police System II (difficult)

This exercise continues the same system idea as *Exercise 2.2 – converting loops*. However, the code is from scratch. In addition, the system is now updated with our newly learned optimizations.

System description:

The police want a system that calculates fines for speeding tickets. The officer wants to provide a list that includes the following: the speed at which the driver was going, whether the driver has a license, and whether the driver was driving recklessly or not. Sometimes, the officer forgets to include something in this list. As a result, the driver might not get a ticket for the crime. Forgetting to include something can be used to exclude certain crimes, too. There should be a list that contains each crime that can be committed. You can find the price of each ticket if the driver commits the crime in each sub-list. Besides the price, there should also be a unique function for each crime that can be used to check whether the driver committed this specific crime or not. A warning should be put into the system's **Output** frame if the ticket price or the unique function is missing. If the driver did not commit a crime, the ticket price would be zero. The ticket price should be displayed in the **Output** frame with the following text: **Ticket Price: 0**. The number depends on the height of the ticket.

Let us analyze the system description together. We see the following things:

- "The police wants a system that calculates fines for speeding tickets." -> This could be a function named `calculateTicketPrice`.

- "The police wants to provide a list that includes the following: the speed at which the driver was going, whether the driver has a license, and whether the driver was driving recklessly or not." -> This could be a dictionary that contains the required items. This dictionary can be given to the previously named function as a parameter.

- "There should be a list that contains each crime that can be committed." -> A global table/dictionary that contains all crimes.

- "In each sub-list, you can find the price of each ticket if the driver committed the crime." -> This global table/dictionary should be multi-dimensional. The sub-table for each crime should contain the ticket price.

- "There should also be a unique function for each crime that can be used to check whether the driver committed this specific crime or not." -> There can be a function within each sub-table per crime. For example, this function could be named isViolating and that receives the previously received data as a parameter.

- "Sometimes, the officer forgets to include something in this list. As a result, the driver may not get a ticket for this crime." -> Each unique function should check whether the data it receives includes the required data to check.

- "If the ticket price or the unique function is missing, a warning should be put into the system's **output**." -> We can make a function to check whether all the required data is within the sub-table for the specific crime.

- "The ticket price should be displayed in the **Output** frame." -> For this, we can use the print function.

> **Note**
>
> Because this is a complex system, in this exercise, you only have to fill out certain system parts. Either way, try to understand the given structure. If you have another idea in mind, feel free to try it. There are a million possible solutions for this system.

Get the fill in code from the GitHub page of this book: https://github.com/PacktPublishing/Mastering-Roblox-Coding/tree/main/Exercises.

Exercise:

1. Create the isViolating() function without checking whether the required data is present.

   Tip for 1: Use simple if statements or expressions to return a Boolean.

2. Update the isViolating() function to check whether all the data you use from the data parameter is present. If not, return false.

3. Create a loop in the calculateTicketPrice() function that loops through the crimeSystem table.

4. Update the isRequiredCrimeDataPresent() function to return false, and give a warning if the ticketPrice variable is not present in the crimeData parameter dictionary.

5. Update the isRequiredCrimeDataPresent() function to return false, and give a warning if the isViolatingFunction variable is not present in the crimeData parameter dictionary.

6. Make an `if` statement that calls the `isRequiredCrimeDataPresent()` function in the loop you created in *step 3*. If `false` is returned, continue to check the next crime.

7. Call the `isViolating()` function in the value variable of your loop. If `true` is returned, increment the ticket price.

Test your system by changing a few variables and check whether the correct result is being displayed. Try to fix any errors that could show up in the **Output** frame. An example answer to this exercise can be found on the GitHub page for this book:

```
https://github.com/PacktPublishing/Mastering-Roblox-Coding/tree/
main/Exercises
```

Summary

Sometimes, we repeat the same piece of code multiple times. Instead of copying and pasting, we can use functions. We learned that functions allow us to repeat the same code multiple times. Additionally, we saw that functions can have parameters. We saw how these parameters could change the function's behavior depending on what conditionals you have. Besides that, we also learned that functions could return data by using the `return` statement. We use the lower camel case naming method, which is similar to variables for function names. We learned how to give the function a fitting name. Additionally, we learned how to split functions if functions have multiple purposes. The same applies when our function gets more than 25 lines. These are all for readability reasons.

Another great way to reduce duplicate code is by using loops. First, we saw how loops repeat the same code a few times. Then, we learned that there are three different loops. We saw that `while` and `repeat` loops could run indefinitely, and they only stop when a particular condition is met. In contrast, `for` loops receive a fixed number of runs until they can stop. We learned that adding a `break` statement or a `return` statement makes it possible to break out of this loop. Finally, we learned that `for` loops are the most common loops in Luau. They are also used when looping through the data in a table.

The last optimization we learned was how to reduce duplicate code over multiple scripts. For this, we used modules. For example, if multiple scripts require the same data or functions, they can be turned into a module. We saw how different scripts could require this module, resulting in you not making the same function multiple times.

Additionally, we learned that there are tables in Luau. We saw how tables allow us to store data in a list. We saw how you could keep specific data connected by having a multi-dimensional table. Each piece of data in a table gets a unique index. We learned that this index is a simple number that keeps counting up. Because these numbers can sometimes be vague, we started using dictionaries. Dictionaries have keys instead of indexes. These keys can be numbers. However, they can also be strings. You can name them whatever you want. Because you can name them anything you want, we immediately noticed an increase in our table's readability without having to explain what each piece of data does.

In this chapter, we learned how to write code more efficiently. In the next chapter, we will start by optimizing our code. We will learn how to use events in combination with everything we learned previously. These events allow us to prevent our code from running when required.

3

Event-Based Programming

In this chapter, we will learn about a specific way of programming, called **event-based programming**. Event-based programming allows us to write more optimized code. That is because our code will only run when a particular event happens. If this event does not happen, our code will not run. We will start by looking at functions that we can execute on instances instead of within scripts. After that, we will start listening to events. Once we know how to do this, we will make our own events. Then, we will learn how to use **bindable events** and **bindable functions** to do this. Finally, we will compare these custom events to modules, and we will even learn how to combine them.

The following topics will be covered in this chapter:

- Introduction to events
- Creating custom events
- Exercise 3.1 – event-based game

By the end of this chapter, you will understand the fundamentals of event-based programming. You will be able to use functions in instances, listen to events, create custom events, and combine custom events with modules. You will even be able to make a simple event-based game.

Technical requirements

To start programming with Luau, you need access to a device with internet access. This can either be a Windows device or a Mac device.

Additionally, you will need to download the following software:

- Roblox Player
- Roblox Studio

All the code examples for this chapter can be found on GitHub at `https://github.com/PacktPublishing/Mastering-Roblox-Coding`.

The CiA video for this chapter can be found at `https://bit.ly/3PDyUwp`.

Introduction to events

Sometimes, you want something to happen when a particular action is performed. This action can be anything. Let us make an application with one of these actions. Throughout the following sections, we will make a system that changes the color of our character once we jump. But this raises a problem: how do we detect whether someone is jumping?

First things first, we need a reference to a **Player** instance. But how do we know which players are in-game? Of course, we can make the system for our character. After all, we know our username. But what if someone else is in the game? We somehow need to detect whether someone joins our game because then, we know who is in our game.

In the following section, we will learn how to use functions on instances. After that, we will learn what events are and what they are used for. Additionally, we will learn how to listen to them. Finally, we will learn what to do when we need an event that does not exist.

Functions on instances

Let us start by solving our first problem. We somehow need to find out who is in our game. Previously, we have worked with **Services** such as the **Workspace, ServerScriptService,** and **ServerStorage** services. But as you can see in the **Explorer** frame, there are many more services. There are even services that do not show up in **Explorer.** For now, that is not important. The service that we need to make our application is called **Players.** This service knows everything about the players in our game. But how do we detect whether someone joins?

A **Player** instance for each player is made when they join our game. This **Player** instance can be found inside the **Players** service. Previously, we learned that parts inside a model, or anything else, are considered **Children.** If a part is directly inside the Workspace service, the part is a child of the Workspace service. Therefore, the **Workspace** service is the parent of this part. So, the `:FindFirstChild()` function is called on the **Parent** instance and looks for a **Child** instance with a particular name. If it can find the instance we are looking for, a reference to this instance is returned.

We know the **Player** instance is inside the **Players** service. Therefore, we can assume that the **Player** instance is a child of the **Players** service. Because of this, we can use the `:FindFirstChild()` function in the **Players** service to find the **Player** instance. Take a look at the following:

```
local Players = game:GetService("Players")


function findPlayer(username)
    local player = Players:FindFirstChild(username)
```

```
    if player ~= nil then
        print(player.Name .. " found!")
    else
        print(username .. " is not in-game.")
    end
end


task.wait(1)
findPlayer("YourUsername")
```

The preceding code works. It finds the **Player** instance based on their username. But we do not know everyone their username. What should we do when we do not know the player's username?

> **Note**
>
> In the preceding code example, we stored the result of our :FindFirstChild() function in a variable. We do this because the :FindFirstChild() function can return nil. In this case, nil is returned if we try to find something that it cannot find. Because nil could be returned, we check whether the variable is not nil on the following line.

The :FindFirstChild() function looks for children that have a specific name. Sometimes, you are not sure what the child's name is, but you do know what type of instance you are looking for. As you might have seen in the properties window, there is a property called **ClassName**. This class name determines what type your instance is. The class name can be **Part**, **MeshPart**, **Decal**, **Player**, or anything else.

Previously, we used the :FindFirstChild() function to find our player. We could've used the :FindFirstChildOfClass() function, too. What this :FindFirstChildOfClass() function does is that, instead of looking for a child with a particular name, the function looks for a child with a specific class name. Take a look at the following:

```
local Players = game:GetService("Players")


function findPlayer()
    local player = Players:FindFirstChildOfClass("Player")
    if player ~= nil then
        print(player.Name .. " found!")
    end
end
```

```
task.wait(1)
findPlayer()
```

With the preceding code, we have solved the problem of not knowing someone's username. However, we do have another problem. Both :FindFirstChild() and :FindFirstChildOfClass() only find the first item that matches your description. If there is another child that matches the description, it gets ignored.

These functions are essential. Almost all instances feature these functions. It does not matter if you execute this function on a **Service** instance, a **Part** instance, a **Model** instance, or any other instance; it works. There are also instance-specific functions. For example, the **Players** service has a function called :GetPlayers(). This function loops through all the children of the service and checks whether the children have the **Player** class name. Then, all the instances matching this description are inserted into a table. Take a look at the :GetPlayers() function:

```
local Players = game:GetService("Players")

function printPlayers()
    -- Getting a table containing all players in our game.
    local players = Players:GetPlayers()

    -- Printing all players
    print("Current players in our game:")
    for _, player in pairs(players) do
        print("- " .. player.Name)
    end
end

task.wait(1)
printPlayers()
```

If we execute the preceding code snippet, we get a list of all of the players in our game. Because our game runs in Roblox Studio, only your username shows up. You can see the code in action in *Figure 3.1*. This new function works much better than the :FindFirstChild() function. It solves two problems: not knowing someone's username and getting more than one player. Nevertheless, we still have issues to address. What if someone joins after 10 minutes? The function only gets executed once. So, how do we solve this? Take a look at the following screenshot:

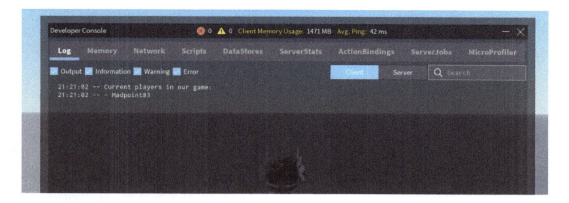

Figure 3.1 – Developer Console containing the player list

Developer Console

The **Developer Console** is the same thing as the **Output** frame. The difference is that the **Output** frame is only for Roblox Studio, whereas the Developer Console can also be accessed in Roblox Player.

To open the Developer Console, press the *F9* key on your keyboard. If you ever play your game on a mobile device, you can also type `/console` into the chat.

Now that we know how to use functions on instances, we can move on to events. In the following section, we will learn what events are and how to use them. Besides that, we will use events to solve the previously described problem.

Listening to events

In the *Programming loops* section of *Chapter 2, Writing Better Code*, we learned about loops. Loops allow us to execute specific code multiple times. One solution to our earlier problem could be to loop over our function constantly. Then, we need a global variable that stores the old player list. If the function detects someone who is not in the global variable, we know that person joined.

You can probably already guess this is a horrible solution. Not only do we have a loop that runs forever, but most importantly, most of the time, it runs for nothing. If no one joins, there is no reason for the function to run. This unnecessary looping is a waste of computer processing power.

Luckily, Roblox implemented a solution for this: **Events**. You can see these events as alarms. For example, when the fire alarm goes off, your action is to evacuate. This alarm is a trigger to do something. This is the same in programming. If something happens, such as a user joining the game, we can start a particular action. There are many of these events. Throughout the book, you will see the most important ones.

Let us take a look at one of those events:

```
local Players = game:GetService("Players")

function playerJoined(player)
    print(player.Name .. " joined the game!")
end


Players.PlayerAdded:Connect(playerJoined)
```

In the preceding code snippet, we can see a .PlayerAdded event. This event gets triggered when someone joins our game. Waiting for this event to get triggered is often referred to as a **Listener**. Using listeners is much better and far easier than the idea we came up with before. In this scenario, events reduce the number of lines we have to code. But most importantly, it also prevents us from looping unnecessarily.

Let us continue with the system we previously described. Our first problem is solved. Now we know what players are in our game. Next, we need to find the character of this player somehow. Luckily, the player parameter we get in our playerJoined() function has a property called **Character**, which references the character. Let us try to see what happens if we try to print the value of this property:

```
local Players = game:GetService("Players")

function playerJoined(player)
    print(player.Character)
end


Players.PlayerAdded:Connect(playerJoined)
```

Unfortunately, if we run the preceding code, nil appears in our **Output** frame. It prints nil because the character of the player does not always exist. The character constantly changes. If the player respawns, a new reference to the character is required. Luckily, there is another event in the **Player** instance. This event is called .CharacterAdded. This event solves our current problem. Let us take a look at the following code:

```
local Players = game:GetService("Players")

function playerJoined(player)
    local function characterAdded(character)
        print(character.Name)
    end
```

```
    player.CharacterAdded:Connect(characterAdded)
end


Players.PlayerAdded:Connect(playerJoined)
```

Notice how we have a nested function? In the *Nested functions* section of *Chapter 2, Writing Better Code*, we learned all about this. We mentioned that, in most scenarios, it is good to avoid this. However, there were a few exceptions. Our current scenario is one of those exceptions. Because we use events that have parameters, we face an issue. For example, the `.CharacterAdded` event has a parameter referencing the user's character. We cannot add an extra parameter because those parameters are fixed for the event. Calling another function would lose the `player` variable from the `playerJoined()` function. Because we use a nested function, we can keep both the character and the player as parameters.

> **Note**
>
> In the *Nested functions* section of *Chapter 2, Writing Better Code*, we learned that we are only allowed to use nested functions if we can be sure that no other function will ever need to call the `characterAdded()` function. In our current scenario, that is the case. Therefore, we are allowed to use a nested function here.

If we run the preceding code, our name gets printed into the **Output** frame. If we reset, the name gets printed again. As previously explained, every time the character respawns, a new character is made. Because we listen to the `.CharacterAdded` event, our function gets executed again every time we reset our character.

Now, we have almost finished our original system. The only thing left to detect is the character jumping. We already have the character. Is there an event on this character that fires when we jump? Unfortunately, there is not. If you are familiar with building basic things in Roblox, you probably know about **Models**. Models group parts together. A character consists of multiple parts grouped by a model. Not all models are characters. Therefore, there is no `.Jump` event on a model. However, there is something inside of this model that makes it unique. It is called a **humanoid**.

Humanoids bring models to models to life. All characters and **Non-Playable Characters** (**NPCs**) have a humanoid. Previously, we learned about the `:FindFirstChild()` and `:FindFirstChildOfClass()` functions. We can use this to find our humanoid:

```
local Players = game:GetService("Players")


function playerJoined(player)
    local function characterAdded(character)
```

```
        local humanoid = character:FindFirstChildOfClass
        ("Humanoid")
        if humanoid ~= nil then
            print("Humanoid found!")
        end
    end

    player.CharacterAdded:Connect(characterAdded)
end

Players.PlayerAdded:Connect(playerJoined)
```

Now that we learned what events are and when to use them, we can move on to the next section. Sometimes, there are no pre-made events for behavior we are trying to listen to. The following section will explain what to do in those scenarios.

Using properties for missing events

Unfortunately, no event gets fired when a character jumps on the humanoid either. However, there is a property named Jump. This property gets set to true if the character is jumping and changes back to false when the character is done jumping. As we mentioned, this is a property, not an event. We cannot listen to when the value of a property gets changed unless we constantly loop over the property's value. Or can we?

There is a really useful function on every instance called :GetPropertyChangedSignal(). This :GetPropertyChangedSignal() function is a special type of function. When we call this function, it returns an event. The reason this is a function is so that we can specify a property. When this property changes, the event that the function returns gets fired. The event allows us to listen to property changes on any instance. Take a look at the following:

```
humanoid:GetPropertyChangedSignal("Jump"):Connect(function()
    print("Jump property changed: " ..
    tostring(humanoid.Jump))
end)
```

If we implement the preceding code into our system and run the game, this message gets printed into the **Output** frame every time we jump. However, for some reason, it gets printed twice. The fact that it gets printed twice actually makes sense. Our listener gets triggered every time the property changes. We know that our property changes to true when we jump, but it gets changed back to false when we finish jumping. Changing our property back to false also triggers our event. There is a simple fix: an if statement.

Take a look at the following code:

```
humanoid:GetPropertyChangedSignal("Jump"):Connect(function()
    if humanoid.Jump == true then
        print(player.Name .. " jumped!")
    end
end)
```

What the preceding `if` statement does is that it checks whether the value of the **Jump** property equals true. If that is the case, the `print()` function gets executed. On the other hand, when the property's value gets changed back to `false`, this statement prevents the rest of the code from being executed.

Now, all we need to do to finish our code is change the avatar's color. First, we need to generate a random color. Previously, we learned about the Color3 data type. We also learned that a **Color3** data type could be made using **RGB** (**Red**, **Green**, and **Blue**). Each color has a number between 0 and 255. Additionally, we learned about the `math.random()` function. This function generates random numbers.

The other thing we need to do is change the children's color inside the character. There is one problem. There are multiple instances inside a character, and we only need to change the parts. This raises another problem, that is, there are many different parts out there, such as **Part**, **MeshPart**, **VehicleSeat**, **Truss**, and **WedgePart**:

Figure 3.2 – Five different BaseParts

All of these classes are grouped together. The group of classes that contain these different types of parts is called **BasePart**. Because there are many classes in the **BasePart** class, it is difficult to check the **ClassName** property for all of them. Luckily, we can use the `:IsA()` function. This function tells us whether an instance, such as a **Part** instance, is inside a class group such as the **BasePart** class group.

If we use the `:IsA()` function, our code will look like this:

```
local Players = game:GetService("Players")


function playerJoined(player)
```

```
local function characterAdded(character)
    -- Looking for the Humanoid in the new Character
    local humanoid = character:FindFirstChildOfClass
    ("Humanoid")
    if humanoid ~= nil then

        -- Listening to the changing "Jump" property on
        -- the Humanoid
        humanoid:GetPropertyChangedSignal("Jump"):
        Connect(function()
            if humanoid.Jump == true then
                -- Printing that someone jumped
                print(player.Name .. " jumped!")

                -- Changing the color of the player's
                -- character
                changeCharacterColor(character)
            end
        end)

    end
end

-- Listening to a new Character
player.CharacterAdded:Connect(characterAdded)
end

function changeCharacterColor(character)
    -- Getting new Color
    local newColor = randomColor()

    -- Changing Color
    for _, part in pairs(character:GetChildren()) do
        -- Checking if the part is in the "BasePart" class
        -- group
        if part:IsA("BasePart") then
```

```
            part.Color = newColor
        end
    end
end

function randomColor()
    local r = math.random(0, 255)
    local g = math.random(0, 255)
    local b = math.random(0, 255)
    return Color3.fromRGB(r, g, b)
end

Players.PlayerAdded:Connect(playerJoined)
```

When we play the game and jump, you should see the color of your character change into a random color:

Figure 3.3 – Changing avatar color

GitHub Code

You can find the preceding code on the GitHub page for this book.

Now we understand what to do when there are missing events, and we have mastered listening to events. We started by looking at how to use functions on instances. After that, we started listening to various events. Finally, we learned what to do when there is no event to listen to. In the next section, we will learn how to create custom events.

Creating custom events

Previously, we learned that no event gets fired when a character jumps. We started listening to a changed event on a property. This works perfectly. Our current script changes the color of the avatar on a jump change. But what if we wanted to create another script that slowly increases the size of the player's head. This script needs to listen to the same **Jump** property, too. Multiple scripts having the same code is a **Bad Smell**. This is where **Custom Events** come in handy.

In the following sections, we will learn how to create custom events using bindable events and functions. After that, we will compare them to modules. Finally, we will combine bindable events and modules.

Using bindable events

To make our custom event, we will make a new script. This script will be responsible for managing the event. Then, other scripts can listen to this new event.

But how do we make a custom event? Roblox has something called **BindableEvents**. These are instances just like any other instance we have seen. The difference is that they have special functions and events. To start listening to BindableEvent, we need a reference to it. Once our reference has been made, we can listen to it using the .Event event. That's great, but because it is a custom event, we need to trigger it somehow. That is where the :Fire() function comes in. Once the :Fire() function has been executed, the .Event event is triggered.

Let us look at the code of the script that handles this custom event. We will call this script JumpedEventHandler:

```
local Players = game:GetService("Players")


function playerJoined(player)
    local function characterAdded(character)
        -- Looking for the Humanoid in the new Character
        local humanoid = character:FindFirstChildOfClass
        ("Humanoid")
        if humanoid ~= nil then

            -- Creating our custom event
            local customEvent =
            Instance.new("BindableEvent")
```

```
        customEvent.Name = "Jumped"
        customEvent.Parent = humanoid

        -- Listening to the .Jumped event on the
        -- Humanoid
        humanoid:GetPropertyChangedSignal("Jump"):
        Connect(function()

            if humanoid.Jump == true then

                -- Firing our Custom Event
                customEvent:Fire()

            end

        end)

        end
    end

    -- Listening to a new Character
    player.CharacterAdded:Connect(characterAdded)
end

Players.PlayerAdded:Connect(playerJoined)
```

The preceding code looks a lot like our original code. The only primary difference is that we now make a custom event and our `:GetPropertyChangedSignal()` function fires an event instead of calling a function.

Let us briefly look at the section that creates our custom event. First, we see a function called `Instance.new()`. What this function does is create a new instance of a specific class. This class is given as an argument in between the parentheses. For our example, this is a BindableEvent. After that, we simply change the values of certain properties. Finally, we name our custom event `Jumped`. This helps us identify the event from other scripts. When the game is running, you can find the bindable event in the **Explorer** frame:

Figure 3.4 – Jumped BindableEvent in the Explorer frame

Now we can start listening to our custom event. This is done from another script. We will call it the JumpedEventListener script:

```
local Players = game:GetService("Players")

function playerJoined(player)
    local function characterAdded(character)
        -- Looking for the Humanoid in the new Character
        local humanoid = character:FindFirstChildOfClass
        ("Humanoid")
        if humanoid ~= nil then

            -- Waiting for Jumped event
            local jumpedEvent =
            humanoid:WaitForChild("Jumped")

            -- Listening to our custom event
            jumpedEvent.Event:Connect(function()
                -- Printing that someone jumped
                print(player.Name .. " jumped!")
            end)
```

```
            end
      end


      -- Listening to a new Character
      player.CharacterAdded:Connect(characterAdded)
end


Players.PlayerAdded:Connect(playerJoined)
```

We have moved all our logic from listening to the property to another script. Something that's noteworthy is the usage of the `:WaitForChild()` function. We have not seen this before. Because one of our scripts creates the event and the other script needs it, there is a chance our script looks for our event before it is created. The `:WaitForChild()` function prevents this.

The `:WaitForChild()` function does something that we call **yielding**. Yielding pauses the current thread until it allows the thread to continue. The `:WaitForChild()` function yields the function for a maximum of 5 seconds. In those 5 seconds, it keeps looking for the instance that we are trying to find.

Previously, we used the `:FindFirstChild()` function. The difference between the `:FindFirstChild()` function and the `:WaitForChild()` function is that the `:FindFirstChild()` function checks whether it can find an instance. If it cannot find this instance, it returns nil. The `:WaitForChild()` function does the same. However, instead of instantly returning nil, it keeps checking to find the instance. This does not mean that you should always use the `:WaitForChild()` function. Let us take a look at the following table to find out how to properly reference instances:

Path	Use case
`workspace.SpawnLocation`	Use the dot (`.`) operator to reference instances when an instance will always be in this location. This has the best performance. If `SpawnLocation` cannot be found, an error is given.
`workspace:FindFirstChild("SpawnLocation")`	Use the `:FindFirstChild()` function if you want to figure out whether an instance is at this location. If `SpawnLocation` cannot be found, `nil` is given.
`workspace:WaitForChild("SpawnLocation")`	Use the `:WaitForChild()` function only if you know an instance is coming soon but might not be there yet. This function might yield forever if `SpawnLocation` never gets created at this location. This function is less efficient than the `:FindFirstChild()` function.

Table 3.1 – Properly referencing instances

With our current script, we can change the avatar's color or increase the size of its head.

Now that we know how to use BindableEvents, we can look at something similar, **BindableFunctions.** In the following section, we will learn what they are and how to use them.

Using bindable functions

We might want to increase the size of our character's head once every five jumps. There are many ways of implementing this. One of the options could be to add a variable into our `JumpedEventListener` script. Another option is to move this variable into the `JumpedEventHandler` script and give the `Jumped` event a parameter that states the number of times the character jumped.

Additionally, we can use **BindableFunctions.** These are very similar to BindableEvents. The difference is that **BindableEvents** can never give something back, whereas BindableFunctions are all about giving data back once completed.

All three of these options have their pros and cons. For now, we are going to explore the BindableFunctions option. To practice, feel free to try and implement these other options.

There are a few differences when comparing BindableEvents to BindableFunctions:

- You can listen to the event of the BindableFunction using `.OnInvoke`. When this is done, a **callback** starts. The primary difference is that a callback must return data, whereas BindableEvents cannot do this.

- To invoke a BindableFunction, you can use the `:Invoke()` function.

- There can only be one script that listens to the `.OnInvoke` event. This makes sense. After all, something must be returned when using the `:Invoke()` function. We cannot get two results from different scripts. When you do listen to the `.OnInvoke` event in multiple scripts, only one result gets used and the rest gets ignored.

Let us change our `JumpedEventHandler` script to implement this BindableFunction:

```
local Players = game:GetService("Players")


function playerJoined(player)
    local function characterAdded(character)
        -- Looking for the Humanoid in the new Character
        local humanoid = character:FindFirstChildOfClass
        ("Humanoid")
        if humanoid ~= nil then
            -- Total Jumps variable
            local totalJumps = 0
```

```lua
            -- Creating custom event
            local jumped, timesJumped =
            createCustomEvents(humanoid)

            -- Listening to the .Jumped event on the
            -- Humanoid
            humanoid:GetPropertyChangedSignal("Jump"):
            Connect(function()
                if humanoid.Jump == true then
                    -- Incremented Total Jumps
                    totalJumps += 1

                    -- Firing our Custom Event
                    jumped:Fire()
                end
            end)

            timesJumped.OnInvoke = function()
                -- Returns the Total Jumps
                return totalJumps
            end
        end
    end
    -- Listening to a new Character
    player.CharacterAdded:Connect(characterAdded)
end

function createCustomEvents(humanoid)
    local jumped = Instance.new("BindableEvent")
    jumped.Name = "Jumped"
    jumped.Parent = humanoid

    local timesJumped = Instance.new("BindableFunction")
    timesJumped.Name = "TimesJumped"
    timesJumped.Parent = humanoid
```

```
    -- Returning events
    return jumped, timesJumped
end


Players.PlayerAdded:Connect(playerJoined)
```

Not much has changed compared to our original script. One of the primary differences is that we now have a new function that creates the BindableEvent and BindableFunction. The reason for this is to prevent our other functions from growing too much in size. Previously, we learned how to make our function only do one thing. Creating events is something that can be done in another function. Because we still need these instances in the other function, our createCustomEvents() function returns the RemoteEvent as the BindableFunction.

Something noteworthy is the way we call our function when the bindable function is invoked. When using .Event, we follow by using :Connect(). After that, we declare our function. Callbacks are a bit different. If you use .OnInvoke, you follow it by an equals (=) operator, and then you declare your function. This is something you need to remember when using BindableFunctions.

To test whether the bindable function works, we can change the code in our JumpedEventListener script, as follows:

```
-- Waiting for Custom Events
local jumped = humanoid:WaitForChild("Jumped")
local timesJumped = humanoid:WaitForChild("TimesJumped")

-- Listening to our custom event
jumped.Event:Connect(function()
    -- Printing that someone jumped
    print(player.Name .. " jumped " .. timesJumped:Invoke()
    .. " time(s)")
end)
```

> **Note**
> The preceding code is just a section of the JumpedEventListener script. Replace this part in the original script.

We can finish our system now that we understand how to invoke bindable functions:

```
-- Waiting for Custom Events
local jumped = humanoid:WaitForChild("Jumped")
```

```
local timesJumped = humanoid:WaitForChild("TimesJumped")

-- Listening to our custom event
jumped.Event:Connect(function()
    -- Calculating Scale
    local headScale = math.floor( timesJumped:Invoke() / 5
    ) + 1

    -- Getting scale value
    local scaleValue = humanoid:FindFirstChild("HeadScale")
    if scaleValue then
        scaleValue.Value = headScale
    end
end)
```

Something noteworthy in the preceding code snippet is the math.floor() function. This function turns decimal numbers into whole numbers. For instance, when we have the decimal number 1.9 and use the math.floor() function, the number gets rounded to the whole number of 1. Now, if we want the number to be rounded up instead of down, we use the math.ceil() function. When using the math.ceil() function, the decimal number of 1.2 gets rounded to 2.

> **Note**
> The preceding code is just a section of the JumpedEventListener script.

The following screenshot shows the increased head size of our player:

Figure 3.5 – Increased head size

Now that we know how to use BindableFunctions, let us compare them to modules. In the following section, we will learn when to use custom events and modules.

Comparing events to modules (advanced)

This section is for those willing to take their knowledge of event-based programming to the next level. Of course, it is perfectly fine to skip this section and only use the knowledge from the previous sections.

Bindable events and functions allow us to execute code in another script. In the *Using modules* section of *Chapter 2, Writing Better Code*, we have seen something that practically does the same, Modules. The only difference is that modules have to be loaded in another script. Once that is done, the module's functions can be used in the script.

You are allowed to use both for any situation. However, there are some common examples where it makes more sense to pick a particular option. Let us walk through them.

When multiple events are somewhat grouped, such as the `Jumped` and `TimesJumped` events from earlier, it might make more sense to create a module. However, if there is just one event, using a BindableEvent or BindableFunction might make more sense. It comes down to preference.

There is one important thing to remember before changing all your BindableEvents to modules. Previously, we made a new BindableEvent inside of the humanoid. Technically, we could have made this BindableEvent anywhere. If we did that, we could have used the BindableEvent for all players instead of making a new one for each character. This means we can implement the usage of BindableEvents and BindableFunctions however we like. On the other hand, modules are a different story.

If you choose to use modules, never copy a module to store it in a specific location. Instead, use one module, even if it will be used for multiple players.

Now that we know when to use modules and when to use custom events, why not combine them? In the following section, we will see how to combine BindableEvents and modules.

Using bindable events in modules (advanced)

This section is for those willing to take their knowledge of event-based programming to the next level. Of course, it is perfectly fine to skip this section and only use the knowledge from the previous sections.

Because we have a custom `Jumped` event and a `TimesJumped` function, we might use a module instead. Previously, we learned that if we choose to use a module, there might only be one for all characters.

Let us start by making a new `ModuleScript`. We place it in **ServerStorage** and name it `CharacterEvents`. Once made, we rename the returning table to `CharacterEvents`. At the end of the module, we return this table. After that, we add a module function called `Jumped`.

The parameter of this function is the reference to the `Player` instance. Currently, our code in the `CharacterEvents` module looks like the following:

```
local CharacterEvents = {}

function CharacterEvents.Jumped(player)

end

return CharacterEvents
```

> **Note**
> The reason the function is called Jumped and, therefore, does not follow the lower camel case naming method is that this function will be an event.

We plan to trigger the Jumped function if the player jumps. Now, you are probably wondering, functions get executed on events, since when can they make events? You are right. They cannot. However, we previously learned about bindable events. bindable events can trigger events. If our function creates a bindable event and returns a listener, the scripts that call this function can start listening to the returned listener.

This most likely sounds very complex. Let us take a look at the full code for the `CharacterEvents` module:

```
local CharacterEvents = {}

function CharacterEvents.Jumped(player)
    -- Creating Event
    local jumped = Instance.new("BindableEvent")

    -- Character Added event
    local function characterAdded(character)
        -- Looking for the Humanoid in the new Character
        local humanoid = character:FindFirstChildOfClass
        ("Humanoid")
        if humanoid ~= nil then

            -- Listening to the .Jumped event on the
            -- Humanoid
```

```
        humanoid:GetPropertyChangedSignal("Jump"):
        Connect(function()
            if humanoid.Jump == true then
                -- Firing our Custom Event
                jumped:Fire()
            end
        end)

    end
end


    -- Listening to a new Character
    player.CharacterAdded:Connect(characterAdded)

    -- Returning Listener
    return jumped.Event
end

return CharacterEvents
```

The preceding code might look really complex. Let us take a better look. So, the only thing that changed compared to the previous code is the function. The first thing the function does is create a new BindableEvent. Then, we have the same code that we have seen a few times. This detects new characters, finds the humanoid, and fires an event depending on the **Jump** property. The BindableEvent that gets fired is what we created at the top of the function.

Below that, we have a listener for the `CharacterAdded` event. We have seen this before, too. Then, we return a listener. Previously, we learned how to listen to BindableEvents. Then, we learned there was an event and a function. This event was named `.Event`. This is exactly what we return here. Typically, after having the `.Event` event, we add `:Connect()`. We do not do this part in our module as we do not want to specify the action based on our trigger here. Instead, we want another script to implement its own action.

Let us look at how we can use this listener. The following script is called the `JumpedEventListener` script:

```
local Players = game:GetService("Players")
local ServerStorage = game:GetService("ServerStorage")

local CharacterEvents = require(ServerStorage.CharacterEvents)
```

```
function playerJoined(player)
    -- Listening to Jumped Event
    CharacterEvents.Jumped(player):Connect(function()
        print(player.Name .. " jumped!")
    end)
end


Players.PlayerAdded:Connect(playerJoined)
```

Our global variables reference the **Players** and **ServerStorage** services. Inside the **ServerStorage** service, we find our module. We require this module so that we can use it in our current script.

At the bottom of our script, we listen to the `.PlayerAdded` event. Once a player has joined our game, we start listening to the `.Jumped` event by calling it on the `CharacterEvents` module. When we were using bindable events, we had to look for the character, then the humanoid, and then listen to an event. We no longer have to do this because the module does this for us. Therefore, our code is a lot cleaner. Now we can quickly implement something by using our very own Jumped event.

If we compare our custom event to a default Roblox event, listening to them is almost identical. See the difference in the following code snippet:

```
Players.PlayerAdded:Connect(someFunction) -- Roblox Event
CharacterEvents.Jumped(player):Connect(someFunction) -- Custom
Event
```

The only difference between calling our custom event and a default Roblox event is the parentheses behind the event's name. This is because we are actually calling a function inside a module.

Now that we know how to combine bindable events and modules, we have finished the advanced sections of event-based programming. As with anything you learn, you might have to practice with this a bit yourself.

In the next section, we will make our very first event-based game in Roblox.

Exercise 3.1 – event-based game

In this exercise, we will make a game based on the knowledge we learned during this chapter. The game will consist of two teams. Each team has to claim as many parts as possible. You can claim parts by simply walking over them. Because this game requires buildings, a premade game has been made. This game is open source. Therefore, anyone can edit the game and create their version. Please bear in mind that the game is not finished. In this exercise, we will finish the game.

You can find the game here:

`https://www.roblox.com/games/8645775042/Event-Based-Game`

Select the three dots next to the name, and click on **Edit** to open this game in Roblox Studio.

Once opened, you will see a square in the Workspace service. The gray area is the playing field. This gray area consists of 144 different parts. In **ServerScriptService,** you will see a script named `TeamAssigner`. This is a premade script; you do not have to change anything here. This script assigns joining players to the team with the least players. This way, the teams are balanced. It is a fairly simple team assigner.

If we play the game, we get assigned to a team. However, nothing happens if we walk over one of the gray parts. This is what we will do in the following exercise. Let us get started.

Exercise:

Follow these steps to create your event-based game:

1. Create a new script in **ServerScriptService**.
2. Create a variable to reference the model named **Map** in **Workspace**.
3. Create a variable to reference the **Players** service.
4. Create the `setup()` function and make a **for loop** to loop through all the child instances of the model by using the `:GetChildren()` function. The index variable of this `for` loop will not be used. This can be an underscore (_). The value of the `for` loop will be a part. The name of this variable can be `part`.
5. Inside the `for` loop, check whether the `part` variable is a part by using the `:IsA("BasePart")` function.
6. Start listening to the `.Touched` event on the `part` variable. The `.Touched` event will fire every time that an instance touches our part. The function that listens to this event has a parameter containing the instance that hits our part. For example, the name of this parameter could be `hit`.
7. We understand that the `hit` parameter has an instance that touches our part. For instance, if a character touches our part, the instance could be a part for the leg of our character. Therefore, the **Character** model would be the parent of this instance. Create a variable to reference the character.

    Tip for 7: `local character = hit.Parent`
8. Get a reference to the Player instance by using a function in the Players service, named `:GetPlayerFromCharacter(character)`.

    Tip for 8: Use the reference to the **Player** service to call the `:GetPlayerFromCharacter()` function. Use the reference to the character as the argument.

9. Get a reference to the player's team and save it in a variable.

   Tip for 9: There is a property on the Player's instance named **Team** that can be used to get a reference to the current team.

10. Get `.TeamColor` of the player's current team and save it in a variable.

   Tip for 10: There is a property on the **Team** instance. Use the variable you created in *step 9* to reference the **Team** instance.

11. Change the **BrickColor** property in the part variable to the `TeamColor` we saved as a variable in *step 10*.

12. Run the game to see whether it works. See *Figure 3.6* to see what a working version could look like:

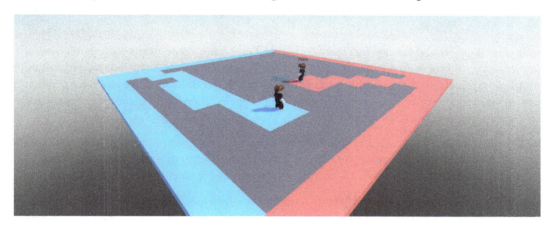

Figure 3.6 – A working event-based game result

If the game works in Roblox Studio, you can upload the game to your own profile and play it with a friend. Another option is to create a local server in Studio to test with two test accounts. You can see two of these test accounts in *Figure 3.6*. You can do this by going to **Test** and selecting **Local Server**. Then, select **2 Players** and press **Start**, as shown in *Figure 3.7*:

Figure 3.7 – Starting a local server in Roblox Studio

If you cannot figure out one of the preceding steps, or your code does not work, please refer to the example solution from GitHub:

`https://github.com/PacktPublishing/Mastering-Roblox-Coding/tree/main/Exercises`

Summary

In this chapter, we learned there are functions on instances. A few common functions are `:GetChildren()` and `:FindFirstChild()`. Both of these events get the children of an instance. But there are way more functions. Previously, we also used the `:GetService()` function to get services such as **Players.** We learned that some of these functions are for all instances, while some are instance-specific.

Besides functions, we also learned that there are events. Once again, some events are found in almost every instance, and there are instance-specific events. Events allow us to write our code in a more optimized way. Instead of constantly checking for certain things to happen, we use events. When using events, our code only gets executed if something happens. Therefore, we learned that our code does not run without anything happening.

We have seen that there are not always events for everything we want to listen to. We learned that in those scenarios, we could look for properties. We learned how to use the `:GetPropertyChangedSignal()` event to listen to property changes. Using this allows us to still to events even if there is no official one.

Using the `:GetPropertyChangedSignal` event, we saw how to make a bindable event and create our own event. Then, we learned how to fire and listen to bindable events. Additionally, we learned about bindable functions. When firing bindable events, we do not get a response. However, if we invoke bindable functions, we do get a response. We saw something similar when we used modules. When using modules, we could also call a function and get a response.

Finally, we learned how to use bindable events in modules. This allows our script to listen to events without messing around with bindable events.

In the next chapter, we will learn about the **Client** and the **Server.** So far, we have only worked with the server. We will learn what the server and the client are and when to use them. Besides that, we will also learn how to securely communicate between the server and the client. Finally, the chapter will explain how to ensure exploiters (hackers) do not gain access to your server.

Part 2: Programming Advanced Systems

This part will go in-depth into complex technologies within Roblox. Understanding the basics of Roblox Luau is a must. When you finish this part, you can make your own game from scratch using complex systems.

This section comprises the following chapters:

- *Chapter 4, Securing Your Game*
- *Chapter 5, Optimizing Your Game*
- *Chapter 6, Creating User Interfaces For All Devices*
- *Chapter 7, Listening To User Input*
- *Chapter 8, Building Data Stores*
- *Chapter 9, Monetizing Your Game*

4
Securing Your Game

In this chapter, we will learn the fundamentals of advanced Roblox programming. We will start by learning what the client and server are. Once we know this, we will learn which part of the system gets implemented where. After that, we will learn how to use RemoteEvents and RemoteFunctions to communicate between the server and client. This is something that hackers and exploiters could abuse as well. This is why we will learn how to implement security measures to prevent this from happening. Finally, we will also look at text filtering to ensure no bad language ends up in your game.

The following topics will be covered in this chapter:

- Understanding the client and server
- Using RemoteEvents and RemoteFunctions
- Implementing security
- Filtering user text
- Exercise

By the end of this chapter, you will understand better how games work. You will know what parts of your system to implement on the server and what parts to implement on the client. In addition, you will know how to communicate between the client and the server securely. Finally, you will know how to filter user text.

Technical requirements

To start programming with Luau, you need access to a device with internet access. This can either be a Windows or a Mac device.

You need to download the following software:

- Roblox Player
- Roblox Studio

All the code examples for this chapter can be found on GitHub at `https://github.com/PacktPublishing/Mastering-Roblox-Coding`.

The CiA video for this chapter can be found at `https://bit.ly/3S6IHwA`.

Understanding the client and server

In the previous chapters, we have repeatedly worked with **Scripts** and not with **LocalScripts**. What is the difference between the two and when do you use them? In this section, we will learn the answers to these questions. In addition, we will also learn what **clients** and **servers** are. On top of that, we will also look into the effect that **LocalScripts** have on the rest of the game. Finally, we will see how the changes made in **LocalScripts** do not **replicate** on the server.

Once we know this, we will learn how to communicate between the server and the client using **RemoteEvents** and **RemoteFunctions**. Because exploiters will try to gain access to the server, we will learn how to secure these RemoteEvents and RemoteFunctions. Besides this, we will learn some additional security tactics we can use to increase the security of our game. Finally, we will learn how to filter text that comes from users.

Introducing LocalScripts

As previously mentioned, we have worked with **Scripts**. When we made our first script, back in *Chapter 1, Getting Up to Speed with Roblox and Luau Basics*, we specifically mentioned not to click on the **LocalScript** option when creating it. Let's start by looking at what would have happened if we did this anyway. Follow these steps:

1. First, create a **Script** in **ServerScriptService** with the `print()` function, which prints the following text: **Printed from the Script**.

    If we play the game and open the **Output** frame, we will see the following line:

    ```
    Printed from the Script   -  Server - Script:1
    ```

2. Now, we will repeat this. This time, we create a **LocalScript** in **ServerScriptService**. Once again, we use the `print()` function; however, we print **Printed from the LocalScript**.

It looks like only the code in the **Script** got executed and not the code in the **LocalScript**. This is because a **LocalScript** runs on the client, whereas a **Script** runs on the server. Both terms are commonly used, but what do they mean exactly?

Everything works with computers. When you join a Roblox game, you are on your own computer. The computer you are on is considered the client. Roblox, on the other hand, has computers too, a lot of them. Roblox's computers are considered servers. When we join a Roblox game, our computer, the client, connects with a Roblox computer, the server.

Figure 4.1 – Client and server

LocalScripts are specifically designed to run on a client. This means that **LocalScripts** run on the computers of the players. When you join a Roblox game, all **LocalScripts** for that game run on your computer. This also means that they do not run on the server.

The same thing applies to **Scripts**. **Scripts** always run on Roblox's servers and never on the client. Now that we know this, let us figure out why our **LocalScript** did not print the message we told it to print.

Technically, we could guess the reason for this by looking at the name of the service, **ServerScriptService**. As the name says, **ServerScriptService** is a service for the server only. The code in **LocalScripts** will simply not get executed when it is in this service. So, where can we run **Scripts** and where can we run **LocalScripts**? Let us take a look at the following table:

Location	Script	LocalScript
Workspace	Yes	No
Character	Yes	Yes
Equipped Tool (in Character)	Yes	Yes
Dequipped Tool (in Backpack)	Yes	No
Lighting	No	No
ReplicatedFirst	No	Yes
ReplicatedStorage	No	No
ServerScriptService	Yes	No
ServerStorage	No	No
PlayerScripts	No	Yes

Table 4.1 – Script and LocalScript locations

The preceding table tells us where **Scripts** and **LocalScripts** run. However, did you notice something strange? **LocalScripts** run inside of characters, which are inside the **Workspace**. However, **LocalScripts** do not run in the Workspace. This is odd but something that makes sense. We, as players, control our characters. We decide when our character moves forward and when it doesn't. We can do this because characters are controlled by the client. Each player controls their own character.

Now that we know where **Scripts** and **LocalScripts** work, let us make one. Let us start by spawning a part in the game using a **LocalScript**. The code for the **LocalScript** would look exactly the same as it would look for the **Script**. The following code snippet is the code in our **LocalScript**, which is placed in the **StarterPlayerScripts**:

```
local part = Instance.new("Part")
part.Position = Vector3.new(0, 10, 0)
part.Parent = workspace
```

When we play our game, we will see a part in the Workspace. So, what is the difference between a **Script** and a **LocalScript** other than them not running in certain spots? Well, something interesting is going on.

Play the game again and switch to the server instead of the client, as shown in *Figure 4.2*:

Figure 4.2 – Switching to the server

When we do this, the part is magically gone, as shown in *Figure 4.3*:

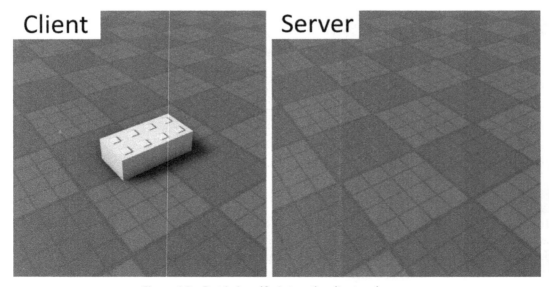

Figure 4.3 – Part in LocalScript on the client and server

> **Understanding the Client and Server**
>
> Use the same code snippet from our **LocalScript** in a **Script** in **ServerScriptService** to see the difference.

We just learned what **LocalScripts** are and how they compare to regular **Scripts**. In addition, we had an introduction to the client and the server. In the next section, we will take a deeper look into why the part does not show up on the server.

FilteringEnabled

In the previous section, we saw how the part we made in our **LocalScript** does not show up on the server or other clients. In September 2017, Roblox introduced something called **FilteringEnabled**. Previously, any changes done by **LocalScripts** would happen to all clients. This means that if we were to remove parts from our game, those parts would be removed for everyone. As you can imagine, this is an extreme security risk that many exploiters took advantage of. Exploiters purposely removed parts from the game to ruin the experience for others.

Roblox's counterdefense was FilteringEnabled. FilteringEnabled stops all changes on the client from happening on the server. For example, if an exploiter removed parts from your game, the parts would be gone for you, but not for anyone else. This is extremely effective in combating exploiters. Unfortunately, this broke numerous games, as some games relied on **LocalScripts** changing the behavior of games. Therefore, another setting was introduced. You were able to choose whether your game used FilteringEnabled or not.

Later, FilteringEnabled was renamed **Experimental Mode**. If your game did not have FilteringEnabled, your game was in Experimental Mode. Later, FilteringEnabled was **deprecated**. Deprecated is a fancy word for saying that something should no longer be used or that it will not work anymore. From that point, every game, including all new games, had to use the FilteringEnabled technology. Developers could not disable it anymore. This means that no game could be in Experimental Mode anymore.

We can now understand the previous behavior when we created the part in our **LocalScript**. Because of FilteringEnabled, the part exists on the client, but it does not replicate to the server. Similar to how parts would not get removed, new parts would not be made either. As a matter of fact, no changes to anything in the game were replicated to the server. We can prove this; let us make a **LocalScript** that changes the **Material** property of the baseplate to **Granite**. Our **LocalScript** would once again be placed in **StarterPlayerScripts** and would contain the following code snippet:

```
local baseplate = workspace:WaitForChild("Baseplate")
baseplate.Material = Enum.Material.Granite
```

If we run the preceding code snippet, we will notice that the **Material** property on the baseplate gets changed from **Plastic** to **Granite**. However, if we change to the server, we will see that the baseplate still has the **Plastic** material:

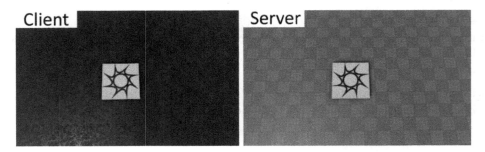

Figure 4.4 – Material on the client and the server

> **Understanding the Client and Server**
> Use the same code snippet from our **LocalScript** in a **Script** in **ServerScriptService** to see the difference.

This is because FilteringEnabled stepped in to prevent this change from happening on the server. However, there are a few things that FilteringEnabled does not prevent from happening.

> **Enums**
> As seen in the previous code snippet, you have to use something called an **Enum** to change the **Material** property on parts. An Enum is basically a **global variable** for every single **Script**. We have previously seen that if we made our variable near the top of our **Script**, it was accessible throughout the entire **Script**. The same thing is true for Enums. You can use them everywhere. The only difference is that Luau has already defined them for us. We will see more usages of Enums throughout the rest of the book.

Now that we know what FilteringEnabled is, we know how Roblox handles the security between the server and clients. We saw how nothing on the client gets replicated to the server. As previously mentioned, a few exceptions still replicate to the server. In the next section, we will cover these exceptions.

Replication exceptions to FilteringEnabled

In the previous section, we learned that FilteringEnabled prevents changes made by **LocalScripts** from happening on the server. We saw the example where we changed the **Material** property of the baseplate to **Granite**. The material only changed on the client and not on the server. Besides that, we learned that exploiters used to remove parts of the map to ruin the experience for other players. FilteringEnabled steps in to prevent both examples from happening on the server, and therefore, on other clients.

Let us take a look at another script. Once again, we will make a **LocalScript** in **StarterCharacterScripts**. Because all instances in the **StarterCharacterScripts** get automatically parented into the character once made, we can assume that the parent of the **LocalScript** is the model's character. The following code snippet will remove a part from our character. This part is called the `RightLowerArm`, like so:

```
local character = script.Parent
local rightLowerArm = character:FindFirstChild("RightLowerArm")
rightLowerArm:Destroy()
```

> **Characters**
>
> This preceding code snippet only works when the character is in **R15**. **R15** is a **body type** that you can pick when creating your avatar. The **R15** avatar consists of 15 unique parts, whereas the **R6** avatar consists of only 6.

If you create the preceding **LocalScript** for yourself and run the game, you will notice something out of the ordinary. If you view the game from the client's perspective, as seen in *Figure 4.5*, nothing special is going on. As expected, the lower arm of your character is gone. However, when we change to the server, something weird happens. The right lower arm part is gone on the server too.

Figure 4.5 – The client's perspective after removing the lower arm

Throughout the past few pages, we continuously mentioned that FilteringEnabled prevents changes made by clients from happening on the server. However, now, we see an example where our change gets allowed. Could it be an accident? No, it was not an accident. FilteringEnabled lets a few changes go through. These changes are for the following categories:

- Some properties of the **Humanoid**
- **Sound** playback (when `SoundService.RespectFilteringEnabled` is set to `false`)

- **ClickDetector** input events

- **AnimationTrack** playback

- **BaseParts** that the client has **network ownership** of

You can find additional information on the **Roblox Developer Wiki** here:

```
https://developer.roblox.com/en-us/api-reference/property/Workspace/
FilteringEnabled
```

Now that we know what changes FilteringEnabled allows, we can clarify why the part of our arm was removed, right? If we take a look at the list, you might think that it has to do with the **Humanoid**. After all, it is a character. However, this is not the case. We removed a **BasePart** class. We did not do anything to the **Humanoid**.

The part that was removed has everything to do with the network ownership. Network ownership determines who handles the properties of parts. Whoever has the ownership is in control of the properties. Each player has ownership of their own character. Therefore, if we remove a part of our character, FilteringEnabled will allow the change. Just remember that **LocalScripts** can perform changes on the character that belongs to the player. If a **LocalScript** were to remove the same arm from someone else's character, it would not happen on the server.

A great way to experiment with FilteringEnabled and its exceptions is to start a local server with two or more players and perform random actions such as removing parts to see what happens on the server and the other client(s). In *Figure 4.6*, you can see how to start a local server:

Figure 4.6 – Starting a local server

Now that we know how the client and server work and how FilteringEnabled works, we understand the fundamentals of securing our game. But what tasks should we perform on the server, and which tasks should we perform on the client? In the next section, we will figure this out.

Client and server responsibilities

Now that we know what clients and servers are, what FilteringEnabled is, and how it works, we understand the fundamentals of the client-server model. However, when do we use the client and when do we use the server? While there is no watertight way of determining what goes on the client and what goes on the server, there are a few dos and don'ts.

In the following subsections, we will learn about these dos and don'ts in detail.

Client responsibilities

Let us start with the client. We basically handle everything that makes our game pretty and the user input on the client. This includes **graphical user interfaces (GUIs)**, animations, effects, listening to input from the keyboard, and clicks on buttons. Of course, there are a few additional use cases where you should use the client. An example of this could be if you only want something visible for one player, but not the rest.

We have not seen many use cases for the client responsibilities in this book so far. In later chapters, we will look at all the previously mentioned responsibilities in detail.

Some things should never be done on the client. These include everything directly related to **data stores**. Besides that, **game logic** should never be done on the client either. What is game logic? Game logic can sometimes be referred to as **business logic**. This sounds really cool, but what is it? Game logic essentially means the game's rules. For example, in our fictive game, we have a **Collect Money** button. Every time someone clicks the **Collect Money** button, a random amount between zero and fifty coins gets added to our account. This is a feature of the game. So, what exactly can we not do on the client here? Calculating the amount someone gets should always be done on the server. We will come back to this example and see why it is essential to perform these actions on the server in the *Implementing security* section.

Server responsibilities

We previously saw what responsibilities the client had—basically, everything that we do not do on the client, we do on the server. For example, we previously read that anything related to data stores should be done on the server. In addition, we heard that business logic should be done on the server too.

Both of these examples are usually done correctly. However, most of the time, us developers tend to overuse the server to make our game look prettier through animations and effects. This is because doing these on the server is just way faster. Therefore, it takes less time to implement them. The problem is that, in these scenarios, our server has to spend time on these effects when it has more important tasks to do. After all, why should the server see these beautiful effects? It is not like someone is viewing the game through the server. In *Chapter 5*, *Optimizing Your Game*, we will learn how to properly implement these effects on the client.

Now that we know the responsibilities of both the server and the client, we truly know everything about the server and the client. As previously mentioned, we can have a scenario where we need to listen to user input and then perform an action on the server. So, how do we make the server and the client work together? We can do this by using **RemoteEvents** and **RemoteFunctions**. In the next section, we will learn how to use these.

Using RemoteEvents and RemoteFunctions

In the previous sections of this chapter, we learned a lot about the client and the server. We also mentioned that sometimes the client and the server have to work together to achieve something. For instance, if a user wants to join a team, they have to use a Team Changer. In this Team Changer, they have to click on the button for the team they want to join.

The code for this team button is programmed on the client. However, the actual team change happens on the server. After all, we want the team change to be visible for all the players, not just one.

In the upcoming sections, we will make this system into reality. We will be using both the client and the server. We will learn how to use **RemoteEvents** and **RemoteFunctions** to communicate between the client and the server.

Setting up the GUI

In this chapter, we will not design and create the GUI ourselves. This has been done for us. The only thing we will do is implement the systems around it. You can get the Roblox Studio file that includes the GUI yourself from the GitHub page here:

`https://github.com/PacktPublishing/Mastering-Roblox-Coding/tree/main/Games`

The game is called **Introducing RemoteEvents and Functions**.

Once you download the fill-in version, open the file using Roblox Studio. It should open like any other game. Once opened, you will see the **Team Changer** GUI in the center of the screen, as seen in *Figure 4.7*:

Figure 4.7 – The Team Changer graphical user interface

In the **Explorer** frame, open the service named **StarterGui**. This Service makes sure all players get the GUIs inside of it. The Service also allows us to see the user interface. For example, if we open StarterGui, we will see a **ScreenGui** called **Team Changer**. A ScreenGui is an instance that groups an entire GUI together. Inside of a ScreenGui we can add other instances such as **TextLabels**, **TextButtons**, **ImageLabels**, **ImageButtons**, and many more.

If we open the **TeamChanger** GUI, we see an **ImageLabel**, as seen in *Figure 4.8*. This ImageLabel is named **MainFrame**. If we select the instance in the **Explorer** frame, an outline will appear around the entire **Team Changer** frame. This image serves as the rounded background for our frame. If we open this image, we see that this image is the parent of a few other instances. The reason that the children, such as the **BlueTeam** and **RedTeam ImageButtons** are parented to the **MainFrame** image has to do with layers and scaling. We will dive deeper into this in *Chapter 6, Creating User Interfaces for all Devices*.

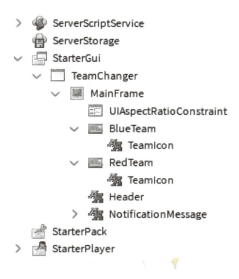

Figure 4.8 – Team Changer GUI structure

For now, it is important to understand there are two buttons in this GUI. The button on the left, with the rocket, is supposed to team you to the Red team. Next to this button, we also have a button with a plane that should team you up with the Blue team. When the player clicks either of these buttons, their team should be changed to whichever button they press.

We have successfully downloaded the Roblox Studio file that contains our Team Changer GUI and we have analyzed its structure. Now, we can start programming it. In the next section, we will learn how to program the Team Changer GUI on the client side.

Client-sided Team Changer

First, we need to make a **LocalScript** inside the TeamChanger ScreenGui. You should give this **LocalScript** a logical name. You can decide what you name it yourself. Once we have made this, we need a reference to both buttons. We have previously made references to instances. However, this time, we need to reference two buttons inside of a GUI. Each player has their own GUI and these GUIs get copied into the `PlayerGui` folder inside each **Player** instance. Then, we can start listening to the `.PlayerAdded` event to get each GUI. While this is possible, there is a better solution.

Our previous references had an **absolute path**. An absolute path starts from the absolute top and works its way down to the desired instance. However, we can have a **relative path** for our reference too. What a relative path does is go from a particular script to its desired instance. Let us look at the reference to both buttons by using a relative path:

```
local blueTeamButton = script.Parent.MainFrame.BlueTeam
local redTeamButton = script.Parent.MainFrame.RedTeam
```

In the preceding code, we start by using the `script` keyword. This starts our reference from the position of our script. Since we made our **LocalScript** directly inside the ScreenGui, we can get the **LocalScript**'s parent to reference the ScreenGui directly using the **Parent** property. After that, we can simply work our way down to both buttons.

Now, we need to start listening to clicks on these buttons. Once someone has clicked, we need to change their team to the correct team color. But how do we see if someone clicked the button? Luckily, an event gets fired when someone clicks on a button. It is called the `.MouseButton1Click` event. Take a look at the following code:

```
local Players = game:GetService("Players")
local player = Players.LocalPlayer
local Teams = game:GetService("Teams")

local blueTeamButton = script.Parent.MainFrame.BlueTeam
local redTeamButton = script.Parent.MainFrame.RedTeam

function switchTeam(teamName)
    -- Getting team
    local team = Teams:FindFirstChild(teamName)

    -- Checking if team exists
    if team ~= nil then
        player.Team = team
    else
        warn("Team [" .. teamName .. "] does not exist!")
    end
end

function swichBlueTeam()
    switchTeam("Blue")
```

```
end

function switchRedTeam()
    switchTeam("Red")
end

blueTeamButton.MouseButton1Click:Connect(swichBlueTeam)
redTeamButton.MouseButton1Click:Connect(switchRedTeam)
```

Let us take a look at the preceding code. At the top of the script, we see something noteworthy. First, we get the `Players` service to get the `LocalPlayer`. What is this? When we used the regular **Scripts**, we had to reference the `Player` by listening to events. However, since **LocalScripts** only run for one player, the `LocalPlayer` references the player on whose device this **LocalScript** is running.

If we test our **LocalScript**, our team gets changed successfully. Therefore, we have successfully implemented our system on the client. However, if we change our view to the server, our change did not happen there. Once again, this is because of FilteringEnabled. So, how do we make sure our change happens on the server? In the next section, we will learn how to use RemoteEvents to make the server change the player's team.

Using RemoteEvents

In our previous code, we need to remove the lines that change the player's team to the new team and add them the server. If we do this, everyone will see that we have changed our team, and not just us, but we need to tell the server to do this somehow. We will use RemoteEvents for this. But first, let us start by making both the server and the client scripts.

We will start by making our server **Script**. We will call our **Script TeamChanger**, and place it in **ServerScriptService**. Let us take a look at the following code:

```
local Teams = game:GetService("Teams")

function switchTeam(player, teamName)
    -- Getting team
    local team = Teams:FindFirstChild(teamName)

    -- Checking if team exists
    if team ~= nil then
        player.Team = team
    else
```

```
            warn("Team [" .. teamName .. "] does not exist!")
        end
    end
```

If we look at the preceding server-side code, we will see the exact function from our **LocalScript**. The only difference is that we now have an **additional parameter** named `player`. Again, this is because we are working on the server; there is no `LocalPlayer` here.

Well, this is great, but how do we make sure this function works if we click the right button? We will use RemoteEvents. RemoteEvents are similar to something we have previously seen in *Chapter 3, Event-Based Programming*. In that chapter, we used something called **BindableEvents**. RemoteEvents are practically the same thing; the only difference is that BindableEvents were for client-client or server-server communication, whereas RemoteEvents are for client-server or server-client communication.

Let us make a RemoteEvent. We can do this in the **Explorer** frame. Usually, RemoteEvents are placed in the **ReplicatedStorage** service. Right-click on the ReplicatedStorage service and add a RemoteEvent. Once you have done this, rename it to **ChangeTeam**. Now, we have successfully created our first RemoteEvent. We still need to configure it a bit, though.

Let us continue on the server **Script**. So what we need to do now is, if our RemoteEvent gets fired, we need to execute our `switchTeam()` function. There is an event on our RemoteEvent called `.OnServerEvent`. We can use this event to listen to incoming requests from the client. We will see this done in the following code:

```
local Teams = game:GetService("Teams")
local ReplicatedStorage = game:GetService("ReplicatedStorage")

function switchTeam(player, teamName)
    -- Getting team
    local team = Teams:FindFirstChild(teamName)

    -- Checking if team exists
    if team ~= nil then
        player.Team = team
    else
        warn("Team [" .. teamName .. "] does not exist!")
    end
end


ReplicatedStorage.ChangeTeam.OnServerEvent:Connect(switchTeam)
```

In the preceding code, we get a reference to the `ChangeTeam` RemoteEvent in ReplicatedStorage. Once this RemoteEvent gets fired, it will now call the `switchTeam()` function. The only thing left for us to do is fire this RemoteEvent from the client. Similar to BindableEvents, there is a function we can call on RemoteEvents that allows us to do this. This function is called `:FireServer()`. Let us implement this function in the **LocalScript** we previously wrote:

```
local ReplicatedStorage = game:GetService("ReplicatedStorage")

local blueTeamButton = script.Parent.MainFrame.BlueTeam
local redTeamButton = script.Parent.MainFrame.RedTeam

function switchBlueTeam()
    ReplicatedStorage.ChangeTeam:FireServer("Blue")
end

function switchRedTeam()
    ReplicatedStorage.ChangeTeam:FireServer("Red")
end

blueTeamButton.MouseButton1Click:Connect(switchBlueTeam)
redTeamButton.MouseButton1Click:Connect(switchRedTeam)
```

If we look at the preceding code, we will see that we changed both the switch team functions to now fire the RemoteEvent. To fire the RemoteEvent, we use the `:FireServer()` function. Inside the parentheses, we have the argument with the team's name that the player needs to switch to. If we look at the server code, we see our `switchTeam()` function actually has two parameters. However, in the preceding client code, we only give one. This is because Roblox provides us with a `player` parameter on the server.

This means every remote event on the server gets the player that fired the remote event as the first parameter, even if we do not give any parameters ourselves. If we add extra parameters, as we did in the preceding code example, we add a string that determines what team the player should be switched to. It will be the second parameter on the server.

We will see the same effect if we test our new client and server code. However, if we change our team now, it gets changed for the rest of the players as well. This means that we have successfully implemented our RemoteEvent. Therefore, we have made our first system that technically works on two devices simultaneously: your device and the Roblox server.

But what if we want to get a response from the server? We have previously seen how to use RemoteEvents in the client-server direction. However, we can do the opposite as well. In the next section, we will learn how to use the `:FireClient()` function on RemoteEvents.

Using RemoteEvents from the server to the client

Let us expand our system to give a warning notification that we cannot change to a team if we are already on it. There is already a TextLabel in the GUI named **NotificationMessage**. We can use this TextLabel to display the message that says they cannot change to a team if they are already on it.

On the server, we will start by writing a simple `if` statement that checks whether the player is already on the team or not. Once we do this, we somehow need to notify the client that the player was already on the team and that a message should be displayed. How do we do this? We can make another RemoteEvent, and this time, instead of the client contacting the server, we can let the server contact the client by using the `:FireClient()` function instead of the `:FireServer()` function. On the client, we then need to listen to the `.OnClientEvent`, instead of the `.OnServerEvent`.

Let us start by making a new RemoteEvent in the ReplicatedStorage. We will call the RemoteEvent **TeamChangerNotification**. Once we have done this, we can make our `if` statement and call the `:FireClient()` function on this new RemoteEvent. Let us take a look at the new server code:

```
local Teams = game:GetService("Teams")
local ReplicatedStorage = game:GetService("ReplicatedStorage")

function switchTeam(player, teamName)
    -- Getting team
    local team = Teams:FindFirstChild(teamName)

    -- Checking if team exists
    if team ~= nil then
        if player.Team ~= team then
            -- Player is not on the team yet
            player.Team = team
        else
            -- Player is already on the team
            ReplicatedStorage.TeamChangerNotification:
            FireClient(player, "You are already on this
            team!")
        end
    else
        ReplicatedStorage.TeamChangerNotification:
        FireClient(player, "Team does not exist!")
    end
```

```
end
```

```
ReplicatedStorage.ChangeTeam.OnServerEvent:Connect(switchTeam)
```

In the preceding code, we called the `:FireClient()` function on the new RemoteEvent every time we wanted a particular message to show up. The first argument for the `:FireClient()` function is the `player` you want to display this message to. After all, the server knows about all players in the game, and we are trying to show it to a specific one. The second argument is the message that we want to show up.

Then, on the client, we have to start listening to this new RemoteEvent. As previously mentioned, we can use the `.OnClientEvent()` event for this. The following code is the new code that has to be placed in the previously made **LocalScript**:

```
local ReplicatedStorage = game:GetService("ReplicatedStorage")
local notificationLabel = script.Parent.MainFrame.
NotificationMessage

function showNotification(message)
    notificationLabel.Text = message
end

ReplicatedStorage.TeamChangerNotification.
OnClientEvent:Connect(showNotification)
```

In the preceding code, we listen to the `TeamChangerNotification` RemoteEvent by using the `.OnClientEvent` event. If we change our team, nothing is different. However, when we try to change to the team that we are already on, we get a notification that we are already on this team as seen in *Figure 4.9*.

Figure 4.9 – "You are already on this team!" notification

Something noteworthy in our code is that once we receive our notification message through the `TeamChangerNotification` RemoteEvent, our function only has one parameter, which is the message. While on the server, we pass two parameters. The first parameter is the player that we want to give this message to, and as the second parameter, we pass the message that we want to display. We only get the message because the first player parameter is used by Roblox internally. We cannot do anything with this parameter ourselves.

Now, we know how to use the `:FireClient()` function on RemoteEvents. However, we now have two RemoteEvents for a tiny system. There is another approach to this problem. We previously learned about **BindableFunctions** as well. These were similar to BindableEvents. However, we were able to return data with them. Luckily, there is something like this to communicate between the client and the server as well. In the next section, we will learn how to use RemoteFunctions in our system to replace both RemoteEvents.

Using RemoteFunctions

Instead of using RemoteEvents, we can use something called RemoteFunctions. But what are RemoteFunctions? In *Chapter 3*, *Event-Based Programming*, we saw something called BindableFunctions. BindableFunctions were almost identical to **BindableEvents**. The only difference was that BindableFunctions could return data, whereas BindableEvents cannot.

Now, let us go back to RemoteFunctions. Similar to BindableFunctions, RemoteFunctions also allow data to be returned. However, RemoteFunctions can be **invoked** from the client and handled on the server. This is the primary difference between RemoteFunctions and BindableFunctions. As mentioned, BindableFunctions only work from the same client to the same client or from the same server to the same server.

To see these RemoteFunctions in action, let us rescript our previously made **Team Changer** and use just one RemoteFunction instead of two RemoteEvents. First, let us make a new RemoteFunction inside the ReplicatedStorage. We will call our RemoteFunction **ChangeTeam**.

> **Note**
>
> Please make sure to remove the RemoteEvents from the game if you decide to implement this system for yourself. The reason for this is that we have both a RemoteEvent and a RemoteFunction with the name **ChangeTeam**. This may lead to weird behavior.

Once we have done this, we will start by updating the code on our server. Let us take a look at the following updated server code that uses a RemoteFunction:

```
local Teams = game:GetService("Teams")
local ReplicatedStorage = game:GetService("ReplicatedStorage")
```

```
function switchTeam(player, teamName)
    -- Getting team
    local team = Teams:FindFirstChild(teamName)

    -- Checking if team exists
    if team ~= nil then
        if player.Team ~= team then
            -- Setting player to the team
            player.Team = team

            -- Returning successful
            return true
        else
            return "You are already on this team!"
        end
    else
        return "Team does not exist!"
    end
end


ReplicatedStorage.ChangeTeam.OnServerInvoke = switchTeam
```

If we look at the preceding code, we see an almost identical function. However, we know we have a `return` statement where we used to fire the other RemoteEvent. This is because a RemoteFunction expects a return value. Like any other function, a return value is specified using the `return` statement. If changing our team was successful, we return a `true` boolean. If it was not successful, for whatever reason, we return a string with an explanation of what went wrong.

Something else that is noteworthy is the last line of our **Script**. When we used BindableFunctions, we learned that BindableFunctions are invoked. However, the way you program this is a tiny bit different. Instead of using the `:Connect()` phrase, we have to put an equals (=) sign and then the name of our function. This is because RemoteFunctions and BindableFunctions use callbacks, as explained in *Chapter 3*, *Event-Based Programming*. Therefore, we use the same **syntax** for RemoteFunctions as with BindableFunctions.

Syntax

The syntax is the way we structure our code. This includes words but also punctuation and special characters. If we refer to the syntax, we mean the sequence in which our code is structured.

Now that we have updated the server code, the only thing left for us to do is the client code. Once again, we need to make sure our client code works with the RemoteFunction. Let us take a look at the following code:

```
local ReplicatedStorage = game:GetService("ReplicatedStorage")
local blueTeamButton = script.Parent.MainFrame.BlueTeam
local redTeamButton = script.Parent.MainFrame.RedTeam
local notificationLabel = script.Parent.MainFrame.
NotificationMessage

function switchTeam(teamName)
    local result = ReplicatedStorage.ChangeTeam:
    InvokeServer(teamName)
    if result ~= true then
        showNotification(result)
    end
end

function swichBlueTeam()
    switchTeam("Blue")
end

function switchRedTeam()
    switchTeam("Red")
end

function showNotification(message)
    notificationLabel.Text = tostring(message)
end

blueTeamButton.MouseButton1Click:Connect(swichBlueTeam)
redTeamButton.MouseButton1Click:Connect(switchRedTeam)
```

In the preceding code, we still listen to `.MouseButton1Click()` event to see if a button was pressed. After that, we execute a function that invokes our RemoteFunction. The parameter for this RemoteFunction is, once again, the name of the team that you want to change to. Like the RemoteEvent, we do not have to specify our **LocalPlayer**. However, it still shows up as the first parameter on the server. Once again, Roblox does this for us.

Interestingly, we store the result of the `:InvokeServer()` inside a variable named `result`. We can do this because a RemoteFunction expects a result. The value of this variable will be what we return in our server code. If we successfully changed our team, this would be a `true` Boolean. If it did not work for whatever reason, we get a string with an explanation.

After that, we check if the variable's value is not `true`. We do this because we know the request was was successful when the value is `true` is returned. However, if we get something other than a boolean, something went wrong on the server. It could be that the team does not exist or that the player is already on this team. When we get a string like this, we call the `showNotification()` function. This function sets the **Text** property of the `notificationLabel` to a given string that was provided as the `message` parameter.

If we add both the new client and the server code, our new system works by using a RemoteFunction. We now know how to communicate between the client and the server by using RemoteFunctions and RemoteEvents. In the next section, we will look at some security implementations.

Implementing security

We already know a lot about the client and the server. We know both their purposes and how to communicate between them. Unfortunately, there are always people trying to ruin the fun by trying to take over your game or exploit it. We already learned how FilteringEnabled prevents a lot of these exploits. However, it cannot stop everything.

So, what can exploiters still do? They are still in control of everything that happens to their own character. Fortunately, this is only the case with their character; they cannot change anything for the characters of other players. The reason for this is because of the network ownership that was explained in the *Replication exceptions to FilteringEnabled* section.

Besides manipulating their own character, exploiters can do anything that we can do with our **LocalScripts**. Exploiters basically "inject" a malicious piece of code into the game. Because this is done on their own computer, this is a client-side script that you could compare to our **LocalScripts**. Us developers cannot detect when this happens. Luckily, Roblox is constantly improving the security of its platform and tries to detect exploiters. Unfortunately, they cannot prevent everything. That is why it is important that we secure our games ourselves too.

Once their code is injected into our game, exploiters might try to gain access to the server. The only way to do this is by using RemoteEvents and RemoteFunctions. Exploiters might look at our **LocalScripts** to see what argument each RemoteEvent and RemoteFunction needs. Then, based on what they read, they could try to fire or invoke these RemoteEvents and RemoteFunctions with false data. They do this in the hope to create unwanted behavior on our server.

Often, games have an in-game currency. This is something that exploiters could target. They will try to find and trick RemoteEvents and RemoteFunctions into giving them free in-game currency. This is just an example of what they could do. As previously mentioned, they can do anything that we can do with our **LocalScripts**.

Of course, this is not something that we want. Therefore, it is important to step up the security in our game. In the following sections, we will learn ways of doing this. In addition, we will learn a few things to keep in mind when making RemoteEvents and RemoteFunctions.

Server checks

In the previous sections, we have already implemented various **server checks**. One of these checks was to see whether a player was already on the team. While this is not a very important check, there is a particular behavior that you do not want your players to do. Let us say we had some sort of check that prevented unbalanced teams. This is important as it would prevent every player from joining a single team. As you can imagine, this is behavior that you do not want, as it might be unfair to other players in our game.

Theoretically, it would not matter whether we had this check on the server or the client in an ideal situation. The `if` statement that prevents unbalanced teams works on either the client or server. However, this is where many beginner developers go wrong. It does matter. Not necessarily for legit players, because it indeed would prevent this behavior for them, but it does not prevent this behavior for exploiters.

Nothing stops these exploiters from firing your RemoteEvent or RemoteFunction. This is why we need these checks on the server. Every single RemoteEvent or RemoteFunction should have checks on it. The more scenarios you can prevent, the more secure your game gets. You need checks for very every parameter that you receive from the client. *Never trust any data from the client.* Always validate whether this data is correct.

Here are a few examples of checks you could implement for your RemoteEvents or RemoteFunctions. Please keep in mind that these are just examples. You will have to come up with checks that work for your game:

- Imagine a RemoteFunction that retrieves data for a shop GUI. This shop GUI can only be opened if the player is standing near the shop building in your game. A possible check could calculate the distance between the character and the shop. If the player is too far away, the request is ignored.

- For a trading system, one of the parameters is the player you will trade with. So, the first check should be to see if this second player is in the game. Then, another check should be to verify that the player is not trying to trade themself. Finally, you also have to check if both players really own the items that they are trying to trade.

- For a shop system, the player wants to purchase an item for 100 coins. A check could verify if this item exists. Another check could be to verify that the player has 100 coins. Maybe your game does not allow the person to have this item multiple times. In this case, a check could verify that the player does not already have this item.

Security Risk

Never, ever have the price of an item as a parameter. Even if there is some individual player discount system, let the server figure this out. Always store the price for each item somewhere on the server. You do not want an exploiter to fire your RemoteEvent with legit data and a price of 0 coins!

- For a restocking system, you want to restock 500 items. The RemoteEvent that gets fired for this purchase will have the number of items that you wish to restock as a parameter. However, one of the checks that is usually forgotten is the one that checks whether this number is negative or not. This is a critical check to implement in your game! If your game does not implement this, there is a good chance that this RemoteEvent could cause an Infinite Money glitch.

These are just a few examples and tips that you have to keep in mind while implementing server checks on your RemoteEvent and RemoteFunction. As previously mentioned, the checks may vary depending on how your game works. Take your time to figure out what incorrect data could be sent. Think outside of the box.

Now that we know why server checks are essential and have seen some examples of server checks, let us look at something else that we can implement to prevent unwanted behavior caused by exploiters. In the next section, we will learn what **debounces** are and how to implement them.

Implementing debounces

Sometimes you have amazing server checks in place, but the function behind this RemoteEvent or RemoteFunction is just really server-intensive. This means that the function can be really complex and has to calculate many difficult things. If we have functions like this, exploiters may intentionally spam fire this with correct data to cause lag on the server.

What can we do to prevent this from creating lag on our server? After all, they might be sending correct data that our server checks would not stop. Sometimes, it is possible to only allow a request to the server once every few seconds or even minutes. But how do we do this? We can do this by creating a **debounce**.

But what is a debounce? Technically, it is just a simple `if` statement and a variable for each player. We will use this variable to store the player's last time using this function. Then, inside our `if` statement, we will use this `time` variable and add a few seconds to it. If this new time is smaller than the current time, the player can use it again. After that, we update our variable so the player cannot use the function for a while. By doing this, we limit the number of times all the complex logic of our function is calculated, which makes spamming the RemoteEvent or RemoteFunction pointless.

Here is an example with a few simple numbers to visualize what the debounce does. Imagine that we have a RemoteEvent that we want a debounce on. Each player can only fire this RemoteEvent once every 5 seconds. The player's last time using this function was when the current time was `10`. Currently, the time is `16`.

First, we get the time that the player last used this function, which is currently 10. Then, we add our debounce duration on top of the last time that they used the function. For our example, the debounce duration is 5. If we combine these, we get the number 15. This means that the current time needs to be 15 or more before the player can use this function again. Currently, that is the case since the time is 16. This means that the player can use this function and does not have a debounce. Finally, we update the last used time to 16, as this is the current time.

Now, let us implement a simple system with a debounce check in place. First things first, we need a variable for each player. How do we store this on the server? We can use a dictionary. Each key will be the player's name in our game and the value will be the last time they used the function. Once the player joins, we will set this value to 0. Our code will look like this:

```
local Players = game:GetService("Players")

local debounceValues = {}

function playerJoined(player)
    debounceValues[player.Name] = 0
end

Players.PlayerAdded:Connect(playerJoined)
```

However, if a player leaves, we need to remove their data. We do not want to build up a massive array of players that are not even in our game. In the following code, we will use the .PlayerRemoving event. This event gets fired right before the player leaves. This allows us to remove the value for this player, like so:

```
function playerLeft(player)
    debounceValues[player.Name] = nil
end

Players.PlayerRemoving:Connect(playerLeft)
```

> **Note**
> All of the code examples in this section, unless specifically stated otherwise, will belong to the same **Script**. We will not be copy-pasting unedited functions or variables. Please view the GitHub repository of this book to see the entire **Script**.

In the preceding code, we see the .PlayerRemoving event. Now, we no longer need to worry about data being stored for players that are no longer in our game.

The last thing we need to do is make our RemoteEvent and add the debounce into it. Create a RemoteEvent in ReplicatedStorage named `DebounceTesting`. After that, we will start listening to this event and add our debounce. If the player is allowed to fire this RemoteEvent, we will simply print **Allowed**, and if they are not, nothing will happen, as demonstrated here:

```
local ReplicatedStorage = game:GetService("ReplicatedStorage")

local DEBOUNCE_DURATION = 5

function debounceFunction(player)
    if ( debounceValues[player.Name] + DEBOUNCE_DURATION )
    < os.time() then
        debounceValues[player.Name] = os.time()
        print("Allowed")
    end
end

ReplicatedStorage.DebounceTesting.
OnServerEvent:Connect(debounceFunction)
```

In the preceding code, there is a bit of highlighted code. This highlighted code is our debounce. First, we get the last time the player used this function from our table. After that, we add the debounce duration, which is 5 seconds. Finally, we check if this combined value is smaller than the current time. We use the `os.time()` function to get the current time. This function gives the exact number of seconds since January 1, 1970 at exactly midnight. This function is ideal when we need to differentiate seconds. On the next line, we update the value for the player that called the function to the current time.

Of course, we still need to test whether our debounce works. Let us make a **LocalScript** inside of **StarterPlayerScript**, or any other location where **LocalScripts** run, with the following code:

```
local ReplicatedStorage = game:GetService("ReplicatedStorage")

function setup()
    while true do
        task.wait(1)
        ReplicatedStorage.DebounceTesting:FireServer()
    end
end

setup()
```

The preceding code snippet has a `setup()` function containing a `while` loop that runs forever. Each second, it fires our RemoteEvent called `DebounceTesting`. However, when we run our game, we will only see the **Allowed** message once every five seconds, as seen in *Figure 4.10*. This means our debounce system works.

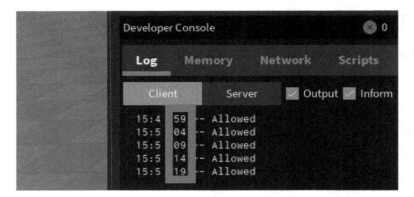

Figure 4.10 – Debounce cooldown

Now that we know what debounces are and how to implement them, let us move on to another thing we can do to boost the security of our game. In the next section, we will learn what **honeypots** are and how they could be useful to boost the security of your game.

Honeypots

We previously learned that exploiters could fire and invoke any RemoteEvent and RemoteFunction. We can use this knowledge and use it to our own advantage. We can make a RemoteEvent or RemoteFunction with an attractive name such as **AddMoney** or **GetPromoCodes**. However, instead of implementing these RemoteEvents or RemoteFunctions, we kick or ban the players that use these. Just make sure that you never give regular players the ability to fire or invoke them.

Honeypots basically trick exploiters into exposing themselves by using these RemoteEvents or RemoteFunctions. After all, normal players will not use them. So, when they do get used, this is the effect of an exploiter.

If you have RemoteEvents or RemoteFunctions like this in your game, they are called **honeypots**. This is not something unique to Roblox. Honeypots are used in many systems. In most other systems, the functionality of these honeypots is way more advanced than what we implement on Roblox. The only thing that matters for us is reducing the number of exploiters in our game.

But how do we implement a honeypot in Roblox? As previously mentioned, we need to implement the server side of the RemoteEvent or RemoteFunction. After that, we can kick them out.

Let us take a look at the following code example:

```
local ReplicatedStorage = game:GetService("ReplicatedStorage")

function kickPlayer(player)
    player:Kick("Do not exploit in our game!")
end


ReplicatedStorage.AddMoney.OnServerEvent:Connect(kickPlayer)
```

Our preceding code snippet is a **Script** in the **ServerScriptService**, which listens to incoming server events for the AddMoney RemoteEvent. If this event is fired, we kick the player out by using the :Kick() function on the player's instance. It might be better to ban these players instead of kicking them out. However, we would need to use data stores for this. We will explain what data stores are and how to use them in *Chapter 8, Building Data Stores*.

> **Note**
> Please make sure that whenever you implement a honeypot in your game, you *never* fire or invoke it in any **LocalScript**. This may cause innocent players to be banned.

Now that we know what honeypots are and how to implement them in our Roblox game, we have finished our third security improvement. We previously also learned about debounces and server checks. Combining all these improvements together with FilteringEnabled should make our game a lot safer. Just like any other thing you learn about programming, it is highly recommended to play around with what you just learned. Only then can you truly master each individual section.

In the next section, we will talk about text filtering. This does not necessarily increase the security in our game; however, it does boost the safety of our players, especially younger ones.

Filtering user text

Most of Roblox's user base consists of younger players. Obviously, we do not want them to see any inappropriate text. Therefore, a lot of text has to be filtered in our games. Roblox already does a lot of text filtering for us, such as when someone sends a message in our game. However, sometimes we decide to make a system that involves text sent by users that can be displayed to other users. In those scenarios, we need to do the text filtering ourselves. If we do not do this, our game might get taken down by Roblox as it would break the **Roblox Community Standards**.

Text filtering is usually considered to be very complicated at first. Therefore, we will slowly walk through each step you have to program to filter messages in our game.

TextObject

To learn how to filter text, we will be using a Roblox game with a premade user interface. Besides this, a partially made server **Script** listens to the `ReceivedMessage` RemoteEvent that the user interface fires. In addition, the **Script** already handles the previously explained security improvements. This way, you can have a good look at how these security improvements are implemented in an actual game. Now, it is our turn to add our final improvement, the text filtering.

You can get the Roblox Studio file that includes all of this from the GitHub page:

```
https://github.com/PacktPublishing/Mastering-Roblox-Coding/tree/
main/Games/Text%20Filtering
```

> **Note**
>
> It is highly recommended that you follow the instructions in the book while implementing them in Roblox Studio yourself. This is the best way to learn, especially since this is a hard-to-understand concept.

Let us begin implementing our game on the server. Inside the **ServerScriptService**, you can find a **Script** called **ServerMessageSystem**. As previously mentioned, we have a `messageReceived()` function that listens to the incoming server requests for our `SendMessage` RemoteEvent. We have two pre-made server checks and a debounce check inside this function. Take a look at these for yourself with the help of the previous sections of this chapter.

Now, we have to fill out the `messageReceived()` function by adding the logic of this function to it. We want this function to filter the `inputMessage` parameter by using the Roblox text filtering system. Once we have filtered this, we will fire the `ReceivedMessage` RemoteEvent for all players in our game. This will ensure everyone gets a new message on their screen.

But how do we filter user text? For any text filtering, we need to make something we will call a **TextObject** (**TextFilterResult**). To do this, we will use a new service called **TextService**. This is the service that is responsible for anything related to text filtering. This service has a unique function called `:FilterStringAsync()`. This function allows us to make our TextObject. Please do not confuse the name, thinking you are done after calling this function.

However, something interesting is going on with this function. So far, all the functions that we have seen always work. Unfortunately, some functions might not always work because they could give an error. `:FilterStringAsync()` is one of these functions that might give an error. Usually, nothing goes wrong while using this function. However, as a programmer, you have to make sure your code works.

So, how do we make sure we can work with this possible error? We have to make a function protected if we know it could give an error. To do this, we use the `pcall()` function.

This function may sound really confusing, so let us just look at the implementation of the `:FilterStringAsync()` function:

```lua
function getTextObject(player, inputMessage)
    -- Variable for the text object
    local textObject = nil

    -- Pcall because the ':FilterStringAsync()' function
        might
    -- return with an error.
    local success, err = pcall(function()
        -- Setting the textObject variable
        textObject = TextService:FilterStringAsync(
            inputMessage,
            player.UserId
        )
    end)

    -- Checking if an error occurred while using the
    -- ':FilterStringAsync()' function.
    if err then
        warn("Something went wrong creating text
        object.\nError: " .. err)
    end

    -- Returning the textObject.
    return textObject
end
```

The preceding code most likely looks complicated. It is a lot of new stuff at once. Let us take a look at it step by step. The first thing we did inside the function is make a variable with the `nil` value. This is not anything new. Then, we see two new variables being made, named `success` and `err`. After that, we call the `pcall()` function we just mentioned. Inside of the `pcall()` function, we make a new function. The argument you have to pass to the `pcall()` function is another function that might give an error. Then, inside this function we have as an argument, we set the previously made `textObject` variable to whatever is the result of the `:FilterStringAsync()` function. The first argument of this function is the message that you want to filter and the second argument is the user ID of the player that sent the message.

That's a lot of information. Unfortunately, that is not all. We have seen the usage of the `pcall()` function now. However, we still do not really know how it works. Why do we need those two variables before it? What the `pcall()` function does is return two values. The first value it returns determines whether there was an error or not. The second value holds the error that was given if something went wrong. This is why we checked if there was an error right after we called our `pcall()` function. If there was an error, we would print a warning. Finally, we return the created `textObject` variable as the purpose of this function was to give a TextObject.

Now that we have finished our `getTextObject()` function, the only thing we have to do is implement it in our `messageReceived()` function. Let us take a look at the following code:

```
function messageReceived(player, inputMessage)

    -- ... Server Checks and Debounce Checks ...

    -- Function logic
    local textObject = getTextObject(player, inputMessage)
    if textObject ~= nil then
        -- ... todo
    end
end
```

The pre-made code was left out of the preceding code snippet, as nothing has changed there. Anyway, we are now calling the `getTextObject()` function inside of our `messageReceived()` function. After that, we checked if the result was not `nil`. We do this because `nil` is returned if something happens while using the `:FilterStringAsync()` function.

We just learned how to make a TextObject. While doing this, we also learned how to make protected functions using the `pcall()` function. But we are not done with filtering the text yet. In the next section, we will see how to finalize this example system.

The GetNonChatStringForBroadcastAsync function

You are probably wondering why we cannot just filter text all at once. This is because there are different types of text filtering in Roblox. For our current example, we want to filter text that gets displayed to every player in our game. Because we want to do this, we need to call the `:GetNonChatStringForBroadcastAsync()` function on our TextObject.

As you might have guessed, the `:GetNonChatStringForBroadcastAsync()` function can also give an error. Therefore, we need to surround it with a **protected function** (`pcall`) once again.

Let us take a look at the implementation of this function in the following code snippet:

```
function filterBroadcastString(textObject)
    -- Variable that stores the filtered message
    local filteredMessage = nil

    -- Pcall because the ':GetNonChatStringForBroadcastAsync()'
    -- function might return with an error.
    local success, err = pcall(function()
        filteredMessage = textObject:
        GetNonChatStringForBroadcastAsync()
    end)

    -- Checking if an error occurred while using the
    -- ':GetNonChatStringForBroadcastAsync()' function.
    if err then
        warn("Something went wrong while filtering message.
        Error: " .. err)
        return "[ Failed to filter message ]"
    end

    -- Returning the filtered message.
    return filteredMessage
end
```

Looking at the preceding code, we see something very similar to the previous function where we made the TextObject. First, we make our variable that will hold the filtered message. After that, we have a `pcall()` function that contains the `:GetNonChatStringForBroadcastAsync()` function. After that, we check if there is an error. If there was, we use the `warn()` function to display it in the console, and we return the `[ Failed to filter message ]` message. This is the message that would appear on the user interface if Roblox went offline, causing there to be an error.

After we have implemented the `filterBroadcastString()` function, we still need to update our `messageReceived()` function so it uses the other function. Let us look at the following code snippet:

```
function messageReceived(player, inputMessage)

    --- ... Server Checks and Debounce Checks ...
```

```
    -- Function logic
    local textObject = getTextObject(player, inputMessage)
    if textObject ~= nil then
        local filteredMessage =
        filterBroadcastString(textObject)
        ReplicatedStorage.ReceivedMessage:FireAllClients(
        player, filteredMessage)
    end
end
```

The pre-made code was left out of the preceding code snippet, as nothing has changed there. We just added the call to the `filterBroadcastString()` function right after our `if` statement. We do not have an extra `if` statement that checks if the result of this function is `nil`. This is because we either return the [Failed to filter message] message, or we have a filtered message. Once we have this, we are ready to send this filtered message to the client. Because we said the message should be given to every player in our game, we will have to fire the `:FireClient()` function for each player. This would require a loop. Luckily, there is a built-in alternative called `:FireAllClients()`, which does this for us, a handy function to remember when making systems like this.

Because the `:FireAllClients()` fires to all clients, we do not have to specify which player we want to send it to. But why do we have a player as our first argument then? We want to inform all the clients whom this message came from. Once we run the game and test our system, we will see our input messages appear on the user interface, as seen in *Figure 4.11*, with the name of the player who sent it above.

Figure 4.11 – Filtered message displayed

However, if we try to test if the filtering actually works, for instance, by sending a swear word, it might not work. If this is the case for you, you are probably testing the game in Roblox Studio. The text filtering does not work in Roblox Studio. Please publish the game and test it by using **Roblox Player** instead. Ensure you do not publicly open the game as you do not want unfiltered messages displayed in the scenario where your scripts do not work.

Now, we know how to use the `:GetNonChatStringForBroadcastAsync()` function on the TextObject, and how to use the `:FireAllClients()` function. As previously mentioned, the `:GetNonChatStringForBroadcastAsync()` function is only used when we need to display text to an entire server. However, there are other instances where two players could have a conversation between them. In this scenario, we use another function on the TextObject. We will learn more about this in the next section.

The GetChatForUserAsync function

As previously mentioned, our current text filtering system is for messages that are sent to all players on our server. However, if we were to rebuild our system and make it for messages only sent to one player, we would have to use another function on our TextObject. In this scenario, we would use the `:GetChatForUserAsync()` function. The reason we have to use this function is that this function actually looks at the context of previous messages for an improved filter experience.

How do we use the `:GetChatForUserAsync()` function? We call this function directly on our TextObject. The creation of the TextObject is not different from when we used the `:GetNonChatStringForBroadcastAsync()` function. The `:GetChatForUserAsync()` function has a parameter. This is the UserId to whom the message is sent. We did not need to specify this again because we previously made the TextObject by providing the UserId of the person who sent the message. Filtering text via the `:GetChatForUserAsync()` function would look like this:

```
function filterPrivateMessage(textObject, recipient)
    -- Variable that stores the filtered message
    local filteredMessage = nil

    -- Pcall because the ':GetChatForUserAsync()' function
    -- might return with an error.
    local success, err = pcall(function()
        filteredMessage = textObject:GetChatForUserAsync(
        recipient.UserId)
    end)

    -- Checking if an error occurred while using the
    -- ':GetChatForUserAsync()' function.
    if err then
        warn("Something went wrong while filtering private
        message. Error: " .. err)
        return "[ Failed to filter message ]"
    end
```

```
    -- Returning the filtered message.
    return filteredMessage
end
```

If we look at the preceding code, there are not many differences between the `:GetChatForUserAsync()` function and the `:GetNonChatStringForBroadcastAsync()` function. The only primary difference is the provided parameter to understand to whom this message is sent.

To summarize, if we want to filter text, we first need to make a TextObject. Once this is done, we need to ask ourselves: *is more than one person in our game going to see this message?* If so, we use the `:GetNonChatStringForBroadcastAsync()` function. However, if only one person sees the message, we should use the `:GetChatForUserAsync()` function.

It is important to filter all the text in our game to protect our users from seeing potentially harmful content. Besides that, it is not really a choice whether we want to do this or not. We have to follow the Roblox Community Standards.

In the next section, we will have an exercise to work with everything we have learned in this chapter.

Exercise 4.1: Securing your game

In this exercise, we will be making a private message system based on all the knowledge we learned throughout this chapter. We need to know how the client and the server work for this exercise. We also need to know how to communicate between them. Besides this, we need to understand how to protect our RemoteEvents by using server checks. Finally, we need to use our knowledge of text filtering to ensure that private messages get filtered. A GUI is provided with a bit of essential code. However, a lot still has to be done in the **LocalScript**. Besides that, we need to completely write the server **Script** ourselves.

You can find the complete and example answer versions of this exercise on the GitHub page here:

`https://github.com/PacktPublishing/Mastering-Roblox-Coding/tree/main/Exercises/4%20Securing%20Your%20Game`

Exercise:

In the **PrivateMessages LocalScript**, inside of the **PrivateMessages** ScreenGui, complete the following exercises:

1. At the bottom of the **LocalScript**, listen to the `.MouseButton1Down` event on the `sendMessageButton` and start the `sendMessage()` function.
2. Inside the `sendMessage()` function, check if input length, for the `playerInput` and `messageInput`, is more than 0 characters by using the `string.len()` function.

3. Directly after the previous `if` statement, check whether the player in the input is actually in-game.

   Tip for 3: Use the **Players** service and the `:FindFirstChild()` function.

4. After the previous two `if` statements, fire the `SendMessage` RemoteEvent in the ReplicatedStorage.

   Argument 1: `playerInput.Text`

   Argument 2: `messageInput.Text`

   In the **PrivateMessages Script**, inside of the **ServerScriptService**, complete the following next steps:

5. At the bottom of the **Script**, listen to the SendMessage RemoteEvent, inside the ReplicatedStorage, and start the `incomingMessage()` function.

6. Inside the `incomingMessage()` function, implement a server check that checks that the `toPlayerName` parameter and the `message` parameter are not `nil` and confirm they are strings. If this is not the case, use the `return` statement.

   Tip for 6: To see if these parameters are strings, use the `typeof()` function.

7. Implement a server check that checks if the `toPlayerName` parameter and the `message` parameter have a length of more than 0 characters. If this is not the case, use the `return` statement.

   Tip for 7: Use the `string.len()` function to get the number of characters.

8. Implement a server check that checks whether the player that the message is sent to is actually on the server or not. If this is not the case, use the `return` statement.

   Tip for 8: Use the **Players** service and the `:FindFirstChild()` function.

9. Implement the `getTextObject()` function using at least:

   - `pcall()`
   - `:FilterStringAsync()`

   Tip for 9: If you have forgotten how this works, look at the *TextObject* section.

10. Inside the `incomingMessage()` function, use the `getTextObject()` function and check whether the result is `nil` or not.

11. Implement the `filterPrivateMessage()` function using at least:

    - `pcall()`
    - `:GetChatForUserAsync()`

    Tip for 11: If you have forgotten how this works, look at the *The GetChatForUserAsync function* section.

12. Inside the `incomingMessage()` function, use the `filterPrivateMessage()` function and store it in a variable named `filteredText`.

13. Use the `ReceivedMessage` RemoteEvent and fire it to the right client.

Argument 1: `toPlayer`

Argument 2: `fromPlayer`

Argument 3: `filteredMessage`

Run the game to see if it works. As previously mentioned in this chapter, text filtering only works in the actual game, not in Roblox Studio. Before opening your game to the public, ensure that the filter works.

An example answer for this exercise can be found on the GitHub page for this book. Please keep in mind there are many ways of solving this exercise. If the example answer is different from your version and your version works, it does not directly mean your version is wrong. Every coder has their own preferred style of coding, which is fine. Just make sure to follow the **best practices**, while avoiding **bad practices** that are explained throughout the book.

Summary

We started this chapter by understanding what the client and the server are. We learned that the client refers to devices, such as your PC, that connect to a server. For Roblox, a client can be a phone, tablet, desktop, laptop, and even an Xbox. Once either of these devices joins a Roblox game, they connect with a server from Roblox. Besides this, we learned that there are two types of scripts, **Scripts** and **LocalScripts**. The **Scripts** run on Roblox servers, whereas **LocalScripts** run on all the devices that are connected to the server.

We also learned about a system that Roblox built called FilteringEnabled. This prevented changes made by clients from happening on the server, and therefore, they do not happen for other clients either. This is one of the security implementations Roblox has made. It prevents exploiters from messing up our game. However, this also means that we strictly need to follow the rules of the client and the server. If we want to start an action from the client, we need to use RemoteEvents and RemoteFunctions to start functions on the server. We learned how to do this, but we also learned that exploiters can abuse these RemoteEvents and RemoteFunctions if we are not careful enough.

We can implement various security measures to ensure that exploiters do not abuse our RemoteEvents and RemoteFunctions. One of the most potent security implementations we can add to our game is server checks. Server checks validate the incoming input from the client to see if a request is legitimate or not. The more useful server checks are, the less chance there is of any exploiter abusing your RemoteEvent or RemoteFunction. Often, you have to think outside of the box to come up with good server checks. We have seen various examples of good server checks throughout this chapter.

Sometimes, server checks are not enough. The function connected to your RemoteEvent or RemoteFunction is very complex. If exploiters spam this, it could cause lag on the server. We learned how to use debounces to prevent this from happening. Debounces allow us only to let certain players execute a particular function every once in a while. Finally, we also learned about honeypots. Honeypots allow us to trick exploiters into using a certain RemoteEvent or RemoteFunction. We use these as bait. We do not actually use these RemoteEvents or RemoteFunctions ourselves. Therefore, if someone uses them, we know they are an exploiter. Once we detect someone using them, we ban them from or kick them out of our game.

But there is another way of securing our game. Children primarily play Roblox. Therefore, we do not want inappropriate messages in our game. We can prevent this from happening by filtering text sent by users. Roblox already takes care of a lot of text filtering. However, if we make our own chat feature, we have to do it ourselves. We learned how to do this, when to use text filtering for an entire server, and when to use text filtering within a private conversation.

In the next chapter, we will learn about optimizing our game. We already learned that specific tasks should be done on the client and others on the server. However, there are more instances where we have to do certain things on the client and not on the server. Doing this improves the performance of our game and allows us to create advanced settings for our users, so they can pick what they want and do not want. Besides this, we will learn about **StreamingEnabled**. **StreamingEnabled** will prevent lag for lower-end devices with big maps.

5

Optimizing Your Game

In this chapter, we will focus on how to optimize our games. Since Roblox games can be played on a wide range of devices, including lower-end devices, we need to ensure everyone can have an amazing time while playing our games. Luckily, there are a few tricks we can follow to boost our games' performance. Besides this, Roblox also has a built-in system called **StreamingEnabled**. StreamingEnabled will automatically remove parts that are far away from the player if that user is lagging. In this way, their performance will go up. However, since these parts get removed, we need to adjust our scripting style a bit in order to deal with this.

In this chapter, we will cover the following topics:

- Using StreamingEnabled
- Working with animations
- Working with Tweens

By the end of this chapter, you will understand how to boost the performance of your game by using StreamingEnabled. Besides this, we will learn how to use animations in our game. In addition, we will learn how to ensure these animations are optimized. Finally, we will learn how to make animations on non-characters, such as doors and other in-game objects, by using Tweens.

Technical requirements

To start programming with Luau, you need access to a device with internet access. This can either be a Windows or a Mac device.

Additionally, you need to download the following software:

- Roblox Player
- Roblox Studio

All the code examples for this chapter can be found on GitHub at `https://github.com/PacktPublishing/Mastering-Roblox-Coding`.

The CiA video for this chapter can be found at `https://bit.ly/3z3ksqk`.

Understanding and using StreamingEnabled

When your game starts growing in map size, we face a problem. Your game might start lagging, the loading times for players might take way longer, and lower-end devices might even crash. Of course, we want as many players in our game as possible. But no one will play a game that keeps crashing, takes too long to load, or just lags overall. All three of these problems can be fixed by using something called **StreamingEnabled**.

So, what is StreamingEnabled exactly? And how does it ensure our players have less lag? Typically, when you join a game, the entire map gets loaded. However, with StreamingEnabled, that is not the case. As a matter of fact, even after you have been playing for a while, there is still a chance that some part of the map will not have been loaded. This is because StreamingEnabled only loads a section of the map near you. In this scenario, the parts of the map that you are not interacting with are just simply not there.

Over the past few years, StreamingEnabled has improved a lot. Many new features have been added, resulting in it becoming even more powerful. However, whatever happens in the future, the essence of StreamingEnabled should remain the same.

In the following sections, we will take a deeper dive into how StreamingEnabled works and what the behavior of StreamingEnabled means for our scripts.

Enabling StreamingEnabled

By default, StreamingEnabled is not active. We have already learned that StreamingEnabled changes the behavior of how our map loads. Because of this, we need to make our scripts a bit different. We will learn about the changes we need to make to our scripts later. First, we need to figure out how StreamingEnabled works exactly. With this knowledge, we can sort of guess all the changes that we need to make in our scripts.

First, let us look at how we even enable StreamingEnabled. Enabling StreamingEnabled is simple; perform the following steps:

1. Open your game using Roblox Studio.
2. In the **Explorer** window, select the **Workspace** service.
3. In the **Properties** window, look for the property named **StreamingEnabled** and select it.

That's it! We have now successfully enabled **StreamingEnabled**. After we enabled it, a few extra properties showed up. Two of these properties are the **StreamingMinRadius** property and the **StreamingTargetRadius** property, as shown in *Figure 5.1*:

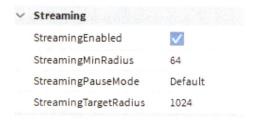

Figure 5.1 – Streaming properties

So, what do both of these properties mean? Well, their names imply what they do already. We know that StreamingEnabled does not load the entire map at once. Instead, it loads the area that the player is near. Knowing this, we can guess what both properties mean. The **StreamingTargetRadius** property determines the distance of the map that will load, measured in **Studs**. Studs are how sizes and distances are measured, similar to us using inches or centimeters in real life. On the other hand, **StreamingMinRadius** is the minimum distance in which the map will load. We know that the size of the map gets loaded and unloaded based on the player's performance. If someone has a lower-end device, the map will get smaller. It is good to mention that the size of the map never gets smaller than the **StreamingMinRadius** property and never bigger than the **StreamingTargetRadius** property.

So, what does this look like for a real game? Let us take a look at *Figure 5.2*. It shows the same map, but there are a few slight differences:

Figure 5.2 – StreamingEnabled scenarios

If we look at *Figure 5.2*, we see three different scenarios going on. The top picture is what the map of this game looks like when **StreamingEnabled** is not turned on. As you can see, the map the player is currently standing in is fully loaded. Even if we look further into the distance, we see a completely new map loaded already. While it might look good, it is not very efficient performance-wise. After all, the player is not even there.

We could argue that we want this other map to be visible from our current map because it might look better. If we want to do this, we could make the **StreamingTargetRadius** property higher. Then, we can still see the second map while using **StreamingEnabled**. In addition, Roblox might automatically scale down the quality of some meshes in the distance. If we were to make a third map behind it, we can still have the one in the middle visible and get rid of the third one. This comes down to a design choice that you will have to make for your own game.

For this example, we only chose to have one map visible at the time. You can see this in the first StreamingEnabled screenshot of *Figure 5.2*. As you can see, the entire current map is visible, but the map cuts off at the bridge. But what if someone was playing on a lower-end device? What would happen to the map? This is the second **StreamingEnabled** picture. We can see that the current map has not been fully loaded. Again, this happens if someone plays your game on a lower-end device.

> **Tip**
> It is best to see **StreamingEnabled** active for yourself. You can see how it works by creating a simple **Baseplate** template and placing many different parts spread around the baseplate. After that, enable StreamingEnabled and set the **StreamingTargetRadius** property to 64. Then, play the game and walk around. You will see how parts in the distance get removed and loaded.

Now we know how to enable **StreamingEnabled** and what its most essential properties do. Besides this, we have seen StreamingEnabled's effects on your map. In the next section, we will learn how to change our scripts to work with the StreamingEnabled behavior.

Programming with StreamingEnabled

As we have heard a few times, we need to change our scripts. This is because the map is not always fully loaded when using **StreamingEnabled**. Let us clear up one possible point of confusion. Practically, we only need to make changes to **LocalScripts** and not **Scripts**. The map is always fully loaded on the server, just not on the client. Actually, there are a few things that we might have to shift to the server, which we would have done on the client, but the way we program on the server does not change.

As mentioned a few times, certain things load instantly when you join the game. However, there are a lot of things that do not load instantly, too. For example, when the player joins a game that uses StreamingEnabled, no part is loaded when the player joins. Instead, the parts are sent later. Please keep in mind that only the parts that fit within the **StreamingTargetRadius** property are sent. So, what is being sent and what is not?

Here is a list of what happens when the player joins:

Class name	Loaded on join?
BasePart	No
Model/folder	Yes
BasePart inside a model/folder	No
Model/folder inside a model/folder	Yes
Model/folder in a BasePart	No
Script	Yes
Script inside a model/folder	Yes
Script inside a BasePart	No
Humanoid	Yes*
Terrain	Yes**

Table 5.1 – List of sent instances while joining the game when using StreamingEnabled

> **Note**
>
> * Humanoids are only loaded if all of their parents are either models or folders.
>
> ** The Terrain object is sent on join. However, the actual terrain is not fully sent.

From this list, we can conclude that, practically, all the structuring classes get sent, but not those that fill the game, such as parts or meshes, which are both **BaseParts**. Additionally, we can conclude that if we had a structure like **Model** > **BasePart** > **Model**, the final model would not be sent when the player joins. Having other BaseParts inside of BaseParts might create some weird streaming behavior. Therefore, it is best to avoid having children inside of a BasePart altogether.

In the following sections, we will learn about the different things we have to do to make our local scripts compatible with StreamingEnabled.

Using WaitForChild

Previously, we learned that parts do not directly load once we join the game. In fact, we can test this ourselves in a simple Baseplate game. Enable StreamingEnabled and create a LocalScript in any location that they work. Once you have done this, enter the following code into your local script:

```
local spawnLocation = workspace:FindFirstChild("SpawnLocation")

print(tostring(spawnLocation))
```

Once we run the game, we will see nil appear in our **Output** frame. This proves that the SpawnLocation does not exist when this script runs. SpawnLocations are BaseParts, too. Therefore, they get sent later than when the player joins.

So, what do we do if we want to reference this part anyway? In *Chapter 3, Event-Based Programming*, we learned about the :WaitForChild() function. We learned that the :WaitForChild() function **yields**. This means that the current thread temporarily pauses, for a maximum of 5 seconds, until the instance can be found. This sounds like the perfect solution to our problem. Let us take a look at the following code:

```
local spawnLocation = workspace:WaitForChild("SpawnLocation")

print(tostring(spawnLocation))
```

Now if we run our game, we will see SpawnLocation appear in the **Output** frame instead of the nil result we previously got. This means that we now successfully referenced the SpawnLocation. If we want to reference objects in the Workspace service when StreamingEnabled is on, we must use :WaitForChild(). Please keep in mind that even if you decide not to use StreamingEnabled, it is best to make your scripts StreamingEnabled compatible anyway. Then, if you ever decide to turn on StreamingEnabled in the future, there is less code to be updated.

But what happens if we accidentally try to use the :WaitForChild() function to find an instance that does not exist? Let us take a look at the following code:

```
local spawnLocation =
workspace:WaitForChild("SomethingThatDoesNotExist")
if spawnLocation ~= nil then
    print("Found!")
else
    print("Couldn't find!")
end
```

In the preceding code, we are looking for an instance named SomethingThatDoesNotExist in the **Workspace** service. As the name implies, this would not actually be something in our game. However, then something interesting happens. If it cannot find the instance, it will give an **Infinite yield** warning in the **Output** frame. However, we actually expected it to print **Couldn't find**, too. For some weird reason, it does not do this. This is expected behavior from the :WaitForChild() function and something you should keep in mind when programming.

However, sometimes, you cannot afford your thread entering the infinite yield state. In those scenarios, you can actually add a second argument to the :WaitForChild() function. This second argument will determine for how long the function might **yield**. If it exceeds this time, it will simply return nil, as the :FindFirstChild() function would. The same code, but now with a second argument, looks like this:

```
local spawnLocation =
workspace:WaitForChild("SomethingThatDoesNotExist", 5)
```

```
if spawnLocation ~= nil then
    print("Found!")
else
    print("Couldn't find!")
end
```

Now that we have specified our **second argument**, we no longer get the **infinite yield** warning, but a `nil` result. As previously mentioned, the second argument determines how long it will keep looking for the instance. We can make this time as short or long as we want.

Now that we know all about the `:WaitForChild()` function, we can move on to the next thing we might have to do when using StreamingEnabled. In the next section, we will look at a useful event called `.ChildAdded`.

Using ChildAdded

Let us imagine a large grid of aligned square parts. All of these parts are stored in a folder called **ColoredParts**. We want to give all of them a random color. But there is one catch; these colors should be different for each client. That means we have to make this coloring script for the client. But first, let us start by making this grid. The following code makes a 50 x 50 grid in our game:

```
local BLOCK_SIZE = 25
local AMOUNT_OF_BLOCKS = 50

local folder = Instance.new("Folder")
folder.Name = "ColoredParts"
folder.Parent = workspace

for x = 1, AMOUNT_OF_BLOCKS do
    for y = 1, AMOUNT_OF_BLOCKS do
        local part = Instance.new("Part")
        part.Parent = folder

        part.Name = x .. ", " .. y
        part.Anchored = true
        part.Size = Vector3.new(BLOCK_SIZE, .25,
        BLOCK_SIZE)

        local positionToCenter = ( (BLOCK_SIZE *
        AMOUNT_OF_BLOCKS ) / 2 )
```

```
        part.Position = Vector3.new(x * BLOCK_SIZE -
        positionToCenter, 1, y * BLOCK_SIZE -
        positionToCenter)
    end
    task.wait()
end
print("Command completed!")
```

But where do we place the preceding code? We can use **Command Bar** to execute this code, as shown in *Figure 5.3*:

Figure 5.3 – Command Bar

Once we have entered our script in **Command Bar**, hit *Enter* on your keyboard. You will see a grid of gray parts spawn in your game. **Command Bar** allows us to execute code in Studio without running the game.

Now that we have our grid, let us turn on StreamingEnabled. First, we will set the **StreamingTargetRadius** property to 64 to test more easily. Implementing this system is not a problem in a game without StreamingEnabled. We could have used the :GetChildren() function and looped through each part to give them a new random color, just like we learned in *Chapter 3*, *Event-Based Programming*. Unfortunately, this is not an option with StreamingEnabled. After all, there is a high chance that not all parts will be loaded once we do this. One solution could be to call the function multiple times.

As we learned in *Chapter 3*, *Event-Based Programming*, this is a bad idea. Just as we learned in this chapter, we should try and look for an event that gets fired once a part is loaded. Luckily, there is one. The event is called .ChildAdded. Let us take a look at the following code:

```
local coloredParts = workspace:WaitForChild("ColoredParts")

function randomRGB()
    local r = math.random(0, 255)
    local g = math.random(0, 255)
    local b = math.random(0, 255)
    return Color3.fromRGB(r, g, b)
```

```
end

coloredParts.ChildAdded:Connect(function(addedInstance)
    if addedInstance:IsA("BasePart") then
        addedInstance.Color = randomRGB()
        print("New instance colored!")
    end
end)
```

The preceding code snippet is used in a LocalScript. If we run our game, we will see some of the grid with colored parts. Once we start walking in a specific direction, more parts spawn. Because we use the .ChildAdded event, these parts automatically get a random color assigned. This means our script is now compatible with StreamingEnabled:

Figure 5.4 – Colored blocks using StreamingEnabled

Because StreamingEnabled prevents all parts from loading at once, we have to make our local scripts more dynamic. The .ChildAdded event is an excellent example of this. In the next section, we will look at how we can start loading a certain part of the map if we know a player will enter this area soon.

RequestStreamAroundAsync function

This time, we have two parts each on the other side of the map. If you touch one of the parts, you get teleported to the other one. Because both parts are on different sides of the map, there is a high chance that the area the player will be teleported to will not be loaded:

```
local Players = game:GetService("Players")

local partA = workspace.PartA
```

```
local partB = workspace.PartB

function teleportPlayer(player, position)
    if playerHasDebounce(player) == false then
        -- Preloading Area
        player:RequestStreamAroundAsync(position)

        -- Teleporting player
        player.Character:SetPrimaryPartCFrame(CFrame.new(
        position + Vector3.new(0, 5, 0)))
    end
end

function teleportA(hit)
    local player = wasHit(hit)
    if player then
        teleportPlayer(player, partA.Position)
    end
end

function teleportB(hit)
    local player = wasHit(hit)
    if player then
        teleportPlayer(player, partB.Position)
    end
end

function wasHit(hit)
    -- Getting Character
    local character = hit.Parent
    if character ~= nil then
        -- Getting Player
        local player =
        Players:GetPlayerFromCharacter(character)
        if player ~= nil then
            return player
```

```
        end
    end
    return false
end


partA.Touched:Connect(teleportB)
partB.Touched:Connect(teleportA)
```

All the functions and variables related to debounces are left out in the preceding code snippet to save space. You can find the complete code on GitHub. Let us analyze what this code does step by step. We will begin with the listeners at the bottom of the script. If something touches `partA` or `partB`, the teleport function gets activated. The reason that `partA` uses the `teleportB()` function is that you want to teleport to the other part. There's no point in teleporting to a part you are already on.

We have a parameter called `hit` in the `teleportA()` and `teleportB()` functions. This parameter contains the instance that touched the part. This can be one of the parts of the player's character. This is precisely what the `wasHit()` function checks. If the `hit` parameter contains a BasePart of a character, the player's character model would be the parent of this `hit` BasePart. Then, if we have a presumed character, we use the `:GetPlayerFromCharacter()` function in the **Players** service that confirms this is actually a character.

Once we confirm an actual player has touched this part, we start the `teleportPlayer()` function. First, this function checks whether the player has an active debounce. We learned about debounces in *Chapter 4, Securing Your Game*. Once again, the functions related to debounces are left out to save space. Then, we use the `:RequestStreamAroundAsync()` function. This function uses a **Vector3** data type, which is the data type we use for positions and sizes. In this case, we use it to define the position that we want to load the area of. Because we do this, the map should be mostly loaded once we teleport them here.

> **Note**
>
> The `:RequestStreamARoundAsync()` function gives an error if you do not have StreamingEnabled.

Finally, we teleport the player using the `:SetPrimaryPartCFrame()` function on the player's character. We can use this function for any model that has a **Primary** part. By selecting a model in the **Explorer** frame, you can specify the **Primary** part in the **Properties** frame. To teleport the player, we use another data type called **CFrame**. CFrame is the data type used to specify a position with a rotation. You can make a CFrame by using the code in the preceding code snippet. Later in this book, we will see more use cases for CFrames.

In this section, we learned about a lot of useful functions. Most importantly, we learned how to use the `:RequestStreamAroundAsync()` function if we were to teleport a player when using StreamingEnabled. We also saw another use case of the `:GetPlayerFromCharacter()` function. Previously, we used this in *Chapter 3, Event-Based Programming*. Finally, we had a short introduction to **CFrames** and the `:SetPrimaryPartCFrame()` function. In the next section, we will take a look at some of the things we have to do on the server when using StreamingEnabled.

Server tasks

In the previous sections, we looked at many ways to change our scripts inorder to make them compatible with StreamingEnabled. However, there are certain things that we could have done on the client that we need to move to the server. Here are a few examples of systems that could have been done on the client, but should now be done on the server, and why:

- Think of a navigation system. You might want to know the distance from your character to a particular object or maybe another player. It is not guaranteed that this object or player is loaded for you when using StreamingEnabled. It will be very difficult to calculate the distance of something that is not there. This system is something you could have done on the client before but now needs to be partially done on the server.

- Have you ever played a Simulator or Tycoon game on Roblox? Usually, there is some sort of pointer toward something that you can or should interact with. This can be the closest upgrade you can buy for your Tycoon or the cheapest. Maybe it is something completely different; who knows. If you want to point a player toward the cheapest upgrade for their Tycoon, you have to know all the possible upgrades. Previously, this could have been done on the client. However, since StreamingEnabled, not all upgrades might be loaded for the player. Therefore, we might have to calculate this cheapest upgrade on the server.

- In the previous section, we looked at a teleporting system. Teleporting is something we could do for the client, too. However, if the part or position is not loaded, it might not be wise to keep it on the client. Therefore, teleporting should be done by the server.

These are just three examples of systems that should be, partially or entirely, done on the server. While there is no fixed list of the things that should be done and where, it is always good to ask yourself: is there a chance that certain instances are not there, and would it matter? This way, you can change your system to make it StreamingEnabled compatible.

In the previous sections, we learned a lot about StreamingEnabled. We learned what it was and how it benefits us. Additionally, we learned that we had to change how we program certain things in our games. We learned about useful functions such as `:WaitForChild()` and `:RequestStreamAroundAsync()`. Besides this, we also learned how to make our scripts more dynamic by using the `.ChildAdded` event.

Now that we know how to use StreamingEnabled, we have the choice to enable it for our games. Enabling StreamingEnabled is optional and requires a few extra thoughts when programming. Whether or not you decide to enable it, it is best to make your scripts compatible with it. From now on, all the scripts that we make in this book will be StreamingEnabled compatible. In the next section, we will learn what **animations** are and how to use them.

Working with animations

Every time we walk, jump, swim, climb, fall, dance, or perform any other action, we use **animations**. Animations are the things that make our characters move. If you type /e dance, in most games, you will start dancing. This dance was animated. In this book, we will not cover how to make animations. Instead, we will learn how to use them in scripts.

In the following sections, we will learn how to load and play animations. Besides this, we will learn about other cool things we can do with animations on both your character and **Non-Player Characters** (**NPCs**).

Uploading animations

Before we can start playing an animation, we need an animation. If you use the *right mouse button* on pretty much any instance in the **Explorer** frame, you will see an **Insert Object...** option. Use this to insert something called an **Animation**. There is a unique property to this animation. This property is called **AnimationId**. This property holds a certain **Roblox Asset ID**. If we upload images, animations, or sounds, we get a unique Roblox Asset ID. Usually, the animators will provide us with the Asset ID or give us something so that we can upload it ourselves. In the scenario where you get an animation sent to you, you can simply press the **Save to Roblox** button in Studio, and it will be uploaded, resulting in you getting a Roblox Asset ID.

If we have a Roblox Asset ID of **4212455378**, we can use this as the **AnimationId** property for our animation. Once we have done this, we will see that it automatically changes into a proper Roblox Asset ID, **rbxassetid://4212455378**. So, we have now successfully set up our animation. But one question remains; where should we place it?

As previously mentioned, we can create it as a child of any instance. But this does not directly mean that we should place them there. While there is no fixed rule on where to place animations, generally, there are two locations used for them, and both have their advantages and disadvantages. The first option is to place the animation in the model or instance that it belongs to. This way, the animation is close to what it will be used for. The disadvantage of this is that this model could be cloned a few times. Then, if we have to change the **AnimationId** property, we have to change it in many places. The other frequently used location for animations is in the **ReplicatedStorage** service. You can create a new folder called **Animations** and place all the animations there. This option solves the disadvantage of the previous one. However, the animation could get a bit vague in a game with many animations. So, what was the dancing animation used for again?

Throughout this book, we will try to center all the animations within a folder inside the **ReplicatedStorage** service. However, feel free to use whatever your preference is. Now that we know how to make animations, we should start programming them. In the next section, we will look at the **Animator** object.

Understanding the Animator object

Now that we have an **Animation** object, let us start it. Unfortunately, there is not a `:Play()` function on the **Animation** object. After all, how would it even know what character it should play the animation on? So, we have to use another object. This is the **Animator** object. We can find the **Animator** object inside the **Humanoid** object.

> **Animation History**
> In the past, animations were loaded into the **Humanoid** object. However, since November 2020, this method of loading animations has been deprecated.

As you might have found out from the previous explanation, we need to load our previously made animation on an **Animator** object. The following code snippet is a **LocalScript** inside the **StarterCharacterScripts** folder:

```
local ReplicatedStorage = game:GetService("ReplicatedStorage")

local character = script.Parent
local animations = ReplicatedStorage:WaitForChild("Animations")
--
function playAnimation()
    local humanoid =
    character:FindFirstChildOfClass("Humanoid")
    if humanoid ~= nil then
        local animator =
        humanoid:FindFirstChild("Animator")
        local animation =
        animations:FindFirstChild("DorkyDance")
        if animator ~= nil and animation ~= nil then
            local animationTrack =
            animator:LoadAnimation(animation)
            -- To be continued
        end
    end
```

```
end
--
task.wait(1)
playAnimation()
```

Let us take a look at the preceding code snippet. Because we placed our local script inside the **StarterCharacterScripts** folder, we can assume that the parent of the script is the player's character. Also, we can conclude from the code snippet that the animations are stored in a folder, called `Animations`, inside the **ReplicatedStorage** service.

In the script, we have a function called `playAnimation()`. The first thing this function does is that it looks for the `Humanoid` object inside of the character. After that, it finds the `Animator` object inside of the `Humanoid` object, and it looks for an animation called `DorkyDance` inside the `Animations` folder in **ReplicatedStorage**. If it finds all of that, it loads the `DorkyDance` animation on the `Animator` object using the `:LoadAnimation()` function. Finally, this function gives us an `AnimationTrack`.

Now that we know what the **Animator** object is and how to use the `:LoadAnimation()` function, we can move on to the next section to dive deeper into `AnimationTrack`.

Programming an AnimationTrack

In the previous sections, we learned about the `Animation` object and the `Animator` object. Besides this, we have seen a code snippet that uses the `:LoadAnimation()` function. As you might have guessed by the variable's name, this function returns something called an `AnimationTrack`. This `AnimationTrack` actually controls the animations.

In the following subsections, we will look at unique functions that we can use on these AnimationTracks.

Starting animation

Now that we have the AnimationTrack, let us start the animation to see whether it works. Take a look at the following code snippet:

```
local animationTrack = animator:LoadAnimation(animation)
animationTrack:Play()
```

You can place the preceding code snippet into the previously made script that we viewed in the *Understanding the Animator object* section. In the preceding code, we simply use the `:Play()` function on the `AnimationTrack` for it to start playing the animation. If we run the game, we will see that our character is now animated, similar to *Figure 5.5*:

Figure 5.5 – The dorky dancing animation

> **Try these animations**
>
> There are many animations you can use. Try the following, too: **rbxassetid://4841405708, rbxassetid://4265725525, rbxassetid://5917459365, rbxassetid://5918726674, rbxassetid://3333387824,** and **rbxassetid://3333331310.**

For this particular animation, the animation keeps playing until we stop it. This is because it is a looped animation. We can choose whether we want to keep it this way or not. There is a simple property on the AnimationTrack, called .Looped, which allows us to specify whether the animation restarts once it is done or not. Let us take a look at the following code snippet:

```
local animationTrack = animator:LoadAnimation(animation)
animationTrack.Looped = false
animationTrack:Play()
```

If we run our game now, the animation still plays. However, after some time, it stops automatically. But what if we wanted to stop the animation before that? For instance, after just a second? In the following section, we will look at how to stop animations.

Stopping animations

What if we only wanted to play the first 2 seconds of the animation? We want to specify at which second the animation should start, let it play, and finally stop it when we want it to stop.

Let us take a look at the following code snippet:

```
local animationTrack = animator:LoadAnimation(animation)

while true do
    animationTrack.TimePosition = 0
    animationTrack:Play()
    task.wait(2)
    animationTrack:Stop()
    task.wait(2)
end
```

In the preceding code, we have a **while loop** that sets the position of the animation to the second 0, which is the beginning of the animation, by using the `.TimePosition` property. Then, it plays the animation for 2 seconds. After that, we use the `:Stop()` function to stop the animation from playing. After that, we wait another 2 seconds, and we repeat the loop.

On a side note, the loop will run indefinitely because we specified `true` as our condition in the `while` loop. After all, `while` loops keep running until the condition is `false`, which can never be the case here.

Now that we know how to start and stop animations, we also understand the essentials of working with animations. In the next section, we will look at how we can change the speed of animations.

Speeding animations

We now understand how to start and stop animations, but there are other cool things we can do with animations. One of these things is changing their speed. Let us take a look at the following code snippet:

```
local animationTrack = animator:LoadAnimation(animation)
animationTrack:Play()
animationTrack:AdjustSpeed(5)
```

The preceding code snippet loads the animation followed by the `:Play()` function. The animation is now playing. After that, we adjust the speed to 5 by using the `:AdjustSpeed()` function. This 5 means that the animation plays five times faster than the original one. If we were to use 2, the animation would play twice as fast, and if we used 1, it would have been the default speed. However, we can also go lower than 1. If we were to use the number 0.5, the duration of the animation would be twice as much compared to the default duration.

Now we know about all the essential functions for AnimationTracks. So far, we have learned how to set up animations, use the `Animator` object, and load animations on the `Animator` object to get an AnimationTrack. Finally, we learned how to use various functions on the AnimationTrack, such as `:Play()` and `:Stop()`, and properties such as `.Looped` and `.TimePosition`. In the next section, we will continue talking about animations. However, this time, we will use these animations on an NPC.

Animations on NPCs

Earlier, we learned how to use animations on our own character. However, what if we wanted to use these animations on NPCs? Luckily, it works almost identically. However, there are a few things we have to keep in mind while doing it.

First, we need to keep in mind that the **Animator** object might not always be inside the **Humanoid** object for NPCs. Luckily, there is a very simple fix: create one yourself. You can do this in the **Explorer** window by inserting it. That's the first possible problem already solved. Let us continue.

For NPCs, we can perform some optimizations for the animations. First, we should perform all animations on each client instead of on the server. That is because NPC animations do not replicate to the server if they are started on the client. This is a good thing. After all, there is no point in having this animation played on the server. This is different from the animations in our own character. They do replicate to the server.

Besides it being a minimal performance gain on the server not to have this animation run, it might not seem very useful. However, the opposite is true. Because we control the animation on each client individually, we can have it interact differently for each player at the same time. For instance, in your game, we have an NPC that is the owner of a clothing store. Every time a player enters the store, the NPC will perform a waving animation. Because we only perform this animation on the client, the player that enters the store will see the animation. Any players that might already be inside will not see it.

Also, we need to keep in mind that NPCs do not have any animations by default. Where our own character plays an idle animation, the NPC would not play any animation when it is not doing anything. If we want to do this, we have to play an idle animation ourselves. Once again, we start this animation on the client. To test all of this, let us set up a testing area. To set this up, follow the following steps:

1. In **ReplicatedStorage**, create a folder called `Animations`. Inside this folder, create two animations named `WaveAnimation` and `IdleAnimation`:

    WaveAnimation Asset ID = **rbxassetid://507770239**

    IdleAnimation Asset ID = **rbxassetid://507766666**

2. Create an R15 dummy NPC using the built-in **Build Rig** plugin in Roblox Studio, as shown in *Figure 5.6*. Make sure you keep the name of this NPC as `Dummy`.

3. Create a **LocalScript** inside the **StarterPlayerScripts** folder. Then, insert the code snippet that follows *Figure 5.6* inside this local script:

Figure 5.6 – The Build Rig plugin

```lua
local ReplicatedStorage = game:GetService("ReplicatedStorage")

local animations = ReplicatedStorage:WaitForChild("Animations")

local npc = workspace:WaitForChild("Dummy")

function setup()
    playAnimation(npc, "IdleAnimation", true,
    Enum.AnimationPriority.Idle)
    task.wait(10)
    playAnimation(npc, "WaveAnimation", false,
    Enum.AnimationPriority.Action)
end

function playAnimation(character, animationName, looped,
animationPriority)
    -- Getting Humanoid and Animation
    local humanoid = npc:WaitForChild("Humanoid", 5)
    local animation =
    animations:FindFirstChild(animationName)
    if humanoid ~= nil and animation ~= nil then
        -- Getting Animator
        local animator = humanoid:WaitForChild("Animator",
        5)
        if animator ~= nil then
            -- Playing Animation
            local animationTrack =
            animator:LoadAnimation(animation)
            animationTrack.Looped = looped
```

```
            animationTrack.Priority = animationPriority
            animationTrack:Play()
        end
    end
end


setup()
```

If we follow the preceding steps, we have an NPC that keeps looking around as their idle animation. Then, after 10 seconds, it starts waving. Once they are done waving, they continue with the idle animation.

Animations stopping for others is actually interesting behavior of animations that we have not covered yet. Before we look into what is going on, let us try to understand what this script does. We have a `setup()` function; this is not anything new. In this `setup()` function, we call the `playAnimation()` function. First, we start playing the idle animation, and after 10 seconds, we use the same function again. However, this time, instead of making it play the idle animation, we play the wave animation. When the wave animation finishes, the NPC magically goes back to the idle animation, even though we did not tell it to do this?

The reason for this is actually pretty straightforward; we never stop the idle animation. But why does it stop the idle animation to play the wave animation instead? This has to do with the priority we gave the animations. The fourth parameter of the `playAnimation()` function determines this priority.

As we can see when we call the `playAnimation()` function, we set the idle animation to loop with the **Idle** priority type. The wave animation gets the **Action** priority type with looping turned off. So, what do these priorities mean? There are four different priority types:

- **Action** (the highest priority)
- **Movement**
- **Idle**
- **Core** (the lowest priority)

For each AnimationTrack, you can specify which priority it has. The animation with the highest priority plays. If another animation with a lower priority already plays, it stops until it is the highest priority animation again. This priority system also works for animations on non-NPCs. Please keep in mind that the priority of the animations has to be specified by using enums. We looked at **enums** in *Chapter 4, Securing Your Game*.

Sometimes, this priority is not enough, or you might want to stop all animations from playing and simply start playing a new set of animations. So, how do we get all the AnimationTracks that are playing on an `Animator` object? To do this, we can use the `:GetPlayingAnimationTracks()` function.

Let us take a look at the following code snippet that uses this function:

```lua
local npc = workspace:WaitForChild("Dummy")

function stopAllAnimations()
    -- Getting Humanoid
    local humanoid = npc:WaitForChild("Humanoid", 5)
    if humanoid ~= nil then
        -- Getting Animator
        local animator = humanoid:WaitForChild("Animator",
        5)
        if animator ~= nil then
            -- Playing Animation
            local animationTracks =
            animator:GetPlayingAnimationTracks()

            -- Looping through animation tracks
            for _, animationTrack in pairs(animationTracks)
            do
                animationTrack:Stop()
            end
        end
    end
end

stopAllAnimations()
```

The preceding code snippet uses the :GetPlayingAnimationTracks() function. This function returns a table of all the AnimationTracks active on this Animator object. Then, we use a **for loop** and loop through all of the AnimationTracks. Then, we use the :Stop() function on each AnimationTrack, which results in all of them stopping.

Previously, we learned all about animations. We combined this information with some additional information about priorities and things to keep in mind when using NPCs. Now we truly understand how animations work. However, what if we wanted to play animations on instances without a Humanoid object? In the next section, we will take a look at **Tweens**.

Working with tweens

Sometimes, we do not want to animate our own character or an NPC. Instead, we would rather animate something else, such as a gate. This could be the gates for a castle that open when you get close to it. It looks way better if these doors open by using some sort of animation rather than just being open instantly. Technically, we could use a hacky way of adding a Humanoid object into a model that contains the gate; then, we could play an animation on it. However, there is a better alternative. We can make **Tweens**.

In the following sections, we will create the previously described animated gate. We will start by making the gate ourselves and looking at **Pivots**. After that, we will start animating the gate.

Setting up the gate

Let us start by making the gate. In *Figure 5.7*, we can see a full gate with two doors. We will be making these doors ourselves:

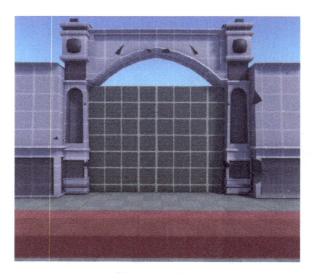

Figure 5.7 – Gate

Follow these steps to make both doors:

1. Create a new part in **Workspace** and name it either `RightGatePart` or `LeftGatePart`.

2. Make sure you anchor the part. This means the **Anchored** property should be set to `true`.

3. Change the **Size** property on the gate part so that the size is equal to `{17.5, 1, 28}`.

4. Change the **Orientation** property on the gate part so that the orientation is equal to `{-90, 0, 0}`.

5. Change the **Material** property on the gate part to **WoodPlanks**.

6. Position the gate somewhere in the Workspace service or next to the other gate part.

Repeat these steps for the other gate part and position them next to each other.

We should have two identical doors for our gate next to each other, similar to *Figure 5.8*:

Figure 5.8 – Creating LeftGatePart and RightGatePart

Now that we have both sides of the door, let us see what needs to happen. We want both sides to rotate 90 degrees, resulting in both sides of the door opening. Before we script this, we can use the **Rotate** tool in Roblox Studio to turn the parts. However, if we rotate both parts by 90 degrees, we will see that they rotated in the center, as shown in *Figure 5.9*, not on the sides, like a typical door:

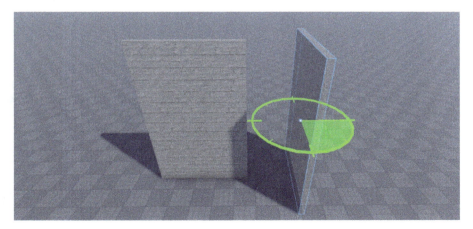

Figure 5.9 – Incorrectly rotated RightGatePart

The reason the part rotates from the center is because of **Pivots**. By default, the pivot of a part, which is the rotation point, is in the center. Rather than having the part rotate from the center, we want it to rotate from the right or left side of the part. For **RightGatePart**, we want the rotation point to be on the part's right side. We can do this by changing the **Pivot Offset Position** property on the part.

Because both gate parts have a width of 17.5 studs, the **Pivot Offset Position** property needs to move to the right-hand side by 8.75 studs. This is because it is in the center by default, so adding half of the width moves the pivot to the side. For **RightGatePart**, our **Pivot Offset Position** property would be {-8.75, 0, 0} and for **LeftGatePart**, our **Pivot Offset Position** property is {8.75, 0, 0}.

Once we have done this, we can easily rotate our door, as shown in *Figure 5.10*:

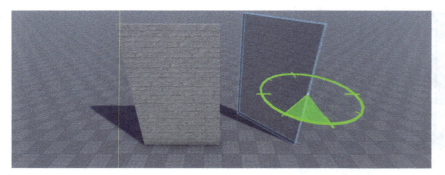

Figure 5.10 – Correctly rotated RightGatePart

We can more easily rotate our gate part because now we have a changed pivot offset. While rotating, we notice the values of the **Position** property and **Orientation** property change. In later sections, we will need these properties.

Now that we have set up our gate parts, let us start scripting them. In the next section, we will set up the server script that we will use for the gate.

Setting up the server scripts

Before tweening our gate, we need to create an action to open the gate. In front of these door parts, we will create another part, named **GateActivation**. The **CanCollide** property of this part should be turned off. The wanted behavior is to make the tween play once we walk through the **GateActivation** part. Because our game works with StreamingEnabled, we choose to make this activation script on the server. However, we could do this for the client, too. In later chapters, we will take a look at how to do this. For now, let us take a look at the following code snippet:

```
local Players = game:GetService("Players")
local ReplicatedStorage = game:GetService("ReplicatedStorage")

local events = ReplicatedStorage.Events

local gateActivation = workspace.GateActivation
```

```
-- GATE FUNCTIONS

function toggleGate(hit)
    -- Server Check
    local distance = ( hit.Position -
    gateActivation.Position ).Magnitude
    if distance >= 25 then
        return
    end

    -- Function Logic
    local player = getPlayerFromHit(hit)
    if player ~= nil then
        if playerHasDebounce(player) == false then
            events.ToggleGate:FireClient(player)
        end
    end
end

function getPlayerFromHit(hit)
    -- Checking variables
    if hit ~= nil and hit.Parent ~= nil then
        -- Getting player
        local character = hit.Parent
        return Players:GetPlayerFromCharacter(character)
    end
    return nil
end

-- DEBOUNCE FUNCTIONS

-- ... debounce functions ...

--

gateActivation.Touched:Connect(toggleGate)
```

The preceding code snippet is a server script located in **ServerScriptService**. Let us take a look at what this script does. At the bottom of the script, we see a `.Touched` event listener. We use this event because we want to know when a player touches our `gateActivation` part. Once someone touches the `gateActivation` part, the `toggleGate()` function is activated.

Inside the `toggleGate()` function, we start with a **Server Check**. You probably did not think of this server check yourself. After all, it seems a bit unnecessary, right? The `.Touched` event only gets fired once someone touches the part. However, exploiters can trigger this event, too. That is why it is wise to have this distance server check either way.

But how does this **Server Check** even work? To calculate the distance, we use two positions. In our scenario, this is the position of the part that hit the `gateActivation` part and the position of the `gateActivation` part itself. We subtract both positions. However, if we do this, we get another **Vector3** value while needing distance. This is where the `.Magnitude` property comes in. Each **Vector3** and **Vector2** data type has the `.Magnitude` property. We can use this to get the distance. Once we get this, we check whether the distance is larger than 25 studs. If that is the case, the player is too far from the `gateActivation` part. Therefore, we stop the function.

If the player is close enough to the part, we continue our function. First, we check whether the part that hit the `gateActivation` part is actually a part of the player's character and not some random part in our game. After that, we check whether this player has an active debounce. To prevent a lengthy code snippet, we have removed the code related to the debounce. This code is included in the GitHub version. If the player does not have a debounce, we fire a `ToggleGate` RemoteEvent inside the **Events** folder in the **ReplicatedStorage** service.

Now we have implemented the trigger to activate the tween on the gate. In the next section, we will start gathering information that the tween will use.

Getting tween data

Now that we have set up the gate and the server event, we can start working on the tween. First, we need to get some values for our tween. What position and rotation should each gate part be once it is closed, and what are they when it is open? You will need to rotate both gate parts yourself and read their properties. Once we have done this, we will store all this data in a **three-dimensional table**. So far, we have never seen this. However, we did see a two-dimensional table. Both work practically the same. Your three-dimensional table could look like this:

```
local GATE_DATA = {
    ["Open"] = {
        ["LeftGatePart"] = {
            ["Orientation"] = Vector3.new(-90, 90, 0),
            ["Position"] = Vector3.new(-40, 15, 83)
        },
```

```
        ["RightGatePart"] = {
            ["Orientation"] = Vector3.new(-90, -90, 0),
            ["Position"] = Vector3.new(-74, 15, 83)
        }
    },
    ["Closed"]= {
        ["LeftGatePart"] = {
            ["Orientation"] = Vector3.new(-90, 0, 0),
            ["Position"] = Vector3.new(-50, 15, 75)
        },
        ["RightGatePart"] = {
            ["Orientation"] = Vector3.new(-90, 0, 0),
            ["Position"] = Vector3.new(-67, 15, 75)
        }
    }
}
```

The preceding code snippet is our three-dimensional table containing a lot of data for our gate parts. First, we differentiate the data from an `Open` gate part and a `Closed` gate part. After that, we differentiate between the left and right gate parts. Finally, we store the **Orientation** and **Position** properties of the parts. Once again, these are just example Vector3 values. You will have to change these to the ones you see in the **Properties** window once you rotate both gate parts.

Now that we have our tween data, we can continue making our tween. In the next section, we will take a look at the `TweenInfo` data type.

Understanding TweenInfo

Now that we have this, we can listen to the `ToggleGate` RemoteEvent. After that, we can use a tween to change the orientation and position. But how do tweens even work? To use **Tweens**, we need to use the **TweenService** service. Besides **TweenService**, we also need `TweenInfo`. This is another data type. Let us take a look at that first:

```
local tweenInfo = TweenInfo.new(
    -- Duration of Tween
    1,

    -- Tween style (EasingStyle)
    Enum.EasingStyle.Quad,
```

```
    -- EasingStyle direction
    Enum.EasingDirection.Out,

    -- Amount of times the tween repeats
    0,

    -- Tween Reverse
    false,

    -- Delay before the Tween starts
    0
)
```

The preceding code snippet contains all the arguments you can provide when creating a `TweenInfo` data type. The values displayed here are the default values. You do not have to provide all of them. Generally, only the first or the first two arguments are provided; they are the most common. We can experiment with all of the different values once we have made our first tween.

Now that we have seen how `TweenInfo` works, let us use it in an actual tween. In the next section, we will make our first tween by combining all the information we have previously learned.

Creating a tween

As previously mentioned, we will listen to the `ToggleGate` RemoteEvent. Once this event is fired, we will start a tween. Let us take a look at the following code snippet:

```
local ReplicatedStorage = game:GetService("ReplicatedStorage")
local TweenService = game:GetService("TweenService")

local events = ReplicatedStorage:WaitForChild("Events")

local GATE_DATA = ...

function toggleGate()
    -- Getting gate parts
    local leftGatePart =
    workspace:WaitForChild("LeftGatePart", 5)
    local rightGatePart =
```

```
        workspace:WaitForChild("RightGatePart", 5)
        if leftGatePart ~= nil and rightGatePart ~= nil then
            -- Opening gate
            animateGate(leftGatePart, "Open")
            animateGate(rightGatePart, "Open")
            --
            task.wait(10)

            -- Closing gate
            animateGate(leftGatePart, "Closed")
            animateGate(rightGatePart, "Closed")
        end
end

function animateGate(gate, doorStatus)
    -- Getting Tween Data
    local tweenData = GATE_DATA[doorStatus][gate.Name]
    local tween = TweenService:Create(gate,
    TweenInfo.new(2), tweenData)
    tween:Play()
end

events:WaitForChild("ToggleGate").
OnClientEvent:Connect(toggleGate)
```

Take a look at the preceding code snippet. At the bottom of the script, we listen to the `ToggleGate` RemoteEvent. Once this `RemoteEvent` gets fired, we start the `toggleGate()` function. In this function, the first thing we do is get a reference to both gate parts by using the `:WaitForChild()` function. Did you notice how we used the second argument for this function? This means that the result will be `nil` if the part cannot be found. That is why we have an `if` statement on the next line, checking whether `nil` was returned. Finally, we use the `animateGate()` function if both gate parts can be found.

The `animateGate()` function has the gate part as the first parameter. This is the part that we will animate. The second parameter is `doorStatus`. This parameter tells us if the door is going to be opened or closed. We use the `GATE_DATA` variable that we made in the *Getting tween data* section. Both parameters are required to select the right piece of data from the `GATE_DATA` variable. Finally, we store this right piece of data in a variable called `tweenData`.

Then, we reach the point where we make our actual tween. We do this by using the `:Create()` function in the **TweenService** service. The `:Create()` function has three arguments. The first argument is the object, in our scenario, the gate part, that we want to tween. The second argument is the `TweenInfo` data type that we saw in the previous section. In our current scenario, we only specify the duration of the tween. Because we only specify the duration, all the other arguments are automatically set to their default values. Finally, we have our `tweenData` variable. The `tweenData` variable is the table containing what is going to be changed. In our current scenario, we are changing the `Position` property and the `Orientation` property, as they are the specified items in our `GATE_DATA` dictionary.

Now, we have our tween. Similar to animations, we still have to start our tween. However, we can simply call the `:Play()` function on the tween. If we combine all the scripts and start the game, we will see that our gate opens once we touch the `gateActivation` part, as shown in *Figure 5.11*:

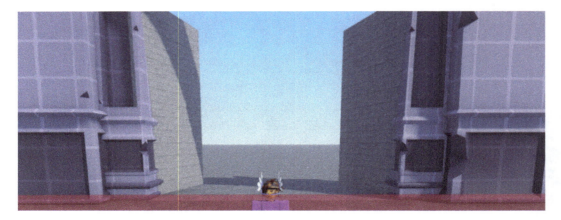

Figure 5.11 – Our first tween

We now know how to make tweens. However, there are a few cool tricks and things we should keep in mind. In the next section, we will look at **Client-Sided Debounces**.

Client-sided debounces

Currently, we already have a debounce on the server. This debounce takes a few seconds. For now, let us say it takes 20 seconds. Our tween on the client side takes 2 seconds to open, with an 8-second extra intermission. The reason there is only an 8-second extra intermission is that the first 2 seconds are already calculated for the opening tweens. Finally, we have another 2 seconds to close. Combined, the tween takes 14 seconds, which means our server debounce is long enough. However, what if we accidentally lowered the debounce on the server or made the tween longer? There might be a chance the server wants the tween to start while it is still performing the previous tween.

We can prevent this from ever being an issue by adding a client-sided debounce. The client-sided debounce is much easier to implement. Let us look at the updated `toggleGate()` function, which now features a client-sided debounce. Please remember that all the function logic has been left out from the following code snippet as nothing has changed there:

```
local debounce = false

function toggleGate()
    if debounce == false then
        debounce = true

        -- Function Logic

        debounce = false
    end
end

events:WaitForChild("ToggleGate").
OnClientEvent:Connect(toggleGate)
```

The preceding code snippet features a client-sided debounce. It is a simple variable with one `if` statement. Once the function starts, it checks whether there is an active debounce. If there is an active debounce, the function ends. However, if there is no active debounce, the `debounce` variable gets set to `true`. Then, the function would do what it would normally do. Once it is done, the `debounce` variable gets set to `false` again.

Even if we were to accidentally make our debounce on the server too short, our client-sided debounce prevents two tweens from starting simultaneously. Yes, the debounce on the server would still think that the action is performed. However, this should not be a serious issue unless you have debounces of a few hours. If that is the case, it is highly recommended that you simply time the duration of your tween or any other action that you might perform that has a client-sided debounce, and ensure your server debounce is longer.

We have seen how to make a client-sided debounce. They give us extra protection against weirdly behaving tweens. However, we can use them for other things, too. Theoretically, you could use client-sided debounces in any function. However, there is no point in implementing one when it is not required. By adding the client-sided debounce, we removed a flaw in our code. However, there is another one. In the next section, we will eliminate this flaw by making **Custom Yielding Functions**.

Custom yielding functions

Let us take a look at the following code snippet:

```
-- Opening gate
animateGate(leftGatePart, "Open")
animateGate(rightGatePart, "Open")
--
task.wait(10)

-- Closing gate
animateGate(leftGatePart, "Closed")
animateGate(rightGatePart, "Closed")
```

The preceding code snippet is a section from the toggleGate() function. In this snippet, we can find a similar problem that we solved in the previous section. In the previous section, we saw that the toggleGate() function could be executed multiple times while already active. Technically, we have this here, too. But what if we decided to make our tween last for 12 seconds? We would have a problem. The door would still be opening while the tween closing the gate already starts.

As mentioned previously, we solved this issue by adding a client-sided debounce. So, could we add one for the animateGate() function, too? Unfortunately, this will not work. If we were to do this, the rightGatePart part would never open. After all, there is a debounce on the animateGate() function. So, how do we solve this issue? One possible solution could be found by taking advantage of **Yielding**. We have heard about yielding functions a few times already. An example of a yielding function is the :WaitForChild() function.

But how would yielding help us? Let us take a look at the updated code:

```
local INTERMISSION_TIME = 5
local TWEEN_DURATION = 2

local GATE_DATA =  ...

local debounce = false

function toggleGate()
    if debounce == false then
        debounce = true

        -- Getting gate parts
```

```
        local leftGatePart =
        workspace:WaitForChild("LeftGatePart", 5)
        local rightGatePart =
        workspace:WaitForChild("RightGatePart", 5)
        if leftGatePart ~= nil and rightGatePart ~= nil
        then
            -- Opening Gate
            animateGate(leftGatePart, "Open", false)
            animateGate(rightGatePart, "Open", true)

            -- Intermission
            task.wait(INTERMISSION_TIME)

            -- Closing gate
            animateGate(leftGatePart, "Closed", false)
            animateGate(rightGatePart, "Closed", true)
        end

        -- Ending client-sided debounce
        debounce = false
    end
end

function animateGate(gate, doorStatus, yield)
    local tweenData = GATE_DATA[doorStatus][gate.Name]
    local tween = TweenService:Create(gate,
    TweenInfo.new(TWEEN_DURATION), tweenData)
    tween:Play()
    --
    if yield == true then
        tween.Completed:Wait()
    end
end

events:WaitForChild("ToggleGate").
OnClientEvent:Connect(toggleGate)
```

The preceding code snippet contains the updated code, which now features a function that might **Yield**. Once again, this is just a snippet of the entire script. The entire script is available on the GitHub page. However, to save space, only the changed code is shown.

The `animateGate()` function now has a third parameter, called `yield`. This parameter will contain a **Boolean** data type. If the Boolean equals `true`, the function will yield. But how do we even make it yield? To make the function yield, we use an event called `.Completed` on the tween. Combining this `.Completed` event with the `:Wait()` function will make our function yield until the `.Completed` event fires.

So, how does this work? As the name implies, the `:Wait()` function waits, and therefore, it yields. However, we can use the `:Wait()` function more than just the `.Completed` event. As a matter of fact, we can use it for any event. Adding the `:Wait()` function on an event will yield the current thread until the event is fired. Using this, we made our `animateGate()` function yield depending on the parameter's input.

However, besides the changes in the `animateGate()` function, we also made a slight change in the `toggleGate()` function. The `toggleGate()` function now provides the third argument when calling the `animateGate()` function. What is noteworthy is that only the second gate part is supposed to yield, not the first one. Try changing both to true yourself, and try to explain why both gate parts wait turns to open and close.

Now we have solved the second flaw in our code. We solved this flaw by taking advantage of what we learned about yielding. We can now make fantastic tweens by combining all the information we learned previously. This section taught us about **TweenService**, **TweenInfo**, **Tweens**, client-sided debounces, yielding functions, and **Pivots**. In the next section, we have an exercise to combine many of the learned aspects of this chapter.

Exercise 5.1 – greeting an NPC

In this exercise, we will make a greeting system compatible with StreamingEnabled. There will be an NPC on the map that constantly plays idle animations. A waving animation will start on the NPC if the player comes near the player. At the same time that the NPC is waving, the player near the NPC should wave, too. The waving animation of the NPC should not replicate in other clients. This means that the NPC is only waving for the player near the NPC, not for other players that see the NPC but are not close to it.

There are multiple ways of implementing this system. There will be steps to make this system next. However, you are not required to follow those steps. If you know a better way or want to experiment yourself, feel free to try it on your own. Just make sure your system meets all the previously mentioned criteria.

Exercise:

We will start by setting up the game from an empty **Baseplate** template:

1. Create an **R15** dummy in **Workspace**, called **Dummy**, using the **Build Rig** plugin. Make sure you create an **Animator** object inside the **Humanoid** object.

2. In **ReplicatedStorage**, make a folder called `Events` and insert a RemoteEvent called `ActivateGreeting`.

3. In **ReplicatedStorage**, make a folder called **Animations** and insert two animations:

    *   **IdleAnimation** with `AnimationId`: **rbxassetid://507766666**

    *   **WaveAnimation** with `AnimationId`: **rbxassetid://507770239**

4. Create a part in Workspace called `GreetingActivation` and ensure the **Anchored** property is set to `true` and the **CanCollide** property is set to `false`. Change the **Size** property of the part to {`15`, `1`, `15`} and position the part on the dummy character. Try to make the dummy character centered on the `GreetingActivation` part.

Now we will make our server script, named `GreetingSystem`, in **ServerScriptService**:

1. Start listening to the `.Touched` event in the `GreetingActivation` part. Connect this listener to a function named `activateGreeting()`. The first and only parameter of this function should be called `hit`.

2. Check whether the `hit` part is within 25 studs of the `GreetingActivation` part by using the `.Magnitude` property on a **Vector3** data type.

3. Confirm an actual player has touched the `GreetingActivation` part by using the `hit` parameter. First, get the character connected to this `hit` parameter. Then, use the `:GetPlayerFromCharacter()` function to get the player and confirm that the result is not `nil`.

4. Make a debounce system that only allows a player to interact with the `GreetingActivation` part once every 30 seconds. While making this system, make sure the cooldown table gets cleared if a player leaves.

5. If the player does not have an active debounce, fire the `ActivateGreeting` RemoteEvent in the **Events** folder for the right player.

Now that the server script is done, we will continue in a local script, called `AnimationHandler`, inside **StarterPlayerScripts**:

1. Create a function called `playAnimation()` with the following parameters:

    `character, animationName, priority, looped, yield`

2. In the `playAnimation()` function, get a reference to the correct animation using the `Animations` folder in `ReplicatedStorage` and the `animationName` parameter.

3. In the `playAnimation()` function, get a reference to the `Animator` object inside the `Humanoid` object.

4. Get the `AnimationTrack` by loading the previously referenced `Animation` object on the `Animator` object. Make sure you set the `priority` property and the `looped` property on the `AnimationTrack` based on the values from the parameters that we made in Step 1. Finally, play the animation.

5. At the bottom of the `playAnimation()` function, check whether the `yield` parameter equals `true` and the `IsPlaying` property on the `AnimationTrack` object equals `true`. If both are `true`, yield the function until the `AnimationTrack` is finished using the `:Wait()` function.

   Tip for 5: There is an event called `.Stopped` on **AnimationTracks**.

6. Create a `setup()` function that starts playing the **idle** animation on the NPC. Make sure the priority of the animation equals **Idle**, the looped parameter equals `true`, and the yield parameter equals `false`.

7. Start listening to the `ActivateGreeting` RemoteEvent and start a function called `greetingSequence()`.

8. In the `greetingSequence()` function, start the **wave** animation for both the player and the NPC. Make sure that the priority of the animation is **Action** and the looped parameter equals `false`. The second time you call the `playAnimation()` function, make sure the yielding parameter equals `true`, while the first one stays `false`.

9. Make a client-sided debounce for the `greetingSequence()` function.

Run the game, walk toward the NPC, and test whether both characters greet each other. An example answer for this system can be found on the GitHub page for this book at `https://github.com/PacktPublishing/Mastering-Roblox-Coding/tree/main/Exercises`.

Exercise 5.2 – falling block

In this exercise, we will create a simple part that we will position in the air. Instead of letting physics do the work of making the block fall down, we will use tweens to make this block fall. Once the Tween is done, we will position the part back to its original position and create another tween. Throughout this exercise, we will use different EasingStyles, as explained in the *Understanding TweenInfo* section. This will give each fall a different effect:

Exercise:

First, we will start by setting up the part that we will create a tween for:

1. Create a new part in the **Workspace** service. Give this part the following properties:

   • **Name:** TweenPart

   • **Size:** {5, 5, 5}

- **Position**: $\{0, \ 2.5, \ 0\}$
- **Anchored**: `true`

Now that we have our TweenPart, let us start creating the tweens.

2. Create a new **LocalScript** in **StarterPlayerScripts**.

3. In our **LocalScript**, create the following global variables:

- `targetPosition`: `Vector3.new(0, 2.5, 0)`
- `startPosition`: `Vector3.new(0, 10, 0)`
- `tweenDuration`: 2

Tip for 3: You can add more global variables if the following steps require them.

4. Create a function, named `tween()`, with the following parameters:

`part, easingStyle, yield`

5. Inside the `tween()` function, change the **Position** property of the part to the position stored in the `startPosition` variable.

6. Inside the `tween()` function, create a new variable named `tweenInfo`. Set the following properties for our `TweenInfo` data type:

- `time`: The `tweenDuration` global variable
- `easingStyle`: The `easingStyle` parameter

7. Create and start a new tween using the `:Create()` and `:Play()` functions on the **TweenService**.

8. Implement a custom yielding system in the `tween()` function. Use the `yield` parameter.

9. Implement a debounce system inside the `tween()` function.

10. Create a new function named `setup()`. Insert the following code in the `setup()` function:

```
while true do
    tween(tweenPart, Enum.EasingStyle.Linear, true)
    tween(tweenPart, Enum.EasingStyle.Bounce, true)
    tween(tweenPart, Enum.EasingStyle.Elastic, true)
end
```

Run the game and watch our part fall with different EasingStyles. An example solution for this system can be found on the GitHub page for this book at `https://github.com/PacktPublishing/Mastering-Roblox-Coding/tree/main/Exercises`.

Summary

We started this chapter by learning about **StreamingEnabled**. We learned that StreamingEnabled is not enabled by default as it changes the way loading in your game works. Normally, when a player joins a game, everything is loaded instantly. However, we learned that only certain instances get sent when the player is joining with StreamingEnabled. Even after the joining process, there is a high chance not everything is loaded on the map. This had to do with the **StreamingMinRadius** property and the **StreamingTargetRadius** property.

Besides the behavior that changes when using StreamingEnabled, we also learned that we have to change our local scripts to be compatible with StreamingEnabled. For example, we learned that we need to use the `:WaitForChild()` function to reference instances in the Workspace service. Sometimes, we cannot rely on the `:WaitForChild()` function because a part might not be loaded unless we are near it. In this scenario, we learned how to use the `.ChildAdded` event. Besides this, we also learned how to use the `:RequeststreamAroundAsync()` function if we want to teleport a player around the map.

However, in this chapter, we did not only learn about StreamingEnabled. We also learned how to use animations. We saw how an **Animation** has an `AnimationId` property, which stores a **Roblox Asset ID**. These animations are uploaded to Roblox. If we want to play an animation, we have to load the animation on an `Animator` object. When we load these animations on the `Animator` object, we get something called `AnimationTrack`. We have seen various functions and properties on this AnimationTrack, such as `:Play()`, `:Stop()`, `.Looped`, and `.TimePosition`.

Finally, we learned about a type of animation that is not played on an `Animator` object. These "animations" are called **Tweens**. We have seen an example where we made our own gate that slowly opens. While doing this, we learned how to make tweens by using **TweenService**, `TweenInfo`, and client-sided debounces, and we even made our own yielding functions. Besides this, we also used the `.Magnitude` property on a **Vector3** data type to calculate the distance. We even made a four-dimensional table that worked exactly like a two-dimensional table.

We have truly learned a lot about programming Roblox games throughout the previous chapters. In the next chapter, we will dive deeper into **Graphical User Interfaces (GUIs)**. In *Chapter 4, Securing Your Game*, we had a short introduction to GUIs. However, in the next chapter, we will take this knowledge to the next level. We will learn how to make GUIs ourselves and how to scale and program them for all devices that Roblox supports.

6

Creating User Interfaces for All Devices

In this chapter, we will learn everything about **graphical user interfaces** (**GUIs**). We will learn about the different types of GUIs, what makes them different, and what they are generally used for. Besides this, we will learn how to properly build GUIs and scale them for all devices on Roblox. Then, we will learn how to use the emulator built into Roblox Studio to test the **user interface** (**UI**) of our game on different devices with different resolutions. Finally, we will also learn about the small things we need to keep in mind when creating our GUIs, such as color blindness and the navigation of our GUIs.

The following topics will be covered in this chapter:

- Creating GUIs
- Testing GUIs
- Small UI improvements
- Exercise 6.1—Creating a shop GUI

By the end of this chapter, you will know how to properly build GUIs for your game that scale on multiple devices. In addition, you will learn about all of the major GUI elements that Roblox has to offer. Besides this, you will know how to test your GUI using the emulator. Finally, you will learn tips that help you take your GUIs to the next level.

Technical requirements

To start programming with Luau, you need access to a device with internet access. This can either be a Windows or a Mac device.

You need to download the following software:

- Roblox Player
- Roblox Studio

All the code examples for this chapter can be found on GitHub at `https://github.com/PacktPublishing/Mastering-Roblox-Coding`.

The CiA video for this chapter can be found at `https://bit.ly/3OygUlv`.

Creating GUIs

In this section, we will learn all the cool things about making GUIs. In *Chapter 4, Securing Your Game*, we already introduced GUIs when we made the team changer. However, we did not make the GUI ourselves back then. So, in this section, we will learn how to make UIs ourselves.

UIs are something we, as players, can interact with. Because players can directly interact with GUIs, this means they are on the client. This is important to remember. Many beginner programmers try to use normal scripts to control aspects of the UI. The worst part is that they somehow manage to get it working. This is an extremely bad practice and should never be done or attempted.

There are multiple types of GUIs. In *Chapter 4, Securing Your Game*, we saw the usage of **ScreenGuis**. However, there are two more that we will cover throughout this chapter. Besides ScreenGuis, we will also learn about **SurfaceGuis** and **BillboardGuis**. In the next subsection, we will start by looking deeper into ScreenGuis.

Using ScreenGuis

Before we can look at what a **ScreenGui** is, we need to look at the service we use for GUIs. This service is called **StarterGui**. This is the service in which we will make all of our ScreenGuis. We previously learned that GUIs are on the client, so why would all the GUIs be in the same location as the StarterGui?

Well, the ScreenGuis we see as players are not the ones in the StarterGui. When we create a ScreenGui inside the StarterGui and run the game, we see that the ScreenGui is still in the StarterGui. While it is true that the ScreenGui is still in the StarterGui, it got cloned to another location. So, inside the **Players** service, open your **Player** instance and look for **PlayerGui.** Inside the PlayerGui, you will see the ScreenGui we just made, plus a few default ScreenGuis that Roblox inserted. The ScreenGui that was cloned to the PlayerGui is the one we see as players.

Now that we know the behavior of the StarterGui, let us look at what ScreenGuis are. Well, they are not something super complex. Remember how we stored parts from the **Workspace** into a **Model**? You could compare ScreenGuis to a Model. ScreenGuis hold different GUI elements. These GUI elements can be various instances such as buttons, text, or images. The ScreenGui itself does not show anything. It needs to get these GUI elements to start showing something.

Now that we know how the StarterGui works and what ScreenGuis are, let us look at all the different GUI elements out there. In the next section, we will look at the most basic GUI element: a **Frame**.

Frame GUI element

Let us insert a new **Frame** into our previously made ScreenGui and see what it does. If we hover over the ScreenGui, we will see a + icon appear next to it, as seen in the following screenshot. If we click on this icon, a menu opens. Look for something called **Frame** in this menu and click on it:

Figure 6.1 – Inserting a new Frame

Once we insert our Frame, we will see a white box with the size of 100x100 pixels appear in the top-left corner. This is our Frame. If we open the **Properties** window, we will see that this Frame has a lot of properties. One of the properties is **BackgroundColor3**. This property allows us to change the color of our Frame. The data type of this property is the **Color3** data type; we have previously used this data type in *Chapter 3, Event-Based Programming*.

If we change the color of our Frame, we see that there is a black outline around our Frame that does not change color. This is your **border pixel**. You can change the color of this by changing the **BorderColor3** property. Most developers do not like this border. Thankfully, we can get rid of this border by changing the **BorderSizePixel** value to 0. When we do this, the border's size will be 0 pixels, making it invisible.

We now know what a **Frame** is and how to create one inside the **ScreenGui**. Besides this, we also learned how to change the color of our Frame and what the **Border Pixel** is. While this is cool, it is way cooler to change the **Size** or **Position** properties of our Frame. The following section will look into the **UDim2** data type used to size and position frames.

UDim2 data type

If we want to change either the **Position** or **Size** values of the Frame, we need to change the designated property on the Frame for this. For instance, to change the size of the Frame, we have to change the **Size** property. While this makes sense, there are some odd numbers inside this property's value. The default size of our Frame looks like this: {0, 100}, {0, 100}. But what does this even mean?

The value inside of the **Size** property is how a **UDim2** data type is structured. The UDim2 data type is what we use when working with GUIs. If we look at the size, we see two numbers surrounded by braces. Then, we see a comma and another two numbers surrounded by braces. This is because a UDim2 data type actually consists of two **UDim** data types. For example, a UDim data type could look like this: {0, 100}.

Now, we know that a UDim2 data type is a combination of two UDim data types. However, we still do not know what both numbers mean. If we look at the **Size** or **Position** properties using the **Properties** window, we can get the answer to this question. Let us take a look at the following screenshot:

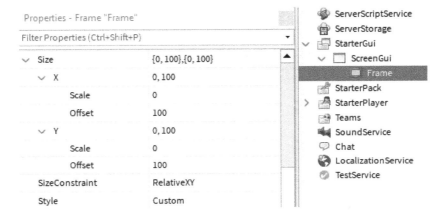

Figure 6.2 – UDim2 displayed on the Size property in the Properties frame

If we open the **Size** property in the **Properties** window, we see **X** and **Y** appear. Those are the names of both **UDim** data types. Once again, the **Size** property is a **UDim2** data type, while both **X** and **Y** are **UDim** data types. If we open the **X** or **Y** UDim data types, we see that the first number is the **Scale** value, and the second number is the **Offset** value.

Most beginner developers do not understand the difference between **Scale** and **Offset**. This results in weird GUIs. Here is a definition and an example use case for both properties:

- **Scale** is deployed to use a percentage of the player's screen. The **Scale** property is a value between 0 and 1. For example, when changing the **Size** property, the value of 0.5 would be half the screen.

- **Offset** is used to use a certain amount of pixels. The size or position will be the same for every player, even if their screen size is not the same. Therefore, misusing the **Offset** property could result in very odd GUIs.

But why do we have two **Scale** and **Offset** properties? They are both in the **X** and **Y** UDim data types. As the name gives away, the **X** UDim data type determines the *x* axis of the screen, which is horizontal. Knowing this, we can guess what the **Y** UDim data type means. The **Y** UDim data type is the *y* axis, which is vertical. If we were to write the full UDim2 data type in text, it would look like this: {x-axis scale, x-axis offset}, {y-axis scale, y-axis offset}.

Still, these properties might seem to be a bit confusing. Let us experiment with them a bit. Give your frame the following **Size** value: {0, 500},{0, 500}. This is a vast square. The size of the square is 500x500 pixels. But what if we make our screen smaller? Make sure Roblox Studio is not in fullscreen mode and try to resize the Roblox Studio window. The square stays the same size, no matter how small we make the Roblox Studio window, as seen in the following screenshot:

Figure 6.3 – Effect of Offset on a Frame

As we can see in *Figure 6.3*, the Frame stays the same size, no matter what. This is the effect that **Offset** has. Now, let us compare this to the **Scale** property. When we change the size of our Frame to {0.5, 0},{0.5, 0}, we will see that the Frame will always be half of the width and height of the screen. It will always stay in these proportions, no matter how small we make Roblox Studio. Let us take a look at the following screenshot:

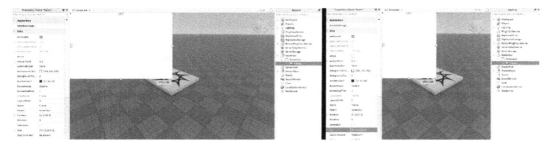

Figure 6.4 – Effect of Scale on a Frame

In *Figure 6.4*, the left Frame has an **AbsoluteSize** value of 479x316 pixels. This is precisely half of the screen. However, if we make Roblox Studio smaller, the Frame stays half of the screen, resulting in the **AbsoluteSize** value of the Frame changing to 254x316 pixels.

We now know about the **UDim2** and **UDim** data types. Besides this, we learned what the difference is between **Scale** and **Offset**. In the next section, we will learn how to position frames and how to use the **AnchorPoint** property.

AnchorPoint property

We want to position our Frame in the center of our screen. First, we need a Frame. We will give this frame a size of {0.25, 0}, {0.25, 0}. Now, we can center the Frame. Our screen might be 1920x1080 pixels, the default for a **high-definition** (**HD**) monitor. If we want the center, we divide both numbers by two. Yes—this will get us the center pixel of our screen. Once again, not everyone has the same screen. Instead of using **Offset**, we have to use **Scale**. **Scale** will always put our Frame in the center, no matter what screen someone has.

If we want to use **Scale**, the center of the screen would be {0.5, 0}, {0.5, 0}. Notice how the Frame is not centered once we put the previously given UDim2 data type as the **Position** type of our Frame? However, the top-left part of the Frame is exactly in the center. Rather than having the top-left part centered, we want to center the entire Frame. We can do some math for this.

We know that the position of the Frame is measured from the top-left part of the Frame. If we want to position it in the middle of our screen, we have to take the current position and subtract half of the size. This would mean that the new position of the Frame is {0.375, 0}, {0.375, 0}. This is true because 0.5 - (0.25 / 2) equals 0.375. If we change the Frame's position to this new position, we see that the Frame is now centered.

Doing this math yourself is very inefficient. If we were to change the size of our Frame, we would have to reposition it again. In *Chapter 5, Optimizing Your Game*, we learned about **Pivots** on **Parts**. We have something similar for GUI elements. For GUI elements, the Pivot is called the **AnchorPoint**. The AnchorPoint of a GUI element is in the top-left corner by default. This means that the AnchorPoint is {0, 0}. The **AnchorPoint** property has a **Vector2** data type. A Vector2 data type has two numbers, **X** and **Y**. For AnchorPoints, both numbers need to have a value between 0 and 1. If both numbers are 0, the AnchorPoint is in the top-left corner. However, if we change both numbers to 1, the AnchorPoint is in the bottom-right corner. This means that if we set the AnchorPoint to {0.5, 0.5} we can easily position our Frame in the center. Now, we can change our position back to {0.5, 0}, {0.5, 0}. We can now easily center our Frame without updating the **Position** value whenever we resize the Frame.

We now know how to position Frames by using **AnchorPoints**. We previously also learned how to size Frames using the **UDim2** data type. In the next section, we will move on to the next GUI element: **TextLabels**.

TextLabel GUI element

As the name implies, a **TextLabel** allows us to display text in our game. Generally, a TextLabel is a child of a Frame. If we insert a TextLabel into our Frame and look at the **Properties** window, we will see that there are once again a lot of properties. We have already seen some of these properties on the **Frame** GUI element. However, some are unique to TextLabels. Some of these similar properties include **AnchorPoint**, **Size**, **Position**, **BackgroundColor**, and many more.

As previously mentioned, there are also new properties. Let us take a look at those. One of the new properties is called **Text**. As the name of this property implies, the value we give will be the text displayed on our TextLabel. There is another property called **Font** that allows us to change what our text looks like. It is also handy to know that we can change the size of the text by adjusting the **TextSize** property. Besides this, we also have a property called **RichText**. If we enable RichText, we can use select **Hypertext Markup Language** (HTML) tags in our **Text** property. For instance, if we want to make a particular word or phrase bold, we can change our **Text** property to this: `This is <b>bold</b>`.

There is another fascinating property called **TextScaled**. This property overrides the **TextSize** property and makes the text as big as possible. If the text does not fit inside the size of your TextLabel, the text will be automatically scaled down.

We now know what a **TextLabel** is. Besides this, we have learned about a few of its properties: **Text**, **TextSize**, **RichText**, and **TextScaled**. In the next section, we will learn how to gain more control over the **TextScaled** property.

UITextSizeConstraint

We previously learned that the **TextScaled** property overrides the **TextSize** property. Unfortunately, this means that we are no longer in control of our text's size. After all, this is what needs to happen if we want to scale the text size automatically. Nevertheless, we might want to have some control over the text size. We can take some of this control back by adding a **UITextSizeConstraint** inside the TextLabel.

We see two exciting properties once we add a **UITextSizeConstraint** and view it with the Properties window—first, the **MinTextSize** property, which allows us to set a minimum size for our text. This property works even if we have the **TextScaled** property turned on. The other property is **MaxTextSize**, which does the exact opposite of the **MinTextSize** property: it allows us to set a maximum text size.

As mentioned, the UITextSizeConstraint works even if we use **TextScaled**, so inserting this constraint gives us back some control over the text size. In the next section, we will look at the next GUI element: **TextBox**.

TextBox GUI element

TextBox elements allow players of our game to insert text. Once they have done that, we can read what they have inserted and do something with it. We see TextBox elements everywhere. When you type a message in a chat, you use a TextBox. In *Chapter 4*, *Securing Your Game*, we saw a TextBox when we learned how to filter text. Back then, we waited for users to insert something to filter it. Let us take a look at how to read data from a TextBox, as follows:

```
local textBox = ...


function textboxChanged()
    print(textBox.Text)
```

```
end
```

```
textBox.FocusLost:Connect(textboxChanged)
```

Let us take a look at the preceding code snippet. At the top of the local script, we have a variable named `textBox`. This variable will have a relative reference to your TextBox, depending on where you place your TextBox in your GUI. At the bottom of the script, we listen to the `.FocusLost` event. If someone is typing in the TextBox, there is a focus on this TextBox. However, once the player is done typing in the TextBox, they lose focus. When the player is done typing, the `.FocusLost` event gets fired. Once it is fired, we start the `textboxChanged()` function. This function simply prints the `.Text` property of the TextBox, and therefore, it prints what we have typed.

Besides this, there is an exciting property worth mentioning. This property is called **PlaceholderText**. This property allows us to display text when the **Text** property is empty. The power of this property is to assist players when there is no given input. For instance, if we make a custom chat GUI, we have a TextBox where players can enter their messages. We can use the **PlaceholderText** property and set its value to display something like this: `Enter your message here`.

We could use the **Text** property to display this message as well. However, the downside of this is that the player can simply send the message, and they would say **Enter your message here**, while if we used the **PlaceholderText** property, the **Text** property would be empty. When using the **PlaceholderText** property, we can check whether the length of the **Text** property is greater than zero characters to prevent players from sending a message zero characters while still showing an assisting message.

We now know how the **TextBox** GUI element works. We learned how to read data inserted by players into the TextBox. In addition, we have seen how the `.FocusLost` event works. Besides that, we also learned about the **PlaceholderText** property that allows us to make our GUI more navigable for our game players. In the next section, we will look at the **ZIndex** property on most GUI elements.

ZIndex property

If you have experimented with GUIs yourself, you might have seen the ZIndex property on a few GUI elements. Maybe you tried to change the number yourself to see what it did. Maybe it did something for you, or maybe it did not. This section will cover what this property does and when we should use it.

Previously, we saw the **UDim2** data type that allowed us to change the *x* and *y* axis of our GUI elements. A GUI is **two-dimensional** (**2D**), as the screens we play on are flat. However, we do have multiple GUI elements that might overlap. The ZIndex property allows us to determine which GUI element should be displayed on top of other GUI elements. The higher the ZIndex value, the more priority a particular GUI element has.

Still, it is a bit more complex than that. For example, on ScreenGuis, there is a property called **ZIndexBehavior**. This property can have one of two values. To explain the difference between both options, we will use the GUI structure shown in the following screenshot:

Figure 6.5 – GUI structure

By default, the TextBox is displayed on top of the Frame. However, we can change this as well. The only requirement is that our ScreenGui has their **ZIndexBehavior** property set to **Global**. Then, we can change the ZIndex value of the Frame to 2, while keeping the ZIndex value for the TextBox at 1. This works because **Global ZIndexBehavior** does not care if the TextBox is a child of the Frame, whereas the other **ZIndexBehavior** option, **Sibling**, does keep this in mind. No matter what we set our Frame's ZIndex property to, the TextBox will always be on top of the Frame when using the **Sibling** behavior.

If we have randomly overlapping GUI elements, we know that we need to change their ZIndex value. We learned what ZIndexes are, and we also learned there are two values for the **ZIndexBehaviors** property: : **Global** and **Sibling**. In the next section, we will look at the **TextButton** GUI element.

TextButton GUI element

Buttons are crucial. We want to register when a user wants to perform a certain action. Roblox has a GUI element called **TextButton**, which is basically a button and a **TextLabel** in one. The TextButton element has events such as `.MouseButton1Down`, `.MouseButton1Click`, `.MouseButton1Up`, and `.MouseEnter`, while also having properties that a TextLabel element has, such as **Text** and **Font**.

To play around with TextButton elements, we will create a simple **Give Feedback** GUI that uses buttons to change what the GUI does. Before we can do this, we will make the GUI ourselves. Follow these steps to make the GUI yourself:

1. In the **StarterGui**, create a new **ScreenGui**.

2. Inside the **ScreenGui**, create a Frame and name it **GivingFeedback**. Set the following properties for this Frame:

   A. **AnchorPoint**: $\{0.5, 0.5\}$

   B. **Position**: $\{0.5, 0\}, \{0.5, 0\}$

   C. **Size**: $\{0.35, 50\}, \{0.3, 25\}$

   D. **BorderSizePixel**: 0

   E. **BackgroundColor3**: Pick a color you like.

3. Inside the **GivingFeedback** Frame, insert a **TextLabel** with the following properties:

   A. **BorderSizePixel**: 0

   B. **Position**: $\{0, 0\}, \{0, 5\}$

    C. **Size:** {1, 0},{0.2, -5}

    D. **Font:** Choose a font you like.

    E. **Text: Feedback**

    F. **TextScaled: True**

4.   Besides a **TextLabel**, insert a **TextBox** into the **GivingFeedback** Frame with the following properties:

    A. **AnchorPoint:** {0.5, 0.5}

    B. **BorderSizePixel:** 3

    C. **Position:** {0.5, 0},{0.5, 0}

    D. **Size:** {0.8, 0},{0.4, 0}

    E. **PlaceholderText:** [Please enter your feedback here]

    F. **TextTruncate:** AtEnd

    G. **TextWrapped:** true

    H. **TextYAlignment:** Top

5.   Inside the **GivingFeedback** frame, insert a **TextButton** with the following properties:

    A. **AnchorPoint:** {0.5, 1}

    B. **Name:** SubmitFeedback

    C. **Position:** {0.5, 0},{1, -5}

    D. **Size:** {0.5, 0},{0.2, -5}

    E. **Font:** Pick a font you like.

    F. **Text:** Submit Feedback

    G. **TextScaled:** true

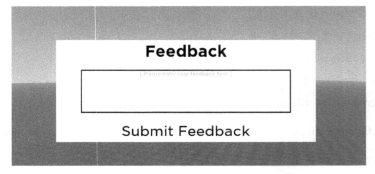

Figure 6.6 – An example GivingFeedback GUI

Congratulations! We have now made our first GUI Frame from scratch. An example solution is shown in *Figure 6.6*. However, feel free to change what your Frame looks like as you wish. However, ensure that the naming of GUI elements and the structure to which GUI elements are parented does not change.

As mentioned, we now have our feedback Frame. Well done! If users want to submit their feedback, it might be nice to see a Frame that says their feedback has been registered. Let us make this Frame as well.

First, change the **Visible** property on the **GivingFeedback** frame to `false`. This way, we can easily make our second Frame without having overlapping Frame. Once you have done this, follow these steps to make our second Frame:

1. Inside the previously made **ScreenGui**, create a new **Frame** and name it `FeedbackReceived`. Set the following properties for this Frame:

    A. **AnchorPoint**: $\{0.5, 0.5\}$

    B. **Position**: $\{0.5, 0\},\{0.5, 0\}$

    C. **Size**: $\{0.2, 50\},\{0.2, 25\}$

    D. **BackgroundColor3**: Pick a color you like.

2. Copy the **TextLabel** we made in the **GivingFeedback** Frame, and insert it into the **FeedbackReceived** Frame. You do not have to change its properties.

3. Create a new **TextLabel** inside the **FeedbackReceived** Frame with the following properties:

    A. **AnchorPoint**: $\{0.5, 0.5\}$

    B. **Position**: $\{0.5, 0\},\{0.5, 0\}$

    C. **Size**: $\{0.8, 0\},\{0.5, 0\}$

    D. **Font**: Pick a font you like.

    E. **Text**: `Thank you for your feedback. Your input has been recorded.`

    F. **TextScaled**: `true`

4. Finally, we will create an additional **TextButton** inside the **FeedbackReceived** Frame. We will call this button **Back**. Give the **Back** button the following properties:

    A. **AnchorPoint**: $\{0.5, 1\}$

    B. **Position**: $\{0.5, 0\},\{1, -5\}$

    C. **Size**: $\{0.5, 0\},\{0.2, -5\}$

    D. **Font**: Pick a font you like.

    E. **Text**: `Back`

    F. **TextScaled**: `true`

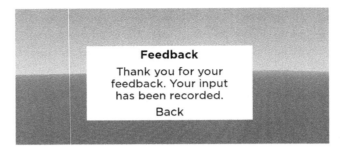

Figure 6.7 – FeedbackReceived GUI

Congratulations! We have now created our second Frame. An example solution is shown in *Figure 6.7*. Once again, feel free to change them to your liking, as long as you do not change the structure or naming. Obviously, these Frames do not do anything when we interact with them. If we want our Frames to change once feedback has been given, we will need to script this. Inside the **ScreenGui**, create a **LocalScript**. Now, let us look at the following code:

```
local screenGui = script.Parent

local givingFeedback = screenGui:WaitForChild("GivingFeedback")
local feedbackReceived =
screenGui:WaitForChild("FeedbackReceived")

function setup()
    givingFeedback.Visible = true
    feedbackReceived.Visible = false
end

function submitFeedback()
    -- Getting the user input
    local textbox = givingFeedback:WaitForChild("TextBox")
    local input = textbox.Text

    -- Checking if the user has provided feedback
    if string.len(input) >= 3 then
        -- Showing feedback recorded frame
        givingFeedback.Visible = false
        feedbackReceived.Visible = true
```

```
        -- Resetting feedback textbox
        textbox.Text = ""
    else
        warn("Cannot submit feedback less than 3
        characters!")
    end
end


function submitMoreFeedback()
    givingFeedback.Visible = true
    feedbackReceived.Visible = false
end


setup()
givingFeedback:WaitForChild("SubmitFeedback").
MouseButton1Click:Connect(submitFeedback)
feedbackReceived:WaitForChild("Back").
MouseButton1Click:Connect(submitMoreFeedback)
```

Let us take a look at the preceding local script. The `setup()` function simply changes the visibility of both Frames to ensure that only the **GivingFeedback** Frame is visible. Only having this Frame visible makes sense as we do not want to thank users for submitting their feedback without giving them the option to give feedback.

The `submitFeedback()` function gets executed once the `.MouseButton1Click` event fires on the **SubmitFeedback** button in our **GivingFeedback** Frame. Once the function starts, the user input is read by reading the `.Text` property. After that, we have an `if` statement that checks whether the `string.len(input)` function returns a value equal to or greater than 3. The `string.len()` function returns the number of characters in a string. Therefore, the user needs to provide feedback containing at least three characters. If the user does this, the **FeedbackReceived** Frame will become visible, and the text in the **TextBox** will be set to an empty string.

Finally, we also have the `submitMoreFeedback()` function. This function gets executed once we click the **Back** button in our **FeedbackReceived** Frame. Once the player presses this button, the **FeedbackReceived** Frame becomes invisible, and the **GivingFeedback** Frame becomes visible again.

Obviously, our current code does not actually record the player's feedback. The reason for this is that it is out of our current scope. If you were to actually implement this system, you could use a **Webhook** or use **Data Stores**. In *Chapter 8*, *Building Data Stores*, we will take a look at what Datastores are and what we can do with them.

Besides this, we also use the `warn()` function to notify the player that their feedback needs to be at least three characters. No player will ever look in the **Developer Console** to see this message. It is highly recommended you make something in your GUIs that allows you to give feedback depending on the actions players of our game take. It would be a great exercise to add this yourself.

We have now seen how **TextButtons** elements work. Besides this, we practiced making GUIs by using: **Frames**, **TextLabels**, **TextBoxes**, and **TextButtons** elements. We have also looked at switching between two Frames by using a **LocalScript**. In the next section, we will look at two more GUI elements: **ImageLabel** and **ImageButton** elements.

ImageLabel and ImageButton

So far, we have looked at many text-related GUI elements, but what is better than seeing images? Most players only look at images and try to avoid as much text as possible. Because of this, it is essential to use clear images to instruct the players of your game. Doing this dramatically increases the user's experience.

Let us start with the **ImageLabel** element. ImageLabel elements have a unique property called **Image**. In the **Image** property, we can insert a **Roblox asset identifier** (**asset ID**). In *Chapter 5, Optimizing Your Game*, we have seen these Roblox asset IDs when using animations. For images, we will use a Roblox asset ID as well. We can upload images on the following page: `https://www.roblox.com/develop?View=13`.

Once uploaded, we can take the ID from the **Uniform Resource Locator** (**URL**), similar to how we got the ID for animations. We can place our ID in the **Image** property on both an **ImageLabel** and an **ImageButton**. But what is the difference between them? We use an ImageLabels to display images to make our GUIs look better. While ImageButton elementss can do the same, the difference is that ImageButton elementss have events such as the `.MouseButton1Click` event, similar to TextButton elementss.

For comparison, an **ImageLabel** is the same as a **TextLabel**. Both display something, either text or an image, but players cannot interact with them. They are static. **ImageButtons**, on the other hand, are more like **TextButtons**. Both are buttons. However, an ImageButton displays an image, whereas a TextButton displays text.

Many beginner developers tend to make an empty TextButton and place a full-sized ImageLabel inside it. However, you are much better off using an ImageButton, optionally adding a TextLabel inside of it if you want to add additional text.

> **Tip**
> Try not to have text in your images. If you want to display text on top of an image, use a **TextLabel** or a **TextButton**. If you keep text in your images, scaling might get weird. Besides this, your game will be challenging to translate into other languages.

Throughout the past few sections, we learned a lot about **ScreenGuis**. First, we learned that ScreenGuis go inside of the **StarterGui**. Inside ScreenGuis, you can have various GUI elements such as a **Frames**, **TextLabels**, **ImageLabels**, **TextButton,s**, **TextBoxes**, and a **ImageButtons**. While learning about these GUI elements, we learned about their properties and unique data types. For example, the **Size** and **Position** properties use a data type called **UDim2**, which consists of **X** and **Y**, both with their **Scale** and **Offset** sub-properties. Because some GUI elements might overlap, there is another property called **ZIndex**. The **ZIndex** property allows you to specify the priority in which GUI elements are displayed.

As mentioned near the beginning of the chapter, there are more types of GUIs. So far, we have seen the **ScreenGui**. In the next section, we will take a look at **SurfaceGuis**. We will learn what they are and what they are used for.

Using SurfaceGuis

Sometimes, we do not want to display something by using a **ScreenGui**. Instead, we might want to have some text on a sign to point players in a certain direction. We could use a **decal** for this. Decals are similar to an ImageLabels that we use in GUIs. However, the difference is that decals are displayed on BaseParts, whereas ImageLabel elements are used in GUIs. If we were to use decals for a sign, this text will be difficult to translate. Besides this, it will be much more difficult to update the sign if we have to change what it says. In this scenario, it is not ideal to use a decal. Never use decals containing text. Having decals that contain text makes it more challenging to translate your game.

The alternative is to use a **SurfaceGui**. A SurfaceGui is basically a model for GUI elements similar to ScreenGuis. However, the difference is that SurfaceGuis go on **BaseParts**, not in the StarterGui. So, let us make a simple **Part** and insert a SurfaceGui into it. In the following screenshot, you can see that we have added a SurfaceGui inside of a Part. Similar to ScreenGuis, there is nothing once we add this:

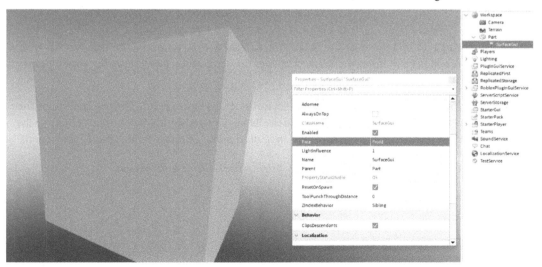

Figure 6.8 – SurfaceGui on a Part

This is because SurfaceGuis rely on GUI elements to display something; there is nothing by default.

An interesting property we can see in *Figure 6.8* is the **Face** property. Because SurfaceGuis are displayed on **BaseParts**, there are multiple "faces" of these BaseParts that the SurfaceGui can be seen on. So, the **Face** property lets you change which of the six sides your SurfaceGui is displayed on.

As mentioned, SurfaceGuis also need GUI elements. All the previously learned GUI elements can be used on SurfaceGuis as well. One of the things many games use SurfaceGuis for is leaderboards. In the following sections, we will make our own leaderboard SurfaceGui.

Making a leaderboard SurfaceGui

In this section, we will make our own leaderboard that will display the players with the most coins in our game. If we take a look at the following screenshot, we will see what the result of this SurfaceGui could be:

Figure 6.9 – Building our own leaderboard

First, we will need a Part that serves as the board. You can change the properties on this Part however you like. Then, we will need to insert the SurfaceGui into this Part. Make sure you set the **Face** property of the SurfaceGui correctly.

Looking at *Figure 6.9*, we can identify two key sections of this SurfaceGui. The top section of the SurfaceGui displays the title of the leaderboard and the name of each column. Below this section, we list all players with their position. For both sections, we should make a **Frame**. Follow these instructions:

1. Create a new Frame inside of the SurfaceGui with the following properties:

    A. **Name**: TopSection

    B. **Size**: {1, 0},{0.2, 0}

    C. **Position**: {0, 0},{0, 0}

2. Create a second Frame inside of the SurfaceGui with the following properties:

    A. **Name**: `PlayersSection`

    B. **Size**: `{1, 0},{0.8, 0}`

    C. **Position**: `{0, 0},{0.2, 0}`

Once we do this, we could have something like this:

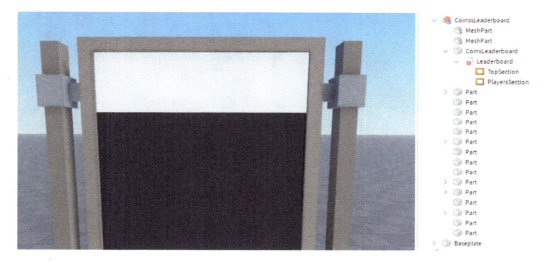

Figure 6.10 – Created Frames

Now, let us make the inside of the **TopSection** Frame, as follows:

1. First, create a **TextLabel** that displays the title of the leaderboard on the top line.

2. Once you have done this, create three more **TextLabel** elements to specify what each column means.

    For the **Rank** and **Coins** columns, reserve **30%** of each width. For the **Name** column, reserve a width of **40%**. Doing this is an excellent exercise for working with GUI elements. Once done, your **TopSection** Frame should look something like this:

Figure 6.11 – Created TopSection Frame

Now that we have finished our **TopSection** Frame, we should work on the **PlayersSection** Frame. This Frame will contain rows with player data. Let us start by making a row for this leaderboard. Once we finish this row, we can copy it a few times. Complete these steps to create your first row:

1. Create a Frame called `Template` with the following properties:

    A. **Position**: {0, 0},{0, 0}

    B. **Size**: {1, 0},{0, 150}

2. Inside the `Template` Frame, create 3 **TextLabel** elements similar to the column names. This time, change the text to an example value instead of the column's name. Make sure the **Size** value of the Frame is {1, 0},{0, 150}.

    Now, we should have something like this:

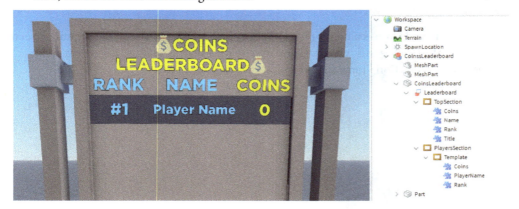

Figure 6.12 – Created leaderboard

We now have our very first SurfaceGui leaderboard. Well done! Obviously, this leaderboard does not actually show the wealthiest players in our game; for now, we are focusing on the UI aspect of the leaderboard. In *Chapter 8*, *Building Datastores*, we will look at **OrderedDataStores** that will allow us to make actual leaderboards.

In this section, we learned how to make our very first **SurfaceGui**, and we practiced making GUI elements. In the next section, we will look at something called an **UIListLayout**.

Using a UIListLayout

In the previous section, we started making our leaderboard. We made one **Template** Frame that will display player data. We do not just want to display one row with player data. We might want a top 10 or a top 20. Every time we copy our **Template** Frame, we have to reposition it. This is too much work. Luckily, there is a solution for this. **UIListLayouts** allow us to position GUI elements in a list form automatically.

If we add an UIListLayout into the **PlayerSection** Frame and copy the **Template** Frame a few times, we will see how the **Template** Frames get positioned automatically, as illustrated in the following screenshot. There is even an option to add spacing between **Template** elements. We can do this by changing the **Padding** property on the UIListLayout:

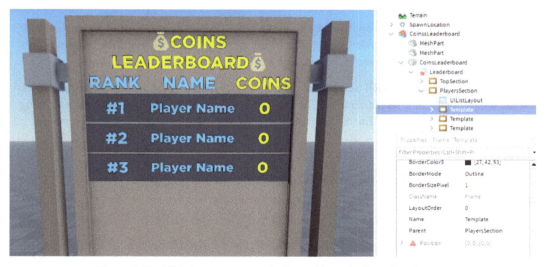

Figure 6.13 – UIListLayout automatically positions the Template Frames

In *Figure 6.13*, we have used padding of 10 pixels. This means there will be a 10-pixel difference between all the GUI elements in this list.

We now know how to use **UIListLayouts**. In the next section, we will look at the **LayoutOrder** and **SortOrder** properties.

LayoutOrder and SortOrder

We have previously seen that the **UIListLayout** manages to position GUI elements for us, resulting in a list. But what is this the order in which GUI elements are displayed based on? On the UIListLayout, there is a property called **SortOrder** option. There are two options for this property: **LayoutOrder** and **Name**. As the name implies, the **Name SortOrder** sorts all GUI elements based on their names. This is alphabetical sorting, meaning a GUI element that starts with the A character is displayed above a GUI element with the starting character, B.

The other **SortOrder** option is based on the **LayoutOrder** property. All GUI elements have a property called **LayoutOrder**. The lower the number, the higher it ends up in the list. Using this **SortOrder** means a GUI element with **LayoutOrder** 1 is displayed above a GUI element with **LayoutOrder** 2. As mentioned, the **LayoutOrder SortOrder** is the default. For our leaderboard example, it is wise to assign the same **LayoutOrder** as the rank. With this, we mean that the **Template** Frame for player #4 has a **LayoutOrder** of 4.

We now know how the sorting is done when using an **UIListLayout**. We learned there are two types of options for the **SortOrders** property: **Name** and **LayoutOrder**. In the next section, we will look at a new GUI element: **ScrollingFrames**.

ScrollingFrame GUI element

Our **SurfaceGui**'s size depends on how big we make our Part. We might want our game's top 20 wealthiest players on the leaderboard. Currently, we use a Frame. Once we reach the bottom of this Frame, the size limit is reached even if we have not yet displayed 20 rows. This is an issue.

Previously, we have seen a lot of GUI elements. However, we skipped one. There are also **ScrollingFrames**. These are almost identical to regular Frames. The only difference is that ScrollingFrames have a scrolling bar when your data does not fit. This is the perfect solution for our previously described problem.

> **Note**
> **ScrollingFrames** can be used in **ScreenGuis** and **BillboardGuis** as well.

Change the Frame into a ScrollingFrame. We will keep the same properties as the Frame.

If we copy our **Template** Frame a few times, we will see that it still goes "hidden" as it does not fit on the Part. However, if we scroll down, we will see that those "hidden" Frames suddenly come up. This is what ScrollingFrames do. If you cannot scroll down without moving your camera in Roblox Studio, try playing the game—this will make controlling the ScrollingFrame much easier.

We now know what **ScrollingFrames** are and what they can be used for. In the next section, we will look at the **CanvasSize** property on ScrollingFrames.

CanvasSize property

In the previous section, we have seen that **ScrollingFrames** allow us to scroll down. At some point, you cannot scroll further down. The total size you can scroll down is based on a property called **CanvasSize**. The **CanvasSize** property has the **UDim2** data type. By default, **CanvasSize** is set to a size of {0, 0}, {2, 0}. This means that the absolute size, which includes all invisible areas of the ScrollingFrame, is twice as much as the displayed size.

> **Tip**
> This might be very difficult to understand by simply reading. It is highly recommended you play around with the **CanvasSize** property by changing the size and see what happens.

Previously, we have seen a solution for manually positioning all of our **Template** Frames. However, if we add many **Template** Frames inside our ScrollingFrame we still have to adjust the **CanvasSize** property to ensure every Frame fits on our ScrollingFrame. There is a solution for this as well. On the ScrollingFrame, there is a property called **AutomaticCanvasSize**. This property has three options: **X**, **Y**, and **XY**. These options determine in which direction the **CanvasSize** property is allowed to be sized automatically.

Currently, we have a list that starts at the top and goes down. Therefore, the option we should pick right now is **Y**. Keep in mind that your set **CanvasSize** property now turns into a **Minimum CanvasSize** property. Even though the **CanvasSize** property is now automatically adjusted, it never gets smaller than the size that the **CanvasSize** property specifies.

In this section, we learned how **SurfaceGuis** work and what they are used for. Besides this, we practiced making GUIs ourselves. In addition, we learned about a new GUI element called **ScrollingFrames** and its properties, such as **CanvasSize** and **AutomaticCanvasSize**. We also learned how to generate a list that automatically positions GUI elements for us by using a **UIListLayout**. In the next section, we will look at another GUI type: **BillboardGuis**.

Using BillboardGuis

So far, we have seen **ScreenGuis** that are constantly visible on your screen and **SurfaceGuis** that are displayed on a face of a BasePart. While both of these already cover a lot of use cases, there is another type of GUI: these are **BillboardGuis**. BillboardGuis go inside of BaseParts, similar to SurfaceGuis. However, instead of being displayed on a face of the BasePart, BillboardGuis behave more like ScreenGuis, while staying on the position of the BasePart.

So, what are BillboardGuis used for? Generally, BillboardGuis display controls, hints, or information about objects you see in-game. For instance, in the following screenshot, we can see a BillboardGui being used to display the price of an instrument in a shop. Please keep in mind that this screenshot contains two pictures of the same BillboardGui with two different angles to display how they work:

Figure 6.14 – BillboardGui displaying the price of an accordion

There are a few interesting properties on the BillboardGui that we should look into. One of these properties is the **AlwaysOnTop** property. If this property is enabled, the UI will be visible even if there is something between your camera and the BillboardGui. We can see the effect of this property in the following screenshot:

Figure 6.15 – Effects of the AlwaysOnTop property

This property is great when you are close to an object. However, if you are on the other side of the map, it might be annoying to see the price of a product. This is where the **MaxDistance** property comes into play. This property allows us to set a maximum distance within which the BillboardGui is visible. If a player is too far from the BillboardGui, it simply becomes invisible to them.

We now know what **BillboardGuis** are and what they are used for. Besides this, we learned what the **AlwaysOnTop** and **MaxDistance** properties do. We will make a BillboardGui ourselves that displays the price in the following sections.

Making a product-price BillboardGui

First, we need a Part that we can insert our BillboardGui into. Once we have done this, we can insert the BillboardGui. Once we insert our BillboardGui, we have to size it. It would be best if you used **Scale** for BillboardGuis. When you use **Scale**, the BillboardGui will keep the same aspect ratio and get smaller as you move away from it. If you were to use **Offset** instead, the opposite happens: the BillboardGui would keep getting bigger and bigger the further you move away from it. An example **Size** value for the BillboardGui could be `{7, 0},{2.5, 0}`.

Once we have sized it, we can insert a Frame. The size of this Frame should be {1, 0},{1, 0}. This Frame will serve as the background of our GUI. Feel free to color it however you like. Once we have done this, we can insert two **TextLabels** elements, one that displays the product's name, and one that informs the player of the price. Feel free to choose any product name and price. Pick a nice **Font** type and **TextColor** property to match your GUI. Make sure the **TextColor** property is not close to **BackgroundColor3** of the Frame, as it will be hard to read.

We practically already have the same BillboardGui as in *Figure 6.14*. The only difference is that the BillboardGui in *Figure 6.14* is rounded and has an outline. In the following sections, we will look at **UICorner** and **UIStroke** instances.

Using a UICorner

If we add a **UICorner** inside a GUI element, the parent of the UICorner gets rounded. This is exactly what we did to round the Frame of our BillboardGui in *Figure 6.14*. The **CornerRadius** property allows us to change the rounding of the GUI element. Once again, a difference is made between **Scale** and **Offset**. However, it does not matter which you use here. However, try to avoid combining **Scale** and **Offset** for UICorners.

> **Performance**
>
> UICorners use more computer power than an image that has rounded corners by default. It is recommended not to overuse UICorners for everything. You could look at the 9-Slices editor if you are very concerned about performance. However, this will not be covered throughout the book.

We now know how to make our GUI elements look rounded by using a **UICorner**. Please keep in mind that UICorners work in a **ScreenGui** and **SurfaceGui** as well. In the next section, we will take a look at **UIStroke**.

Using a UIStroke

We can also add strokes around our GUI elements. Perhaps you are wondering why we aren't using the **BorderSizePixel** property. Sometimes we can, and sometimes we cannot. For example, if we use a **UICorner**, we can no longer use the **BorderSizePixel** property. On the other hand, when we use a square Frame without the UICorner, we would be perfectly able to use the **BorderSizePixel** property.

But a **UIStrokes** can do more than just give a border around a Frame. If we create a UIStroke, we see a property called **ApplyStrokeMode**. The value of this property can either be **Contextual** or **Border**. This is where the real advantage of UIStrokes comes into play. We can use UIStrokes in a **TextLabel**, **TextButton**, and **TextBoxe** as well.

We can use UIStrokes to give an outline to text by using the **Contextual ApplyStrokeMode**. Please keep in mind that UIStrokes do not work with **RichText** at the time of writing this book. A UIStroke works on GUI elements in **BillboardGuis**. However, they work in a **ScreenGuis** and **SurfaceGuis** as well.

So far, we have learned a lot about GUIs already. We learned what a **ScreenGui, SurfaceGui,** and **BillboardGui** is. Besides this, we learned about many GUI eElements that we can use inside these GUIs, such as a **Frame, ScrollingFrame, TextLabel, ImageLabel, TextButton, ImageButton,** and **TextBox**.

Besides this, we learned about many properties of these GUI elements, such as **Size, Position, ZIndex, LayoutOrder, CanvasSize,** and many more. We also learned about useful UI constraints that allow us to give our GUI more structure or a better design. A few of these UI constraints are **UITextSizeConstraint, UIListLayout, UICorner,** and **UIStroke**. Long story short, we now know how to make proper GUIs ourselves. In the next section, we will look at a small optimization we can do in our GUIs for better performance of our game.

Optimizing UIs

There is a small optimization we can implement when making GUIs. While this optimization only increases the speed of our GUIs by a few milliseconds, it is actually important, especially for lower-end devices and mobile devices. So, how can we optimize GUIs? To answer this question, we first need to know how GUIs work.

Previously, GUIs were computed every Frame. By default, Roblox is capped to 60 **frames per second (FPS)**. In an ideal situation, this means that GUIs were recomputed 60 times per second, even when there are no changes compared to the previous Frame. For instance, if we were to use a **UICorner** inside of our GUI, all the math assigned with the UICorner would be recomputed, even when there is no change. As you can see, this is not ideal and wastes a lot of computer power.

Luckily, Roblox came up with a solution. Instead of recomputing GUIs every Frame, they are now only recomputed if the GUI or something inside the GUI changes. So, for instance, if no property is changed and no new instances are inserted or removed, the GUI does not get recomputed. However, if we were to change the visibility of—for example—a Frame, the GUI would get recomputed.

This, on its own, is a major performance upgrade for everyone's game, and the great part is that we did not have to change anything for it. So, what is the small optimization we can implement? We know that GUIs do not get recomputed unless there is a change. Well, we can use this knowledge to improve the performance of our game even more. So, how do we do this? We can simply create separate GUIs for certain Frames instead of having our entire UI inside one single ScreenGui.

For example, we may have a Frame called **PurchaseCurrency** that allows users to purchase our in-game currency in exchange for Robux, and another Frame called **SettingsFrame** that allows our users to change their in-game settings. Both Frames are completely different from each other. It is very unlikely that the **PurchaseCurrency** Frame updates when someone changes a setting.

Imagine if they were inside the same ScreenGui—in this scenario, the PurchaseCurrency Frame would be recomputed if we changed a setting. This is very inefficient. Instead, we should separate both Frames into different ScreenGuis. Then, the **PurchaseCurrency** Frame does not get recomputed when we change a setting in the **SettingsFrame** Frame. We should keep this small performance optimization in mind when creating **a ScreenGui, SurfaceGui,** or **BillboardGui**.

We just learned how GUIs work internally. By understanding the internal working, we figured out how to optimize our own GUIs. In the next section, we will learn how to test our own GUIs to see whether they scale correctly on different devices using the **emulator**.

Testing GUIs

Nothing is more annoying and unprofessional than GUIs that do not scale properly. We have already learned how to scale GUIs properly using the **Scale** property in the **UDim2** data type throughout this chapter. Doing this already makes our GUIs scale properly across different-sized screens.

But there are many devices that you can play Roblox on. Roblox even supports consoles that might be connected to enormous TVs but also supports phones and tablets. While they keep getting bigger, there are still a lot of very small phones out there, and our job is to make our GUIs look fantastic on all of these devices.

Obviously, we cannot purchase every device to see whether our GUIs look good on them, yet we still want to see what they would look like on these devices. Luckily, there is a solution for this. Roblox Studio has a built-in **emulator** that allows us to pretend to be another device. This way, we can see what GUIs look like, and much more, which we will come back to in a later chapter.

In the top-right corner of the window that displays the game's map, there is a button displaying two different devices. Clicking this allows you to change into a different device. This way, you can see what the GUIs look like as well. In addition, you can start playing the game to get a proper view of how your game would work on this device, including device-specific controls. In the following screenshot, we can see the emulator in action:

Figure 6.16 – Playing a game inside of the emulator

> **Tip**
>
> If you are designing a GUI for a phone, the buttons need to be big to be comfortable. Therefore, it is highly recommended you play your game on your own phone before releasing your game. Generally, if the buttons look big enough on the emulator, it is still too small. A way to automatically get your GUIs bigger on phones is to use a combination of **Scale** and **Offset**. Use **Scale** to properly scale your GUI while adding a bit extra using the **Offset** property. This will increase the size of your GUIs for smaller screens such as those on phones.

When making GUIs for your phone, a good practice is to play random games on it. Once you find a game with a comfortable layout, take a screenshot of it. Then, use an image-editing program on your PC and compare your UI to your screenshot. Take a look at sizing and position differences that you might be able to improve on.

We now know how the **emulator** works. This will allow us to test our GUIs better. In the next section, we will look at minor improvements to help us take our GUIs to the next level.

Small UI improvements

So far, we have learned a lot about GUIs and how to scale and test them properly. However, there are a few small things we can improve in our GUIs to increase the quality of our UI tremendously. In the following subsections, we will dive deeper into all these small improvements we can make. We will start by looking at improving our GUIs for color-blind players. After that, we will look at the controls and navigation on GUIs, and we will also talk about images. In addition, we will use Tweens on GUIs and a few other small improvements.

Working with color-blindness

When picking colors for GUIs, people tend to forget that there are color-blind people. How amazing would it be to make our UI easy to use for color-blind players? If you have some previous experience with making GUIs, you most likely used the color combination of red and green. While this is a super-basic color combination for most of us, this is a very troubling color combination for people that are color-blind. Instead of using red and green, try using red and blue or blue and yellow.

But there is more you can do to improve your GUIs. Here is a list of tips when making your GUIs:

- As previously mentioned, research your color combinations.
- Do not solely rely on colors. How many games have you played where you can pick between the red or blue team? Most likely, a lot. While this is not a troubling color combination, it would be better to have an icon inside these teams. For instance, the red team could be a pirate or robbers team. Having a simple icon that matches the theme of your game can do wonders.

- Similar to the previous one, try to add patterns or text. For example, if you have a grid of colored blocks and players have to walk to a specific color, this might be difficult. However, if random patterns were on these blocks as well, it would be much easier to differentiate. For instance, if blue has stripes, red has dots, and yellow has a cross, it is easier to see for everyone.

Keeping these tips in mind will help color-blind people enjoy your game, but the best part is that this does not only benefit those who are color-blind. These tips make our GUIs and games better for everyone. In the next section, we will learn how to make the controls displayed in our game more dynamic, depending on the device.

Displaying controls

Some GUIs display controls for certain actions that players can perform. We do not want to display controls for a device that the player is not on. As a matter of fact, we are not allowed to display incorrect controls to players that are playing on consoles. If we do this anyway, our game might get taken down. However, the problem is that there is no real way to detect which device a player is on. So, which controls do we display?

Instead of trying to display controls for the device the player is on, we should make our GUIs dynamic for any device controls. We have to make them able to change depending on what input is being used. So, how do we see this? There is a service called **UserInputService** that has many functions related to user input. In *Chapter 7*, *Listening to User Input*, we will learn more about this service. For now, we will use one event: .LastInputTypeChanged. This event gives us an **UserInputType** enum. Let us take a look at the following client-sided example code:

```lua
local UserInputService = game:GetService("UserInputService")

local ui = script.Parent
local controlsText = ui:WaitForChild("ControlsText")

local previousInputType = nil

function updateControls(lastInputType)
    -- Checking if anything has changed
    -- Small optimization in case this function gets bigger
    -- overtime.
    if previousInputType == lastInputType then
        return
    end
```

```
    -- Changing controls
    if lastInputType == Enum.UserInputType.Gamepad1 then
        -- Player is using a gamepad.
        -- Console or someone using a gamepad?
        previousInputType = lastInputType
        controlsText.Text = "Press [X] to confirm"

    elseif lastInputType == Enum.UserInputType.Touch then
        -- Player is using a touchscreen, phone/tablet?
        previousInputType = lastInputType
        controlsText.Text = "Click here to confirm"

    elseif lastInputType == Enum.UserInputType.Keyboard
    then
        -- Player is using keyboard.
        previousInputType = lastInputType
        controlsText.Text = "Press Enter to confirm"


    end
end

UserInputService.LastInputTypeChanged:Connect(updateControls)
```

As we can see in the preceding code snippet, we change a fictive `controlsText` **TextButton** whose text depends on the last input type. This is how we make the displayed controls as dynamic as possible. This way, even if someone is playing on their desktop with a controller connected, they switch between which controls they want to use. As a matter of fact, they could even switch while playing the game without any issues.

Making sure the controls in your game are dynamic takes your GUIs to the next level. It is highly recommended you spend some extra time perfecting your GUIs by implementing this. In the next section, we will talk about improving navigation in your GUIs.

Improving GUI navigation

This may sound really obvious, but make sure your GUIs are easy to navigate. Many developers tend to forget that new players have never used these GUIs and have no clue what each button does. Of course, the GUIs are straightforward for you, but a new person might not know what a music button does. In the following screenshot, we can see an excellent solution for this issue. When players hover over a music icon, they will instantly know what this button will do:

Figure 6.17 – Text displaying the purpose of a button once hovered over

This greatly improves the navigation of your GUIs. However, there is another common problem with GUIs. Generally, there are two ways to close Frames in games. You either press a button to open and close it or there is an opening button and closing button. Some games might add both for ease of use. However, you must not switch this behavior throughout your game. For instance, do not make the **Change Music** Frame open and close with the same button, while the **Shop** Frame has to be opened with button **A** and closed with button **B**.

> **Tip**
> For console users, make sure your Frames close when the **Back** button on the controller is pressed. This functionality is adapted in most games. It would be annoying for players if your game did not have this commonly used feature. In *Chapter 7, Listening to User Input*, we will learn how to do this.

We now know how to improve the navigation of our GUIs. In the next section, we will look at the use of images in GUIs.

Using images

When designing your GUIs, make sure you use enough images. Players do not want to take a look at a bunch of text explaining they need to press a particular key to open a door. Instead, it is highly recommended you show an image that shows the before-and-after scenario while displaying the controls.

> **Tip**
> Do not insert controls in images. Instead, add a **TextLabel** on top of the **ImageLabel** that displays the controls. This way, you can use the same image for multiple devices.

Besides players actually looking at images, your GUI will also look much better. You can make these images yourself or hire artists to make them for you. The second option is recommended but might not work, depending on your game's budget.

In the next section, we will take a look at **Tweens** on GUIs.

Using Tweens

In *Chapter 5*, *Optimizing Your Game*, we learned about **Tweens**. We used these Tweens to animate a gate. In addition, we practiced making a Part fall in an exercise. But what does this have to do with GUIs? Well, we can use Tweens on GUI elements too. For example, if we want to make a certain Frame show up, we might want it to become bigger or change its position.

We can use Tweens the same way we learned in *Chapter 5*, *Optimizing Your Game*. For example, in the following client-side code snippet, we have a function that tweens the **Position** property of a Frame using the TweenService. Let us analyze this, as follows:

```
local TweenService = game:GetService("TweenService")

local ui = script.Parent
local frame = ui:WaitForChild("SomeFrame")

function openMenu()
    -- Setting frame out of the screen
    frame.Position = UDim2.new(0.5, 0, 1.5, 0)

    -- Making frame visible
    frame.Visible = true

    -- Setting up TweenInfo
    local tweenInfo = TweenInfo.new(
        -- Duration of Tween
        1,
        -- Tween style (EasingStyle)
        Enum.EasingStyle.Quad,
        -- EasingStyle direction
        Enum.EasingDirection.Out,
        -- Amount of times the tween repeats
        0,
        -- Tween Reverse
        false,
        -- Delay before the Tween starts
        0
    )
```

```
    local tween = TweenService:Create(frame, tweenInfo,
    {Position = UDim2.new(0.5, 0, 0.5, 0)})
    tween:Play()
end


openMenu()
```

In the preceding code snippet, we use a function called openMenu(). First, we set the **Position** property of the Frame to **UDim2** with a y-axis scale greater than 1. This means that the Frame will not be visible from this position. After that, we set the visibility of the Frame to true. This still does not show the Frame as it still has the **Position** property outside of our screen, but most developers set the **Visible** property to false if they are not in use.

After that, we create a new variable that will store TweenInfo for the tween we will make. This has many arguments. As explained in *Chapter 5, Optimizing Your Game*, you do not have to use all of these. The ones displayed in the preceding code snippet are the defaults. Finally, we create our Tween using the :Create() function on the **TweenService**. Once we have this Tween, we use the :Play() function to start the Tween.

This is how we would create a Tween on GUI elements, using what we previously learned. However, Roblox has two functions on these GUI elements called :TweenPosition() and :TweenSize() that allow us to easily tween that GUI element.

In the following code snippet, we create the exact same Tween as before. However, this time, we will use the :TweenPosition() function instead of the **TweenService**. Let us take a look at this here:

```
local ui = script.Parent
local frame = ui:WaitForChild("SomeFrame")

function openMenu()
    -- Setting frame out of the screen
    frame.Position = UDim2.new(0.5, 0, 1.5, 0)

    -- Making frame visible
    frame.Visible = true

    -- Moving frame into the screen
    frame:TweenPosition(
        -- (Required)
        -- Target Position
```

```
        UDim2.new(0.5, 0, 0.5, 0),

        -- (Optional)
        -- EasingStyle Direction
        Enum.EasingDirection.Out,

        -- (Optional)
        -- Tween Style (EasingStyle)
        Enum.EasingStyle.Quad,

        -- (Optional)
        -- Duration of the Tween
        1,

        -- (Optional)
        -- Set to true if you want to
        -- override a Tween that might
        -- be active on the Frame right now.
        false,

        -- (Optional)
        -- Function that gets executed
        -- once the :TweenPosition finished.
        function()
            print("Tween has finished!")
        end
    )
end

openMenu()
```

In the preceding code snippet, we use the same openMenu() function. Once again, we start by setting the **Position** property of the Frame to a **UDim2** with a *y*-axis scale greater than 1. After that, we set the visibility of the Frame to true.

So far, this was the same as when using the **TweenService**, but here's where the difference starts. Instead of creating TweenInfo, we use the :TweenPosition() function with quite a few arguments. Some of these arguments are similar to those from TweenInfo, but the order is mixed.

First, we specify the target position. This is basically the position that the Frame will be in once the Tween is over. This argument is required. Then, we get optional arguments; we could leave these out. Feel free to try all the differences out. The last argument is noteworthy, though. Here, we can make a function. This function gets executed once the Tween ends. Some common use cases for this function are to disable a client-side debounce, as explained in *Chapter 5, Optimizing Your Game*.

We have now learned how to use Tweens on GUI elements. Please keep in mind that you can use "normal" Tweens, as explained in *Chapter 5, Optimizing Your Game*, instead as well. In the next section, we will look at the **core GUIs** from Roblox.

Core GUIs

Before we can get to the improvement of this section, we first need to understand what the **CoreGui** service even is. Roblox has a few GUIs that are in every game by default that combined are called the core GUIs. These core GUIs include **Chat**, **Backpack**, **Leaderboard**, and more. Sometimes, you do not want to use these because you want to make a custom version, or maybe they overlap with your own GUIs. Generally, we try to avoid overlapping GUIs/Frames as it looks very chaotic.

Thankfully, we can disable some of the core GUIs. While there is no **ScreenGui** in the **PlayerGui** of which we can change the visibility, there is a function we can call. On the **StarterGui** service, there is a function called :SetCoreGuiEnabled(). In the following client-side code snippet, we will disable the **Chat** core GUI:

```
local StarterGui = game:GetService("StarterGui")

StarterGui:SetCoreGuiEnabled(Enum.CoreGuiType.Chat, false)
--                           Enum.CoreGuiType.Health
--                           Enum.CoreGuiType.PlayerList
--                           Enum.CoreGuiType.Backpack
--                           Enum.CoreGuiType.EmotesMenu
--                           Enum.CoreGuiType.All
```

In the preceding code snippet, we disable the chat using the :SetCoreGuiEnabled() function. To specify that we want to disable the **Chat** GUI, we use an **enum**. The second argument of this function is a Boolean. Currently, we provide the false Boolean. This means we want to disable the **Chat** GUI. If we were to reactivate the **Chat** GUI, we would have to put true as the second argument.

We now know what the core GUIs are. Besides this, we learned how to enable and disable them in our game. Besides the core GUIs, we also learned how to improve our GUIs for color-blind players. After that, we learned how to show the proper controls based on the player's device. In addition, we learned how to improve the navigation of our GUIs. After that, we also learned how to play Tweens on GUI elements. In the next section, we will practice everything that we have learned throughout this chapter.

Exercise 6.1 – Creating a shop GUI

In this exercise, we will be creating a GUI that will allow users to purchase **Game Passes** in our game. Please remember that we will just be creating the GUI; we will not sell **Game Passes**. In *Chapter 9, Monetizing Your Game*, we will learn how to do this.

In the following screenshot, we see an example result for this exercise. Feel free to follow the steps or recreate this GUI on your own by looking at the example:

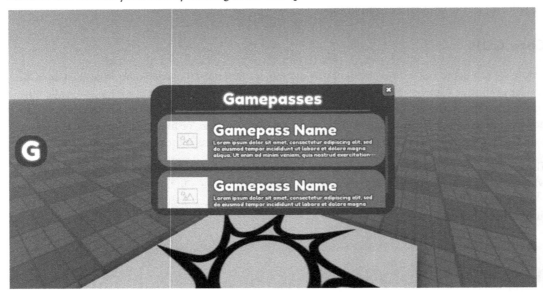

Figure 6.18 – Example result for this exercise

As mentioned, the GUI shown in *Figure 6.18* is an example solution. You can mix up things if you prefer another style. Throughout the exercise, no properties will be given. You have to decide for yourself what the value of certain properties will be. Sometimes, there will be a hint toward you picking a certain property; in this case, it is recommended you do this. As for **Sizes**, **Positions**, and **AnchorPoints** properties, you will have to pick something that works. Use the **emulator** to see whether the chosen properties work for all devices. You will have to experiment with this a lot. No one picks the correct properties all the time. Take your time to perfect this.

Exercise

First, we will start by making the GUI. Proceed as follows:

1. Create a **ScreenGui** named GamepassUI inside the **StarterGui**.

2. Inside GamepassUI, create a Frame named MainFrame. Make sure this Frame gets a nice color, correct sizing, and rounded corners.

3. Inside the **MainFrame** Frame, create two Frames. The first Frame should be named `Header` and will contain the title of this Frame. The second Frame should be a **ScrollingFrame** Frame named `Body`.

4. Inside the **Header** frame, create a **TextLabel** that will display the text `Gamepasses`. Give this text an outline with a **Thickness** value of 3.

5. Make sure the **Body ScrollingFrame** Frame automatically gets the correct **CanvasSize** value without you having to change the **CanvasSize** value manually. The minimum **CanvasSize** value should be `{0, 0}, {0, 0}`.

6. Make sure the **Body ScrollingFrame** Frame automatically makes a list of all its child GUI elements without you having to position each GUI element manually.

7. Inside the **MainFrame** Frame, create a **TextButton** named `Close` that displays **X**. The **Close** button must have rounded corners. Besides this, **X** must have an outline.

8. Inside the **Body ScrollingFrame** frame, create a **TextButton** that has the same width as the **Body ScrollingFrame** frame, but subtract the size of the **ScrollingBar**. Rename this **TextButton** `GamepassButton`.

   Tip for 8: **ScrollingFrames** have a property called **ScrollBarThickness**. This is the size in pixels of the **ScrollingBar**.

9. Inside the **GamePassButton**, create an **ImageLabel**. Feel free to add an actual image. Make sure the **ScaleType** property is set to **Fit**.

10. Inside the **GamepassButton**, create a **TextLabel** that displays the name of the gamepass. Choose a bold font for this. Make sure this **TextLabel** has an outline with a **Thickness** value of 2.

11. Inside the **GamePassButton**, create another **TextLabel** that displays the description of the gamepass. Make sure this **TextLabel** has an outline with a **Thickness** of 2. Besides this, the text has to be set to **Scaled**. However, the **TextSize** value may never be smaller than 15 nor greater than 25. If the text does not fit, three dots have to appear at the end of the **TextLabel**.

    Tip for 11: All the specified information can be done by inserting UI elements or changing properties. There are no scripts required for this.

We have now finished the **GamePassUI** ScreenGui. Next, we will create a button that will allow us to open and close the **MainFrame** Frame. Follow these next steps:

1. Create a **ScreenGui** named `SideButtons` inside the **StarterGui**.

2. Inside the **SideButtons**, create a **TextButton** named `OpenGamepasses`. The **TextButton** must have rounded corners.

3. Make sure the **OpenGamePasses TextButton** displays the **G** character. This character should have an outline with a **Thickness** value of 3.

We have now finished designing our GUI. Up until this point, you did not have to use any scripts. If you did, you probably forgot about a property. We will start scripting this GUI so that the Frame becomes visible and invisible when certain actions are performed. Read the following requirements and create **LocalScripts** that will meet the set requirements:

1. When the **OpenGamePasses** button inside the **SideButtons** ScreenGui gets pressed, the **MainFrame** Frame inside the **GamepassUI** changes visibility.

2. If the **MainFrame** Frame is already visible when the **OpenGamePasses** button is pressed, then the **MainFrame** Frame should become invisible.

3. The transition of becoming visible or invisible should be done using **Tweens**. The type of **Tween** you choose is up to you.

4. When the **Close** button inside the **MainFrame** Frame is pressed, the **MainFrame** Frame should close. Make sure using the **Close** button does not bug the **OpenGamePasses** button.

   Tip: Create a **LocalScript** or **Module** inside the **GamePassUI** that is responsible for opening and closing the **MainFrame** Frame. Then, use this **Module** or make **BindableEvents** to open and close this Frame. Here is a list of optional functions, **BindableEvents**, and **BindableFunctions**:

   • For **Modules**: `:OpenFrame()`, `:CloseFrame()`, `:IsOpen()`

   • For **BindableEvents**: `OpenFrame`, `CloseFrame`

   • For **BindableFunctions**: `IsOpen`

If you forgot how **Modules** or **BindableEvents/BindableFunctions** work, go back to *Chapter 3*, *Event-Based Programming*.

Test the game to see whether it works. Do not worry if you did not manage to complete parts of this exercise. This was a very large and complicated exercise. It is highly recommended that you try to do everything in the best possible way. Once you think you are done, take a look at the default example result and try to learn from it. Preferably, try to redo this exercise after that.

Two example answers can be found on the GitHub page for this book, at `https://github.com/PacktPublishing/Mastering-Roblox-Coding/tree/main/Exercises`. The second example answer contains more advanced code that might be harder to understand. This example is meant for those wanting to script better GUIs.

Summary

We started this chapter by learning more about GUIs. We learned there are three types of GUIs, and these are **ScreenGuis, SurfaceGuis**, and **BillboardGuis**. Each of them has a different purpose. We learned that these GUIs do not display anything themselves—they need GUI elements for that. We learned about the: **Frame, ScrollingFrame, TextLabel, ImageLabel, TextButton, ImageButton**, and **TextBoxe** GUI elements. We have seen how each of them works.

While learning about all of these GUI elements, we have used a lot of properties as well. The two most common properties were **Size** and **Position**. We learned that both properties use a unique data type called **UDim2**. We have seen that a UDim2 data type is built from two **UDim** data types. There is one **UDim** data type for the *x* axis and one for the *y* axis. Besides this, we have seen how a UDim data type is built up by **Scale** and **Offset** properties. **Scale** allows us to keep players' screen size, whereas **Offset** is measured in pixels. These pixels are the same for everyone. We have seen that GUIs could be outside of players' screens when the developer accidentally uses **Offset** instead of **Scale**.

Besides this, we learned how to add constraints to our GUIs without any scripting. A few examples of the constraints we have seen are **UITextSizeConstraint** and **UIListLayout**. Besides those two, we have also learned about useful properties such as **AutomaticCanvasSize**, which automatically handles the size of the **CanvasSize** property without manually changing it.

Not only did we learn how to build GUIs, but we also learned how to optimize them by creating multiple ScreenGuis for frames that are not connected. In addition, we learned how to test our GUIs by using the **emulator** built into Roblox Studio. We have seen how the emulator allows us to pretend to be another device to see what our GUIs would look like. While doing this, we learned that we could use scale and add a bit of offset to automatically make our GUIs bigger for smaller devices such as phones. This makes it easier for players to read text and press buttons.

Finally, we also looked at a few things to keep in mind while making our GUIs. These things take little effort to implement yet have a massive impact on the quality of our GUIs. For instance, we have looked at how to design color-blind-friendly GUIs, improve navigation, and add **Tweens** to GUIs.

While GUIs are not very complex, they take a lot of practice. You might not be a pro in making GUIs just yet. However, the more you practice you have with it, the easier it gets, and the better your GUIs will become. In the *Displaying controls* section, we had a short introduction to the **UserInputService** service. In the next chapter, we will learn how to listen to user input using this service.

Listening to User Input

In this chapter, you will learn many ways of listening to user input. We will start by looking at simple ways of listening to user input, such as by using **ClickDetectors**, **ProximityPrompts**, and **Tools**. Then, we will create simple systems to experiment with these ways of listening to user input. Once we understand these methods, we will move on to more complex ways of listening to user input. We call this **advanced user input**. We will learn how to listen to input from a keyboard and mouse. Besides this, we will learn to listen to input from various gamepads. Finally, we will learn how to use the **ContextActionService** to make these advanced user inputs easier.

The following topics will be covered in this chapter:

- Working with ClickDetectors, ProximityPrompts, and tools
- Implementing advanced user input
- Choosing how to listen to user input
- Exercise 7.1—Eating food

By the end of this chapter, you will know how to listen to user input using ClickDetectors, ProximityPrompts, and tools. Besides this, you will know how to listen to keyboard, gamepad, and mouse input by using the **UserInputService**. Finally, you will also have learned to listen to user input using the **ContextActionService**. Besides listening to user input, you will know how to use leaderboard, particle, tool, and SpotLight instances. In addition, you will know how to use the Lighting and HapticService services.

Technical requirements

To start programming with Luau, you need access to a device with internet access. This can either be a Windows or a Mac device.

You need to download the following software:

- Roblox Player
- Roblox Studio

It is highly recommended to have a Microsoft Xbox controller that you can connect to your PC.

All the code examples for this chapter can be found on GitHub at `https://github.com/PacktPublishing/Mastering-Roblox-Coding`.

The CiA video for this chapter can be found at `https://bit.ly/3z5ZsPI`.

Working with ClickDetectors, ProximityPrompts, and tools

In *Chapter 6, Creating User Interfaces for All Devices*, we have listened to user input from **Graphical User Interfaces (GUIs)**. An example of when we did this was when we listened to the `.MouseButton1Click` event. We used this event to see when a player clicked on either a **TextButton** or an **ImageButton**. While this is a very powerful event that you will use a lot throughout your development career, there are way more inputs that users can give. In the following sections, we will look at how to listen to user input by using **ClickDetectors**, **ProximityPrompts**, and **tools**. First, we will start with ClickDetectors.

Working with ClickDetectors

Sometimes, we want our players to interact with objects in our game. For instance, we could make a system where players have to press a button for a door to open or pick up a particular item. **ClickDetectors** allow us to do all of this. The only thing that is stopping you is your imagination.

So, how do ClickDetectors work? When you add a ClickDetector inside a **BasePart**, this BasePart becomes clickable. In the following screenshot, we can see that a special cursor icon appears when we hover over this **BasePart** that contains a **ClickDetector**:

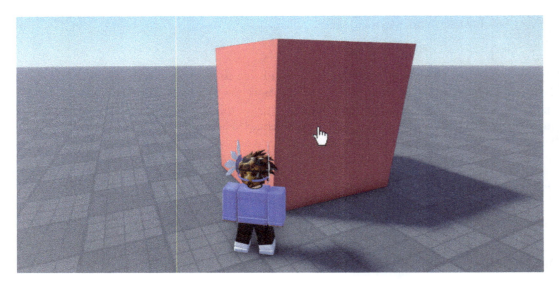

Figure 7.1 – Part containing a ClickDetector

In *Figure 7.1*, a unique cursor icon tells the player that this Part is clickable. While it is essential to inform our players that we can interact with this Part, this icon might not fit everyone's game genre. Luckily we can customize this cursor icon. On the ClickDetector, we can change the **CursorIcon** property. When we change this to a valid **Roblox asset identifier** (**asset ID**), this will become the cursor icon. Please keep in mind that this Roblox asset ID has to belong to an Image.

We now know the basics of **ClickDetectors**. However, we have not seen them in action just yet. In the next section, we will use ClickDetectors to increase a value in the player list **leaderstats**.

Increasing leaderstats

In the previous section, we said we would use a **ClickDetector** to increase a value in the **leaderstats**. Before implementing this system, we first need to understand what leaderstats are and how ClickDetectors work. In the next section, we will take a look at what leaderstats are. After that, we will make a simple script that works with a **ClickDetector**. This way, we understand how both systems work separately. Once we get both systems working, we have a **proof of concept** (**POC**) that proves what we want is possible to implement. Finally, we will combine both systems and make an increasing leaderstats value.

Understanding leaderstats

So, what are **leaderstats**? In *Chapter 6*, *Creating User Interfaces for All Devices*, we briefly mentioned that Roblox has a few **core GUIs**. These core GUIs include a **PlayerList** that displays the name of all the players that are connected to the same server as you. We can turn this PlayerList into a **leaderboard**.

So, how does this work? Let us take a look at the following code snippet:

```lua
local Players = game:GetService("Players")

function newPlayer(player)
    local leaderstats = Instance.new("Model")
    leaderstats.Name = "leaderstats"
    leaderstats.Parent = player

    local statistic = Instance.new("IntValue")
    statistic.Name = "SomeStatistic"
    statistic.Parent = leaderstats
    statistic.Value = 0
end

Players.PlayerAdded:Connect(newPlayer)
```

Let us analyze the preceding code snippet. Once a player joins our game, we create a model inside of their `Player` object. This model is called `leaderstats`. After that, we create an `IntValue` instance. We call our `IntValue` instance `SomeStatistic` and parent it to the previously made `leaderstats` model. `IntValue` is an instance that allows us to store whole numbers such as 1, 5, 10, and 25. An `IntValue` instance does not allow decimal numbers.

We have now made our very first leaderboard. So, when we play our game and take a look at the player list, it could look like this:

Figure 7.2 – Created leaderboard

We now know what **leaderboards** and **leaderstats** are. With this knowledge, we have solved the first problem in making our increasing leaderstats based on **ClickDetector** input. In the next section, we will figure out how ClickDetectors work.

Understanding ClickDetectors

Next, we will figure out how **ClickDetectors** work. Previously, we learned that ClickDetectors go inside of **BaseParts**. Therefore, let us start by creating a **Part** inside of the **Workspace**. We will call our Part **ClickablePart**. Once we have done this, we will insert a **ClickDetector** into this Part.

Great—we have now set up everything we need for a ClickDetector to work, but how do we check when someone presses it? Luckily, there is an event for this. This event is called a `.MouseClick` event. Let us take a look at the following code snippet:

```
local clickDetector = workspace.ClickablePart.ClickDetector

function clicked(player)
    print(player.Name)
end

clickDetector.MouseClick:Connect(clicked)
```

In the preceding code snippet, we listen to the `.MouseClick` event. Once this event gets fired, we execute the `clicked()` function. When the `.MouseClick` event gets fired, the first parameter is the `Player` object that used our **ClickDetector**. We use this parameter to print the player's name that has used the **ClickDetector**.

If we use this piece of code and run our game, our **Developer Console** could look like this:

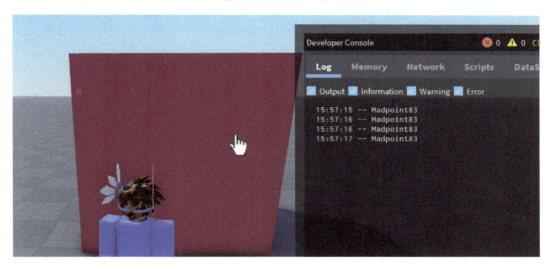

Figure 7.3 – Listening to the ClickDetector

In *Figure 7.3*, we can see that your username gets printed every time we use the **ClickDetector**. Try this for yourself if you have not already.

We now know how to listen to input on the **ClickDetector**. We can now combine this knowledge with the previously learned information about leaderstats. In the next section, we will combine both systems to create one system that increases a leaderstats value when the ClickDetector is used.

Increasing leaderstats using a ClickDetector

Let us go over the system we want to make once more. We need a **leaderboard** that displays the number of **clicks**. When someone clicks on a Part with a **ClickDetector**, the number of clicks has to be increased by one. We know that the leaderstats are saved in a model inside the `Player` object. Besides this, we have seen that the first parameter of our `clicked()` function will contain the player that interacted with the **ClickDetector**. We will use this parameter to find the leaderstats and increment it. Let us take a look at the following code snippet:

```
local Players = game:GetService("Players")

local clickDetector = workspace.ClickablePart.ClickDetector
```

```
function newPlayer(player)
    local leaderstats = Instance.new("Model")
    leaderstats.Name = "leaderstats"
    leaderstats.Parent = player

    local clicks = Instance.new("IntValue")
    clicks.Name = "Clicks"
    clicks.Parent = leaderstats
    clicks.Value = 0
end

function incrementClicks(player)
    local leaderstats =
    player:FindFirstChild("leaderstats")
    if leaderstats ~= nil then
        local clicks = leaderstats:FindFirstChild("Clicks")
        if clicks ~= nil then
            clicks.Value += 1
        end
    end
end


Players.PlayerAdded:Connect(newPlayer)
clickDetector.MouseClick:Connect(incrementClicks)
```

In the preceding code snippet, we have two functions. The newPlayer() function gets executed when a new player joins our game. This function creates leaderstats for us. The other function is the incrementClicks() function. This function gets executed once someone interacts with the ClickDetector. In this function, we find the leaderstats model and the Clicks IntValue instance. If those can be found, we increment the value of the Clicks IntValue instance by 1.

When we play our game and use the **ClickDetector**, we will see our **Clicks** stat increase every time we press it.

Throughout the previous sections, we learned how to work with **ClickDetectors** and **leaderstats**. But more importantly, we learned what to do if we need to make a system that includes elements that we are unfamiliar with. First, we split up our system into separate subsystems. Then, we made **Proof of Concepts** (**POCs**) for each subsystem to determine how and if they work. Finally, we used what we learned to create a working system. In the next section, we will stick with ClickDetectors for a bit longer and figure out when to listen to the `.MouseClick` event on the client and the server.

Activating particles

In the previous sections, we made a system that increases the Clicks leaderstat every time we used the ClickDetector. This time, instead of working with leaderstats, we will use particles.

What are particles? There are a ton of different types of particles on Roblox. We can use **Sparkle**, **Smoke**, **Explosion**, **Fire**, and **Beam** particles. These are just a few examples of relatively simple particles. There are also **ParticleEmitters** particles that have a lot more customization. ParticleEmitters allows you to create spectacular particles for your game. This book will not cover how to make these particles as this is not something programmers tend to do. Generally, there are **visual effects** (**VFX**) **designers** who design particles for your game.

In *Chapter 5*, *Optimizing Your Game*, we learned that it is important to figure out what you do on the client and the server. Since particles improve the looks of our game, this is something you would do on the client. Doing this allows us to remove stress from the server.

Let us say we want to toggle a **Fire** particle for a furnace in a kitchen. The **Fire** particle needs to be changed on the client. What we could do is create a script that listens to the `.MouseClick` event on the **ClickDetector**. Then, we could use a **RemoteEvent** that tells a specific client to toggle the **Fire** particle. While this works, it is a lot of work, especially since there is a much better alternative.

So far, we only listened to the `.MouseClick` event on the server, but why do we even want to do this? In the previous section, we had to change a leaderboard value; this had to be done on the server. However, particles need to be done on the client, so why don't we just make our entire system on the client?

Clients can listen to events as well. We are much better off creating our entire system on the client for this system. Let us take a look at the following client-side code snippet:

```
local furnace = workspace:WaitForChild("KitchenFurnace")

local clickDetector = furnace:WaitForChild("ClickDetector")
local fire = furnace:WaitForChild("Fire")

function clicked()
    fire.Enabled = not fire.Enabled
end

clickDetector.MouseClick:Connect(clicked)
```

In the preceding code snippet, we have a Part called KitchenFurnace inside of the **Workspace**. This KitchenFurnace part has a **ClickDetector** and a **Fire** particle inside of it.

At the bottom of this **LocalScript**, we listen to the .MouseClick event. When a player uses the **ClickDetector**, the Enabled property on the **Fire** particle gets changed. The Enabled property is a Boolean that determines if the **Fire** particle is enabled or not. To toggle this property, we use the not construction. First, we read the current value of this property, which could be true. Then, this true value gets changed to false because the not keyword switches Booleans. This construction allows us to toggle Boolean properties easily.

> **StreamingEnabled**
>
> When using StreamingEnabled, the preceding code snippet should be adjusted depending on your game. It is recommended to use some sort of .ChildAdded construction to ensure the ClickDetector can always be found.

When we run our game and click on the KitchenFurnace Part, we will see that the **Fire** particle turns on or off, depending on its current state. We can see what should happen in the following screenshot:

Figure 7.4 – Toggling a Fire particle for a furnace

> **Note**
>
> Because we chose to listen to the .MouseClick event on the client, the state of the **Fire** particle will not change on other clients. Suppose you want the **Fire** particle to change for everyone. You will have to listen to the .MouseClick event on the server and use a RemoteEvent that uses the :FireAllClients() function.

In this section, we had a short introduction to **particles**. First, we learned how to use the **Fire** particle. It is recommended you change the **Fire** particle to one of the other particles to see how they work. Besides this, we learned that sometimes it is better to listen to certain events on the client rather than the server. In the next section, we will learn how to listen to user input by using **ProximityPrompts**.

Working with ProximityPrompts

In the previous sections, we have looked at **ClickDetectors** to listen to user input. Throughout the following sections, we will take a look at **ProximityPrompts**. ProximityPrompts were released in December 2020 and are relatively new. Even though they have not been around for a long time, they were quickly adapted into many games as they allow us to listen to user input for various devices exceptionally easily.

So what are ProximityPrompts? ProximityPrompts look very similar to the **BillboardGuis** we saw in *Chapter 6, Creating User Interfaces for All Devices*. To use ProximityPrompts, we insert them into **BaseParts**. In the following screenshot, we can see what a ProximityPrompt looks like:

Figure 7.5 – ProximityPrompt

> **ProximityPrompt not visible**
>
> **ProximityPrompts** do not show while developing in Roblox Studio. If you cannot see them, try playing the game. When you play the game, it should show up.

In the previous screenshot, we can see a ProximityPrompt inside of a **Part**. On the left side of the ProximityPrompt, we can see the E character. This means we have to press the *E* key on our keyboard to interact with this ProximityPrompt. You are most likely wondering: What if someone does not have a keyboard? Roblox handles all of this for us. Phones and tablets have to press the ProximityPrompt to interact with them. For PCs and consoles, there are two properties. These are the **GamepadKeyCode** and **KeyboardKeyCode** properties. We can change these to a key of our choosing. In the following screenshot, we can see both properties:

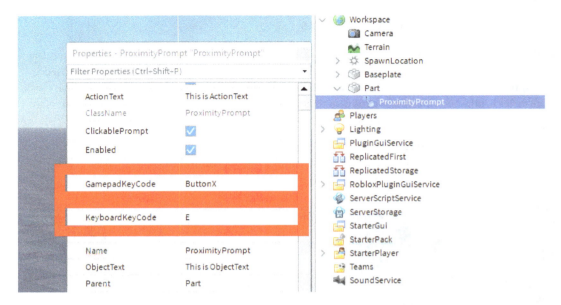

Figure 7.6 – Properties of a ProximityPrompt

Besides the previously mentioned properties, there are more noteworthy properties. These are the **ActionText** and **ObjectText** properties. The **ActionText** property is the primary text that is displayed. This property is used to inform players what this ProximityPrompt will do. For instance, if we want to use this ProximityPrompt to open a shop menu, we could change the **ActionText** value to **Open Shop**. If we need an additional explanation, we can use the **ObjectText** property.

While it may sound like there are no customization options for ProximityPrompts, this could not be further from the truth. We can change the looks of ProximityPrompts a lot. For example, in the following screenshot, we can see a customized ProximityPrompt that fits the game's design. We will not cover how to change the looks of ProximityPrompts throughout the book, but it is good to know that this is possible:

Figure 7.7 – Customized ProximityPrompt

We now know what **ProximityPrompts** are. We have seen how they work and how to change the keybindings for different devices. In addition, we learned about the **ActionText** and **ObjectText** properties. In the next section, we will make a system that picks up a tool using a ProximityPrompt.

Picking up a tool using ProximityPrompts

In the previous section, we learned what **ProximityPrompts** are. However, we still do not know how to listen to any input that users might give. Therefore, in the following sections, we will create a **tool** that players can get in their inventory using a ProximityPrompt.

We have never worked with tools before. Because of this, we will first look at what tools are and how they work. This will be a short introduction. Later in this chapter, we will have a more in-depth look at how we can listen to user input using tools. Once we know how tools work, we will create a simple flashlight tool that players can use. After we get this working, we will look at the code that allows users to get this flashlight using a ProximityPrompt.

Explaining tools

Tools can be anything that a player uses in-game. You can make any tool you can think of. For instance, if you were to make a farming game, you could make the following tools: forks, rakes, and shovels.

When you create a **tool**, you can insert it into the **StarterPack** service. Every player automatically gets this tool in their inventory when you do this. Inside each `Player` object, there is a folder called `Backpack`. In the `Backpack` folder, we store all the tools that are not currently used but are in the player's inventory. When a player equips this tool, the tool is parented to this player's character model. Therefore, if there is a tool inside of the character model, we can conclude this is the active tool.

When using a tool, we need to hold them in our avatar's hand at a specific position. The position we hold the tool is based on a BasePart called **Handle**, which should be inside each tool. There must be one BasePart directly inside of the tool with this name. If this BasePart is missing, the tool will not work. In a later section, we will learn more about the **Handle** part.

We now know what **tools** are. Besides this, we learned about the **StarterPack** service. We learned that inactive tools are stored in the `Backpack` folder, which can be found inside the `Player` object. When a player is using a tool, they get parented to the player's character model. In the next section, we will learn how to create a flashlight.

Creating a flashlight

Let us make a simple flashlight that brightens the map when it is dark. Because this book focuses on programming, we will not explain how to model an excellent-looking flashlight. Instead, we will keep it simple while making it work. Regardless of this, if you know how to model or how to weld Parts together, feel free to make a better-looking flashlight.

Follow these steps to create our very first tool:

1. Create a new **tool** and name it **Flashlight**. Keep this in the **Workspace** as we will need to see what it looks like.

2. Inside the tool, create a **Part** and name it **Handle**. Resize this Part to the following size: {0.5, 0.5, 2}. Make sure that the **Handle** Part is not anchored.

3. Inside the **Handle** Part, create a **SpotLight**. Spotlights create light. Ensure the **Face** property is set correctly; the SpotLight should face forward. Next, change the **Brightness** property to 5.

> Lighting
>
> The **Lighting** service allows us to change anything related to the lighting in our game. To easily test if the **SpotLight** is faced correctly, it might be easier to change the time to midnight. Change the **ClockTime** property on the **Lighting** service to 0.

4. Parent the tool to the **StarterPack** service.

We have now created our very first tool. That was pretty easy, right? When we play the game, we will see that our flashlight lights up the area in front of us. This is because of the **SpotLight** that we added inside of the **Handle** Part. In the following screenshot, we can see what it could look like:

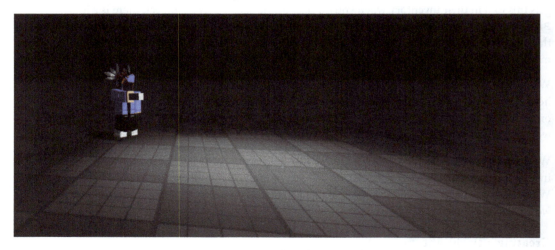

Figure 7.8 – Working flashlight

In this section, we learned how to create a **tool**. Besides this, we learned what **SpotLights** are, and we have seen a few of their properties. In addition, we had a short introduction to the **Lighting** service. In the next section, we will learn how to pick up this tool using a ProximityPrompt.

Picking up a flashlight

Right now, we have our flashlight stored in the **StarterPack** service. This means that every player has this flashlight by default. However, we might want this flashlight to be an item that players can pick up. For instance, if we are making a maze, there are multiple routes; one of these might lead to a flashlight that will help players navigate the maze more easily.

In this section, we will learn how to pick up this flashlight using a ProximityPrompt. First, we need to remove the flashlight from the **StarterPack** service. But where should we place it? Generally, there are two locations where tools get stored. Tools are either stored somewhere in the **ReplicatedStorage** or **ServerStorage** service. So, what is the difference? Let's find out:

- The client can see what is in the **ReplicatedStorage** service. We can use this to make our GUIs display a preview of certain tools. For instance, we might want to make a GUI that displays a list of all the tools players could purchase. In this situation, we use the **ReplicatedStorage** service.

- The **ServerStorage** service is not accessible to the client. Therefore, if we do not need clients to access the tool directly—we store it here.

Now that we know where tools are generally stored, we can move our flashlight. But where do we move it to? Right now, we have no intention of showing the tool in a GUI. Therefore, we will store our flashlight in the **ServerStorage** service to keep it a bit more organized.

To set up our flashlight, follow these steps:

1. First, create a folder called `Tools` inside the **ServerStorage** service.
2. Move your flashlight into this folder.

Now, all we need is a ProximityPrompt. Follow these steps to create our ProximityPrompt:

1. Create a **Part** somewhere in the **Workspace**. Name this Part `FlashlightGiver`.
2. Insert a **ProximityPrompt** named **GiveTool**.
3. Change the **ActionText** property to **Get a Flashlight!**
4. Optionally, you could change the **HoldDuration** property on the ProximityPrompt to `1`. Changing the **HoldDuration** to `1` makes players hold the specified key for 1 second.

Now that we have this, let us analyze the following code snippet:

```
local ServerStorage = game:GetService("ServerStorage")

local toolsStorage = ServerStorage.Tools

local flashlightGiver = workspace.FlashlightGiver
local proximityPrompt = flashlightGiver.GiveTool
```

```
function proximityPromptTriggered(player)
    -- Checking if flashlight is in ServerStorage > Tools
    local flashlight =
    toolsStorage:FindFirstChild("Flashlight")
    if flashlight ~= nil then
        -- Cloning flashlight
        local toolClone = flashlight:Clone()

        -- Parenting tool to Backpack
        toolClone.Parent = player.Backpack
    else
        warn("Flashlight tool is not in the Tools folder!")
    end
end


proximityPrompt.Triggered:Connect(proximityPromptTriggered)
```

In the preceding code snippet, we start by making a few variables. These are references to certain instances in our game, such as the ProximityPrompt that we previously made. At the bottom of the script, we use this `proximityPrompt` reference to listen to the `.Triggered` event. This event gets fired when a player interacts with the ProximityPrompt. Once this event gets fired, we start the `proximityPromptTriggered()` function. This function provides the `Player` object, which interacts with the ProximityPrompt as the first parameter.

In the `proximityPromptTriggered()` function, we first check if we can find the Flashlight tool inside the **Tools** folder that we made in the **ServerStorage** service. If this tool can be found, we refer to the Flashlight tool and execute the `:Clone()` function. What the `:Clone()` function does is create an exact copy of the instance and all its **descendants**. Descendants include children and children of children, and so on.

When we have a clone of the flashlight, we can parent the clone to the **Backpack** of folder the player. Here is a question that you can experiment with yourself: What would have happened if we cloned the flashlight to the player's **Character** model instead of the **Backpack** folder?

In our previous code, we used a **Script**. However, in the *Activating particles* section, we learned that we were able to listen to these events on the client as well. Could we have listened to the ProximityPrompt `.Triggered` event on the client? Yes and no. Yes, we can listen to the `.Triggered` event on the client. However, since our code clones a tool, we have to do this on the server. For starters, our flashlight is stored in the **ServerStorage** service; **LocalScripts** cannot access this service. Besides this, if we were to clone tools on the client and parent them to the **Backpack** folder, the tool would be visible to you, but not to anyone else. This is because of **Filtering Enabled**, which we learned about in *Chapter 4*, *Securing Your Game*.

In this section, we learned how to listen to user input coming from **ProximityPrompts**. Besides this, we learned where to store tools in our game. While doing this, we learned what the `:Clone()` function does. The `:Clone()` function allows us to make an exact copy of any instance that includes all of their descendants. Finally, we also thought about where to implement this system. We used the information we learned about **Filtering Enabled** to determine that we should implement our system on the server. In the next section, we will learn how to prevent duplicate tools in the players' inventory.

Preventing duplicate tools

In the previous section, we made a ProximityPrompt that allows players of our game to get a flashlight. The thing is, they can use this ProximityPrompt as many times as they want. There is no limit. We might want to limit the number of times this flashlight gets cloned per player, so how do we do this? Let us take a look at the following code snippet:

```
function proximityPromptTriggered(player)
    -- Checking if the player already has this tool
    if not playerHasTool(player, "Flashlight") then
        -- ... function>s code
    end
end


function playerHasTool(player, toolName)
    local character = player.Character
    local backpack = player.Backpack
    --
    local characterTool =
    character:FindFirstChildOfClass("Tool")
    if
        backpack:FindFirstChild(toolName)
        or
        ( characterTool ~= nil and characterTool.Name ==
        toolName )
    then
```

```
        -- Player already has this tool
        return true
    end
    -- Player does not have this tool
    return false
  end
```

In the preceding code snippet, we have introduced a new function compared to our previous script. Please keep in mind that we have only shown the new code. This new function is the `playerHasTool()` function. The second parameter, the `toolName` parameter, allows us to specify a tool's name that we want to check. Because tools can be either inside of the **Backpack** folder or **Character** model, we have to look for this tool in both places.

First, we check if the tool can be found inside the **Backpack** folder. We simply use the `:FindFirstChild()` function that we have seen multiple times throughout this book. However, to check if a tool can be found in the **Character** model, we do something exotic. First, we use the `:FindFirstChildOfClass()` function to find any tool. If any tool can be found, we check if the name of this tool matches the tool we want to find. While it is fun to analyze a more complex `if` statement, there is a reason we do this.

Inside of the **Backpack** folder are pretty much only **Tools** and **LocalScripts**. We can easily use a `:FindFirstChild()` function here; just make sure you do not name your scripts after tools. However, inside the **Character** folder are a bunch of different things. These include **accessories**. Roblox has so many different accessories, especially with the **user-generated content** (UGC) program getting bigger and bigger; there might be an accessory with the same name as your tool. Because we use the `:FindFirstChildOfClass()` function, only one tool comes up. This way, all accessories and other instances are automatically filtered out.

This section taught us how to check if a player already has a particular tool. By doing this, we prevent players from having duplicate tools. We did this by checking both the player's **Character** model and **Backpack** folder. We now know how to properly use **ProximityPrompts** to listen to user input. In the next section, we will learn how to listen to user input by using **tools**.

Working with tools

In the previous sections, we learned how to listen to user input by using **ClickDetectors** and **ProximityPrompts**. While learning about ProximityPrompts, we had an introduction to **tools**. While tools are not very complex, they will definitely come in handy when you start making games that have tools.

How can we listen to user input by using tools? There are only four events on tools that we have to know about. These are the following events:

Event	Purpose
.Equipped	This event is fired when the tool is parented to the player's **Character** model. We use this event to figure out when they equip the tool.
.Unequipped	This event is fired when the tool gets parented to the **Backpack** folder. We use this event to figure out when the player stops using the tool.
.Activated	This event gets fired when the player starts using the **Tool**. The same events get fired for any device. You do not have to worry about other types of user input depending on the device. For PCs, this event could be compared to the .MouseButton1Down event on GUI elements.
.Deactivated	This event gets fired when the player stops using the **Tool**. Similar to the .Activated event, this event works for all devices. For PCs, this event could be compared to the .MouseButton1Up event on GUI elements.

Table 7.1 – Important tool events

We now know the most common events for tools. Throughout this chapter, we have asked ourselves multiple times if we should listen to these events on the client or server. Once again, it depends on the use case. For example, if we want to play a particular animation once someone uses a tool or if we want to update something on one of our GUIs, we should do this on the client. However, if there is more complex logic or behavior that everyone on the server should see, it should be done on the server.

Maybe you remember that back in *Chapter 4, Securing Your Game*, we said that **LocalScripts** do not work inside the **Workspace**. However, when tools are active, they are inside the **Character** model, which is inside the **Workspace**, yet LocalScripts still work if we insert them into tools. This is because the Character objects were one of the exceptions to the Workspace rule. LocalScripts do work when they are inside of Character model. Therefore, LocalScripts work when they are inside tools, a child of the Characters model.

Now that we know about the most common events for **tools**, we can start using them. We will continue on the previously made Flashlight tool in the next section. We want the flashlight to turn on or off when we use the tool, depending on its current state.

Toggling the flashlight on and off

Before we can implement this system, we first have to ask ourselves: will we implement this on the server or the client? For our current tool, the flashlight, it will depend on what we want as developers. Maybe we do not want other players to benefit from the flashlight, in which case we could do it on the client. However, maybe we want the flashlight to change for all players. Or even better, perhaps there are monsters in our game. When the flashlight is off, the monsters cannot see the player. In this scenario, we would have to implement our system on the server.

For now, we will implement our system on the server as this makes the most sense. Let us take a look at the following code snippet:

```
local tool = script.Parent
local handle = tool.Handle

function activated()
    local spotlight = handle:FindFirstChild("SpotLight")
    if spotlight ~= nil then
        spotlight.Enabled = not spotlight.Enabled
    end
end


tool.Activated:Connect(activated)
```

In the preceding code snippet, we listen to the .Activated event on the tool. Once this gets fired, we start the activated() function. Inside the activated() function we find the **SpotLight** inside the **Handle** Part using the :FindFirstChild() function. If this SpotLight can be found, we toggle the .Enabled property. We have seen this toggle using the not keyword in the *Activating particles* section.

We have now seen how to use the .Activated event on tools. Try experimenting with tools yourself. There is most likely a tool you can think of that interests you. An obvious pitfall is to instantly make a complex tool. Instead, try keeping it simple. When working with simple systems, you figure out what works and what does not. If you were to jump into something complex instantly, there could be many things that might not work. This usually results in most developers quitting trying. Please keep it simple. Try combining it with the knowledge you already have. For instance, make a tool that plays a random animation when the .Activated event gets fired. Perhaps you could combine it with the .Deactivated event and work your way up from there.

Implementing advanced user input

So far, we have seen many ways to detect user input. For instance, in *Chapter 6, Creating User Interfaces for All Devices*, we have already seen how to listen to user input on **GUIs**. Besides this, we have already learned how to listen to user input by using **ClickDetectors**, **ProximityPrompts**, and **tools**. These are the most commonly used ways of detecting user input for mobile devices. However, there are other ways to detect "input" from phones, such as by using the **Gyroscope** or **Accelerometer** sensors. However, these are not used very often.

For consoles and PCs, there are more ways of getting input. We will consider these types of inputs "advanced" inputs. This is because we have to worry about more elements when listening to these than, for example, tools. When we used tools, Roblox made one event: the .Activated event that would get fired when a player interacted with it. We did not have to worry about the device that this player was playing on; this was all handled for us. We will have to do this ourselves with all the upcoming user inputs. Besides this, all the inputs we will listen to have to be programmed on the **client**. We have to do this on the client because the **server** does not get the events that we will use.

In the next sections, we will learn how to listen to input from a player's **mouse**, **keyboard**, and **gamepad**. We will start by listening to keyboard input.

Keyboard input

To listen to keyboard input, we need to use a service called **UserInputService**. This service knows everything related to the inputs of our players. In *Chapter 6, Creating User Interfaces for All Devices*, we briefly introduced this service. Back then, we used this service to figure out which controls to display for a player using the .LastInputTypeChanged event.

As previously mentioned, we have to listen to this service on the **client**, but where do we listen to it? On the **UserInputService** service, there are two events that we should look into. These are the .InputBegan and .InputEnded events. The .InputBegan event fires when the user presses down a key, whereas the .InputEnded event fires when the user releases this key. Let us look at a simple script that uses the .InputBegan event, as follows:

```
local UserInputService = game:GetService("UserInputService")

function inputBegan(inputObject, gameProcessedEvent)
    print(gameProcessedEvent, inputObject.KeyCode)
end

UserInputService.InputBegan:Connect(inputBegan)
```

In the preceding code snippet, we listen to the .InputBegan event. Once this event fires, we start the inputBegan() function. The parameters of this function are inputObject and gameProcessedevent. So far, we have no clue what either is. However, from the print() function, we can conclude that we can print gameProcessedEvent and that we can print some **KeyCode** that is inside of the inputObject.

If we run the game with this script and start clicking with our mouse, we will see a bunch of Enum. KeyCode.Unknown lines show up in our **Developer Console**. However, if we start pressing keys on our keyboard, **enums** that fit the keys we press show up in the Developer Console, as seen in the following screenshot:

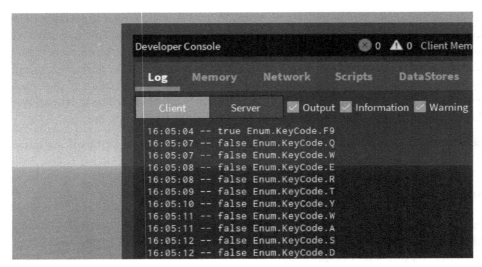

Figure 7.9 – Printing gameProcessedEvent and KeyCode

In *Figure 7.9*, we can see that the correct enum **KeyCodes** get printed if we use our keyboard. However, we still do not know what this gameProcessedEvent Boolean means. The gameProcessedEvent parameter tells us if Roblox already registered this input for something else. As shown in *Figure 7.9*, gameProcessedEvent is true when we open the Developer Console after pressing the *F9* key. This is because Roblox already used this key to open the Developer Console. Therefore, we can conclude that we should not listen to any user input when gameProcessedEvent is true, as this input already resulted in something else.

So far, we know how to listen to these events. However, not everyone has a keyboard connected to their device. How do we handle this? It would be bad to listen to events for a peripheral that is unavailable for them. Let us take a look at the following code snippet:

```
local Players = game:GetService("Players")
local UserInputService = game:GetService("UserInputService")

local player = Players.LocalPlayer

function setup()
    -- Checking if Keyboard is enabled
    if UserInputService.KeyboardEnabled == true then
        -- Listening to the .InputBegan event
        UserInputService.InputBegan:Connect(inputBegan)
    end
```

```
end

function inputBegan(inputObject, gameProcessedEvent)
    -- Checking if Roblox used this event already
    if gameProcessedEvent == false then
        -- Checking if the <B> key was pressed
        if inputObject.KeyCode == Enum.KeyCode.B then
            -- Creating (client-sided) explosion
            local explosion = Instance.new("Explosion")
            explosion.Parent = player.Character.PrimaryPart
            explosion.Position = explosion.Parent.Position
        end
    end
end

setup()
```

In the preceding code snippet, we use the `setup()` function when we start the script. The reason we do this is to check if a keyboard is connected. To see if a keyboard is connected, we read the `.KeyboardEnabled` property on the **UserInputService** service. When we first mentioned we had to check if a keyboard was enabled, you may have thought: Okay, we will do this inside of the `inputBegan()` function. This is a pitfall that developers often fall into. Doing this is actually the opposite of what you should be doing. If you were to check if a keyboard is enabled, you have to do this before a connection to the `.InputBegan` event was made, not after. Doing this after would defeat the point of checking if a keyboard is enabled.

Once the `inputBegan()` function starts, we check if `gameProcessedEvent` is `false`. After all, we do not want to do anything if this key is used for something else. Then, we check if the **KeyCode** inside of `inputObject` matches the *B* key. If this is the case, we create an explosion particle. This is a standard particle that Roblox offers.

> **Note**
>
> For the simplicity of this example, a client-sided explosion is made. Because of **Filtering Enabled**, this explosion will not be visible to other players.

We now know how to listen to user input from keyboards by using the **UserInputService** service. We learned about the `.InputBegan` and `.InputEnded` events. In addition, we learned about the parameters that both events provide: the `inputObject` and `gameProcessedEvent` parameters. Besides this, we learned how to check whether a keyboard has been enabled or not. Finally, we have also seen how to use the **Explosion** particle. In the next section, we will learn how to listen to user input that comes from a gamepad.

Gamepad input

In the previous section, we covered how to listen to user input from keyboards. However, Roblox supports many devices, including various consoles. These consoles do not have keyboards. Instead, consoles use gamepads. Roblox games support up to 10 different gamepads at the same time. Obviously, these 10 gamepads are per device. Generally, there is only one gamepad used for most games. However, it is good to know that you could make a game that supports multiple gamepads.

For now, let us focus on just one gamepad. How do we listen to this gamepad? It is actually very similar to keyboards. Just keep in mind that gamepads do not have the same keys as keyboards. When writing this book, only **Microsoft Xbox** consoles are supported on Roblox. This might change in the future.

In the following code snippet, we will continue the previously made code that creates an explosion and add console support. Let us take a look at the code here:

```
local Players = game:GetService("Players")
local UserInputService = game:GetService("UserInputService")
local player = Players.LocalPlayer

function setup()
    -- Checking if Keyboard is enabled
    if
        -- Checking if Keyboard is enabled ...
        UserInputService.KeyboardEnabled == true
        -- ... or a Gamepad is enabled.
        or UserInputService.GamepadEnabled == true
    then
        -- Listening to the .InputBegan event
        UserInputService.InputBegan:Connect(inputBegan)
    end
end

function inputBegan(inputObject, gameProcessedEvent)
    -- Checking if Roblox used this event already
    if gameProcessedEvent == false then
        if
            -- Checking if the <B> key was pressed (Keyboard)
```

```
            inputObject.KeyCode == Enum.KeyCode.B
            -- Checking if the <X> key was pressed (Gamepad)
            or inputObject.KeyCode == Enum.KeyCode.ButtonX
        then
            -- Creating (client-sided) explosion
            local explosion = Instance.new("Explosion")
            explosion.Parent = player.Character.PrimaryPart
            explosion.Position = explosion.Parent.Position
        end
    end
end

setup()
```

Let us look at the changes we made in the preceding code snippet compared to the code snippet from the previous section. For starters, we now check if either the .KeyboardEnabled property or the .GamepadEnabled property is set to true. Because both inputs use the .InputBegan and .InputEnded events, we can combine them. Besides this change, we had to change something in the inputBegan() function. Here, we now check if the **KeyCode** matches Enum.KeyCode.B, which is the *B* key on your keyboard, or Enum.KeyCode.ButtonX, which is the *X* button on Xbox controllers.

Testing is going to be a bit more complex. We either need to publish our testing game to Roblox and test it on an actual Xbox or we can connect an Xbox controller wirelessly to our PC. Keep in mind that not all PCs or controllers support this wireless connection—you might have to purchase an adapter for this. If you purchase an adapter, you have to plug in the adapter before starting Roblox Studio. The same applies to the wireless connection; this connection has to be made before you start Roblox Studio.

We now know how to listen to user input that comes from a controller. We used the .GamepadEnabled property on the **UserInputService** service to see if a controller was connected. Then, we still used the .InputBegan event to listen to the incoming user input. We simply added an extra check for a different **KeyCode** enum to support a gamepad key. We now know the basics for listening to gamepad user input. In the following sections, we will expand our knowledge related to gamepads. First, we will look at how to support multiple gamepads for your game. Next, we will look into **haptic feedback** on controllers.

Multiple gamepads

In the previous section, we learned how to listen to gamepad input. Each Roblox client can have up to 10 different gamepads connected. While this is not a likely scenario, it would be a fun game concept or family game to play. So, how do we listen to multiple gamepads? No change needs to happen to our current code for this, but there are a few things we should look into.

We previously used the `InputObject` parameter to read which key was pressed using the `KeyCode` property. However, `InputObject` has way more data than we can read. Another property we can read is the `UserInputType` property. Let us look at the following code snippet:

```lua
local UserInputService = game:GetService("UserInputService")

function inputBegan(inputObject, gameProcessedEvent)
    print(inputObject.UserInputType)
end

UserInputService.InputBegan:Connect(inputBegan)
```

The preceding code snippet is a very simple function that listens to the `.InputBegan` event and prints the `UserInputType` property from the `inputObject` parameter. If we add this **LocalScript** to our game and start pressing keys on our gamepad, keyboard, or mouse, we will see that an `UserInputType` enum is printed, as seen in the following screenshot:

Figure 7.10 – Different UserInputTypes values

We can use the `UserInputType` enum to differentiate which input is given. One of the enums we can see is the `Gamepad1` enum. This is the first gamepad that Roblox supports. There are 10 different versions of this enum: `Gamepad1`, `Gamepad2`, up until `Gamepad10`. We can use this knowledge to create certain actions for certain gamepads.

In the following code snippet, we will make sure that only `Gamepad1` can create an explosion when the **X** button is pressed:

```lua
function inputBegan(inputObject, gameProcessedEvent)
    -- Checking if Roblox used this event already
    if gameProcessedEvent == false then
        if
            -- Checking if the <B> key was pressed (Keyboard)
            inputObject.KeyCode == Enum.KeyCode.B
```

```
            -- or checking if a valid gamepad key was
            -- pressed
            or
            (
                -- Checking if input came from Gamepad1 ...
                inputObject.UserInputType ==
                Enum.UserInputType.Gamepad1
                -- ... and if the <X> key was pressed (Gamepad)
                and inputObject.KeyCode ==
                Enum.KeyCode.ButtonX
            )
        then
            -- ... Creating (client-sided) explosion ...
        end
    end
end
```

Please remember that the preceding code snippet is just a section of the previously made explosion script. As we can see in the preceding code snippet, we can get an explosion by either the *B* key on our keyboard or by pressing the **X** button on Gamepad1.

We now know how to use the UserInputType enum to differentiate between where a particular input came from. We have seen that we can use this enum to differentiate between multiple gamepads as well; doing this allows us to support multiple gamepads for one player. In the next section, we will learn how to use **haptic feedback** on controllers.

Haptic feedback

In the previous sections, we have learned a lot about gamepads already. Maybe you have played with gamepads as well. If you did, you might know about **haptic feedback**. Haptic feedback is the vibration your phone or controller makes to notify you about something that happened. We can make players' controllers vibrate when a particular action happens. To do this, we use the **HapticService**.

Before we can start a vibration, we have to know a few things. For starters, we must somehow specify which gamepad we want this vibration to start from. In the previous section, we learned about the UserInputType enum. We will use this enum to specify which gamepad will vibrate. Besides this, it is good to know that there are multiple **motors** inside of a gamepad. Once a motor starts, the vibrating on the gamepad starts. However, not every gamepad has all the motors; we will learn more about this later.

Now that we know this, let us take a look at the following code snippet:

```
local HapticService = game:GetService("HapticService")

HapticService:SetMotor(
    -- UserInputType
    Enum.UserInputType.Gamepad1,

    -- Vibration Motor Enum
      Enum.VibrationMotor.Large,
    --Enum.VibrationMotor.Small
    --Enum.VibrationMotor.LeftHand
    --Enum.VibrationMotor.RightHand
    --Enum.VibrationMotor.LeftTrigger
    --Enum.VibrationMotor.RightTrigger

    -- Intensity (0-1)
    0.5
)
```

In the preceding code snippet, we use the `:SetMotor()` function on the `HapticService`. The `:SetMotor()` function has three parameters: a `UserInputType` enum, a `VibrationMotor` enum, and the `Intensity`. The `UserInputType` enum determines on which gamepad this vibration will start. Then, we have to specify which `VibrationMotor` we want to use; picking this should be based on the action that takes place. Please keep in mind that most controllers only have a `Small` and `Large` vibration motor. Finally, we also have to specify the intensity of this vibration motor. This has to be a number between 0 and 1. When the number is 0, the vibration motor is off.

As previously mentioned, not all controllers support each motor. As a matter of fact, some controllers do not even support vibration at all. Luckily there are some functions on the `HapticService` that help us figure this out. Let us take a look at the following code snippet:

```
local HapticService = game:GetService("HapticService")

function giveHapticFeedback(inputType, vibrationMotor,
duration, ...)
    if
        -- Checking if Vibration is supported ...
        HapticService:IsVibrationSupported(inputType) ==
        true
```

```
        -- ... and if Motor is supported
        and HapticService:IsMotorSupported(inputType,
        vibrationMotor) == true
    then
        -- Setting Gamepad Motor
        HapticService:SetMotor(inputType, vibrationMotor,
        ...)

        -- Waiting for duration
        if duration > 0 then
            task.wait(duration)
            HapticService:SetMotor(inputType,
            vibrationMotor, 0)
        end
    end
end

giveHapticFeedback(
    Enum.UserInputType.Gamepad1, -- inputType
    Enum.VibrationMotor.Large, -- vibrationMotor
    .5, -- duration
    .5 - intensity
)
```

In the preceding code snippet, we have created a function named `giveHapticFeedback()`. This function has four parameters: `inputType`, `vibrationMode`, `duration`, and **three dots**. These three dots are how we display a **variable number of parameters**, also referred to as **tuple parameters**. These three dots literally mean we can give this function an unlimited amount of arguments. Let us quickly take a look at the following example using a variable number of parameters:

```
function printEverything(...)
    local arg = {...}
    for _, data in pairs(arg) do
        print(tostring(data))
    end
end

printEverything("Hey!")
```

```
printEverything("Hey, ", "how are ", "you?")
printEverything("Numbers", 124)
printEverything({"table data"})
```

In the preceding code snippet, we can see that we turn the variable amount of parameters into a table stored in a variable named `arg`. Then, we use a `for` loop that loops through this table and prints everything that was given to the function. Now that we know how to use a variable amount of parameters, let us continue with the original code snippet.

In the original code snippet, we use two functions on the `HapticService`. These are the `:IsVibrationSupported()` and `:IsMotorSupported()` functions. Both functions return a Boolean that needs to be `true` for a vibration to be possible. The `:IsVibrationSupported()` function returns `true` when this gamepad supports haptic feedback. However, since there are different motors, we need to check if this gamepad supports the motor we attempt to start. We can check this by using the `:IsMotorSupported()` function.

If the gamepad supports what we are trying to do, we can use the `:SetMotor()` function. This results in haptic feedback happening.

In the previous sections, we learned how to listen to gamepad input. We have now learned how to give feedback to the player using their gamepad. In addition, we have learned how to use a variable number of arguments using three dots (. . .). In the next section, we will learn how to listen to user input that comes from a mouse.

Mouse input

In the previous sections, we learned how to listen to user input from keyboards and gamepads. However, the mouse plays a vital role for most PC players. While we have already learned many ways to listen to mouse input, such as by using the `.Activated` event on **tools**, and by using **ClickDetectors**, we can listen to more advanced input as well. Before we can look into this, we have to ask ourselves something first. When listening to keyboard and gamepad input, we use a `KeyCode` enum. However, there are no **KeyCodes** for mouse input. This is because mouse input has a unique `UserInputType` enum for each input. Let us take a look at all the `UserInputType` enums that are related to the mouse, as follows:

Enum	Meaning
`Enum.UserInputType.MouseButton1`	Left mouse button
`Enum.UserInputType.MouseButton2`	Right mouse button
`Enum.UserInputType.MouseButton3`	Mouse wheel button
`Enum.UserInputType.MouseMovement`	Mouse movement
`Enum.UserInputType.MouseWheel`	Mouse wheel movement

Table 7.2 – Mouse input enums

Now that we know about the `UserInputTypes` from *Table 7.2*, let us take a look at the following code snippet:

```
local UserInputService = game:GetService("UserInputService")

function inputBegan(inputObject, gameProcessedEvent)
    print(inputObject.UserInputType)
end


UserInputService.InputBegan:Connect(inputBegan)
```

We have seen the preceding code snippet in the section about multiple gamepads as well. However, this time, we will check which mouse `UserInputType` enums get fired.

Once we tested this, we noticed that only the `MouseButton1`, `MouseButton2`, and `MouseButton3` enums work. Why does nothing happen when we move or scroll with our mouse? The reason for this is because we use the `.InputBegan` event.

In the previous sections, we have worked primarily with the `.InputBegan` event. However, for the `MouseWheel` and `MouseMovement` enums, we have to use another event on the `UserInputService`. This is the `.InputChanged` event. This actually makes sense; a mouse always has a position. There is no beginning or ending to this position; it just changes. Let us look at how to listen to `MouseMovement` and `MouseWheel` enums in the following example:

```
local UserInputService = game:GetService("UserInputService")

function inputChanged(inputObject, gameProcessedEvent)
    print(inputObject.UserInputType)
end


UserInputService.InputChanged:Connect(inputChanged)
```

Not much has changed in the preceding code snippet compared to the previous one. The only things that have changed are the event and the name of the function; the rest is still the same. Now, when we try to scroll or move our mouse, the correct enum gets printed.

But what can we do with these mouse inputs? One of the possibilities is to make a Frame that follows your mouse position. Every time your mouse would move, the frame would follow. Besides this, we might want the color of the frame to change every time we use the left mouse button. Let us make this system using the `UserInputService`.

Before we can implement this system, we first need to make a simple GUI. Follow these steps to make our GUI:

1. Create a **ScreenGui** inside of the **StarterGui**.

2. Create a frame inside of the **ScreenGui**. Make sure this frame stays named `Frame`.

3. Inside of the **ScreenGui**, create a **LocalScript**. Do not worry about the code; we will create this later.

Now that we have our GUI, let us start scripting our system. Before we can do this, we need to figure out a way to get the mouse's position on our screen. Luckily, there is a function on the `UserInputService` that gets this for us. This is the `:GetMouseLocation()` function. This function returns a `Vector2` value with the **X** and **Y** offset of the mouse. Now that we know this, let us implement this system, as follows:

```lua
local UserInputService = game:GetService("UserInputService")

local ui = script.Parent
local frame = ui:WaitForChild("Frame")

function setup()
    -- Checking if the device has a mouse
    if UserInputService.MouseEnabled == true then

        -- Handling mouse input
        local function listenToMouseInput(inputObject,
        gameProcessedEvent)
            -- Checking if Roblox handled this event
            if gameProcessedEvent == false then
                if inputObject.UserInputType ==
                Enum.UserInputType.MouseMovement then
                    -- Mouse has moved
                    repositionFrame()
                elseif inputObject.UserInputType ==
                Enum.UserInputType.MouseButton1 then
                    -- Left mouse button has been pressed
                    changeFrameColor()
                end
            end
```

```
            end

            -- Listening to the .InputBegan event
            UserInputService.InputBegan:Connect(listenToMouseIn
            put)

            -- Listening to the .InputChanged event
            UserInputService.InputChanged:Connect(listenToMouse
            Input)
        end
    end

function changeFrameColor()
    local r = math.random(0, 255)
    local g = math.random(0, 255)
    local b = math.random(0, 255)
    frame.BackgroundColor3 = Color3.fromRGB(r, g, b)
end

function repositionFrame()
    -- Getting the mouse location
    local mouseLocation =
    UserInputService:GetMouseLocation()

    -- Setting frame position
    frame.Position = UDim2.new(0, mouseLocation.X, 0,
    mouseLocation.Y)
end

setup()
```

Let us take a look at the preceding code snippet. Inside the `setup()` function, we check if this device has a mouse connected by checking the `.MouseEnabled` property on the `UserInputService`. If this device does have a mouse, we start listening to the `.InputBegan` and `.InputChanged` events. We will use the `.InputBegan` event to listen to clicks, and we use the `.InputChanged` event to see when the player moves their mouse. Because both events have a very similar function, we have chosen to use a **nested function**. We learned about nested functions in *Chapter 2, Writing Better Code*.

Inside of our nested function, we check if the `UserInputType` equals `MouseMovement` or `MouseButton1`. When the left mouse button gets pressed, we start the `changeFrameColor()` function. This function is responsible for changing the `BackgroundColor3` property on our frame. When the mouse has moved, we use the `repositionFrame()` function. This function uses the `:GetMouseLocation()` function on the `UserInputService` to determine where the mouse is positioned. As previously mentioned, this function gives a `Vector2` value containing the **X** and **Y** offset of the mouse. We use this data to create a `UDim2` data type that positions the frame correctly.

When we test our game, the frame will follow our mouse, and when we press the left mouse button, we see that the color of the frame changes into a new random color, as illustrated in the following screenshot:

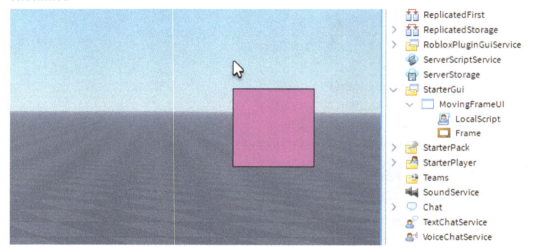

Figure 7.11 – Frame following our mouse

Best Practice

When looking for information about mouse input online, you will see many code examples using `Player:GetMouse()`. Try to avoid using this, as difficult as it might be. While this method is not **deprecated**, as of writing this book, the `UserInputService` is a better alternative as it makes it easier to develop for various devices.

In this section, we learned how to listen to user input that comes from a mouse. First, we figured out which enums to use as there were no `KeyCodes` for mouse input. Once we figured this out, we learned that we have to use the `.InputChanged` event for certain enums as they do not work with the `.InputBegan` and `.InputEnded` events. Once we got this working, we made a system that updates a frame's position based on the location of our mouse. In addition, we made this frame change color every time we pressed the left mouse button, and all of this by using the input from the **UserInputService**.

We now know how to listen to advanced user input from keyboards, gamepads, and even mice. In addition, we learned how to ensure that we do not create connections to the `UserInputService` if a certain peripheral, such as a gamepad, is not connected. Currently, these controls are always active, no matter the context. While we can make some advanced `if` statements that determine when these controls should work, there is a better alternative. In the next section, we will learn about the **ContextActionService.**

ContextActionService

We learned how to listen to advanced user input in the previous sections. While this is super useful, it is not always very efficient. We have already looked at how to prevent unnecessary connections when certain peripherals are not connected, yet it does not prevent unnecessary fires on the `.InputBegan`, `.InputEnded`, and `.InputChanged` events. We have seen that these events get fired many times throughout the previous sections. As a matter of fact, they even fired when Roblox had already handled these inputs. All of this starts our functions many times when it might not even be required. For instance, we might want a shop menu to come up when a player presses *E*. However, this menu is only allowed to open when the player is inside the shop.

The previously described scenario will start many unnecessary functions. Imagine if a player is on the other side of the map. Every time the *E* key gets pressed, we have to ignore the input. Now, we could add some smart code that connects and disconnects listeners to the `.InputBegan` event, but there is a much better alternative out there: the **ContextActionService**.

So, what is the **ContextActionService?** The **ContextActionService** allows us to easily listen to certain user input when the player is in a specific "context". For example, we can start listening to the *E* key when the player is inside of the shop using the **ContextActionService,** then we stop listening when the player leaves our shop.

The **ContextActionService** has two primary functions: the `:BindAction()` and `:UnbindAction()` functions. The `:BindAction()` function allows us to start listening to user input, and the `:UnbindAction()` allows us to stop listening to this input.

We now know what the **ContextActionService** is. In the following sections, we will create a system that opens a shop frame when a player is inside of a shop, using the **ContextActionService.** First, we will figure out a way to see if a player is inside the shop. Then, we will use the **ContextActionService** to toggle the visibility of this frame. Once we have this working, we will look at how the **ContextActionService** works for phones and tablets.

Entering and leaving a shop

The **ContextActionService** is used when a player is inside of a certain context. This context can be anything. For our current scenario, the context is a shop. Players should only be able to open the shop frame if they are inside the shop. So, how do we do this?

There are various ways of detecting if a player is within a certain area. As a matter of fact, there are even open source modules that help developers solve this issue. We will not look into these modules, as we will focus on developing everything using standard Roblox **application programming interfaces (APIs)**. So, what are our options? Let's take a look:

- We could make a `while` loop that constantly checks the player's position; if the player is within a certain distance, the shop could be opened
- Another option is to use `workspace:GetPartBoundsInBox()`

Both options have their pros and cons, but something that they have in common is that they are both very intensive to calculate constantly. So, how can we fix this?

There is a "hacky" way to figure out if a player is at a certain location. On **Humanoid** objects inside of each Character model, there is a property called `FloorMaterial`. We can make an invisible part inside our map and give this a material that is not used in our game. Optionally, we can add an extra `if` statement that checks the distance in case there are multiple shops. Please keep in mind that this option will not always work for your game. Feel free to try the previously mentioned options.

Let us see how this would work, as follows:

```
local Players = game:GetService("Players")

local character = Players.LocalPlayer.Character
local humanoid = character:WaitForChild("Humanoid")

function setup()
    -- Listening to changes on the FloorMaterial property
    humanoid:GetPropertyChangedSignal("FloorMaterial"):
    Connect(function()
        -- Checking if player is standing on <Foil>
        -- We use this as a simple method to detect if the
        -- player is
        -- in a certain location
        if humanoid.FloorMaterial == Enum.Material.Foil
        then
            -- Player is in <Context>
        else
            -- Player is out of <Context>
        end
    end)
```

```
end

setup()
```

In the preceding code snippet, we created a custom event that fires every time the `FloorMaterial` property changes, using the `GetPropertyChangedSignal()` function. Once this event fires, we check if the player is standing on a BasePart with the `Foil` material. `Foil` is the material that we chose to figure out if a player is inside of the shop. We still have to make an invisible Part near our shop and give it the `Foil` material to make this work. An example `Foil` Part can be seen in the following screenshot. *Figure 7.12*. If the player is standing this BasePart, the player is in `'Context'`; if not, the player is out of `'Context'`:

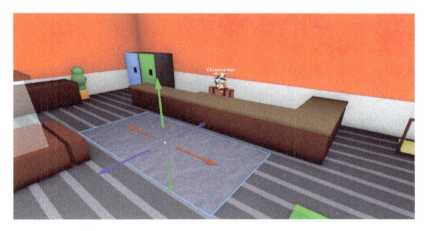

Figure 7.12 – Created Foil Part (visible for demonstration)

We now know how to figure out if a player is at a particular location using the `FloorMaterial` property. As mentioned in this section, there are various ways to determine if the player is in context. This is just an example solution. Each solution has its pros and cons, so feel free to experiment with other solutions. In the next section, we will toggle the shop frame using the `ContextActionService`.

Opening a Frame using ContextActionService

In the previous section, we figured out when a player is "in context". This was a required condition for our system. Now, we can use the `:BindAction()` and `:UnbindAction()` functions on the `ContextActionService`. However, we need to create a simple GUI that will serve as our shop frame first. Follow these steps:

1. Inside of the **StarterGui**, create a new **ScreenGui**.
2. Inside the **ScreenGui**, create a new Frame named **ShopFrame**.
3. Inside the **ScreenGui**, create a new **LocalScript**.

We have now created a super-simple GUI. If you wish to practice a bit more with making GUIs, feel free to add `TextLabels`, `TextButtons`, and other GUI elements.

As previously mentioned, we need to use the `:BindAction()` function when the player is in context. Once the player leaves context, this action has to be unbound by using the `:UnbindAction()` function. But how do these functions even work? Let us take a look at the required arguments for both functions, as follows:

```
local ContextActionService =
game:GetService("ContextActionService")

function someFunction()
end

ContextActionService:BindAction(
    -- Action Name
    "ToggleShop",

    -- Function Name
    someFunction,

    -- Touch Button
    true,

    -- (Variable Arguments)
    -- KeyCodes or UserInputTypes
    Enum.UserInputType.MouseButton3,
    Enum.KeyCode.ButtonX,
    Enum.KeyCode.E
)

ContextActionService:UnbindAction(
    -- Action Name
    "ToggleShop"
)
```

In the preceding code snippet, we can see the required arguments that we must provide for using the `:BindAction()` and `:UnbindAction()` functions. For the `:BindAction()` function, we need to provide an **action name**; this can be anything. It is recommended you give it something related to the action while keeping it unique from other actions. Then, we need to specify the **function's name**, without parentheses, that will be fired once this action happens. The third argument is a Boolean that specifies whether a button has to be made for phones and tablets as they do not have keyboards or gamepads. Finally, we can specify an unlimited number of `KeyCodes` and `UserInputType` enums to activate this action.

Now that we know about the required arguments, let us continue our previously made system. Let us analyze the following code snippet:

```lua
local Players = game:GetService("Players")
local ContextActionService =
game:GetService("ContextActionService")

local ACTION_NAME = "ToggleShop"

local ui = script.Parent
local shopFrame = ui:WaitForChild("ShopFrame")

local character = Players.LocalPlayer.Character
local humanoid = character:WaitForChild("Humanoid")

function setup()
    -- Listening to changes on the FloorMaterial property
    humanoid:GetPropertyChangedSignal("FloorMaterial"):
    Connect(function()
        -- Checking if player is standing on <Foil>
        if humanoid.FloorMaterial == Enum.Material.Foil
        then
            beginAction()
        else
            endAction()
        end
    end)
end

function beginAction()
    -- Starting ContextAction
    ContextActionService:BindAction(ACTION_NAME,
```

```
        toggleShop, true, Enum.KeyCode.E, Enum.KeyCode.ButtonX)
    end

function endAction()
    -- Stopping ContextAction
    ContextActionService:UnbindAction(ACTION_NAME)

    -- Closing shop (if open)
    closeShop()
end

function toggleShop(actionName, inputState, inputObject)
    -- Checking if this is the Begin action
    if inputState == Enum.UserInputState.Begin then
        -- Toggling frame
        shopFrame.Visible = not shopFrame.Visible
    end
end

function closeShop()
    -- Checking if shop is open
    if shopFrame.Visible == true then
        -- Closing shop
        toggleShop(ACTION_NAME, Enum.UserInputState.Begin)
    end
end

    setup()
```

In the preceding code snippet, we have copied the setup() function from the previous section. However, this time, we start the beginAction() and endAction() functions inside of the setup() function. The beginAction() function uses the :BindAction() function, whereas the endAction() function uses the :UnbindAction() function. Besides this, the endAction() function also calls the closeShop() function, which will simply change the Visible property on the shopFrame frame to false.

The toggleShop() function is something we should look into a bit more. This is the function that the :BindAction() calls when user input is given. As we can see, the toggleShop() function has three parameters: `actionName`, `inputState`, and `inputObject`. For our current system, only the `inputState` parameter is used.

The `:BindAction()` function fires the `toggleShop()` function, twice per input. The first time is when the input starts, and the second time is when the input ends. The `inputState` parameter allows us to check if this function was started on `Begin` or `End`. For our current scenario, we only want to toggle the frame once the input begins; we do not want to toggle the frame again when the input ends. Not having this `if` statement would only make the shop frame visible when the input key is pressed; you could try this if it interests you.

When we test our game, we have to press the *E* key on our keyboard when standing on our `Foil` BasePart. If we do this, the shop frame will become visible. However, once we move away from our `Foil` BasePart and press the *E* key, the shop frame will not become visible; this is because we are not in "context" in this scenario.

We now know how to use the `:BindAction()` and `:UnbindAction()` functions on the `ContextActionService`. In the next section, we will take a look at the button that phones and tablets will interact with when using the `ContextActionService`.

ContextActionService for phones and tablets

As we have seen in a previous section, there is a parameter on the `:BindAction()` function that we referred to as `Touch Button`. This parameter will create a button for phones and tablets so they can start this action as well. We will call this button the **ContextAction** button.

We can test to see if this parameter works by using the **emulator**. We learned about the emulator in *Chapter 6, Creating User Interfaces for All Devices*. In the following screenshot, we can see the button that gets generated if we set the `Touch Button` parameter to `true`:

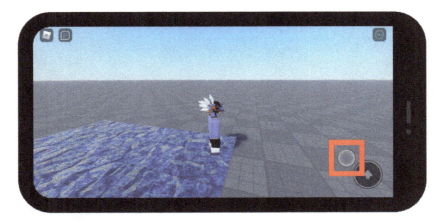

Figure 7.13 – Generated ContextAction button for a phone

In *Figure 7.13*, we can see a highlighted button next to the **Jump** button. This is our **ContextAction** button that gets generated when enabling the `Touch Button` parameter. As we can see in *Figure 7.13*, this button is very blunt and simple. Players will have no clue what this button does. Luckily, we can change this. There are various functions on the **ContextActionService** that allow us to change this, as outlined here:

Function Name	Behavior
`:SetTitle()`	This function will change the text inside of the mobile button.
`:SetImage()`	This function will add an image inside of the mobile button.
`:SetPosition()`	This function will change the position of the mobile button. Recommended using when multiple binding actions could occur at the same time.
`:GetButton()`	This function will get a reference to the mobile button. You can use this reference to redesign what the button looks like entirely. Please keep in mind that this function will return `nil` if there is no mobile button; this could be because the player does not play on a phone or tablet.

Table 7.3 – Functions on the ContextActionService that change the mobile button

In *Table 7.3*, we can see the functions that allow us to change what our mobile button looks like. One of these functions is worth looking into more. This is the `:SetPosition()` function. But to which position are we supposed to reposition our button? This will come down to your preference. Here is a list of commonly used positions:

1. `{1, -150},{1, -77}`
2. `{1, -135},{1, -128}`
3. `{1, -83},{1, -145}`

The preceding positions are shown in the following screenshot:

Figure 7.14 – Common ContextAction buttons positioned

Now that we know about the functions we can use to change the looks of these **ContextAction** buttons, let us look at how we use these functions in a script. In the following code snippet, we will use the `:SetTitle()` and `:SetPosition()` functions for our previously made shop system. Please keep in mind that just the `beginAction()` function is shown, not the entire script:

```
function beginAction()
    -- Starting ContextAction
    ContextActionService:BindAction(ACTION_NAME,
    toggleShop, true, Enum.KeyCode.E, Enum.KeyCode.ButtonX)

    -- Changing Mobile Button
    ContextActionService:SetTitle(ACTION_NAME, "Shop")
    ContextActionService:SetPosition(ACTION_NAME,
    UDim2.new(1, -150, 1, -77))
end
```

In the preceding code snippet, we can see that both functions require two arguments. The first argument is the **action name**. This argument is required because there might be multiple **ContextAction** buttons; we do not want to change the title or position for all of them. The second argument specifies what we want to change our property to. For the title, this will be the text that will appear inside of the **ContextAction** button. As you might have guessed, the second argument for the `:SetPosition()` is the position the **ContextAction** button gets positioned to.

Now that we know how **ContextAction** buttons work, we know all the fundamentals of the `ContextActionService`. In the next section, we will compare all the learned input methods to figure out when to use which input.

Choosing how to listen to user input

The previous sections taught us many different ways to listen to user input. We started by looking into **ClickDetectors**, **ProximityPrompts**, and **tools**. All of these had their own use cases. After that, we looked at keyboard, gamepad, and mouse input using the `UserInputService`. Finally, we also learned about the `ContextActionService`, which was similar to the functions we have seen on the `UserInputService`. So, what do we use, and when?

First, we will take a look at ClickDetectors and ProximityPrompts. Both are very similar. ClickDetectors work when a player clicks on the BasePart that the ClickDetector is in. The ProximityPrompt shows a GUI when the player is near the BasePart that the ProximityPrompt is in. Unlike the ClickDetector, ProximityPrompts work based on key input, whereas ClickDetectors work on a *left mouse click* or something similar for consoles and phones. So, when choosing between ClickDetectors and ProximityPrompts, base it on whether you want the interaction to happen based on keys or clicks.

When we have something visual such as a flashlight, fireworks, a lawnmower, or anything else, use a tool. Tools have the most basic functionality that suits almost any interaction. However, sometimes you want to take your tools to the next level. For example, maybe you want your flashlight to turn on or off when the player presses the *E* key. This cannot be done by using just a tool. To do this, you need to use the `UserInputService` or `ContextActionService`. But how do we pick between both?

Both the `UserInputService` and the `ContextActionService` allow us to listen to specific keys using the `KeyCode` enum. As explained, we use the `ContextActionService` when there is any form of "context". This can be anything. Maybe the player needs to have an equipped tool, own a certain game pass, have a certain amount of money, and so on. If this is not the case, we use the `UserInputService`.

Let us put all of this information into a diagram to easily get an overview of when to pick what. You can see this here:

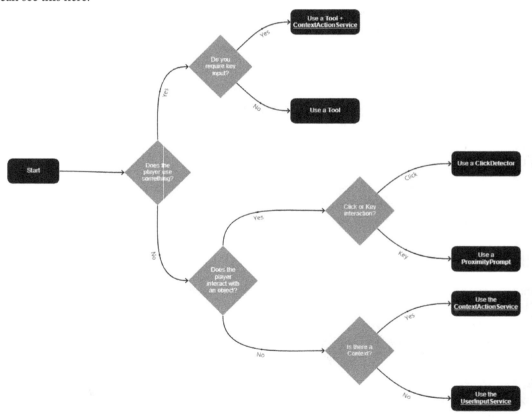

Figure 7.15 – User input decision visualized

We now know how to decide when to use different methods of listening to user input. In the next section, we will practice everything we learned throughout this chapter.

Exercise 7.1 – Eating food

In this exercise, we will combine a lot of the previously learned information about user input. The system you will have to make in this exercise will require some experimenting with combining certain features into one.

In this exercise, we will make `leaderstats` containing the number of pizzas a player has eaten. To eat a pizza, the player must equip the **Pizza** tool and hold their *left mouse button*, *X button* for gamepads, or *touch* their screen for at least 5 seconds. If the player holds their mouse for 3 seconds, for example, then stops and holds it for another 2 seconds, the pizza is not eaten. After a pizza has been eaten, the player can directly eat a new pizza.

A GUI will contain a progress bar that tells the player when to release their input. For phones, this progress bar should be displayed on the right side of the screen. However, for devices with a mouse, the progress bar needs to be displayed next to the mouse icon and the position should be updated every time the mouse moves.

Once the progress bar is full, a `RemoteEvent` has to be fired, which will increase the `leaderstats`. On the server, there needs to be at least two server checks. The first server check will be a 5-second cooldown, and the second one will ensure that this player has the **Pizza** tool equipped.

On the GitHub page for this book, we provided a **Fill In** version of this exercise, which contains the **Pizza** tool, GUI, and the `RemoteEvent` that you must use for this exercise.

There are multiple ways of implementing this system. There will be steps to make this system shown next. However, you are not required to follow these steps. If you know a better way or want to experiment yourself, feel free to try it yourself. Just make sure your system meets all the previously mentioned criteria.

Exercise

We will start by making the leaderstats for each player. Follow these steps:

1. Create a script in the `ServerScriptService` and give it a fitting name.
2. Listen to the `.PlayersAdded` event on the `Players` service and create a model with the name `leaderstats` inside of each `Player` object.
3. Inside of each `leaderstats` model, create an `IntValue` named **Pizzas Eaten**. Of course, you could change this name. However, we will keep referring to it as the **Pizzas Eaten** leaderstat.

We have now created our leaderstats. Next, we will set up a `RemoteEvent` that will increase these leaderstats, as follows:

1. Create a new script or continue with the previously made script.
2. Listen to the `.OnServerEvent` event on the `PizzaEaten` `RemoteEvent`. This `RemoteEvent` can be found in the **Events** folder inside the `ReplicatedService` service.

3. Create a cooldown that verifies that the player can only send a request once every 5 seconds.

    Tip for 3: If you have forgotten how cooldowns work, look at *Chapter 4, Securing Your Game*.

4. Create a **server check** that verifies the player is currently using the **Pizza** tool.

    Tip for 4: When a tool is in use, it is parented to the player's charactermodel.

5. Increment the **Pizzas Eaten** leaderstat by 1.

We have now ensured that our **Pizzas Eaten** leaderstat gets incremented once the `PizzaEaten` RemoteEvent gets fired. Next, we will start working on our **Pizza** tool located inside the `StarterPack` for the **Fill In** version. Proceed as follows:

1. Create a new `LocalScript` inside of the tool.

2. When the tool is equipped, the player should be able to start the 5-second timer. It is not allowed to use the `.Activated` event on the tool to register the input. Choose between using the `UserInputService` or `ContextActionService`. Ask yourself if you should always listen to this input to figure out what to use. Listen to the following enums:

    A. `Enum.UserInputType.MouseButton1`

    B. `Enum.KeyCode.ButtonX`

    C. `Enum.UserInputType.Touch`

    Tip for 2: Use the `.Equipped` event on the tool to see when the player equips it.

    To start a timer, store the starting time, using the `os.time()` function, in a variable. You can use this variable to calculate if the player held their key for at least 5 seconds.

3. When the tool is equipped, set the `Enabled` property on `EatingPizzaGui` to `true`.

4. When the tool is unequipped, set the `Enabled` property on `EatingPizzaGui` to `false`.

5. When the player starts giving input, a **Tween** on the **ProgressBar** frame, inside the GUI, should start. This Tween should have the following properties:

    A. `TargetPosition`: `UDim2.new(1, 0, 1, 0)`

    B. `EasingDirection`: `Out`

    C. `EasingStyle`: `Linear`

    D. **Duration**: 5

    E. **Override**: `true`

    Tip for 5: Use the `:TweenSize()` function on the **ProgressBar** frame.

6. When the player stops giving input, the **Size** value of the **ProgressBar** frame should change to `UDim2.new(1, 0, 0, 0)`.

   Tip for 6: To cancel a possible ongoing Tween, start a new Tween using the `:TweenSize()` function, which has the **Override** value set to `true`. Make sure this Tween has a duration of `0`.

7. When the player stops giving input, the **PizzaEaten** `RemoteEvent` should be fired, with no parameters. However, this event may only be fired if the player held their input for longer than 5 seconds.

   Tip for 7: To see if the player held their input for more than 5 seconds, use the previously made variable that stored the time of when the player began their input. The current time should be greater than the starting time plus the required hold duration.

8. When the tool is equipped, the **LocalScript** should check if this device has a connected mouse. If a mouse is connected to this device, the following sizes of the GUI should be changed:

   A. **ProgressFrame**: `UDim2.new(0, 10, 0, 30)`

   B. **ProgressSpace**: `UDim2.new(1, -4, 1, -4)`

9. To continue on from *step 8*, when the tool is equipped, and a mouse is enabled, the **ProgressFrame** should be repositioned every time the mouse moves. Choose between using the `UserInputService` or the `ContextActionService`. Ask yourself if you should always listen to this input to figure out what to use. Listen to the following enum:

   A. `Enum.UserInputType.MouseMovement`

   Tip for 9: To reposition the **ProgressFrame**, use the `:GetMouseLocation()` function on the **UserInputService** to get the position, in `Offset`, of the mouse.

10. When the tool is unequipped, all connections to the **UserInputService** or **ContextActionService** should be disconnected or unbinded.

We should now have the described system. However, it would be cool if something changed visually after a player ate their pizza. Inside the **Humanoid**, there are **NumberValues**—these are very similar to **IntValues** but allow decimal numbers. These **NumberValues** determine the size of the player's character model. It would be fantastic if these values increased every time the player ate. Doing this will result in the player growing in size every time they eat a pizza. The example answer on GitHub will include this feature.

Test the game to see if it works. Do not worry if you did not manage to complete parts of this exercise. This was a very large and complicated exercise. It is highly recommended that you try to do everything in the best possible way. Once you think you are done, take a look at the default example result and try to learn from it. Preferably, try to redo this exercise after that.

In the following screenshot, we can see what the exercise could look like for PC users:

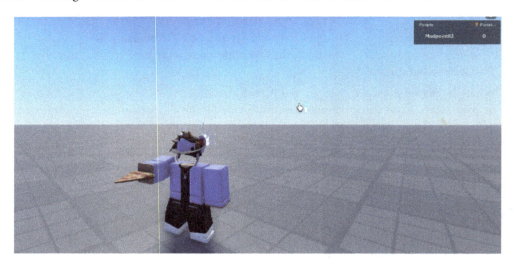

Figure 7.16 – Possible outcome for our system on PC

When playing on phones, the GUIs should look a bit different. In the following screenshot, we can see what it could look like:

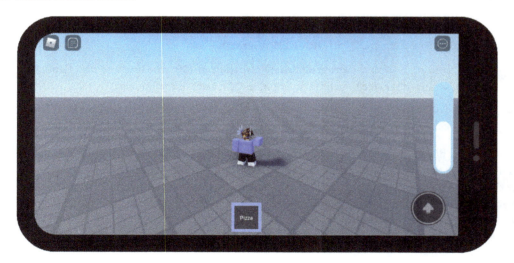

Figure 7.17 – Possible outcome for our system on a phone

An example solution for this exercise can be found on the GitHub page for this book, at https://github.com/PacktPublishing/Mastering-Roblox-Coding/tree/main/Exercises.

Summary

In this chapter, we learned so much about listening to user input. While we already knew how to listen to user input from **GUIs**, we can now make advanced systems that rely on user input. Throughout this chapter, we learned how to listen to user input from **ClickDetectors**, **ProximityPrompts**, and **tools**. All three of these allow us to easily listen to user input without worrying about the device that the user is playing on. Roblox handles all of these complexities for us.

When we looked into how ClickDetectors work, we learned more than just listening to user input. In addition to listening to user input, we learned how **leaderstats** work. We have seen how leaderstats allow us to easily display progress inside of the player list, which is a core GUI in every Roblox game. Besides leaderstats, we have also looked at the default particles that Roblox offers, such as **Explosions** and **Fire**.

Besides particles, we have also learned how to work with tools. In this chapter, we have made a very simple flashlight tool, with a **SpotLight** inside the handle, allowing us to light up our game during nighttime. To change the time in our game, we used the **Lighting** service that we had not used before.

Besides all of this, we have also learned how to listen to advanced user input using the **UserInputService.** While this service was not entirely new to us, we now have a much better understanding of its functions. We have learned how to listen to user input that comes from a keyboard, one or multiple gamepads, and a mouse. In addition, we learned about everything to keep in mind when doing this, such as checking whether this peripheral is even connected to the player's device.

While learning about gamepads, we have also learned how **HapticService** works. We have seen that **HapticService** allows us to enable **motors** inside of the gamepads. We have seen how these motors create a vibration inside the gamepad, allowing us to give players **haptic feedback**. We have seen that not every gamepad contains these motors. Because of this, we learned to check whether a controller has the specified motor before enabling it.

Finally, we have also looked into **ContextActionService.** We learned that **ContextActionService** allows us to easily listen to user input when a player is in a certain context. The biggest drawback we noticed when using **UserInputService** is that we always listen to user input. While we could make advanced checks that only listen to events when players are in a context, we have seen that **ContextActionService** makes all of this really easy.

We now know how to properly listen to user input by using various methods. In the next chapter, we will learn about **data stores**. Data stores will allow us to save player data even when they leave a game.

8
Building Data Stores

In this chapter, you will learn how to let players make progress in your game and continue building on this progress even if they decide to leave and rejoin the game. You will learn how to do this by using **data stores**. We will start with an introduction to data stores that will teach us the basics of how to save and load data. This will help us understand how data stores work. Once we know this, we will learn best practices to make our data stores safer and prevent data loss. Finally, we will learn how to use **ordered data stores**, which will allow us to make leaderboards that feature the best players of our game.

The following topics will be covered in this chapter:

- Introduction to data stores
- Writing safer data stores
- Working with ordered data stores
- Exercises

By the end of this chapter, you will know how to build data stores using best practices. You will know how to save, load, and remove data. In addition, you will know how to make proper error handling for these actions. You will understand the limitations that data stores have, such as size and request limits. While doing this, we will repeat many previously learned subjects, such as loops, modules, and custom events.

Technical requirements

To start programming with Luau, you need access to a device with internet access. This can be either a Windows or a Mac device.

You need to download the following software:

- Roblox Player
- Roblox Studio

All the code examples for this chapter can be found on GitHub at `https://github.com/PacktPublishing/Mastering-Roblox-Coding`.

The CiA video for this chapter can be found at `https://bit.ly/3cMQ3oR`.

Introduction to data stores

When playing a game, you build progress. This progress can range in measure from the amount of in-game currency to the amount of furniture in a house, to a purchased car, or to anything else. For example, when a player completes certain tasks in your game, they may be rewarded with some coins. These coins are in-game currency, which can be used to unlock various items, such as upgrades or accessories for their avatar.

The average playtime for Roblox games is around 8-20 minutes, depending on the quality and genre of your game. This means that there is a significant chance that players will not finish your game in one run. The problem is that every time the player rejoins your game, their progress is back at zero. This is something we do not want. So, we need to find a way to save the progress that the players of our game make so that they can continue to expand on what they have previously done once they decide to play our game for a second time.

So, how do we do this? Roblox has something called **data stores**. Data stores allow us to save and load data at any time. We can use these data stores to save the progress that players have made once they leave the game or to load it when they rejoin. This way, players can continue where they left off. Please keep in mind that data stores only work on the server. There are no client-side data stores.

Now that we know why we need data stores, let us figure out how they work. In the following sections, we will introduce the basics of data stores. We will learn how to save and load data. Besides this, we will practice creating data stores with many small examples.

Saving data

First, we will learn how to save data. After all, it makes no sense to load data if it is not there. Before we do this, we have to change the settings in Roblox Studio. Although data stores do not work inside Roblox Studio by default, they always work in real games. We will enable data stores in Roblox Studio for testing purposes by changing a specific setting. Follow these steps:

1. Open Roblox Studio and publish your game to Roblox

2. Then, open the **Game Settings** menu, as shown in *Figure 8.1*

3. Once this menu is open, go to the **Security** tab inside this menu and enable the **Enable Studio Access to API Services** setting

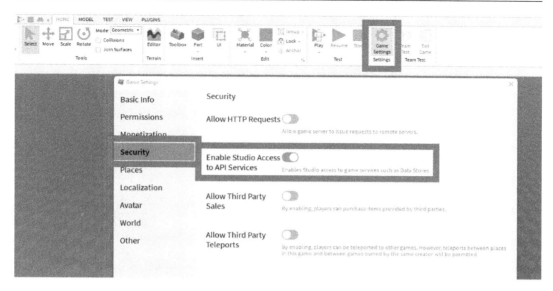

Figure 8.1 – Enabling the Studio API Access setting

Now that we can use data stores inside of Roblox Studio, let us start saving data. First, we need to know about the service that is used when working with data stores. This is the **DataStoreService**. The DataStoreService has all the primary functions that we use when loading and saving data.

So, how do we save data? First, we need to get a specific data store. We can save many different things that do not relate to each other at all. One data store might store all the player data, while another might have things related to game statistics; this is up to you. The following code snippet shows you how to get a specific data store:

```
local DataStoreService = game:GetService("DataStoreService")
local DataStoreTesting =
DataStoreService:GetDataStore("DataStoreTesting")
```

In the preceding example, we got the DataStoreTesting data store. When making a real system or game, please make sure your data stores name are related to their purpose.

Now that we have our actual data store, we can try to save something inside it. To save something inside of a data store, we use the :SetAsync() function on the data store. The :SetAsync() function had two primary arguments. The first argument is the **Key** and the second is the data you wish to save. Let us start by explaining what the Key argument is. So far, we have a data store. This data store is the same for every player in our game. We somehow need to differentiate data for each player. To do this, we use a key, which has to be unique for every player. Generally, to ensure that the Key is unique, we use the **UserId** of the player. After all, there can never be two players with the same UserId.

Now that we know about the two primary arguments of the :SetAsync() function, let us take a look at the following code snippet:

```lua
local Players = game:GetService("Players")
local DataStoreService = game:GetService("DataStoreService")

local DataStoreTesting =
DataStoreService:GetDataStore("LastPlayed")

function playerLeft(player)
    -- Saving the second the player leaves
    -- We can use this second to figure out the last time
    -- the player joined.
    DataStoreTesting:SetAsync(
        -- Key
        "Plr_" .. player.UserId,

        -- Data
        os.time()
    )
end

Players.PlayerRemoving:Connect(playerLeft)
```

In the preceding code snippet, we listen to the .PlayerRemoving event on the **Players** service. Often, developers choose to save data the moment that the player leaves. However, there are many other times we can choose to save the player data; we will get back to this in the *Autosaving* section of this chapter. For now, we will save the player data the moment that they leave.

In our preceding code example, we have a data store called LastPlayed. We use this data store to save the time that the player last played our game. When the player rejoins, we can use this data to calculate how many minutes, hours, or even days the player takes to rejoin our game. Obviously, this is just a simple example to explain what we can do with data stores. We will see much more interesting things we can do with data stores throughout this chapter.

In the code snippet, we used the :SetAsync() function with a Key that starts with Plr_ and ends with the UserId of the player. This ensures that the Key is always unique. The Plr_ part of the Key is used to inform developers that a UserId is used and not some other random number. The data that we save comes from the os.time() function, which we worked with when making server check debounces in *Chapter 4, Securing Your Game*. The result of this value is what we will use in later sections to calculate the last time the player joined, as explained previously.

> **Important note**
> If you used the preceding code snippet yourself, you most likely noticed that nothing happens when using this script. This is correct; do not worry about this for now.

We now know the basics of saving data in data stores. First, we had to get a specific data store using the `:GetDataStore()` function. Once we have our data store, we can use the `:SetAsync()` function, which requires a unique key and the data you wish to save. However, a lot can go wrong while trying to save data. Therefore, proper error handling is required. In the next section, we will learn how to do this.

Error handling

We saved data using the `:SetAsync()` function in the previous section. While this hopefully works fine, there are a lot of things that could go wrong while saving or loading data. A few examples of why data stores might fail are: saving data that cannot be stored in data stores, saving data that exceeds the size limit, saving or loading data too often, or maybe Roblox data stores going offline due to an outage. Anything can happen and it is our job to handle it. After all, we do not want our players to lose their progress.

So, how do we do this? In *Chapter 4*, *Securing Your Game*, we learned about the `pcall()` (**protected call**) function. This function is able to see what errors are happening without completely stopping the active thread. We can use this to print whatever error is happening so that we can change our scripts. Obviously, it would be better if we acted on whatever error happens; we will do this in the *Improving error handling* section, which goes more in-depth on error handling. For now, we will simply print the error that happens.

In the following code snippet, we can see how to use the `pcall()` function when using data stores:

```
local Players = game:GetService("Players")
local DataStoreService = game:GetService("DataStoreService")

local DataStoreTesting =
DataStoreService:GetDataStore("LastPlayed")

function playerLeft(player)
    -- Saving the second the player leaves
    -- We can use this second to figure out the last time
    -- the player joined.
    local suc, err = pcall(function()
        DataStoreTesting:SetAsync(
            -- Key
```

```
            "Plr_" .. player.UserId,

            -- Data
            os.time()
        )
    end)
    if not suc then
        warn(err)
    end
end


Players.PlayerRemoving:Connect(playerLeft)
```

The preceding code snippet is an improved version of what we saw in the previous section. In this code snippet, we have included our `pcall()` function. When an error happens, the `suc` variable will not be `true`. When the `suc` variable is `false`, it means that an error has occurred. The error message for the error that occurred is stored in the `err` variable.

Whenever an error happens, we get a warning in the **Developer Console** frame or the **Output** frame. From now on, we will be using the `pcall()` function whenever necessary. This includes setting and loading data.

We now know a lot can go wrong when using data stores. To get informed about what goes wrong, we use the `pcall()` function to print the error message without stopping the entire thread. So far, we have seen how to save data but we cannot do anything with it since it has never been loaded. In the next section, we will learn how to load data from a data store.

Reading data

So far, we know how to save data and how to print errors that might occur while this happens. However, saving data is useless if we never load it. So, how do we read data that is saved? To do this, we will use the `:GetAsync()` function on our data store. This way, the saved data can be read. Whatever the `:GetAsync()` function returns should be saved in a variable. Once we do this, we can use the loaded data.

Just as a lot can go wrong when saving data, the same is true for loading data. Therefore, we have to wrap our `:GetAsync()` function inside `pcall()` as well.

To see how loading and reading data from a data store works, let us look at the following code snippet. The following code snippet continues from the `LastPlayed` data store, which we made in previous sections:

```lua
local Players = game:GetService("Players")
local DataStoreService = game:GetService("DataStoreService")

local DataStoreTesting =
DataStoreService:GetDataStore("LastPlayed")

function playerJoined(player)
    -- Getting data from data store
    local currentPlayingSecond = os.time()
    local lastPlayingSecond = nil

    local suc, err = pcall(function()
        lastPlayingSecond = DataStoreTesting:GetAsync(
            -- Key
            "Plr_" .. player.UserId
        )
    end)
    if not suc then
        warn(err)
    else
        -- Using data
        print("It has been [" .. currentPlayingSecond -
        lastPlayingSecond .. "] seconds since you last
        played!")
    end
end

Players.PlayerAdded:Connect(playerJoined)
```

In the preceding code snippet, we used the :GetAsync() function on the DataStoreTesting data store, using the same key that we saved our data with. If you ran the saving data script before using this one, you should have seen a message telling you how many seconds it had been since you last played, as shown in *Figure 8.2*.

Figure 8.2 – Print displaying the seconds since you last played

If you get an error that includes something with nil, restart the game and try again; this should fix it. We will get back to the reason for this error in the next section.

> **Code snippet**
> In the preceding code snippet, the code related to saving data has been left out. The full script can be found on the GitHub page for this chapter.

We now know how to load the data previously saved in our data store using the :GetAsync() function. However, because a lot can go wrong while using the :GetAsync() function, we have to wrap this function in a pcall() function as well. Obviously, there won't be any data if a player joins for the first time ever; this could cause some errors. We can solve this by creating default player data. In the next section, we will learn how to do this.

Creating default player data

Every player has a moment when they join your game for the first time. Because you do not know if this is their first time or not, you use the :GetAsync() function in an attempt to load their data. Obviously, this function returns nothing when they have never played your game. When you try to use data that did not load, it usually results in some error as something essential is missing. This is why it is essential to use default player data when there is no data to load.

So, how do we make default player data? Well, it is actually not as complex as you might think. When the :GetAsync() function returns nil, just set your variable to something else or make an if statement that starts an alternative path. Let us take a look at the following code snippet to put what this means into context:

```
function playerJoined(player)
    -- Getting data from data store
    local currentPlayingSecond = os.time()
    local lastPlayingSecond = nil
```

```
    local suc, err = pcall(function()
        lastPlayingSecond = DataStoreTesting:GetAsync(
            -- Key
            "Plr_" .. player.UserId
        )
    end)
    if not suc then
        warn(err)
    else
        -- Using data
        if lastPlayingSecond ~= nil then
            print("It has been [" .. currentPlayingSecond
            - lastPlayingSecond .. "] seconds since you
            last played!")
        else
            print("It is your first time playing!")
        end
    end
end
```

We have the same system in the preceding code snippet as in the previous section. Please remember that this is just a section of the entire code snippet. The difference in this code snippet compared to the previous one is that we now check whether the `lastPlayingSecond` variable is `nil` or not. When this variable is `nil`, the system prints that it is the player's first time playing our game. This is a great example of a system that starts an alternative path when the loaded data is `nil`.

Another solution would've been to use default player data, as shown in the following code snippet:

```
if not suc then
    warn(err)
else
    -- Default Player Data
    if lastPlayingSecond == nil then
        lastPlayingSecond = currentPlayingSecond
    end

    -- Using data
```

```
        print("It has been [" .. currentPlayingSecond -
        lastPlayingSecond .. "] seconds since you last
        played!")
    end
```

In the preceding code snippet, we checked whether the `lastPlayingSecond` variable was `nil`. If it is `nil`, we set the `lastPlayingSecond` variable to the `currentPlayingSecond` variable. This will cause the system to tell us that we last played our game zero seconds ago.

It probably makes more sense to use the example where we printed that it was the player's first time playing. However, this is not always the case. For instance, when we make a system that loads and saves money, we do not want it to say that it is their first time playing. Instead, we would rather have the player receive 500 in-game coins to start the game with.

Throughout the previous sections, we learned how to save and load data using the `:SetAsync()` function and the `:GetAsync()` function. In addition, we learned how to handle possible errors that could occur while doing this. Finally, we also learned how to use default player data. In the next section, we will combine all of this knowledge and create a leaderboard that displays the amount of in-game money a player has, which is saved and loaded.

Making a saving money leaderboard

With all the previously learned information, we can now make a simple system that saves a player's money and shows it in a leader stat in the player list. This section will start by making the **leader stats**, as discussed in *Chapter 7, Listening to User Input*. Once we have our leader stats in place, we will load and save data using data stores. Finally, we will make a system that increases the amount of in-game money every minute.

Creating leader stats

As previously said, we will start by making our leader stats. Because we were taught how to do this, we will not go into full details on how to do this. However, here is the code snippet that we will use:

```
local Players = game:GetService("Players")

function playerJoined(player)
    -- Creating leader stats
    createLeaderStats(player)
end

function createLeaderStats(player)
    local leaderstats = Instance.new("Model")
```

```
        leaderstats.Name = "leaderstats"
        leaderstats.Parent = player

        local money = Instance.new("IntValue")
        money.Name = "🎖 Money"
        money.Parent = leaderstats
        money.Value = 0
end

function getLeaderstatValue(player, leaderstat)
        local leaderstats =
        player:FindFirstChild("leaderstats")
        if leaderstats ~= nil then
            local statistic =
            leaderstats:FindFirstChild(leaderstat)
            if statistic ~= nil then
                return statistic.Value
            else
                warn("Statistic named [" .. leaderstat .. "]
                does not exist!")
            end
        end
        return 0
end

function incrementLeaderstat(player, leaderstat, value)
        local leaderstats =
        player:FindFirstChild("leaderstats")
        if leaderstats ~= nil then
            local statistic =
            leaderstats:FindFirstChild(leaderstat)
            if statistic ~= nil then
                statistic.Value += value
            end
        end
```

```
end


Players.PlayerAdded:Connect(playerJoined)
```

In the preceding code snippet, we listen to the `.PlayerAdded` event at the bottom. Once a new player joins, the `playerJoined()` function starts. For now, the only thing this function does is call the `createLeaderStats()` function. This is nothing new compared to what we learned in *Chapter 7*, *Listening to User Input*.

However, there are two more functions that are worth mentioning. The `getLeaderstatValue()` function allows us to get the value of any leader stat easily. This function has a parameter named `leaderstat`, which makes the function useful in case we decide to add more leader stats in the future. Besides this function, there is an additional function we made. This is the `incrementLeaderstat()` function. As the name of this function implies, this function increments the value of a leader stat. Please keep in mind that this function will only be useful for **NumberValues** and **IntValues**.

We have now implemented our leader stats. We can continue building our system by saving and loading data using data stores now that we have this. After that, we will finish our system by incrementing the amount of money each player has every minute.

Using data stores

For our system, we will need a data store that saves the money that a player has. Because money is a currency, we will call our data store `CurrencyData`. The reason we give our data store such a general name will be explained later.

First, we will start by making the data save when the player leaves. Please keep in mind that this is just a portion of the code; all the code examples related to the money leaderboard are one script. The full script can be found on the GitHub page for this book.

Let us take a look at the following code snippet:

```
local Players = game:GetService("Players")
local DataStoreService = game:GetService("DataStoreService")


local CurrencyDataStore =
DataStoreService:GetDataStore("CurrencyData")


function playerLeft(player)
    local suc, err = pcall(function()
        local money = getLeaderstatValue(player, "💰
        Money")
        if money >= 0 then
```

```
        CurrencyDataStore:SetAsync(
            "Plr_" .. player.UserId,
            money
        )
    end
end)
if not suc then
    warn(err)
end
end
        )

Players.PlayerRemoving:Connect(playerLeft)
```

In the preceding code snippet, we listen to the .PlayerRemoving event. When this event fires, we start the playerLeft() function. This function uses the :SetAsync() function on our CurrencyDataStore and saves the player's current amount of money. However, if we look ahead, there might be an issue we could face. If something goes wrong while loading, we do not want to save this data. If we did save the data when it failed to load, it would override real data with data that did not load. This would be a massive issue. So, how can we stop this from happening?

We could make it so that our game does not allow players to have a negative balance. Then, we can use this constraint to our advantage. For example, we could set the player's amount of money to a negative number when it fails to load. This way, we can detect if something went wrong while loading their data. If we do this, we can conclude that something went wrong while loading when a player has a negative amount of money. As we do not want to override their real data, we just do not save it when it is negative. This is why we check if the money is equal to or greater than zero in the preceding code snippet.

Obviously, we still need to get this player's current amount of money. To do this, we use the getLeaderstatValue() function. We made this function in the previous section while creating our leader stats.

Now that we have saved our data, we should load it when a player joins. As learned in the previous sections, we will have to wrap our :GetAsync() function inside a pcall() function. However, when something goes wrong while loading data, we will kick this player out of the game and set their money to a negative number so that it does not save.

Let us take a look at the new playerJoined() function:

```
local STARTER_MONEY = 500

function playerJoined(player)
```

```
    -- Creating Leaderstats
    createLeaderstats(player)

    -- Loading Data
    local loadedCurrency = nil

    local suc, err = pcall(function()
        -- Getting data store value
        loadedCurrency = CurrencyDataStore:GetAsync("Plr_"
        .. player.UserId)
    end)
    if not suc then
        -- Printing error
        warn(err)

        -- Making leaderstat negative
        incrementLeaderstat(player, "🪙 Money", -
        (getLeaderstatValue(player, "🪙 Money") + 1))

        -- Kicking player
        player:Kick("\n[Data Failed]\nFailed to load data.
        Please rejoin")
    else
        -- Setting default data
        if loadedCurrency == nil then
            loadedCurrency = STARTER_MONEY
        end

        -- Setting leaderstat
        incrementLeaderstat(player, "🪙 Money",
        loadedCurrency)
    end
end
```

Please remember that the preceding code snippet is just a part of the entire script. At the beginning of the playerJoined() function, we start by making our leader stats. Once this is done, we start loading our data. First, we define a new variable named `loadedCurrency`. This variable will store the result of our `:GetAsync()` function. Then, we start our `pcall()` function. Inside of the `pcall()` function, we use the `:GetAsync()` function with the same key we used while saving data.

Once the `pcall()` function is done, we check whether an error occurred while loading the data from the data store. We use the `warn()` function to print the error if this is the case. After that, we increment the money leader stat with a negative number, which is the current amount of money plus one. This causes the amount of money that the player has to always be negative. For our current script, `-1` would have been enough to make the amount of money negative, as the default is `0`. However, if in the future something changes, which makes it so that the leader stat is not initialized on `0`, but `500`, for example, this script would still make it negative. After the money is set to a negative number, causing our `:SetAsync()` function to not save the player's data, we kick the player out of our game using the `:Kick()` function on the **Player** object.

However, most of the time, nothing goes wrong while loading data. If it successfully loads, we get to the `else` part of our `if` statement. Here, we check whether the `loadedCurrency` variable equals `nil`. If this is the case, it is the player's first time playing. When a player joins our game for the first time, they will be given `500` starter money. We can change the amount of starter money in our `STARTER_MONEY` constant variable, which is located at the top of our script. Finally, we increment the leader stat so that the player gets the same amount of money as the previous time they played.

> **Set versus increment**
>
> In our current example, we use the `incrementLeaderstat()` function to set the player's amount of money when joining. This only works if the leader stat is set to `0` by default. If this is not the case, you should consider writing a `setLeaderstat()` function, which sets the leader stat to a specific value rather than incrementing it.

We are now done with the basics of our system; we created our leader stats, saved and loaded the amount of money the player has, and updated the leader stat. We even implemented a way to prevent data loss by using negative numbers. However, we still need to give a player a way of earning money. We have chosen to give a player 10 coins for every 30 seconds they play. In the next section, we will see how to implement this.

Making a playtime reward

There are two common ways to implement a playtime reward. One option is to make a single `while` loop. We could implement this `while` loop in the `setup()` function that rewards each player every 30 seconds. This way, everyone in the game gets rewarded at the same time. The other option is to make a unique `while` loop for each player in our game. This would mean that players do not necessarily get rewarded simultaneously. Both solutions are OK. Whichever you decide to implement comes down to your gameplay or preference.

For this example system, we will choose to create an individual `while` loop for each player that joins our game. So, how do we implement this? There are many ways of implementing this. However, it is crucial to keep this system on the server only. When some developers hear that something has to be unique for each player, they instantly think of doing something partially on the client. Do not do this when it is directly involved with a data store. If you were to implement something like this partially on the client, you would have to make a **RemoteEvent**, which exploiters could abuse. While it is true that you could then protect this RemoteEvent, this is so much more work. So, how do we implement this system entirely on the server, while keeping it unique to each player?

We already have a function that gets called when the `.PlayerAdded` event gets fired. We can simply build on this function. Because every event creates a new thread, creating a `while` loop at the end of this function does not stop the rest of the script from running. Let us take a look at how to implement this:

```
local REWARD_INTERVAL = 30
local REWARD_AMOUNT = 10

function playerJoined(player)
    local suc, err = pcall(function()
        -- ...
        -- Previous code is left out to save space
        -- ...
    end)
    if not suc then
        -- ...
        -- Previous code is left out to save space
        -- ...
    else
        -- ...
        -- Previous code is left out to save space
        -- ...

        enablePlayingReward(player)
    end
end

function enablePlayingReward(player)
    while player:IsDescendantOf(Players) do
        task.wait(REWARD_INTERVAL)
```

```
        incrementLeaderstat(player, "🐾 Money",
        REWARD_AMOUNT)
    end
end
```

In the preceding code snippet, we have a new function named `enablePlayingReward()`. This function has a `while` loop that runs while the player is a descendant of the **Players** service. We check if the player is still a descendant of the **Players** service because we do not want to continue this loop after a player has left the game.

This function uses two global variables that are constant. These are the `REWARD_INTERVAL` constant and the `REWARD_AMOUNT` constant. We can easily change these constants to change the behavior of the playtime reward without having to look at the code itself.

It is important to understand that we have to call the `enablePlayingReward()` function at the end of the function. This is because the `while` loop keeps running until the player leaves the game. If you do not exactly understand why this is recommended, try placing a few `print()` statements after calling this function to see what happens. Please keep in mind that you need to start a **local server** instead of a **simulation**.

We have now finished a money leaderboard that actually loads and saves data using data stores. Congratulations if you managed to recreate the system yourself. If you could not follow every step, please take a look at the full script, which can be found on the GitHub page for this book. Data stores are complex and require a lot of practice. It is highly recommended to play around with data stores to truly understand how they work.

In the next section, we will learn how to save tables with data stores.

Saving tables

So far, we have only saved one single number for each player in one single data store. However, if we take a look at the limitations of data stores, we will see that each key in a data store can store up to 4 million characters. In comparison, if we save the number `100`, we only use three characters. This means we can use 3,999,997 more characters for this key. Therefore, it seems like a waste to only store one number or string per data store key.

Generally, developers tend to store more data in one data store. How would we store multiple strings or numbers in just one variable if we think outside of data stores? We would use a table. For data stores, we do the same. Instead of saving one string or number, we save an entire table. Unless you are storing a tremendous table, it will most likely not exceed the data store limit.

Maybe we have a survival game where players can craft tools. We might not want our players to lose their tools when they rejoin the game. The solution is to make a data store that saves all the tools that a player has in a table.

Let us take a look at how we would do this:

```lua
local Players = game:GetService("Players")
local DataStoreService = game:GetService("DataStoreService")

local BackpackDataStore =
DataStoreService:GetDataStore("BackpackData")

function playerJoined(player)
    -- Initializing tool dequip on reset
    initializeUnequipTools(player)
end

function playerLeft(player)
    -- Getting Tools
    local tools = getTools(player)

    -- Saving Tools
    local suc, err = pcall(function()
        BackpackDataStore:SetAsync(
            "Plr_" .. player.UserId,
            tools
        )
    end)
    if not suc then
        -- Printing error
        warn(err)
    end
end

function initializeUnequipTools(player)
    player.CharacterRemoving:Connect(function(character)
        local humanoid =
        character:FindFirstChildOfClass("Humanoid")
        if humanoid ~= nil then
            humanoid:UnequipTools()
        end
```

```
        end)
    end


    function getTools(player)
        -- Tools variable
        local tools = {}

        for _, tool in pairs(player.Backpack:GetChildren()) do
            if tool.ClassName == "Tool" then
                table.insert(tools, tool.Name)
            end
        end

        -- Returning Tools
        return tools
    end

    Players.PlayerAdded:Connect(playerJoined)
    Players.PlayerRemoving:Connect(playerLeft)
```

Let us analyze what is going on in the preceding code snippet. We start the `playerJoined()` function when a player joins the game. The only thing this function does is call the `initializeUnequipTools()` function. The reason we do not directly call this function is because we might want to do more when a player joins in the future.

The `initializeUnequipTools()` function starts listening to the `.CharacterRemoving` event. Every time the character resets, this event gets fired. When this happens, we unequip all the tools that a player has equipped right before the character actually gets removed. We do this because the character gets removed when the player leaves the game as well. However, the issue is that the character gets removed before the `.PlayerRemoving` event gets fired. Because of this, we cannot access the **Character** in the `playerLeft()` function. Because of this, we listen to the `.CharacterRemoved` event as a workaround.

Finally, when a player leaves the game, all the tools are inside the **Backpack**. After all, the character was removed and the `:UnequipTools()` button made sure all tools inside of the Character were now in the Backpack. The only thing left for us to do is loop through the Backpack and store all the instances with the tools' `ClassName` properties inside a table. All of this is done in the `getTools()` function, which gets called inside of the `playerLeft()` function.

After all of the tool names are stored in a table, we use the `:SetAsync()` function to update the data store and save all of the tools that a player has in their Backpack. When a player rejoins our game, we can use the `:GetAsync()` function to load all of their tools. In the preceding code example, this has not been done. However, feel free to practice doing this yourself.

We now know how to save tables inside of a data store. However, what about **dictionaries**? Can we save them in data stores as well? We will find out in the next section.

Saving dictionaries

In the previous section, we learned how to save tables. This allowed us to store more of the data of items that are related to each other in one data store. However, the data store limit is still way higher than that of the average table we make. So, what if we make a dictionary? This will allow us to store way more data that might not even be related. For instance, if we use a dictionary, we can save data related to player currency, statistics on how many times the player has played our game, and even more data.

Let us take a look at the following code snippet:

```
local Players = game:GetService("Players")
local DataStoreService = game:GetService("DataStoreService")

local TestDataStore =
DataStoreService:GetDataStore("DictionaryTest")

function playerLeft(player)
    local randomDictionary = {
        ["Coins"] = 5,
        ["Gems"] = 0,
        ["PlayTime"] = 0,
        ["TimesPlayed"] = 0
    }

    local suc, err = pcall(function()
        TestDataStore:SetAsync(
            "Plr_" .. player.UserId,
            randomDictionary
        )
    end)
    if not suc then
        warn(err)
```

```
        end
    end


Players.PlayerRemoving:Connect(playerLeft)
```

In the preceding code snippet, we save a random dictionary to prove that this works. A real-world example would look slightly different, as it would not be a static dictionary with fixed values. In the *Caching data* section later in this chapter, we will see more examples of how to properly do this.

Saving dictionaries is precisely the same as saving single data types and tables. However, this allows us to store way more data in one data store. Therefore, this method of saving data is preferred among all developers. Please keep in mind that if your data stores get very large, and certain data is not related to each other, it is perfectly fine to create a new data store altogether. There is no requirement to have all your data in one single data store. Feel free to choose something that works for your game. Just make sure you do not create unnecessary data stores.

Now that we know that saving dictionaries is possible and that this is the preferred way of saving data, we can move on to the next section. In the next section, we will learn how to save certain data types, such as **Color3** and **Vector3**.

Saving user data in data stores

Have you been practicing with data stores and received the following error: "104: Cannot store Dictionary in data store. Data stores can only accept valid UTF-8 characters?" Or, "104: Cannot store int in data store. Data stores can only accept valid UTF-8 characters?" You are most likely very confused. Basically, what is causing this error is that you are trying to save **user data** inside a data store.

Saving user data? What is wrong with that? I thought data stores were supposed to save the data of the players in our game? Yes, that is true. Unfortunately, this is not what user data means here. Throughout the chapters, we learned about many data types. We learned about three primary data types in *Chapter 1, Getting up to Speed with Roblox and Luau Basics*. These were **Strings**, **Numbers**, and **Booleans**. These are the data types that we can save inside data stores. Other data types such as **Vector3**, **Color3**, **BrickColor**, **Region3**, **TweenInfo**, **UDim2**, **CFrame**, and the other data types that we learned about, are considered to be user data. They cannot be saved in data stores.

Other than these, we cannot save instances or references to instances in data stores either. This means that we cannot save a certain chair that a player positioned on a certain spot, for example.

We might not be able to save all of this directly, but we have a workaround to save this data anyway. We need to convert whatever user data we are trying to save back to the three primary data types. For instance, a Vector3 data type consists of three numbers: **X**, **Y**, and **Z**. We could save these three numbers individually.

> **Data type properties**
>
> We are used to seeing that instances such as Parts or TextButtons have properties. However, data types can have properties as well. For instance, we can get the X-axis of a Vector3 by reading the **X** property, like this: print(Vector3.new(10, 20, 30).X).

Let us take a look at the following code snippet:

```
DataStore:SetAsync(
    "Plr_" .. player.UserId,
    {
        [1] = {
            ["item_type"] = workspace.PlacedItems.Chair,-->
            Error!
            ["position"] = Vector3.new(100, 200, 300) -->
            Error!
        },
        [2] = {
            ["item_type"] = "Chair", --> Allowed!
            ["position"] = {100, 200, 300} --> Allowed!
        }
    }
)
```

The preceding code snippet is the :SetAsync() function of a fictitious game where players can place anything they want in a game. In the code example, we are trying to save what the player has built so that they can continue building on it the next time.

In the preceding code snippet, we are trying to save a dictionary with two tables. Each table represents a placed object from the player. Both tables have two properties: item_type and position. The item_type property specifies what the player has placed in our game and the position property specifies where the player placed it. In the first table, we are trying to save a reference to the player's chair, combined with a Vector3 data type representing where the player tried to place it. Unfortunately, we cannot do this as we cannot save references, nor can we save user data in a data store. Therefore, this will result in an error.

In the second table, we take a different approach to our problem. Instead of trying to save a reference to the chair, we save the name of the object that the player has placed, which is a chair, in our current scenario. Besides this, we do not save a Vector3 data type. Instead, we use all three numbers that a Vector3 data type has and place them in a table. This time, there will be no error since we are not using a reference or user data in our second table. We can save what we stored in our second table.

Since we did not save a real `Vector3` data type as the position of our chair, we have to convert it back to a `Vector3` data type when we load the player's data for them. In the following code snippet, we can see how to do this:

```
local data = DataStore:GetAsync("Plr_" .. player.UserId)
local chairPosition = Vector3.new(
    data[2]["position"][1], --> 100
    data[2]["position"][2], --> 200
    data[2]["position"][3]  --> 300
)
```

In the preceding code snippet, we convert the position table of the previous code snippet into a `Vector3` data type. We do this because we could not save a `Vector3` data type, so we saved the **X**, **Y**, and **Z** numbers individually in a separate table.

In this section, we learned what user data is and that we cannot save these data types in data stores. We have seen what we can do as a workaround to save certain data types anyway. For instance, we have seen that we can split up a `Vector3` data type into three separate numbers that represent the **X**, **Y**, and **Z**-axis. Because these three axes are now normal numbers, we can store them inside the data store. This is because we can only save strings, numbers, and Booleans.

In previous sections, we have learned about getting data and setting it in data stores. However, what about removing data? In the next section, we will learn how to remove data from a data store.

Removing data

Sometimes we want to remove data from our data stores. There can be many reasons for this. For example, maybe we want to test what it would look like for a completely new player to join our game, or maybe we have to remove a player's data because of their **right to erasure** request.

Right to erasure

Everyone has the right to have their online data deleted. You can contact companies, including Roblox, to remove all the data that they have about you. If you do this, your Roblox account will be removed, and the developers that stored data about you in their data stores will be notified that they have to get rid of it. When we developers get these requests, we have to remove the data of the specified player.

So, how do we remove the data from a data store? In the previous sections, we have worked with the `:SetAsync()` function and the `:GetAsync()` function. However, there is another function, the `:RemoveAsync()` function. To remove all the data from a data store, we need to specify which key we want to remove the data from.

Let us take a look at the following code example:

```
local DataStoreService = game:GetService("DataStoreService")

local PrimaryDataStore =
DataStoreService:GetDataStore("PrimaryDataStore")
local SecondaryDataStore =
DataStoreService:GetDataStore("SecondaryDataStore")

function removeAllPlayerData(userId)
    local suc, err = pcall(function()
        PrimaryDataStore:RemoveAsync("Plr_" .. userId)
        SecondaryDataStore:RemoveAsync("Plr_" .. userId)
    end)
    if not suc then
        warn(err)
    end
end
```

In the preceding code snippet, we have two data stores. For now, they have been given general names, as this is just an example. We also have a `removeAllPlayerData()` function. This function uses the `:RemoveAsync()` function on all the data stores we have. We can use this function to remove all the data for a specific user, such as when we get a right to erasure request.

The only argument the `:RemoveAsync()` function requires is the key that we used in our data stores. When the `:RemoveAsync()` function is executed, the data is removed. However, Roblox keeps it for 30 more days before it is permanently removed. This does not mean that the `:GetAsync()` function still loads the data until these 30 days have passed, nor does it mean that you cannot set new data on this key. The `:RemoveAsync()` function simply sets all the data to `nil`.

We now know what the `:RemoveAsync()` function does and why it is useful. Besides this, we have learned about the right to erasure, which players of Roblox and those outside of Roblox have. Throughout the previous sections, we have learned all the basics about data stores. We learned how to read, set, and remove data. Besides this, we learned about error handling on data stores to prevent the entire thread from stopping if an error occurs. In addition, we learned how to use default player data when a player joins for the first time.

However, we also learned that a lot could go wrong while working with data stores. Therefore, we must ensure they work correctly. We can implement many more tricks and best practices to ensure that our data stores become safer. In the following sections, we will learn how to do this.

Writing safer data stores

We will learn helpful best practices to keep in mind when creating data stores in the upcoming sections. These best practices will assist us in the small chance that something goes wrong, which hopefully occurs as infrequently as possible! However, even though it might not occur as often, we still need to prepare for when it happens.

In this section, we will expand on our knowledge about saving tables and dictionaries by learning how to cache data. After that, we will improve our data stores by making our data stores autosave. We will also learn how to improve our error handling by implementing retries. Once we understand this, we will learn more about the limitations that data stores have.

The previously mentioned improvements will greatly improve the quality of our data stores. However, all these improvements will make our scripts very lengthy. If we were to have multiple scripts that handled our data stores, we would have a lot of duplicate code. This is a bad practice. To prevent this, we will learn how to create a **DataManager** module, which will ensure that all the complexities of our data stores are covered in a standalone module. Finally, we will also learn how to improve our data stores when multiple servers are trying to update the same player's data.

Caching data

In the previous sections, we learned that it is preferable to use tables or dictionaries. However, we have not exactly seen how we make these tables or dictionaries. The reason for this is that we cache these tables or dictionaries.

But what is **caching**? In our scenario, we use caching to store data inside a table rather than constantly getting it using the `:GetAsync()` function. This means that we will have a dictionary called `playerData` near the top of our script, which will hold all the data for each player that is in-game. Then, when we have to change this player's data, we simply change it in the `playerData` dictionary. Finally, when we have to save the player's data, we read what is inside the `playerData` dictionary and save it.

To keep it clear, we will first take a look at the code snippet related to loading data. Once we understand this, we will continue by taking a look at how to update and save the data. Let us take a look at the first code snippet:

```
local Players  = game:GetService("Players")
local DataStoreService = game:GetService("DataStoreService")
local DataStore = DataStoreService:GetDataStore("PlayerData")

local DEFAULT_PLAYER_DATA = {
    ["coins"] = 500,
    ["gems"] = 0,
```

```lua
        ["times_played"] = 0
}

local playerData = {}

function playerJoined(player)
    -- Getting and Caching data
    playerData[player.Name] = get(player)
end

function get(player)
    local loaded = nil
    local suc, err = pcall(function()
        loaded = DataStore:GetAsync("Plr_" ..
        player.UserId)
    end)
    if not suc then
        warn(err)
    end
    --
    if loaded == nil then
        return copyTable(DEFAULT_PLAYER_DATA)
    else
        return loaded
    end
end

function copyTable(toCopy)
    local copy = {}

    -- Looping through toCopy table
    for i, v in pairs(toCopy) do
        if typeof(v) == "table" then
            -- Copying nested table/dictionary
            v = copyTable(v)
        end
```

```
        -- Inserting value into copied table
        copy[i] = v
    end

    return copy
end


Players.PlayerAdded:Connect(playerJoined)
```

Let us take a look at the preceding script. The `playerJoined()` function gets called when a player joins the game. Inside of this function, we use the `get()` function that we made. The `get()` function returns the result of the `:GetAsync()` function. This is nothing new. However, at the bottom of the `get()` function we use the `copyTable()` function.

Why do we make a copy of the `DEFAULT_PLAYER_DATA` variable? If we did not do this, we would update both the `playerData` dictionary and the `DEFAULT_PLAYER_DATA` table when a player does not have data. This is something that may sound very weird. After all, we are not even updating the `DEFAULT_PLAYER_DATA` variable; we are updating the player data.

Let us take a look at the following piece of code:

```
-- Normal variable behavior
local variableA = 5
local variableB = variableA
variableB += 1
print(variableA) --> Still 5
print(variableB) --> 5 + 1 = 6

-- Table behavior
local tableA = {5}
local tableB = tableA
tableB[1] += 1
print(tableA[1]) --> 6
print(tableB[1]) --> 6
```

When `variableB` is set, a copy of the value in `variableA` is made. However, this is not what happens when using tables. When you reference a table, it simply uses the same table in the memory of Luau instead of copying the entire table. Therefore, we have to manually copy tables ourselves.

Now that we know this behavior of tables, let us continue with the previous code example. Once we return the loaded data or a copy of the DEFAULT_PLAYER_DATA variable, we save this inside of the playerData variable. This way, the player data is cached.

Now, if we want to update the data for the player, we can change it inside of the playerData variable. Let us take a look at the second code snippet for our script:

```
function playerJoined(player)
    -- Getting and Caching data
    playerData[player.Name] = get(player)

    -- Updating times_played
    playerData[player.Name]["times_played"] += 1
    print(playerData[player.Name]["times_played"])
end

function playerLeft(player)
    -- Saving data
    save(player)

    -- Removing cached data
    playerData[player.Name] = nil
end

function save(player)
    local suc, err = pcall(function()
        DataStore:SetAsync(
            -- Key
            "Plr_" .. player.UserId,
            -- Cached data
            playerData[player.Name]
        )
    end)
    if not suc then
        warn(err)
    end
```

```
end

Players.PlayerAdded:Connect(playerJoined)
Players.PlayerRemoving:Connect(playerLeft)
```

In the `playerJoined()` function, we now increment the `times_played` statistic by 1. This way, our statistics are updated inside our cached `playerData` variable. Even though the changes are made in our variable, and not in the data store directly, they still get saved. This is because of the `playerLeft()` function. Here, we call the `save()` function that uses the `:SetAsync()` function. As a result, our cached data gets updated in the data store.

We have now seen a full example of a working data store script that uses caching. In the next section, we will learn how to make our data stores **autosave**.

Autosaving

One of our current script's flaws is that it only saves the data when the player leaves the game. Because a lot can go wrong while saving data, relying on just one save attempt is a bad idea. A solution for this is to save while the player is still in-game. For instance, we could decide to save the player data once every 30 seconds. Let us implement this:

```
local AUTO_SAVE_INTERVAL = 30

function autoSave()
    while true do
        -- Waiting for auto-save interval
        task.wait(AUTO_SAVE_INTERVAL)

        -- Getting players
        for _, player in pairs(Players:GetPlayers()) do
            -- Checking if data is cached
            if playerData[player.Name] ~= nil then
                -- Auto-Saving
                task.spawn(function()
                    save(player)
                end)
            end
        end
    end
```

```
        end
    end


task.spawn(autoSave)
```

The preceding code snippet is just a section of the entire script. Everything related to autosaving is supposed to be in the same script we saw in the *Caching data* section.

In the preceding code snippet, we have a new function named `autoSave()`. This function has a `while` loop that runs forever. Inside of this `while` loop, we loop through all the players that are currently in-game. Then, we call the `save()` function for each of these players. This results in all the cached data being saved every 30 seconds. It is not such a big deal if something goes wrong while saving. After all, we will retry in 30 seconds anyway.

There is one more thing that is worth mentioning. Instead of directly calling the `autoSave()` function and the `save()` function, we call them inside of the `task.spawn()` function. The `task.spawn()` function creates a new thread. If we did not create a new thread for this, anything after the `autoSave()` function would never run. This is because we have an infinite `while` loop inside of the `autoSave()` function. The same thing applies to the `save()` function. If we did not do a thread, the autosaving would work on one player at a time, whereas it works on all of them pretty much simultaneously now.

We now know how to autosave our data. In addition, we learned how to create our own thread using the `task.spawn()` function when calling another function. In the next section, we will learn how to improve our error handling using **retries**.

Improving error handling

So far, we have improved our data stores by adding autosaves. This greatly improves the safety of our data stores. However, there is one thing we already do that we could improve. This is our error handling. Currently, we use the `pcall()` function to detect whether or not an error occurred. Yet, the only thing we do with this information is print it into the **Output** frame. So, what else could we do? We could use **retries**.

A retry is basically a `repeat` loop that repeats a certain function until it works. This means we have a repeat loop that has a condition based on the result of the `pcall()` function. Then, when the `pcall()` function detects that an error has occurred, we simply retry it. This does not sound that complicated, right? Let us take a look at the following code snippet:

```
function get(player)
    local loaded = nil
    local suc, err
    --
```

```
    repeat
        suc, err = pcall(function()
            loaded = DataStore:GetAsync("Plr_" ..
            player.UserId)
        end)
        if not suc then
            -- Printing warning
            warn(err)

            -- Small wait period in between retries
            task.wait(6)
        end
    until
    suc
    --
    if loaded == nil then
        return copyTable(DEFAULT_PLAYER_DATA)
    else
        return loaded
    end
end

function save(player)
    local suc, err
    repeat
        suc, err = pcall(function()
            DataStore:SetAsync(
                -- Key
                "Plr_" .. player.UserId,

                -- Cached data
                playerData[player.Name]
            )
        end)
        if not suc then
            -- Printing warning
```

```
        warn(err)

        -- Small wait period in between retries
        task.wait(6)
      end
    until
    suc
  end
```

We see the `get()` function and the `save()` function in the preceding code snippet. This time, we have modified them so that they include a `repeat` loop. This `repeat` loop simply repeats the entire function until the `suc` variable is set to `true`. Please remember that you have to declare a new variable for `suc` and `err` before you start the `repeat` loop. This is because of the scope of the `until` condition.

There is one more thing that we have added to both the `get()` function and the `save()` function. Besides just printing the error that has occurred, we now also wait six seconds. This is because we do not want to retry the same operation instantly.

We have now seen how to improve our error handling by retrying the function when an error occurs. We do this by using a `repeat` loop. Before retrying, we first wait six seconds. This is because of data store limitations. In the next section, we will learn more about data store limitations.

Data store limitations

In the *Saving tables* section, we talked about the size limit of data stores. This was 4 million characters per data store. However, there are many more limitations. Some of these limitations are related to how often we can use the `:GetAsync()` function, the `:SetAsync()` function, and the `:RemoveAsync()` functions. Let us take a look at *Table 8.1*:

Functions	Limitation (per minute)
`:GetAsync()` – any Key	60 + (players in-game x 10)
`:SetAsync()` – any Key	60 + (players in-game x 10)
`:UpdateAsync()` – any Key	
`:RemoveAsync()` – any Key	
`:SetAsync()` – same Key	6 seconds cooldown
`:UpdateAsync()` – same Key	
`:RemoveAsync()` – same Key	

Table 8.1 – Data store limitations

Please keep in mind that the data in *Table 8.1* is as of writing this book. These limitations could change in the future. For the most up-to-date information, please view the developer documentation here: `https://create.roblox.com/docs/scripting/data/data-stores#limits`.

In *Table 8.1*, we can see the limitations per key. When functions are in the same column, they share the same limitation limit. This means the same limit goes down when using the `:SetAsync()` function and the `:RemoveAsync()` function. Something else we can see in *Table 8.1* is that some functions have a six-second cooldown between requests. In the previous section, *Improving error handling*, we had a `task.wait()` function that waits for six seconds for this exact reason.

We now know what the limitations are. Even though we already have a wait of six seconds, multiple requests might overlap, causing the request to queue until there is a **budget**. The problem with this is that this queue can be full. When this happens, an error is thrown.

So, how would we prevent this? There is a function called `:GetRequestBudgetForRequestType()` that knows how many times each function is called. This data is then used to give us a budget. This budget tells us whether or not there is space for this request to happen. Let us take a look at the following code snippet:

```
function save(player)
    -- Waiting for budget
    yieldUntilBudget(Enum.DataStoreRequestType.SetIncrement
    Async)
    --                 Enum.DataStoreRequestType.GetAsync
    --                 Enum.DataStoreRequestType.UpdateAsync


    -- Saving data
    local suc, err
    repeat
        suc, err = pcall(function()
            DataStore:SetAsync(
                -- Key
                "Plr_" .. player.UserId,
                -- Cached data
                playerData[player.Name]
            )
        end)
        if not suc then
            -- Printing warning
            warn(err)
```

```
            -- Small wait period in between retries
            task.wait(6)
        end
    until
    suc
end


function yieldUntilBudget(dataStoreRequestType)
    while
        DataStoreService:GetRequestBudgetForRequestType(
        dataStoreRequestType) <= 0
    do
        task.wait(1)
    end
end
```

In the preceding code snippet, we have a new function named yieldUntilBudget(). This function has a while loop that waits until the :GetRequestBudgetForRequestType() function returns a number greater than 0. We do this because the :GetRequestBudgetForRequestType() function returns the number of requests that we can make for a certain DataStoreRequestType based on the limitations we have seen before.

Inside the save() function, we execute the yieldUntilBudget() function, before starting with the :SetAsync() function. This way, we never execute the :SetAsync() function without having the budget for it. Please remember that you have to provide the yieldUntilBudget() function with the correct DataStoreRequestType enum. This means we have to give the GetAsync enum when we use the :GetAsync() function, and so on.

We now know about the data store limitation requests. In addition, we learned how to use the :GetRequestBudgetForRequestType() function so that we can yield before attempting to execute a function on the data store. In the next section, we will take a look at the advantages of creating a **DataManager**.

Creating a DataManager

The number of functions related to data stores is starting to grow rapidly. If we also want to add game logic into the same script, such as increasing statistics for the number of times they played our game, the script starts growing even further. Most developers create a DataManager or something with a similar name to prevent this.

This `DataManager` is simply a module containing all the functions related to data stores. We have a few functions that other scripts can call, such as `:Get()`, `:Set()`, and `:Increment()`. The module itself will handle errors, data store limitations, (auto)saving, and caching. This way, scripts can use the `DataManager` without worrying about any of the complexities that come with it. Let us take a look at what a snippet of the `DataManager` could look like:

```
local DataManager = {}

local DataLoadedEvent = Instance.new("BindableEvent")

function playerJoined(player)
    -- Getting and Caching data
    playerData[player.Name] = get(player)

    -- Firing data loaded event
    DataLoadedEvent:Fire(player)
end

function setupEvents()
    DataManager["PlayerAdded"] = DataLoadedEvent.Event
end

function DataManager:DataLoaded(player)
    -- Checking if the data was loaded already
    return playerData[player.Name] ~= nil
end

function DataManager:Set(player, key, value)
    -- Checking if data is loaded
    if DataManager:DataLoaded(player) ~= true then
        error("[Data Not Loaded]: Use the
        DataManager.PlayerAdded event in favor of the
        Players.PlayerAdded event!")
    end

    -- Setting data
    playerData[player.Name][key] = value
```

```
end


return DataManager
```

As mentioned, this DataManager is just a snippet of what the entire script looks like. You can find the entire script on the GitHub page for this book.

Let us cover what makes this DataManager unique. The first thing to notice is that we made a **custom event** inside this module. This event is called .PlayerAdded. In *Chapter 3*, *Event-Based Programming*, we explained how our modules could make custom events using **BindableEvents**. If you skipped these sections before, you should read them before continuing with this chapter.

The reason we made a custom .PlayerAdded event is because this DataManager uses the :GetAsync() function with retries and yields for a budget. Because this might take some time, the data might not load instantly. Therefore, it is recommended to listen to the DataManager.PlayerAdded event instead of the Players.PlayerAdded event. When you do this, you never handle players without data. Thus, there can be no data loss.

The :Set() function we see in the preceding code snippet also checks whether the data has loaded before attempting to set the data. Once again, this is to prevent possible data loss in case the developer decides to listen to the Players.PlayerAdded event anyway. When the :Set() function gets called before the data is loaded, it uses the error() function. We have not seen this function before. This function, as the name implies, gives an error. This means that you have to use pcall() when calling the :Set() function as it might give an error.

We have now seen a portion of a DataManager module. Once again, on the GitHub page for this book, you can find all the code for this DataManager, which includes the missing functions. Besides this, it also includes additional functions, such as: :Get() and :Increment(). While learning about a DataManager, we have seen another use case for **custom events**. Besides this, we have also seen how to give a real error using the error() function. In the next section, we will learn about the :UpdateAsync() function.

Setting versus updating data

In previous sections, we learned how to set data using the :SetAsync() function. However, this function has some major problems when we start looking at scenarios where player data might be changed on different servers.

Let us imagine a scenario where a player has 500 coins. Our game has a feature that allows players to donate to other players that are not currently in-game or on different servers. If we decide to donate them, we would use the :GetAsync() function to get the current money this player has. Then, we would increment this by 100 using the :SetAsync() function. The new amount of money the player has would be 600.

However, the problem is that the player who received the donation is currently playing our game. This player joined the game having 500 coins. While they were playing, they earned 10 coins, which would make their new balance 510. However, this player does not know that they were given 100 extra coins. This is because we never used the :GetAsync() function to see if our 500 coins were still up to date.

Finally, the player decides to leave with a total of 510 coins. We use the :SetAsync() function to save this new balance. Doing this would override the data store that currently holds a balance of 600 coins, as they got donated. The final result: the player did not lose the money that they earned while playing. However, they never received their donation, as it got overwritten. In addition, the player that donated might have paid Robux for this donation, which was never received.

So, how would we fix this previously described problem? We could use the :GetAsync() function before every time we try to save. However, doing this also has a very slim chance of something going wrong. Potentially, another server could update the data between you running your :GetAsync() function and your :SetAsync() function. While there is a very slim chance of this happening, it is possible. So, if this is not good either, what are we supposed to do?

Instead of using the :SetAsync() function, we should use the :UpdateAsync() function. The first thing the :UpdateAsync() function does is get the current data from the data store. Then, you are able to change this retrieved data and set it, all of this while preventing other :SetAsync() functions from happening in between.

OK, this sounds really complex. Let us take a look at how the :UpdateAsync() function works with a code example:

```
SomeDataStore:UpdateAsync(
    -- Key
    "Plr_" .. player.UserId,

    -- Update function
    function(oldData)
        -- Getting current data
        local data = oldData or 0

        -- Updating data
        data += 1

        -- Returning new data
        return data
    end
)
```

In the preceding code snippet, we use the `:UpdateAsync()` function on `SomeDataStore`. This is a random data store that we will use for this example.

In the code snippet, we can see that the first argument of the `:UpdateAsync()` function is the key. This is the same key we use when using the `:SetAsync()` function and the `:GetAsync()` function. However, the second argument is a function. This function has a parameter named `oldData`. The `oldData` parameter contains the current data in the data store. You could see this as the result of the `:GetAsync()` function.

Once we have our `oldData` parameter, we have to check whether it is `nil` or not. If it is `nil`, the player has never joined our game. This means that we will have to use default player data instead. In our current scenario, the default player data is the number `0`. We set this default player data using the `or` operator. In the previous sections, we used an `if` statement to see whether it was `nil` or not. However, we can write this shorter by using `or`. If we use `or`, we must specify the most important data first. In our current example, the most important data is the `oldData` variable. However, if this `oldData` is `nil`, the `or` operator will make sure that we use our backup data, which is the number `0` in the current scenario.

In essence, the `or` operator and the full `if` statement are the same. The `or` operator is just shorter. To prove that the `or` operator works, execute the following code: `print(nil or 5)`. This should print the number 5, as the first piece of data is `nil`.

We now have our old data, which is a random number. The point of our `:UpdateAsync()` function is to increment this number by 1. We do this by doing `data += 1`. This will increment our data variable by 1. Once we have updated our data, we return it. Doing this will result in the data store being updated with the new data.

> **Aborting :UpdateAsync()**
>
> Sometimes you are updating the data but then it turns out that you do not want to change it. An example of when this happens could be to prevent players from getting a negative balance. In that scenario, you might want to abort your update. To do this, you can simply return `nil` at any point to cancel the update.

We now know how to use the `:UpdateAsync()` function. In addition, we have seen what makes this better than using both the `:GetAsync()` function and the `:SetAsync()` function when your game manipulates other players' data.

We went from having almost no knowledge about data stores to writing complex and safe data stores throughout all the previous sections. We learned how to make a DataManager module that features data caching, autosaving, retries, and budget yielding, all of this is to save data for players. However, Roblox has more than just data stores. They also have ordered data stores. In the next section, we will learn more about this.

Working with ordered data stores

In the previous sections, we have worked with regular data stores. However, sometimes we want to make a leaderboard with the wealthiest players for our game. It is going to be very difficult to load all the data for all the players that played our game from these regular data stores. Luckily, there is a different type of data store, ordered data stores.

As the name implies, these ordered data stores have the ability to order all the data. This means we can use a single function to get the top 25 players. Since it is another data store, we have to use the :SetAsync() function to fill this ordered data store. Because this entire data store is just for a leaderboard, there is no need to save this every 20 seconds. It is enough to update this when the player leaves. After all, there can be no data loss, as it is simply a copy of the real data store.

> **Important note**
> Never use the :UpdateAsync() function when using ordered data stores. As mentioned, ordered data stores contain a value that is copied from the real data store. The real data store should handle all of the complexities that were explained in the previous section.

Let us take a look at how ordered data stores work. We will split the script that handles the ordered data stores in half. First, we will take a look at how we update data in the ordered data store. Once we understand this, we will take a look at how to read the data from an ordered data store:

```
local RichestPlayers =
DataStoreService:GetOrderedDataStore("RichestPlayers")
local DataManager = require(PATH_TO_DATAMANAGER)
local LEADER_BOARD_SIZE = 25

function updatePlayer(player)
    -- Getting coins
    local coins = nil
    local suc, err = pcall(function()
        coins = DataManager:Get(player, "coins")
    end)

    -- Checking if data was retrieved
    if coins ~= nil then
        yieldUntilBudget(Enum.DataStoreRequestType
        .SetIncrementSortedAsync)
        local suc, err
```

```
        repeat
            suc, err = pcall(function()
                RichestPlayers:SetAsync(
                    player.UserId,
                    coins
                )
            end)
            if not suc then
                warn(err)
                task.wait(6)
            end
        until suc
    end
end
```

Please remember that the `yieldUntilBudget()` function, some global variables, and the events have been left out of this code snippet. You can find the complete script on the GitHub page for this book.

Let us take a look at the preceding code snippet. Something worth mentioning is that we use the `:GetOrderedDataStore()` function instead of the `:GetDataStore()` function. Now that we know this, let us take a look at the `updatePlayer()` function. This function is responsible for updating the ordered data store. One of the things we can see is that we use most of the previously learned practices, such as yielding for budget and retries for ordered data stores as well. Please remember that we need to use the `SetIncrementSortedAsync` enum instead of the `SetIncrementAsync` enum when working with data stores.

Other than the previously mentioned differences, it is very similar to how we would update normal player data. The real difference comes when we want to retrieve the data from the data store. Let us take a look at the second code snippet for this script:

```
function printRichestPlayers()
    yieldUntilBudget(Enum.DataStoreRequestType
    .GetSortedAsync)

    -- Getting richest players
    local richest = {}
    local suc, err
    repeat
        suc, err = pcall(function()
            local ascending = false
```

```lua
            local pages =
            RichestPlayers:GetSortedAsync(ascending,
            LEADER_BOARD_SIZE)
            local page = pages:GetCurrentPage()
            --
            for rank, data in pairs(page) do
                -- Declaring data
                local userid = data.key
                local coins = data.value
                local username = "[ Account Deleted ]"

                -- Getting username
                pcall(function()
                    username =
                    Players:GetNameFromUserIdAsync(userid)
                end)

                -- Updating richest table
                richest[rank] = {["username"] = username,
                ["coins"] = coins}
            end
        end)
        if not suc then
            warn(err)
            task.wait(6)
        end
    until suc


    -- Printing table
    print(richest)
end
```

Now, let us take a look at the `printRichestPlayers()` function. Here, we start by calling the `yieldUntilBudget()` function as well. After that, we make a new variable named `richest`. This variable will be a table containing a dictionary. This table will be sorted with the top 25 richest players. To get these players, we use the `:GetSortedAsync()` function. However, the difference compared to the `:GetAsync()` function is that the `:GetSortedAsync()` function returns **pages** instead of a table.

You could compare pages to models. A model in **Workspace** groups a few instances, such as parts, together. Pages do the same. However, instead of parts, they hold one or more pages. This page is usually a table. Inside the `printRichestPlayers()` function, we get the pages by calling the `:GetSortedAsync()` function. Then, to get the first page, we use `:GetCurrentPage()`. This is all we need to know for now.

Once we have a page, we loop through it using a `for` loop. Because we use a `for` loop, we get an `index` variable and a `value` variable. We have renamed these `rank` and `data`. After all, the index is the rank of the player in the top 25, since the `:GetSortedAsync()` function has sorted this for us. The `data` variable is a dictionary that consists of a `key` and a `value`. `key` is the key we used when we called the `:SetAsync()` function. As you might have guessed, the `value` variable is the value that we set when using the `:SetAsync()` function. In our scenario, this is the number of coins that the player has.

Since we might use this data to create a leaderboard, we somehow need to get the username of the player to whom this data belongs. The thing is that we never stored their username. However, we do have the UserId since this is the key we used. In the **Players** service, there is a function called `:GetNameFromUserIdAsync()`. This function allows us to get the username based on a UserId.

You might be wondering, why did we make a new `pcall()` function inside of something that is already in a `pcall()` function? This is because the `:GetNameFromUserIdAsync()` function might give an error when the UserId is incorrect or if the user does not exist anymore. We do not want the entire function to fail and retry forever simply because a username cannot be found.

We have now seen how ordered data stores work. In addition, we have seen that we need to apply some of the previously learned best practices, such as retries, and yielding for a budget to ordered data stores as well. Throughout the previous sections, we learned a lot about data stores and ordered data stores. In the next section, we will practice making data stores from scratch.

Exercise 8.1 – Building and testing data stores

We will create a `DataManager` module from scratch by following a few steps in this exercise. You can use the example `DataManager` that we made earlier in the chapter to help you. However, it is highly recommended that you try to mix whatever you have learned from the individual sections.

Once we have created our `DataManager`, we will create a server script that handles incoming requests to purchase tools. This way, we learn how to verify incoming requests from a client that is directly involved with the data stores.

Exercise

We will start by making our DataManager module. Follow these steps:

1. Create a new **ModuleScript** inside of the **ServerScriptService** service and name it `DataManager`.

2. Inside `DataManager`, create a table named `DataManager` at the top of the script and return this table at the bottom of the script.

3. Declare a new variable named `DataStore` with the name `PlayerData` using the `:GetDataStore()` function.

4. Declare a new variable named `playerData` and set it to an empty table. This table will contain all the cached player data.

5. Declare a new constant named `DEFAULT_PLAYER_DATA`. This constant will be our default player data. Make sure the default player data has the following values:

   - `coins = 500`

   - `tools = {}`

6. Create a function named `get()`. This function gets the `player` parameter.

   The function will return the data that is loaded from the data store using the `:GetAsync()` function. Make sure the function uses the following best practices: retries and budget yielding. When the `:GetAsync()` function returns `nil`, return a table copy of the `DEFAULT_PLAYER_DATA` table.

   Tip for 6: Create a new function called `yieldUntilBudget()`. Copy the `copyTable()` function that we have seen throughout this chapter. You do not have to write it yourself. This is such a standard function. Tip: Save this function somewhere on your PC; you never know when you will need it.

7. Create a function named `save()`. This function gets the `player` parameter. The function will save the data that is stored in the `playerData` table using the `:SetAsync()` function. Ensure the function uses the following best practices: retries and budget yielding.

8. Create a function named `playerJoined()` and make it listen to the `.PlayerAdded` event on the **Players** service. Inside of the `playerJoined()` function, call the `get()` function with the `player` parameter. Save the result of this function inside the `playerData` table.

9. Create a function named `playerLeft()` and make it listen to the `.PlayerRemoving` event on the **Players** service. Inside the `playerLeft()` function, call the `save()` function with the `player` parameter. Once this is done, remove all the cached data related to this player from the `playerData` table.

10. Make a new function named `autoSave()`. Inside the `autoSave()` function, make a `while` loop that runs indefinitely. Inside this `while` loop, use the `task.wait()` function to only run the loop once every 30 seconds. Besides this, loop through each player that is currently in-game using the `:GetPlayers()` function on the **Players** service. Check whether this player has cached data inside of the `playerData` table. If this is the case, call this player's `save()` function. Make sure you call the `autoSave()` function at the bottom of the `DataManager`. Make sure you create a new thread while calling this function using `task.spawn()`.

11. At the top of the `DataManager`, create a new BindableEvent using the `Instance.new()` function. Then, create a new function named `setupEvents()`. Inside this function, set up the new event using the BindableEvent that we previously made. Once this is done, fire the BindableEvent inside the `playerJoined()` function after the loaded data is inserted into the `playerData` cache.

12. Create a new function named `DataManager:Get()`. This function should have the following two parameters: `player` and `key`. Inside of the function, ensure the player has data inside of the cache and check whether the key exists. If either of these conditions is not met, throw an error using the `error()` function. If no error is thrown, return the data that belongs to this key.

13. Create a new function named `DataManager:Set()`. This function should have three parameters: `player`, `key`, and `value`. Inside the function, ensure that the player has data inside the cache. If this condition is not met, throw an error using the `error()` function. If no error is thrown, set whatever data is provided in the value parameter as on the provided key.

14. Create a new function named `DataManager:Increment()`. This function should have three parameters: `player`, `key`, and `value`. Inside the function, ensure that the player has data inside of the cache, that the key exists, and that the data type for this key is a number. If either of these conditions is not met, throw an error using the `error()` function. If no error is thrown, increment the key with the provided value.

Congratulations, we have now created our own `DataManager` that uses all the best practices. If you got stuck while writing the `DataManager`, please look at the `DataManager` that we made inside of the *Creating a DataManager* section.

While it is great to have a `DataManager` with working data stores, it is also crucial that we know how to work with this `DataManager`. In the following steps, we will create a script that allows players to purchase new tools while changing the coins and tools data inside the data store:

1. Create a new Script inside the **ServerScriptService** service.

2. Declare a new variable and initialize the `DataManager` module that we made previously using the `require()` function on this variable.

3. Create a new constant named TOOL_PRICES. This constant is a dictionary with the following values:

   - `ToolA = 400`

   - `ToolB = 600`

4. Create a new function named `playerJoined()` and make it listen to the `.PlayerAdded` event on the DataManager.

5. Create a new function named `purchaseTool()` with the following parameters: `player` and `toolName`.

6. Add a server check in the `purchaseTool()` function that checks if the `toolName` can be found in the `TOOL_PRICES` table. If not, use the `warn()` function and finally use the `return` statement to cancel the function.

7. Get the current amount of money and owned tools by using the `:Get()` function on the `DataManager` and store the result in a variable. Please keep in mind that the `:Get()` function can throw an error. Make sure you wrap your call inside of a `pcall()` function.

8. If no error occurred while retrieving the requested data using the `:Get()` function, check whether the player does not own the tool yet. If the player does own the tool, use the `warn()` function and finally use the `return` statement to cancel the function.

    Tip for 8: Use a `for` loop that loops through all the current tools that a player has. If the current tool matches `toolName`, cancel the function.

9. Check whether the player can afford this tool by comparing the tool's price with the amount of money the player has.

    Tip for 9: We previously received the player's amount of money in *step 7*. Use this data.

10. Insert the `toolName` parameter into the previously loaded table in *step 7*.

11. Update the tools key inside using the `:Set()` function on the `DataManager`. Please keep in mind that the `:Set()` function may throw an error. So, make sure you wrap your call inside of a `pcall()` function.

12. Decrease the number of coins the player has based on the chosen tool. Use the `:Increment()` function.

    Tip for 12: To lower an amount using an increment function, provide a negative number rather than a positive one.

13. Inside the `playerJoined()` function, include the following code snippet:

    ```
    purchaseTool(player, "ToolA")  --> Success
    purchaseTool(player, "ToolA")  --> Already own this tool
    error
    purchaseTool(player, "ToolB")  --> Insufficient money
    error
    purchaseTool(player, "ToolC")  --> Tool does not exist
    error
    ```

We have now finished our script. When we run the game, the data store should work, and you should not run into errors other than the ones that were expected, as shown in the comments in the preceding code snippet.

> **Removing data**
>
> Make sure you remove your data from the data store using the `:RemoveAsync()` function. The test code in the preceding code snippet only works the first time the player joins.

If you did not manage to complete the exercise because you ran into an issue, please take a look at the example answer that is provided on GitHub at `https://github.com/PacktPublishing/Mastering-Roblox-Coding/tree/main/Exercises`.

Exercise 8.2 – Simple obby

One of the most iconic types of Roblox game is **obbies**, short for **obstacle courses**. Throughout the years, they have increased a lot in quality. However, we will script a simple and iconic obby using data stores in this exercise.

In the previous exercise, we made a `DataManager`. In this exercise, we will focus on creating a game that uses the `DataManager`. There is a **Fill In** version of our simple obby with three stages. This **Fill In** version can be found on the GitHub page for this book:

`https://github.com/PacktPublishing/Mastering-Roblox-Coding/tree/main/Exercises`

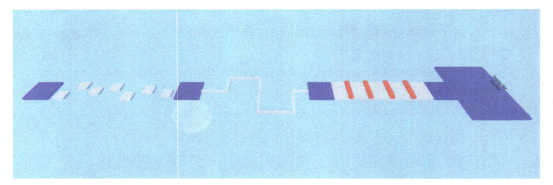

Figure 8.3 – Our obby

As previously mentioned, our current obby only has three stages. This is not much. However, it is enough to understand the concept of an obby. Feel free to include additional stages.

Inside the ServerScriptService, you can find two scripts: our `DataManager` module and a script named `KillParts`. We will use the `DataManager` module to save how far the player has progressed in our obby. This `DataManager` has a key named `stage`. This key contains the number of stages the player has completed.

KillScripts is the script that will kill players when they touch **kill parts**. They are usually red-colored bricks. When players step on them, their character will respawn. We do not have to script the KillScripts script ourselves. However, feel free to practice if you are up for a challenge.

Exercise

First, we will start by setting up our game. Follow these steps:

1. Download the **Fill In** version of the obby from the GitHub page for this book.
2. Publish the **Fill In** version to Roblox.
3. Enable the **Enable Studio Access to API Services** setting in the **Game Settings** menu.

Now that we have set up our game, let us start scripting the system that will save the player's progress:

1. Create a new **Script** in the **ServerScriptService**.
2. When a player joins the game, wait until their character is loaded. When their character is loaded, teleport them to the correct obby part. Each stage has its own **ObbyPart**, which you can find in the `ObbyParts` folder in the Workspace. To teleport the player's character to them correctly, follow these steps:

    A. Get the current progress using the `DataManager:Get(player, "stage")` function.
    B. Use the `:FindFirstChild()` function to find the correct **ObbyPart** inside the `ObbyParts` folder. If none can be found, use the `warn()` function.
    C. Use the `:SetPrimaryPartCFrame()` function to teleport the character for the player to the position of the **ObbyPart** that you found in *step 2B*.

Teleporting does not work

If your character keeps spawning at the first stage while being at a later stage, and when no errors appear, use the `task.wait(1)` function before using the `:SetPrimaryPartCFrame()` function.

    Tip for 2: To get all the characters, including the future characters, use the `.CharacterAdded` event on the **Players** service.

3. For each BasePart inside the `ObbyParts` folder, listen to the `.Touched` event. When this event gets fired, do the following:

    A. Use the `hit` parameter that the `.Touched` event provides to determine whether a player touched one of the obby parts.
    B. When the player touches an **ObbyPart**, check whether the **ObbyPart** is of a stage that is greater than the player's current stage.

C. For example, when the player's `stage` key in the `DataManager` is 2, the **ObbyPart** named `1` is smaller than the player's current stage.

D. Update the `stage` key in the `DataManager` to the number of the new stage.

Tip for 3: To determine if the `hit` parameter belongs to a player, use the `Players:GetPlayerFromCharacter(hit.Parent)` function.

Key does not exist

When programming, you can make the mistake of setting the key in the `DataManager` to `nil` accidentally. This can result in many weird behaviors. When this happens, check whether your `:Set()` function could give `nil` as the new value. If this happens, remove your data using the `:RemoveAsync()` function.

If you did not manage to complete the exercise because you ran into an issue, please take a look at the example answer that is provided on GitHub at `https://github.com/PacktPublishing/Mastering-Roblox-Coding/tree/main/Exercises`.

Summary

In this chapter, we went from almost no data store experience to an advanced level. We started the chapter with an introduction to data stores. Here, we have seen how to use the primary data store functions, such as `:GetDataStore()`, `:GetAsync()`, `:SetAsync()`, and `:RemoveAsync()`. While using these functions, we learned that many things could go wrong working with data stores. As programmers, we have to prepare ourselves for the worst-case scenario. Because of this, we learned how to implement basic error handling using the `pcall()` function.

We have learned that it is best to use as few separate data stores as possible. We aim to create just one or two data stores per game. To achieve this, we have seen how to use tables and dictionaries for the data that is saved in data stores.

Because of limitations, we learned to use caching because we cannot keep getting and setting tables and dictionaries from the data store. We have seen how to load and cache player data in a table. We learned to change this in the cache when we have to update certain data in the data store.

During the introduction into data stores, we only saved the player data once they had left the game. We have seen that this is very insecure; what if it might not save this one time? We learned about two additional best practices: autosaving and retries to prevent this from happening. We have seen how to implement both autosaving and retries to ensure that the amount of data loss is minimized as much as possible.

We have also looked into the limitations that data stores have. We learned that there is a 4 million character limit per key for a data store. Besides this, we have seen that we cannot use functions, such as the `:SetAsync()` function, every single second. We learned that some cooldowns and budgets prevent us from doing this. To work with this, we created a function called `yieldUntilBudget()`. We have seen that this function yields until we can make our request.

Finally, we also looked at how our data stores would work when multiple servers were to manipulate them. We have seen that the `:UpdateAsync()` function allows us to make changes that respect any previous changes that could have been made in different servers.

In the next chapter, we will learn how to implement monetization features into our game. Besides this, we will learn about the **PolicyService**, which helps us determine what monetization methods are allowed depending on age, location, and platform.

Monetizing Your Game

In this chapter, you will learn how to implement monetization features in your game. You will learn about different ways of monetizing your game, such as by implementing game passes, developer products, Premium Benefits, and third-party sales. In addition, you will learn how to use best practices when it comes to the previously named implementations. This way, your players can easily enjoy their purchased power-ups.

The following topics will be covered in this chapter:

- Programming game passes
- Implementing developer products
- Giving Premium Benefits
- Third-party sales
- Exercise 9.1 – building a currency system

By the end of this chapter, you will know how to implement game passes in your game to give players a permanent power-up. Besides this, you will learn how to create temporary power-ups or how to let players purchase in-game currency by implementing developer products. In addition, you will learn how to make your game comply with government laws. You will also learn about the Roblox Premium subscription and its benefits. You will know what the common implementations of Premium Benefits are and how to implement them in your own game. Finally, you will learn how to earn commissions through third-party sales.

Technical requirements

To start programming with Luau, you need access to a device with internet access. This can either be a Windows or a Mac device.

You will need to download the following software:

- Roblox Player
- Roblox Studio

All the code examples for this chapter can be found on GitHub at `https://github.com/PacktPublishing/Mastering-Roblox-Coding`.

The CiA video for this chapter can be found at `https://bit.ly/3Jb9t2x`.

Programming game passes

Throughout the previous chapters, we learned everything about programming Roblox games. We learned how to secure and optimize our game, build data stores, listen to user input, and work with **graphical user interfaces** (**GUIs**). While it is true that all of these categories are essential while creating a game, there also needs to be a monetization aspect of your game.

There are many ways to monetize your game. Throughout this chapter, we will cover the most popular ones. One way to start earning from your game is by creating **game passes**. Roblox allows developers to sell game passes, which act as permanent power-ups for your game. We are allowed to implement the effects of these game passes ourselves. A few examples of game passes are admin commands, double money, bigger plots, exclusive cars, and anything else that fits your game genre.

Each published Roblox game has a **Store** section, as shown in the following screenshot. Inside this **Store** section, we can see all the game passes that a game has:

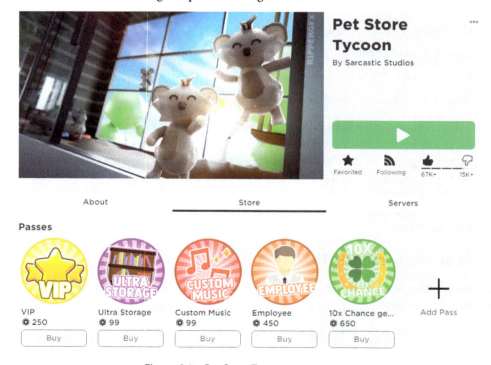

Figure 9.1 – Pet Store Tycoon game passes

Players can purchase game passes to receive an in-game power-up. For instance, the following screenshot shows a **2x Cash** game pass. As the description of this game pass specifies, this game pass provides twice the amount of money for each paycheck that the player gets:

Figure 9.2 – 2x Cash game pass

.Players can purchase game passes with a virtual currency called **Robux**. Instead of directly purchasing something with real-world currency, such as USD or euros, you pay with Robux for everything on the platform. So, whether you purchase a new accessory for your avatar, a game pass, or advertisements for your game, you always pay in Robux.

You can directly purchase Robux with real-world money or get a subscription to **Roblox Premium**. Roblox Premium gives you Robux every month. In addition, you unlock the ability to trade limited accessories, and you will receive **Premium Benefits** in various games. Later, in the *Giving Premium Benefits* section of this chapter, we will learn more about Roblox Premium and Premium Benefits.

Now that we know more about Robux, let us continue with game passes. As previously mentioned, developers can create their own game passes. This includes setting a price for them. When a game pass is purchased, Roblox takes 30% of the revenue; we get 70% of each sale that's made for our game.

We now know that we can monetize our game using game passes. We have learned that game passes allow players to get a permanent power-up inside our game. Now that we know this, let us try to implement a game pass in our game.

In the next section, we will create a game pass prompt that allows players to easily purchase a game pass while playing our game. Once we have implemented this, we will learn how to reward players that have purchased those game passes.

Prompting game passes

Previously, we learned that players can purchase game passes from the **Store** section for a particular game. However, most of the time, players will decide that they want to purchase a specific game pass while playing your game. Therefore, it is highly recommended that we create a GUI or **SurfaceGui** somewhere in our game that allows players to purchase game passes. An example of a GUI that allows you to purchase game passes can be seen in the following screenshot:

Figure 9.3 – Purchasing in-game game passes

When a player opens the **Premium Shop** area for this game, they will be presented with all the game passes that this game has. It also includes a **Purchase** button. When a player presses this button, a game pass prompt will appear that allows the player to purchase this game pass while in-game, as shown in the following screenshot:

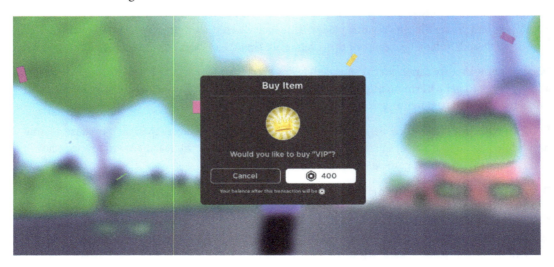

Figure 9.4 – Purchase game pass prompt

We now know the desired outcome: the game pass prompt. However, how do we make it? Similar to all the previous chapters, there is a primary service that we will use throughout this chapter. When monetizing your game, you need the **MarketplaceService** service. The **MarketplaceService** service provides every function related to monetizing your game.

If we want to create a game pass prompt, we need to use the `:PromptGamePassPurchase()` function. We can use this function both on the Server and the Client.

> **Prompting Game Passes on the Client**
>
> Please remember that the Client can only call the function on themselves. This means that **Player1** cannot prompt a game pass purchase for **Player2**.

Let us create a simple GUI that features a button that will prompt a random game pass. Follow these steps:

1. Inside **StarterGui**, create a new **ScreenGui**.

2. Inside **ScreenGui**, insert **TextButton** that is positioned somewhere on your screen. Then, change the **Text** property on **TextButton** to **Purchase**. Then, change the **Name** property to **PurchaseButton**.

3. Create a new **LocalScript** inside **ScreenGui**.

   Feel free to style your GUI however you like. Your GUI could look something like this:

Figure 9.5 – Created Purchase button

Now that we have our GUI, let us script it so that it starts the game pass prompt. Take a look at the following code snippet:

```
local Players = game:GetService("Players")
local MarketplaceService =
game:GetService("MarketplaceService")


local screenGui = script.Parent
```

```
local purchaseButton = screenGui:WaitForChild("PurchaseButton")

function purchaseGamePass()
    MarketplaceService:PromptGamePassPurchase(
        -- Player that will receive the prompt
        Players.LocalPlayer,

        -- Game Pass Id
        123456789
    )
end

purchaseButton.MouseButton1Click:Connect(purchaseGamePass)
```

In the preceding code snippet, we call the purchaseGamePass() function when the .MouseButton1Click event on PurchaseButton fires. Inside the purchaseGamePass() function, we call the :PromptGamePassPurchase() function. This function requires two arguments. The first argument is player – that is, the player who will receive the prompt. Since this is a LocalScript that runs on the Client, it should always be LocalPlayer. The second argument is game pass id, which is the ID of the game pass that you are trying to tell the player about.

When you click on the **TextButton** property that we made, you will receive a game pass prompt.

> **Game Pass Prompt Error**
>
> If you try the preceding code snippet and run into an unexpected error, please change the game pass ID inside the script. Regardless, your code will work if this message shows up; you are just using a non-existing game pass ID.

We now know how to create a game pass prompt using the :PromptGamePassPurchase() function on the **MarketplaceService** service. In addition, we practiced making a simple GUI that features a **TextButton** that we scripted. While it is great to know how to prompt a game pass in your game, it is also very important to give the players what they paid for. In the next section, we will learn how to reward players who own game passes in our game.

Rewarding game passes

We now know how players can purchase game passes. They can either purchase them via the **Store** section on the game's page or via a prompt that we can script ourselves. However, we have not implemented a reward for these game passes yet. After all, it is just as essential to implement the reward as the prompts.

So, how do we detect whether someone owns a certain game pass? In **MarketplaceService**, there is a function that tells us exactly this. Let us take a look at `:UserOwnsGamePassAsync()`:

```
if
    MarketplaceService:UserOwnsGamePassAsync(
        -- User Id
        player.UserId,

        -- Game Pass Id
        123456789
    )
then
    -- Implement game pass reward
end
```

In the preceding code snippet, we use the `:UserOwnsGamePassAsync()` function, along with its arguments, inside an `if` statement. As mentioned previously, this function only checks whether a player owns a particular game pass, nothing else. Therefore, if we wish to reward a player with something, we must script this ourselves.

> **Cache**
>
> The result of calling the `:UserOwnsGamePassAsync()` function for the first time gets cached in the function internally. There is nothing you can do to change this behavior. While this is not a big issue, it is important to remember that this function may still return `false` when the player has just purchased the game pass.

Imagine that we have a game pass that gives a player a certain tool. How would we make this? First, we need to create this tool. Because this example is not about the tool itself, we will create an empty tool without using any parts or scripts. Follow these steps to reward a game pass:

1. Inside the **ServerStorage** service, create a new folder named `Tools`.

2. Inside the previously made folder, create a new tool and name it `GamePassTool`. You do not have to change anything about the tool.

3. Inside the **ServerScriptService** service, create a new script with the following piece of code:

    ```
    local Players = game:GetService("Players")
    local ServerStorage = game:GetService("ServerStorage")
    local MarketplaceService =
    game:GetService("MarketplaceService")
    ```

```
local tools = ServerStorage.Tools

function playerJoined(player)
    if
        MarketplaceService:UserOwnsGamePassAsync(
            -- User Id
            player.UserId,
            -- Game Pass Id
            123456789
        )
    then
        tools.GamePassTool:Clone().Parent =
        player.Backpack
        tools.GamePassTool:Clone().Parent =
        player.StarterGear
    end
end


Players.PlayerAdded:Connect(playerJoined)
```

With that, we have implemented our game pass reward script. Let us take a look at what it does.

Here, we call the `playerJoined()` function when a player joins the game. Inside this function, we check whether the players own the game pass by using an ID of `123456789`. Once again, this is just a fictitious game pass ID. Please change this number to your game pass ID that was generated when you created a new game pass.

If a player owns this game pass, we can use the `:Clone()` function on the `GamePassTool`. To get this `GamePassTool`, we must use the `tools` variable that we declared at the beginning of the script. The `tools` variable references the `Tools` folder inside the **ServerStorage** service.

But why do we clone `GamePassTool` twice? The first time we clone `GamePassTool`, we parent it to `Backpack`, which can be found inside the player. The second clone goes into the `StarterGear` folder. What is the difference between both? As we learned in *Chapter 7, Listening to User Input*, we use `Backpack` to store all the tools that a player does not currently use. When a player does use a tool, it gets parented to the character of the player instead.

But what about the `StarterGear` folder? While learning about the `Backpack` folder in *Chapter 7, Listening to User Input*, we saw what the **StarterPack** service does. When we parent tools to this service, every player gets these tools inside their `Backpack` by default, even when they reset. The

`StarterGear` folder is very similar to **StarterPack**. The only difference between them is that the `StarterGear` folder is unique to a certain player, whereas **StarterPack** is for all players.

Because we parent our `GamePassTool` to both `Backpack` and `StarterGear`, we can simply reward the game pass once. This means we will never have to worry about it again, not even when a player decides to respawn their character.

With that, we've learned how to reward a game pass tool to a certain player using the `:UserOwnsGamePassAsync()` function on **MarketplaceService**. However, in our code example, we are listening to the `.PlayerAdded` event. This event only gets fired when a player joins the game. What should we do when a player decides to purchase a new game pass while playing the game, for instance, by purchasing it through a game pass prompt? In the next section, we will learn how to reward game passes instantly when the player is playing our game.

Instant game pass reward

When a player buys a game pass, you want to ensure the player immediately gets rewarded with whatever that game pass promises. However, when you look away from the front-page games, you will see that many games require users to reset or even rejoin the game. This is a bad practice. Not only is it an inconvenience for your players, but it also lowers the average play time of your game.

So, how do we ensure that players get instantly rewarded when purchasing a game pass in-game? In **MarketplaceService**, there is an event called `.PromptGamePassPurcahseFinished`. This event gets fired when the player purchases or cancels a game pass prompt. Let us take a look at this event:

```
local MarketplaceService =
game:GetService("MarketplaceService")

function purchaseFinished(player, gamePassId, purchased)
    if purchased == true then
        -- Getting game pass product info
        local productInfo =
        MarketplaceService:GetProductInfo(
            gamePassId,
            Enum.InfoType.GamePass
        )

        -- Printing message
        print(
            player.Name .. " just purchased a game pass"
            .. " named [" .. productInfo.Name .. "]."
```

```
        )
    end
end


MarketplaceService.
PromptGamePassPurchaseFinished:Connect(purchaseFinished)
```

In the preceding code snippet, we listen to the .PromptGamePassPurchaseFinished event. This event provides us with the following three parameters:

- The player that interacted with the prompt

- The game pass that was prompted

- A Boolean that determines whether the game pass was purchased or not

We can use these parameters to figure out everything that we need. We can use the gamePassId variable to get the name of the game pass by using the :GetProductInfo() function, as shown in the preceding code snippet.

Now, let us take a look at a system that instantly rewards players, even when they purchase a game pass while playing:

```
local Players = game:GetService("Players")
local ServerStorage = game:GetService("ServerStorage")
local MarketplaceService =
game:GetService("MarketplaceService")

local tools = ServerStorage.Tools

local gamePasses = {
    [123456789] = function(player)
        tools.GamePassTool:Clone().Parent = player.Backpack
        tools.GamePassTool:Clone().Parent =
        player.StarterGear
    end
}

function playerJoined(player)
    -- Looping through all game passes
```

```lua
    for gamePassId, rewardFunction in pairs(gamePasses) do
        -- Checking if game pass was purchased
        if
            MarketplaceService:UserOwnsGamePassAsync(
                -- User Id
                player.UserId,

                -- GamePass Id
                gamePassId
            )
        then
            -- Rewarding game pass
            rewardFunction(player)
        end
    end
end

function purchaseFinished(player, gamePassId, purchased)
    if purchased == true then
        -- Checking if game pass reward was programming
        if gamePasses[gamePassId] == nil then
            warn("GamePass [" .. gamePassId .. "] reward
            was not programmed")
            return
        end

        -- Rewarding game pass
        gamePasses[gamePassId](player)
    end
end

Players.PlayerAdded:Connect(playerJoined)
MarketplaceService.
PromptGamePassPurchaseFinished:Connect(purchaseFinished)
```

In the preceding code snippet, we have a dictionary called `gamePasses`. This dictionary has the game pass ID as the key and a reward function as the value. The `playerJoined()` function gets called when a player joins the game. We loop through the `gamePasses` dictionary in this function and check whether a player owns this game pass. When they do, we execute the rewarding function, which is the value of each key in the dictionary. Because we do this, we automatically reward every game pass that a player owns when they join the game.

We also need to reward the player when they purchase an item in-game. To do this, we must listen to the `.PromptGamePassPurchaseFinished` event. When this event is fired, we call the `purchaseFinished()` function. Inside the `purchaseFinished()` function, we check whether the player purchased the game pass. If they did, we execute the reward function that is inside the `gamePasses` dictionary. This way, we reward the player instantly after they purchase a game pass.

In the previous sections, we learned a lot about game passes. We learned that implementing game passes allows us to monetize our game. Besides this, we learned that game passes can be used as permanent power-ups for players. They only have to pay once to receive a permanent effect.

After learning what game passes are, we learned how to implement them in our game. We learned how to create a prompt that allows players to purchase game passes while playing the game. In addition, we learned how to instantly reward players that own these game passes using the `:UserOwnsGamePassAsync()` function and the `.PromptGamePassPurchaseFinished` event.

Now that we know about game passes, let us try a different way of monetizing our game. As mentioned previously, game passes are a one-time permanent power-up. But what if we want the power-up to be for a limited time only and allow players to purchase it multiple times? In that case, we should use **developer products**. We will learn what these are and how to program them in the following sections.

Implementing developer products

Throughout the previous sections, we learned how to monetize our games by implementing game passes. Similar to game passes, we have **developer products**. These, unlike game passes, can be purchased an unlimited number of times, though generally, the effects of developer products are temporary. They can be used to implement money boosts or an adrenaline shot for extra health. However, developer products can have other implementations as well. For example, they can be used to purchase a revival or purchase in-game currency quickly rather than saving up by playing the game.

To create a new developer product, follow these steps:

1. Open the **Game Settings** menu in Roblox Studio.
2. From this menu, open the **Monetization** tab and scroll down to **Developer Products**, as shown in the following screenshot:

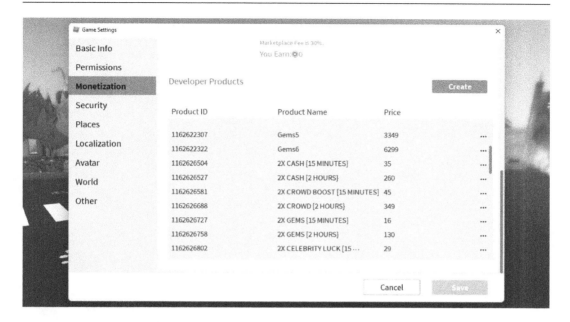

Figure 9.6 – The Developer Products section in the Game Settings menu

Here, we can see the **(Developer) Product ID**, **Product Name**, and **Price** (in Robux) properties for each developer product in this game. This data will be helpful when we start programming our developer product in the next section.

When we create a new developer product by clicking the **Create** button, a new developer product shows up in the list.

3. To edit the product, click on the three dots (**…**) and click **Edit**, as shown in the following screenshot:

Developer Products

Product ID	Product Name	Price	
(Not Saved)	Developer Product 51	1	•••
1162621968	Cash1	16	Edit
1162621985	Cash2	50	•••

Figure 9.7 – The Edit button for a newly created developer product

4. When we press the **Edit** button, we have the option to set the name and price for our developer product, as shown in the following screenshot. Ensure that the name of your developer product fits its purpose; players will see the name you put here when attempting to purchase it.

5. Finally, press the **Save** button when you are done:

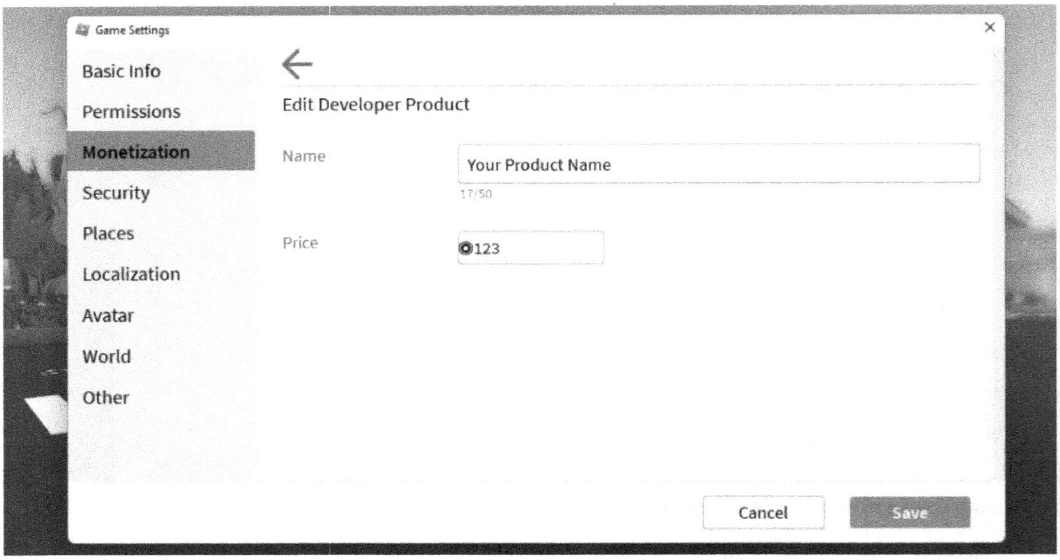

Figure 9.8 – Editing a developer product

We now know how to create a developer product. However, we do not know how to implement it in our game. In the next few sections, we will follow the same path we followed when learning about game passes. First, we will learn how to create a developer product prompt so that players can purchase a developer product. Then, we will learn how to reward players for purchasing this developer product. Rewarding players when they purchase a developer product will be a bit more complex than it is for game passes, but we will get to this later. Finally, we will learn about **PolicyService**, which will make our game monetization compliant in countries with restrictions.

Prompting developer products

Unlike game passes, developer products cannot be purchased on the **Store** page of your game. Instead, developer products can only be purchased in-game through prompts. Similar to game passes, we can create these prompts by scripting.

In the *Prompting game passes* section, we created a GUI with `LocalScript` that prompted a game pass. We will use the same GUI in this section. However, we will make it prompt a developer product instead. Let us take a look at how to create a prompt for a developer product:

```
local Players = game:GetService("Players")
local MarketplaceService =
game:GetService("MarketplaceService")
```

```
local screenGui = script.Parent
local purchaseButton = screenGui:WaitForChild("PurchaseButton")

function purchaseProduct()
    MarketplaceService:PromptProductPurchase(
        -- Player that will receive the prompt
        Players.LocalPlayer,

        -- Developer Product ID
        123456789
    )
end


purchaseButton.MouseButton1Click:Connect(purchaseProduct)
```

Let us take a look at the preceding code snippet. Near the top of the script, we reference `PurchaseButton`, which is a **TextButton** in our GUI. At the bottom of the script, we listen to the `.MouseButton1Click` event on this button. When this event gets fired, we call the `purchaseProduct()` function. In this function, we call the `:PromptProductPurchase()` function on **MarketplaceService**. This is very similar to how we created a game pass prompt. The only difference compared to prompting a game pass is the function we use; we now use the `:PromptProductPurcahse()` function instead of the `:PromptGamePassPurchase()` function.

We now know that players cannot purchase developer products on the **Store** page of our game. Instead, they have to purchase them via prompts. We covered an example of how to create a developer product prompt. However, we still need to reward the players when they purchase this developer product. In the next section, we will learn how to do this.

Rewarding developer products

In the previous section, we learned that prompting game passes and developer products are similar in terms of how they are coded. The real difference comes when we want to reward them. When we want to reward game passes, we check whether a player owns the game passes. However, you cannot own a developer product. So, how do we do this?

Remember how we instantly rewarded game passes in the *Instant game passes reward* section? Rewarding developer products is very similar to this. When a developer product is processed, the `.ProcessReceipt` callback is fired on **MarketplaceService**. We can use this event to reward developer products.

Before we can take a look at the .ProcessReceipt callback, let us think of a good developer product that we can implement in our game. A widespread implementation of developer products is to purchase in-game currency. If we want to implement this, we need to use the **DataManager** module we created in *Chapter 8, Building Data Stores*. **DataManager** needs to save the money key for each player. This can be done by including the money key inside the DEFAULT_PLAYER_DATA variable.

With that, we have set up everything we need to implement our developer products. Because the .ProcessReceipt callback is usually considered difficult to understand, we will take a look at it next.

Analyzing the ProcessReceipt callback

First, we will listen to the event to see what we have to work with:

```
local Players = game:GetService("Players")
local MarketplaceService =
game:GetService("MarketplaceService")

local DataManager = require(PATH_TO_DATA_MANAGER)

function processReceipt(receiptInfo)
    return Enum.ProductPurchaseDecision.NotProcessedYet
end

MarketplaceService.ProcessReceipt = processReceipt
```

The preceding code snippet is the start of what we will use to reward players when they purchase a developer product. At the bottom of the script, we listen to the .ProcessReceipt callback. You could compare this to how we used **BindableFunctions** and **RemoteFunctions** in *Chapter 3, Event-Based Programming*, and *Chapter 4, Securing Your Game*.

Because this is a callback, it is expected that we return something. When using .ProcessReceipt, we are expected to return a ProductPurchaseDecision Enum. This Enum has two options, NotProcessedYet and PurchaseGranted. When anything goes wrong while rewarding the developer product, we return the NotProcessedYet Enum. Only when everything goes correct can we return PurchaseGranted. Never return the PurchaseGranted Enum if something goes wrong.

> **Callback Limitation**
> Callbacks can only be set once. This means that we can only have one script that listens to the .ProcessReceipt callback. Because of this, we must program all of our developer products in the same script.

Besides the Enum that we have to return, there is one more noteworthy item that we can find in the preceding code snippet. Our `processReceipt()` function has a parameter named `receiptInfo`. This parameter comprises a dictionary that contains data that might be useful. Let us take a look at the following table, which shows what is inside this dictionary:

Key	Description
CurrencySpent	This key holds the amount of currency based on the `CurrencyType` key that the player spent on this developer product.
CurrencyType	This key holds the currency that the player used to pay for the developer product. This will always be Robux. In the past, Roblox had another currency called Tix; this does not exist anymore.
PlaceIdWherePurchased	This is the `PlaceId` property in which this purchase took place.
PlayerId	The `UserId` property of the player that purchased this developer product.
ProductId	The developer product ID that was purchased.
PurchaseId	A string that is unique to this developer product sale.

Table 9.1 – Keys provided in the receiptInfo dictionary

With that, we've analyzed how the `.ProcessReceipt` callback works. We have learned that we must return a `ProductPurchaseDecision` Enum in our `processReceipt()` function. Besides this, we learned that callbacks should only be set once per game. This means that no more than one script should listen to the same callback. Finally, we looked at the `receiptInfo` parameter, which is provided in the `processReceipt()` function. In the next section, we will set up each developer product's functions.

Setting up rewards

As mentioned in the previous section, all our developer products must be handled in the same script. To prevent our `processReceipt()` function from flooding with all the reward codes, we will do something similar to what we did in the *Instant game pass reward* section. There, we made a variable named `gamePasses()` that contained a reward function for each game pass.

Let us take a look at the following code snippet:

```
local developerProducts = {
    -- 500 money developer product
    [123456789] = function(player)
        DataManager:Increment(player, "money", 500)
    end
}
```

In the preceding code snippet, there's a new dictionary named `developerProducts`. This dictionary should contain a reward function for each developer product in our game. For now, we only have one developer product. This developer product will increment the amount of money a player has by `500` by using the `:Increment()` function on `DataManager`, which we set up in the *Rewarding developer products* section.

For those that remember, the `:Increment()` function uses the `error()` function internally. This means we should wrap our function call in `pcall()`. We will get back to the reason why we did not do this in the *Giving developer product rewards* section.

With that, we have made a new dictionary containing a reward function for each developer product. Now that we have this, let us continue building the `processReceipt()` function. In the next section, we will implement checks to verify whether a developer product can be successfully rewarded.

Setting up ProcessReceipt checks

Because the `.ProcessReceipt` callback only fires once, we must ensure that we can successfully reward the developer product to the player. As we saw in the *Analyzing the ProcessReceipt callback* section, our `processReceipt()` only has the `receiptInfo` parameter. This means we still have to determine which player purchased the developer product. During this process, things can go wrong. When this happens, we must return the `NotProcessedYet` Enum.

Let us start by looking at some of the checks that we must implement in the `processReceipt()` function:

```
function processReceipt(receiptInfo)
    -- Getting player
    local userId = receiptInfo.PlayerId
    local player = Players:GetPlayerByUserId(userId)
    --
    if player == nil or not player:IsDescendantOf(Players)
    then
        -- Player is not in-game anymore
        return Enum.ProductPurchaseDecision.NotProcessedYet
    end

    -- Checking if the developer product is programmed
    local purchasedDeveloperProduct = receiptInfo.ProductId
    --
    if developerProducts[purchasedDeveloperProduct] == nil
    then
```

```
         -- Developer product was not programmed
         warn("Developer Product [" ..
         purchasedDeveloperProduct .. "] was not
         programmed!")
         return Enum.ProductPurchaseDecision.NotProcessedYet
      end

      -- ... todo ...
   end
```

Let us analyze what we have done here. We get the player at the top of the processReceipt() function. Because one of the keys inside receiptInfo is PlayerId, we can use the :GetPlayerByUserId() function to get a reference to the player that purchased this developer product. If we cannot get this reference, we must return the NotProcessedYet Enum. After all, we could not determine which player purchased this developer product.

We can continue if we can figure out who purchased the developer product. Finally, we reached our second check. First, we get the developer product's ID and store it in the purchasedDeveloperProduct variable. Then, we have an if statement that checks whether it can find a reward function for this developer product. We use the warn() function to display this in the **Developer Console** area if it cannot. Besides this, we return the NotProcessedYet Enum. After all, we will be unable to reward this developer product if we have never scripted it.

When we pass all of these checks, we have got everything we need. We know which function we need to call to provide the reward, and we know which player to call this function for. In the next section, we will implement this in our processReceipt() function.

Giving developer product rewards

The only thing left is to call the correct function for the correct player. However, there is one more thing we have to keep in mind: errors. When calling these reward functions, things could go wrong due to a scripting mistake or because the underlying functions use the error() function. When this happens, we need to return the NotProcessedYet Enum.

Let us take a look at the updated processReceipt() function:

```
function processReceipt(receiptInfo)
    -- Getting player
    local userId = receiptInfo.PlayerId
    local player = Players:GetPlayerByUserId(userId)
    if player == nil or not player:IsDescendantOf(Players)
    then
```

```
        -- Player is not in-game anymore
        return Enum.ProductPurchaseDecision.NotProcessedYet
    end

    -- Checking if the developer product is programmed
    local purchasedDeveloperProduct = receiptInfo.ProductId
    if developerProducts[purchasedDeveloperProduct] == nil
    then
        -- Developer product was not programmed
        warn("Developer Product [" ..
        purchasedDeveloperProduct .. "] was not
        programmed!")
        return Enum.ProductPurchaseDecision.NotProcessedYet
    end

    -- Rewarding developer product
    local suc, err = pcall(function()
        developerProducts[purchasedDeveloperProduct](
        player)
    end)

    -- Checking if reward was successful
    if not suc then
        -- An error occurred while trying to reward
        warn(err)
        return Enum.ProductPurchaseDecision.NotProcessedYet
    else
        -- Rewarding successful
        return Enum.ProductPurchaseDecision.PurchaseGranted
    end
end
```

In the preceding code snippet, we call the reward function inside pcall(). Then, we use the suc and err variables to determine whether an error occurred while calling the reward function. If an error did occur, we use the warn() function to print the error that occurred in the **Developer**

Console area. However, if no errors occur, we return the `PurchaseGranted` Enum. Once again, it is essential that we only return the `PurchaseGranted` Enum when we are confident that the developer product was successfully rewarded.

> **Full Script**
>
> You can find the full script we made in the previous sections in this book's GitHub repository. The link was provided in the *Technical requirements* section.

In the previous sections, we learned a lot about developer products. We learned that developer products are used to provide limited-time boosts or boosts that can be purchased multiple times, such as purchasing in-game money. We learned how to prompt developer products and compared it to how we made a prompt for game passes; this was very similar. The fundamental difference between both comes when we want to implement the reward. Because developer products can be purchased many times, we have to reward them for using the `.ProcessReceipt` callback.

Working with PolicyService

Roblox games can be played in many different countries. However, some of these countries have restrictions that impact video games. To make our games comply with the laws of these countries, we must use **PolicyService**. This helps us figure out what we can and cannot implement for certain players based on their country, device, and age.

So, how does PolicyService work? PolicyService has a function called `:GetPolicyInfoForPlayerAsync()`. Let us take a look at what this function returns. First, we need to create `LocalScript`. Once we have this, we must insert the following code inside it:

```
local Players = game:GetService("Players")
local PolicyService = game:GetService("PolicyService")

local player = Players.LocalPlayer

print(PolicyService:GetPolicyInfoForPlayerAsync(player))
```

When we execute this, we get a dictionary with a few keys. The following table explains what each key tells us:

Key	Description
AllowedExternalLinkReferences	This key contains a table that provides all the external references that are allowed to be displayed to this player. At the time of writing, these references can be Discord, YouTube, Twitch, and Facebook.
ArePaidRandomItemsRestricted	This key contains a Boolean that determines whether random paid items are allowed. For example, many games feature loot boxes, which can be purchased for Robux or an in-game currency. However, when the value for this key is true, none of this is allowed, and the loot boxes will be blocked.
IsPaidItemTradingAllowed	This key contains a Boolean that determines whether trading items that were purchased with Robux or an in-game currency are allowed. When the value for this key is true, trading these items is not allowed.
IsSubjectToChinaPolicies	Roblox (LuoBu) is available in China. However, games have many restrictions there. Therefore, there are too many restrictions to name in this book. Besides this, these restrictions may change in the future. At the time of writing, your games will be unavailable in China unless you have submitted your game via an application. Therefore, you do not have to worry about this key unless your game participates in this program.

Table 9.2 – PolicyService restrictions

So, how do we implement PolicyService in our game? First, we should just make the game the way we want. Then, we should implement PolicyService in the scripts that we have already made. For instance, if we had a loot box that players can purchase with in-game currency, we would check whether the ArePaidRandomItemsRestricted key equals false. If it happens to be true, we will simply not allow players to interact with this loot box. An example of this can be seen in the following screenshot:

Figure 9.9 – PolicyService implementation

Here, we can see that PolicyService is implemented in a GUI. However, if a player decides to purchase a pet, `RemoteEvent` gets fired. Exploiters in countries with restrictions could still do this, even when we do not let them interact with the GUI. Therefore, it is required that we implement PolicyService on both the Server and the Client. On the Server, we use the same `:GetPolicyInfoForPlayerAsync()` function.

> **Note**
>
> If your game is centered around pets, and players can only purchase them through loot boxes, you may have to rethink how players can collect these pets.

In the previous sections, we learned about developer products. In addition, we learned that we could not sell or implement anything in our game. Our game must comply with laws that may vary based on the country a player is in. To do this, we can use the `:GetPolicyInfoForPlayerAsync()` function on **PolicyService**. In the next section, we will learn about another way many developers earn money through their games: **Premium Benefits**.

Giving Premium Benefits

In September 2019, Roblox released a new subscription: **Roblox Premium**. This subscription gives users a fixed amount of Robux each month. In addition, users unlock the ability to trade, get discounts on catalog items, and access Premium-only items. While these are great, Roblox also promises that users can receive **Premium Benefits** inside games. These Premium Benefits can be anything. We are allowed to decide this ourselves. We do not even have to implement them if we do not want to.

But what's in it for us? Are we just supposed to give benefits to Premium members and get nothing in return? Fortunately, Roblox thought of a way to compensate us. Every game, even those that do not implement any Premium Benefits, gets an additional source of income under the **Premium Payout** category.

> **Income**
>
> Premium Payout is an extra income source that gets paid in Robux. However, this does not reduce the amount of Robux you get for selling game passes or developer products.

Your Premium Payout is based on the engagement of your game. The more Premium users play your game, the higher your Premium Payout will be. In the **Creator Dashboard** area, you can see how much Robux you will receive and the projected amount that is expected in the future. These statistics are unique for each of your games:

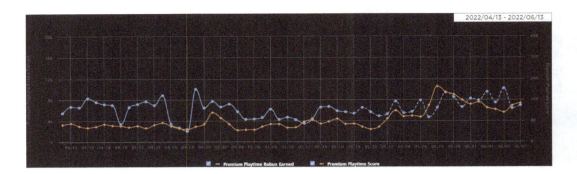

Figure 9.10 – Premium Payout statistics in the Creator Dashboard area

You can find **Creator Dashboard** here: `https://create.roblox.com/`.

So, what kind of rewards are we supposed to implement? As mentioned previously, this is totally up to us. A few common practices are an additional daily Premium Reward next to the **Daily Reward** and **Group Reward** chests. Something else could be that Premium users get a 10% discount on selected in-game items. Alternatively, there could be entire sections in your game that are Premium only. While these examples are fine, the best benefits are the ones that seamlessly fit into your game.

Now that we know what Premium Benefits and Premium Payouts are, let us try to implement one of these Premium Benefits.

Implementing Premium Benefits

Most games have a **Daily Reward** system in their games. This system is designed to let players come back every day. After all, they get something for free by simply joining. Games have different implementations of this Daily Reward system; this could be a GUI, a chest, a minigame, or anything else. The following screenshot shows a game with three chests: **Daily Reward**, **Group Reward**, and **Premium Reward**. When players walk up to one of these chests, they get a reward, and a timer starts that tells them they can claim this reward again after 24 hours:

Figure 9.11 – The Daily Reward, Group Reward, and Premium Reward chests

When a player that does not have the Premium membership walks to the Premium Reward chest, the following message will appear:

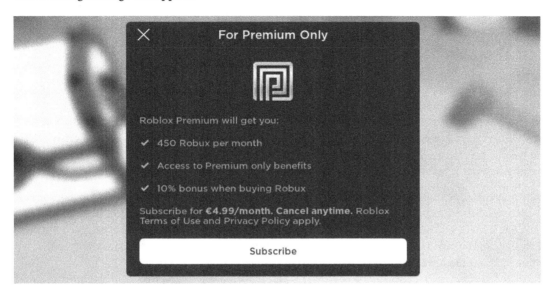

Figure 9.12 – For Premium Only GUI

The **For Premium Only** GUI is not something we have to make ourselves. There is a function on **MarketplaceService** named :PromptPremiumPurchase() for this. Let us take a look at this function:

```
local Players = game:GetService("Players")
local MarketplaceService =
game:GetService("MarketplaceService")

function promptPremium()
    -- Getting player
    local player = Players.LocalPlayer

    -- Checking if player owns Premium
    if player.MembershipType ~= Enum.MembershipType.Premium
    then
        -- Player is not subscribed to Premium
        MarketplaceService:PromptPremiumPurchase(player)
    else
```

```
        -- Player is subscribed to Premium
        print("You are already subscribed!")
    end
end


promptPremium()
```

In the preceding code snippet, there's a function called `promptPremium()`. In this function, we check whether the `MembershipType` property of the player is `Premium` or not. If it is not, we use the `:PromptPremiumPurchase()` function. This will enable the **For Premium Only** GUI that we saw previously. When the player does have Premium, we simply use the `print()` function to verify that our script works. This `print()` function is not required in an actual implementation.

In the previous code snippet, we saw a Client-side implementation of our Premium Benefit that prompts unsubscribed users to purchase Premium. We also have to verify that this player is eligible for this Premium Benefit on the Server. To do this, we can use the same `if` statement that we used on the Client. We simply need to check whether the `MembershipType` property matches the `Premium` Enum. When it does, we apply our benefit. That is all there is to it.

In this section, we learned that one of the perks of subscribing to the **Roblox Premium** subscription is to receive in-game **Premium Benefits**. These benefits can be anything that we want to implement. We are not required to implement them at all. We learned how to create a prompt that allows players to subscribe to Roblox Premium, and we have learned how to verify that players are subscribed. In the next section, we will learn how to monetize our game using third-party sales.

Third-party sales

Another way you can monetize your game is by selling **avatar items**. avatar items are sometimes referred to as **Catalog Items** as well. In the **Avatar Shop** area, players can purchase new accessories and clothing to customize their avatar:

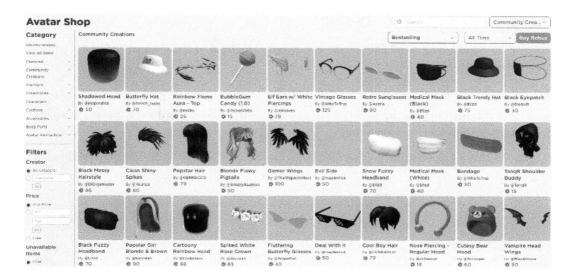

Figure 9.13 – Avatar Shop

But how do we earn money through these avatar items? When we sell these avatar items in our game, we get paid a **commission**. This commission is our "thank you" for selling someone else their avatar item. Commissions get paid as a percentage. This means that we get a portion of the money the player spent on this avatar item when they buy it in our game. Let us take a look at these percentages:

Avatar Item	Percentage
Classic Clothing (Classic Shirt, Classic Pants, and Classic T-Shirt)	10%
3D Clothing (Shirt, Sweaters, Jackets, Pants, Shorts, Dresses and Skirts, Shoes, and T-Shirts)	40%
Accessories (Head, Face, Neck, Shoulder, Front, Back, Waist, and Gear)	40%

Table 9.3 – Avatar items

The preceding percentages are when a player purchases an avatar item in your game that you do not own. You get more when this is your own avatar item.

> **Limited Avatar Items**
>
> Roblox has limited avatar items. These avatar items can be bought and sold by players. We do not get a commission when we sell a limited item in our game.

Now that we know how to earn money through selling third-party items, let us try to implement one in our game.

Implementing third-party sales

Before we can start selling third-party items in our game, we need to change a setting in our game. Follow these steps:

1. Open the **Game Settings** menu in Roblox Studio.

2. From this menu, open the **Security** tab and enable the **Allow Third Party Sales** setting, as shown in the following screenshot:

Figure 9.14 – Enabling the Allow Third-Party Sales setting

3. Finally, press the **Save** button.

> **Security**
>
> When you enable this setting, a message will appear that states **Enabling security bypasses may make your experience vulnerable to third-party attacks**. This message warns you that you allowed players in your game to purchase items that are not yours. If exploiters gain control over your game, they could start selling their items in your game. If you do not use malicious plugins or free models and follow the best practices taught in *Chapter 4, Securing Your Game*, this should not be an issue.

Now that we have enabled the setting for our game, let us create a prompt for an avatar item. To do this, we need to use the :PromptPurchase() function on **MarketplaceService**. In the *Prompting game passes* section, we created a GUI with a LocalScript that prompted a game pass. We will use the same GUI in this section. However, this time, we will change it so that it uses the :PromptPurchase() function.

Let us take a look at the following script:

```
local Players = game:GetService("Players")
local MarketplaceService =
game:GetService("MarketplaceService")

local screenGui = script.Parent
local purchaseButton = screenGui:WaitForChild("PurchaseButton")

function purchaseAvatarItem()
    MarketplaceService:PromptPurchase(
        -- Player that will receive the prompt
        Players.LocalPlayer,

        -- Avatar Item Id
        123456789
    )
end


purchaseButton.MouseButton1Click:Connect(purchaseAvatarItem)
```

Let us take a look at the preceding code snippet. Near the top of the script, we reference PurchaseButton, which is a **TextButton** in our GUI. At the bottom of the script, we listen to the .MouseButton1Click event on this button. When this event gets fired, we call the purchaseAvatarItem() function. In this function, we call the :PromptPurchase() function on **MarketplaceService**. This is very similar to how we created a game pass and developer product prompt. The only difference is that we now use the :PromptPurchase() function.

Now that we know how to earn money using third-party sales, we know about four different ways we can monetize our game. In the next section, we will practice implementing monetization features.

Exercise 9.1 – building a currency system

In this exercise, we will create a simple currency system that uses the previously learned information. First, we need to make a **data store** that contains **money**. Then, players should be able to purchase a **2x Cash** game pass. Besides this, players should be able to purchase 500 coins through a developer product. If players purchase this developer product while owning the **2x Cash** game pass, they should get 1,000 coins instead of 500. In addition, we must implement a Premium Benefit. For our current game, we will give Premium users 10% more in-game money when they purchase it through a developer product. This means that Premium users without the double money game pass will get 550 coins and that the players with the game pass will receive 1,100 coins.

Now that we know what system we will implement, let us start making it. First, we will create a new game. Follow these steps:

1. Open **Roblox Studio** and create a new **Baseplate**.

2. Publish your **Baseplate** to Roblox.

3. Open the **Game Settings** menu. Navigate to the **Security** tab and enable the **Enable Studio Access to API services** setting.

4. Navigate to the **Monetization** tab in the **Game Settings** menu and create a new developer product. Make sure you set a proper name for your developer product. Set the price of your developer product to 19 Robux.

5. On the Roblox website, go to the game page for the game you just published. Then, open the **Store** section on your game's page and create a new game pass. Make sure you put your game pass on sale for 199 Robux after you finish making your game pass.

Next, we will create our **DataManager** module. Follow these steps:

1. Create a new **ModuleScript** in **ServerScriptService** or **ServerStorage**, depending on your liking. Name it DataManager.

2. Use the **DataManager** code we made in *Chapter 8, Building Data Stores*.

3. Make sure we have a data field named money in **DataManager** for each player. The data type for this should be a number.

   Tip for 3: Change the DEFAULT_PLAYER_DATA variable so that it includes the money field.

Next, we will create a simple GUI that allows us to purchase game passes and developer products in-game. Follow these steps:

1. Insert a new **ScreenGui** into the **StarterGui** service.

2. Inside the previously made **ScreenGui**, insert two **TextButton** properties. Then, change the **Name** and **Text** properties of the TextButtons to **DevProduct** and **GamePass**.

3. Create a new **LocalScript** inside **ScreenGui** with the following functionalities:

    *   When a player clicks on the **GamePass** TextButton, create a game pass prompt for the previously made game pass

    *   When a player clicks on the **DevProduct** TextButton, create a developer product prompt for the previously made developer product

Next, we will create a script that handles the game passes for our game. Follow these steps:

1. Create a new **Script** in the **ServerScriptService** service.

2. Declare a variable named gamePasses. This variable should contain a dictionary with the **2x Cash** game pass ID as the key and a reward function as the value.

3. Inside the reward function for the **2x Cash** game pass, use the :SetAttribute() function on the player. Use the following code to do this:

```
player:SetAttribute("2xCash", true)
```

4. When the player joins the game, check whether this player owns the game pass by using the :UserOwnsGamePassAsync() function on **MarketplaceService**. If the player owns this game pass, execute the reward function for this game pass.

5. Listen to the .PromptGamePassPurchaseFinished event on **MarketplaceService** and call the reward function for the game pass that was just purchased.

Next, we will create a script that processes developer product purchases. Follow these steps:

1. Create a new **Script** in the **ServerScriptService** service.

2. Declare a variable named developerProducts. This variable should contain a dictionary with the 500 cash developer product ID as the key and a reward function as the value.

3. Inside this reward function, apply the Premium Benefit and game pass boost to the base 500 cash. The Premium Benefit will increase the amount of money by 10%. When the player owns the game pass, the money should be doubled. Both boosts must stack.

    Tip for 3: Use the multiplier operator (*) to apply boosts. To add a 10% increase, use * 1.1. To double the amount of money, use * 2.

4. Call the :Increment() function on **DataManager** and increase the amount of money the player has.

5. Listen to the .ProcessReceipt event on **MarketplaceService**.

6. Confirm that the player that just purchased the developer product is in-game and that the developer product ID can be found inside our developerProducts variable. If either of these conditions is not met, return the NotProcessedYet Enum.

7. If the previously mentioned conditions are met, execute the reward function in `pcall()`. If an error occurs while rewarding the player, return the `NotProcessedYet` Enum. When there are no errors, return the `PurchaseGranted` Enum.

We have now finished the currency system that we monetized. You can test your system using the GUI we made during this exercise. Optionally, you could include some `print()` statements to test that your script is working properly. Purchasing game passes and developer products do not cost Robux when done in Roblox Studio. Feel free to include other features or expand the system by adding, for instance, a new premium Gem currency.

If you did not manage to complete this exercise because you ran into an issue, please take a look at the example answer that is provided on GitHub: `https://github.com/PacktPublishing/Mastering-Roblox-Coding/tree/main/Exercises`.

Summary

In this chapter, we learned how to monetize our game. We started by looking at **game passes**. We saw that players can purchase game passes in our game for a permanent power-up. These power-ups can be anything. Furthermore, we saw that players can purchase these game passes via the **Store** section on our game's page or via an in-game prompt. We can create prompts in our game to sell game passes. This way, players can conveniently purchase them without quitting or tabbing out of the game to go to the **Store** section.

Once players have purchased a game pass, we need to reward them with this permanent power-up. We learned how to use the `:UserOwnsGamePassAsync()` function on **MarketplaceService** to determine whether players own the game pass. Then, we can reward them with a tool or anything else that the game pass offers. Because the `:UserOwnsGamePassAsync()` function caches its data internally, rewards may not be instant when we use this function. We also do not want our players to rejoin to claim a game pass. Therefore, we have learned to listen to the `.PromptGamePassPurchaseFinished` event, which allows us to instantly reward players when they purchase a new game pass in-game.

Besides game passes, we learned about **developer products**. Unlike game passes, developer products are usually temporary. They can be used for short boosts or to purchase items such as in-game currency. After all, players can purchase developer products multiple times through prompts. Because of this, we saw that it is a bit more difficult to reward the benefits of developer products compared to game passes.

To reward players for purchasing developer products, we must listen to the `.ProcessReceipt` callback. This allows us to see which developer product was just bought and by whom. We learned that it is essential to return a `ProductPurchaseDecision` Enum in our `processReceipt()` function. This Enum determines whether we were able to successfully reward the effect of our developer product.

Finally, we learned about the **Roblox Premium** subscription. We learned that one of the perks of this subscription is receiving in-game **Premium Benefits**. We have the option to include these benefits in our game. We saw that we get paid a **Premium Payout** as a reward for attracting Premium users to our game. This is an additional income source for our games where the player doesn't have to pay for anything. We get paid simply by having Premium users play our games.

Throughout the previous chapters, we have learned so much about Roblox and Luau. We started this book by learning the basics of Luau, such as working with `if` statements, loops, functions, and tables. After that, we quickly improved our programming skills by securing and optimizing our games. Besides this, we learned how to create and program GUIs, listen to user input, build data stores, and how to script the monetization aspect of our games.

Most of the time, we learned about an individual item, such as a data store, that was not necessarily connected to, for instance, user input. Because of this, we have not looked at any examples where all of these systems work together. This is why we will create a **Simulator** game in the next chapter. By doing this, we will see how all of the systems we learned about throughout this book work together. This will result in a fully functioning game that you can be proud of.

Part 3: Creating Your Own Simulator Game

This part will focus on the development process a Roblox Programmer goes through when creating a game. Once completed, you will have a good understanding of all the required steps. In addition, you will have learned tricks to overcome development struggles.

This section comprises the following chapter:

- *Chapter 10, Creating Your Own Simulator Game*

10

Creating Your Own Simulator Game

In this chapter, you will create your very own simulator game. You will use many of the systems that you learned about in previous chapters. Besides this, you will learn how to combine all of these individual systems into one complete game. This way, you will learn, for example, how your GUIs can display data that is stored in your data stores by creating safe RemoteEvents or RemoteFunctions.

The following topics will be covered in this chapter:

- Introduction to the game
- Creating data stores
- Implementing server scripts
- Programming GUIs
- Updating your game

By the end of this chapter, you will have made your own simulator game based on several requirements that your employer could provide you with. You will know how to create proper data stores that will save all the data required for your game. In addition, you will learn how to create the server scripts for all the systems in your game. Besides this, you will know which RemoteEvents and RemoteFunctions to implement to ensure that all the user actions can be performed. Finally, you will also learn how to use these RemoteEvents and RemoteFunctions to make your GUIs work.

Technical requirements

To start programming with Luau, you need access to a device with internet access. This can either be a Windows or a Mac device.

You need to download the following software:

- Roblox Player
- Roblox Studio

This chapter's code examples can be found on GitHub at `https://github.com/PacktPublishing/Mastering-Roblox-Coding`.

The CiA video for this chapter can be found at `https://bit.ly/3OD2wsp`.

Introduction to the game

Because we learned a lot about scripting in Luau throughout the previous chapters, we will create an entire game together in this chapter. Therefore, this chapter is divided into multiple sections. Each section creates a part of our game. However, before we can start creating this, we need to understand the game we will make.

In this chapter, we will create a **simulator** game. Simulators are a popular genre on Roblox. In essence, players collect some sort of currency in their backpacks. Then, they can sell this currency for in-game money. When they do this, they can purchase upgrades, pets, or even rebirth their character to restart the game with a money boost.

Now that we know what simulators are, let us look at the game we will make ourselves. Because this book is about programming, we will provide a great map that was uniquely made for this book. This map was made by Cole Tucker (1Coai):

Figure 10.1 – Our simulator map

You can download this map and the GUIs from the GitHub page for this book: `https://github.com/PacktPublishing/Mastering-Roblox-Coding/tree/main/Games`.

> **Permission**
>
> Because we will make a game in this chapter, you might want to release it once you have finished creating it. This is perfectly fine. You are allowed to use the map and the code that was provided in the example answer for your own game.

Now that we know what a simulator game is and in which map we will create our game, let us look at the game's specifications. In our game, we will have **orbs**. Orbs are the circles on the map that players must collect. Players can convert these orbs into money at a selling point. With this money, they can upgrade the speed of their character. When players upgrade their speed, they will walk faster and therefore be able to collect more orbs in a shorter amount of time. Besides this, players can purchase an orb multiplier. When players upgrade their orb multiplier, they get more orbs when collecting orbs.

Besides upgrades, players must also have the ability to rebirth. Rebirthing in a simulator resets all the progress that they have made. This includes all the orbs, money, and upgrade progress. When players rebirth, they get more money from the selling point in their "second" life. Rebirths should stack. This means that players can rebirth multiple times. The more they rebirth, the higher the multiplier at the selling point becomes.

Because programmers that make a game usually get a list of requirements that need to be implemented into a game, we will follow one as well. Here is the list of requirements for our game:

General requirements:

- You must use the simulator map made by Cole Tucker (1Coai) with the `Orbs`, `RebirthParts`, and `SellParts` folders. You can change the map to your liking.
- The game must be compatible with **FilteringEnabled** and **StreamingEnabled**.
- The game must have a **money** and **orb** currency.
- Players must be able to purchase money through developer products.
- Players must be able to purchase a game pass that doubles their money when selling.
- Players must be able to upgrade their walking speed.
- Players must be able to upgrade their orb multiplier.
- Players must be able to rebirth, which increases their orb selling multiplier.
- All player data must be reset when rebirthing except for the rebirth multiplier.
- When rebirthing, the rebirth price and multiplier must increase for the next rebirth.
- When players touch a `BasePart` inside of the `Orbs` folder, the number of orbs the player has must be increased by 1. This number can go higher depending on the **orb multiplier**.

- When players touch a `BasePart` inside the `SellParts` folder, all the orbs must be converted into money. The amount of money can be more than the number of orbs, depending on the `rebirth` multiplier and game passes.

- When players touch a `BasePart` inside of the `RebirthParts` folder, a GUI has to pop up, allowing players to rebirth.

- **Leader stats** in the player list must show each player's number of **orbs**, **money**, and **rebirths**.

- Players must be able to teleport to the nearest sell point by clicking a button.

- When any player claims an orb, it becomes invisible for five seconds. When the orb is invisible, it cannot be claimed by anyone else either.

The previous *General requirements* are usually provided by the person that hires you. Since they generally do not know much about programming-related specifications, they are usually not provided. Regardless, we want to create high-quality scripts. Therefore, these will be our additional programming-related requirements:

Data store requirements:

- There must be a **DataManager** module that handles everything related to data stores. The DataManager needs to be created so that other scripts do not need any knowledge about data stores other than the data keys that they can use, for instance, `money`, `orbs`, and so on.

- The DataManager must **cache** all the data or the frequently updated data.

- The DataManager must use **retries** when functions fail.

- The DataManager must **yield** until there is enough **budget** for the requested action.

- The DataManager must implement **auto-saving**.

GUI requirements:

- GUIs that are unrelated to each other must be separated into different **ScreenGuis**.

- GUIs may not overlap with each other.

- When opening GUIs, the current GUI, if there is one open, must be closed before the new GUI can open.

- When opening GUIs, you must use **tweens**.

Security requirements:

- All RemoteEvents must implement **server checks**.

- All RemoteEvents and RemoteFunctions must implement **cooldowns**.

- Everything directly related to data stores must be implemented on the server.

- All prices must be calculated on the server. This means that there must not be any parameters on **RemoteEvents** or **RemoteFunctions** that include the prices of items.

Monetization requirements:

- Game pass rewards must be instant.

- When an error occurs while rewarding a developer product, the `NotProcessedYet` enum must be returned.

All these requirements may seem overwhelming. However, if you followed all the **best practices** throughout the book, none of the technical requirements would surprise you. The only thing we need to pay much attention to is the general requirements. After all, this is what we must make. So, to assist you in getting a better view of what our final product will be, here is the published Roblox game that we will make:

`https://www.roblox.com/games/9917292298/Simulator`

We now know what sort of game we are expected to make. Like all the exercises in this book, you can try and make this game without following this chapter's steps. However, remember that this game is far from easy to implement. In addition, we highly encourage you to improve upon and give your personal touch to the game. Finally, remember that this is a complete game, and it will likely take multiple days for you to finish it. Therefore, do not get frustrated if you cannot do multiple sections of this chapter daily.

Throughout the following sections, we will look at our game's aspects. We will look at what we are expected to make and implement it. Because we have explained all the systems, such as datastores and GUIs, in other chapters, we will not explain how they work but rather how we can perfect them for our game. We will start by creating the data stores.

Creating data stores

In this section, we will look at how to design our data stores. In *Chapter 8, Building Data Stores*, we made a base DataManager in the *Creating a DataManager* section. We will use this base version for our game. However, there are still a few things we have to change. First, we must figure out which data we will save in our data stores.

Getting keys for our data stores

When we look at the requirements for our game, we can conclude that we need to implement a key for the following items:

- Money
- Orbs

- Speed upgrade multiplier

- Orb upgrade multiplier

- Rebirths

For money and orbs, we will obviously use **number** as the data type. However, what about the others? You might think of storing the multiplier value for the upgrades and rebirths. This could be something like 1.1 for a 10% bonus. While this might be your initial thought, this is a **bad practice**. Rather than storing the effect, you should store the number of rebirths, for example, that the player has done. This way, you must constantly convert the number of rebirths into a multiplier. As a result, you can change the multiplier for rebirths or upgrades without having to change anything in the data stores.

Just imagine that we would store the multiplier for the speed upgrade in the data stores. The default walking speed for players is 16. Maybe we initially thought it would be a good idea to double the walking speed every time that the player upgraded. This would mean that the new walking speed is 32 when the player upgrades once. But then we figure out that by the fifth upgrade, the walking speed is way too high. Unfortunately, we have already shipped the game and have many players playing. How would we fix this? Do we load their data and divide each player's walking speed by half? But what if they upgraded with the new multiplier rate?

As you can imagine, this becomes a complete mess. Therefore, we should never store multiplier values in our data stores. Instead, we store the number of upgrades. When the player has upgraded two times, we store the number 2. Then, when we load the data, we might multiply this number by 16. This means that the walking speed is 32 again. But when we want to change our multiplier and change it to 8, we still get the number 2 from the data store and multiply it with the new multiplier, which is 8. This results in a new walking speed of 16 for each player, whether they played before our change or not.

Knowing this, we can conclude that for each key we originally thought of, we must save a number. If we change the DEFAULT_PLAYER_DATA constant in the DataManager, it will look like this:

```
local DEFAULT_PLAYER_DATA = {
    -- Currency data
    ["money"] = 0,
    ["orbs"] = 0,

    -- Upgrade data
    ["speed_upgrade"] = 0,
    ["orb_multiplier"] = 0,

    -- Rebirth data
    ["rebirths"] = 0
}
```

Now that we know which keys and data types to use, let us continue by looking at which functions we need in our `DataManager` module.

DataManager functions

In the base version of our **DataManager**, we already have a few functions. These are the `:DataLoaded()` function, the `:Get()` function, the `:Set()` function, and the `:Increment()` function. While this covers everything that we might need, there is one thing that we might need to take a look at. Most of these functions may throw an error. Therefore, we should wrap our calls in a `pcall()`. While this is not a big deal, we get a lot of duplicate code when we use the `:Get()` function in a `pcall()`. This is because when an error occurs, we might want to set some sort of `default` value, like this:

```
local money
local suc, err = pcall(function()
    DataManager:Get(player, "money")
end)
if not suc then
    warn(err)
    money = 0 -- Default value
end
```

The preceding code snippet is all the code that is required when we use the `:Get()` function. As you can imagine, this results in a lot of duplicate code fairly quickly. Therefore, we should introduce a new function into our DataManager. This is the `:GetWithDefault()` function. The `:GetWithDefault()` function will use the `:Get()` function and will basically do what we showed in the preceding code snippet.

When we use the `:GetWithDefault()` function, we try to load the data using the `:Get()` function. However, when an error occurs, we return the `default` value. This could be a parameter. Let us take a look at the following code snippet:

```
function DataManager:GetWithDefault(player, key, default)
    -- Declaring variable
    local data

    -- Default parameter
    if default == nil then
        default = 0
    end
```

```
    -- Querying data store
    local suc, err = pcall(function()
        data = DataManager:Get(player, key)
    end)
    if not suc then
        warn(err)
        return default
    end

    -- Returning data
    return data
end
```

We removed many possible duplicate codes by implementing this function into our DataManager but you might be wondering why we do not just replace the :Get() function to have a default. This is because errors are not always a bad thing.

Imagine we are writing code that relies on the :Get() function having an actual result. When the :Get() function fails, we might want to stop changing the data stores completely. When using the :GetWithDefault() function, we will always continue as if an error would never occur.

We have now looked at the functions in the DataManager and updated them so they meet the required criteria for our game. We prevented possible duplicate code by implementing a new :GetWithDefault() function. If you are making the game while reading, please do not forget to implement this function in your own code. In the next section, we will analyze whether the events in our DataManager suffice.

DataManager events

The base version of the DataManager has just one event, the .PlayerAdded event. This event gets fired when the player data gets successfully loaded. We need to use the DataManager.PlayerAdded event in favor of the Players.PlayerAdded event. After all, we cannot let players play our game without their data being loaded. However, are there more events that we might need?

When we look at the requirements for our game, we see that we must make leader stats for our game. The DataManager is the module that knows when this data changes. Therefore, we need to do something in the DataManager so that the leader stats update. Now, we have two methods of doing this:

- Let the DataManager handle everything related to leader stats
- Create an event that fires when data in the DataManager is updated

When we include everything related to leader stats in our DataManager, the module starts doing two things. First, it handles everything related to data stores and leader stats. Generally, module scripts should only have one purpose. This way, the name of the module can contain everything it does. Other developers should instantly know what to expect from this module without looking at the code. This is no longer the case if we decide to include leader stats. Therefore, this is not the best option.

The other option is to create an additional event. This event fires when data for a player is updated. This means that we need to fire our event in both the `:Set()` function and the `:Increment()` function. This also means that we would fire this event when keys are not necessarily in the leader stats. This is fine. After all, if we were to prevent this, the DataManager would know which keys are used in the leader stats. This would once again mean that the DataManager knows the leader stats. We do not want this, as we want the DataManager to be a standalone module.

Let us look at what we need to change in our DataManager to add our new event:

```
local DataLoadedEvent = Instance.new("BindableEvent")
local DataUpdatedEvent = Instance.new("BindableEvent")

function setupEvents()
    DataManager["PlayerAdded"] = DataLoadedEvent.Event
    DataManager["DataUpdated"] = DataUpdatedEvent.Event
end

function DataManager:Set(player, key, value)
    -- ... Function code ...

    -- Firing data updated
    DataUpdatedEvent:Fire(player, key, value)
end

function DataManager:Increment(player, key, value)
    -- ... Function code ...

    -- Firing data updated
    DataUpdatedEvent:Fire(player, key, cachedData[key])
end
```

Please remember that the preceding code snippet is just the updated code in our base `DataManager` module. Do not forget to include this in your own DataManager.

In the preceding code snippet, we created a new `DataUpdatedEvent` BindableEvent. In the `setupEvents()` function, we ensured that other scripts can listen to this new event. Then, in both the `:Set()` function and the `:Increment()` function, we fired the event with the following three arguments:

- The player whose data just got updated
- The key of the data that just got updated
- The new value for the previously mentioned key

Now, we have set up all the events that might be useful when making the rest of our game. Throughout the previous sections, we looked at which keys our data store needs and whether we implemented all the functions and events in the DataManager. This means we have now finished with everything related to our data stores. In the following sections, we will build the rest of our game. This will rely heavily on our data stores. After all, we want their progress to be saved. Luckily, we did a standalone module. This means we only have to use the functions and events of this module without having to worry about any of its internal complexities.

Implementing server scripts

Now that our data stores are finished, we can implement the scripts that run on the server. This means we will start thinking of **RemoteEvents** and **RemoteFunctions** that the client will need to use. Then, we will implement these.

Implementing this will be a lot of work without seeing any visible results. When making your own game from scratch, you might make systems feature-based. This means that you would make both the client and server sides at the same time, instead of making the entire server side first. However, to improve the readability of this chapter, we have chosen to start with the server side and finish this in its entirety. Then, once our server side is finished, we have finished **RemoteEvents** and **RemoteFunctions** that we can call from the client that will instantly work.

In the following sections, we will analyze what has to be programmed together. After that, we will provide steps similar to the way we have done with the exercises in the previous chapters, which will help you script what we just analyzed.

Implementing leader stats

First, we will implement leader stats into our game. According to the requirements that were specified in the *Introduction to the game* section, we need leader stats for the following data keys:

- Money
- Orbs
- Rebirths

Since all the data types for these keys are numbers, we must create `NumberValues` inside the `leaderstats` model. We will create this `leaderstats` model when the player joins the game. Please keep in mind that you must listen to the `DataManager.PlayerAdded` event instead of the `Players.PlayerAdded` event. This is because there is no point in getting leader stats when the data that has to be displayed has not loaded yet.

Of course, we must also listen to the `DataManager.DataUpdated` event. In the *DataManager events* section, we made this event so that we could update our leader stats whenever data was updated.

Now that we know this, let us try to implement this script. Follow these steps:

1. Create a new script in the **ServerScriptService** service. Make sure you name this script accordingly.

2. Inside this script, create a new function that creates the `leaderstats` model inside the `Player` instance. Besides this, ensure all the required `NumberValues` are made and parented to the `leaderstats` model.

3. Listen to the `.PlayerAdded` event and call the function mentioned in the previous step when this happens.

4. Ensure that the leader stats display the latest information directly after they are created.

5. Listen to the `.DataUpdated` event on the DataManager and ensure the correct data is updated in the leader stats. Use these three parameters that the `.DataUpdated` event provides:

    *   `player`

    *   `key`

    *   `newData`

When you implement the previous steps, your leader stats should be created and updated accordingly. Then, of course, we need to test whether this works. Because the rest of our game is not completely done yet, we cannot play the game to see whether it works. Therefore, we have to execute a small test. Create a new script in `ServerScriptService` that includes the following code snippet:

```
local ServerScriptService =
game:GetService("ServerScriptService")

local DataManager = require(PATH_TO_DATAMANAGER)

DataManager.PlayerAdded:Connect(function(player)
    DataManager:Set(player, "money", 1)
    DataManager:Increment(player, "orbs", 1)
    DataManager:Set(player, "rebirths", 10)
    task.wait(5)
```

```
    DataManager:Increment(player, "money", 100)
    DataManager:Set(player, "orbs", 5)
    DataManager:Increment(player, "rebirths", 1)
end)
```

When you run the preceding code snippet, you should see changes in the leader stats. If this does not happen, look at possible errors in the **Developer Console** frame or the **Output** frame and try to solve them. It is highly recommended that you try to figure out what goes wrong. If, for whatever reason, you are unable to understand what is going on, look at the example answer, which can be found on the GitHub page for this chapter. The link for the GitHub page can be found in the *Technical requirements* section.

Congratulations, you just made your first script for your very own game!

Implementing monetization scripts

Next, we will implement the monetization scripts for our game. Usually, this is something you do last. However, we will implement this first to prevent us from having to implement the monetization aspects of our game while working on different systems.

There are not many complicated things that we must implement into our game to meet the set of requirements regarding monetization. As for game passes, we must create one that doubles the money when selling orbs. This is the only game pass we have to implement. You are free to add more if you'd like. A few example game passes could be **Instant Sell**, **Double Orbs**, **Double Speed**, or anything else that comes to mind. While implementing these is an outstanding practice, it is recommended that you wait until we have finished the game before you implement them.

Besides game passes, we must also implement a few developer products that allow players to purchase in-game money. To create a bit of variation, we will create three developer products. These developer products will give 500, 1,000, or 2,500 coins.

> **Base scripts**
>
> In *Chapter 9, Monetizing Your Game*, we created a base script for game passes and developer products. We will use these scripts. This way, we do not have to remake something we already made.

We now know which game passes and developer products we have to implement. Follow these steps:

1. Ensure your game is published to Roblox so you can create game passes and developer products.

2. Create a new game pass named **Double Money**. You can create a new game pass on the **Store** page for your game. First, make sure this game pass is put on sale. Then, you can decide the price for the game pass yourself.

3. Create a new script in `ServerScriptService` and ensure it contains the base version of the game pass script we made in *Chapter 9*, *Monetizing Your Game*.

4. In the `gamePasses` variable, create a new key with the game pass ID for the previously made game pass. The value of this key should be a `reward()` function. This `reward()` function should change the `2xMoney` attribute on the `Player` instance to `true`. To do this, use the `:SetAttribute()` function.

   Tip for 4: In the exercise of *Chapter 9*, *Monetizing Your Game*, we did something similar.

5. Next, create three new developer products that will reward players with in-game money. Give these developer products a fitting name and price.

6. Create a new script in `ServerScriptService` and ensure it contains the base version of the developer products scripts we made in *Chapter 9*, *Monetizing Your Game*.

7. In the `developerProducts` variable, create three new keys with the developer product IDs you made in *Step 5*. The value for each key should be a `reward()` function. In the `reward()` function, you should use the `:Increment()` function on the DataManager to increment the player's money.

   Tip for 7: According to the requirements, there are no multipliers through game passes or premium benefits that would reward players with more money. Therefore, you can just increment their money with the same amount as the developer product specifies.

This is everything we need to do to implement monetization features into our game. Obviously, future scripts will still have to look at whether players own this game pass, but this is something for later.

We need to perform two tests to check that our script works. First, to test whether the developer products work, we can simply create a prompt for each developer product to check whether the money increases. Since our leader stats work, we can simply see whether these increase.

Then, to test game passes, we must do something else. If you created the game pass yourself, you should have this in your own inventory. This means you own the game pass. You can check whether you own the game pass by clicking on the game pass from the **Store** section of your game. Then, you should see a message that says **Item Owned**. You can see this in *Figure 10.2*:

Figure 10.2 – Item Owned

If you own this game pass, use the **Properties** frame in Roblox Studio to verify that the **2xMoney** attribute on your Player instance is checked, as seen in *Figure 10.3*:

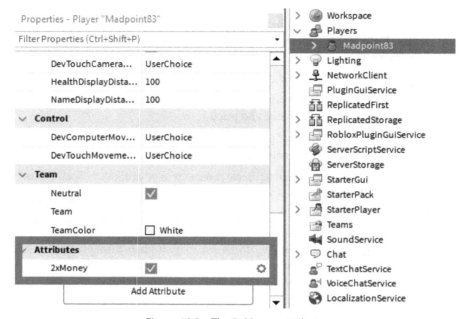

Figure 10.3 – The 2xMoney attribute

When both tests work, we can continue to the next section. If either does not work, try to look for errors in the **Developer Console** frame or the **Output** frame. If, for whatever reason, you are unable to understand what is going on, look at the example answer, which can be found on the GitHub page for this chapter. The link for the GitHub page can be found in the *Technical requirements* section.

Implementing character upgrades

Next, we will create the most complex system of the entire game: character upgrades. Even though it is the most complex system, do not worry; we will walk through it step by step. According to the requirements specified in the *Introduction to the game* section, we need to make two upgrades for characters. Players must be able to upgrade their speed and orb multiplier. In our data stores, we save an **upgrade number**. We have to convert these upgrade numbers into a multiplier. Because there is no requirement that there should be an infinite number of upgrades, we can just decide ourselves how many upgrades we want to implement.

First, we will create a dictionary that stores the price and multiplier for each upgrade. This dictionary will store all the upgrade data for each individual upgrade. Please keep in mind that this is not the player's data. The player's data will refer to one of these indexes. This is what a dictionary that contains all the upgrade data looks like:

```lua
local upgrades = {
    ["speed_upgrade"] = {
        [0] = { price = 0, multiplier = 1 }, -- Default
        -- ...
        [10] = { price = 25_000, multiplier = 5 }
    },
    ["orb_multiplier"] = {
        [0] = { price = 0, multiplier = 1 },  -- Default
        -- ...
        [10] = { price = 75_000, multiplier = 15 },
    }
}
```

In the preceding code snippet, we can see the upgrade data for both the **speed upgrade** and the **orb multiplier upgrade**. The data that is on index 0 is the default data. This means that when the player has never upgraded, their multiplier will be 1.

When a player wants to upgrade, we look at the upgrade number that is one higher than the current number. When we want to check how much it costs to upgrade, we add 1 to the current upgrade number, for example, 0 + 1 equals 1. Then, we check if this upgrade number exists. If it does not, the player cannot upgrade any further. However, if this new index does exist, the player can upgrade. When the upgrade does exist, we look at the price key for this upgrade. This way, we know how much it costs to upgrade to this new level.

Now that we know how to implement the data structure for the upgrades, let us implement it into our game. Follow these steps:

1. Create a new UpgradeService script in the ServerScriptService service.

2. Create a dictionary containing all the upgrade data. Each upgrade should have at least 10 upgrades. For each upgrade, you should determine the multiplier and price.

3. Now that we have implemented the data structure for our upgrades, let us create the RemoteEvents and RemoteFunction that we will need for our system. Please keep in mind that you must create these in the **Explorer** window of Roblox Studio, not in a script. Create an Events folder in **ReplicatedStorage**. Inside this folder, create the following instances:

    *   An Upgrade RemoteEvent

    *   A GetUpgradeData RemoteFunction

    *   An UpgradeDataUpdated RemoteEvent

Now that we have created our RemoteEvents and RemoteFunction, let us start implementing them. First, we will create our RemoteFunction. This RemoteFunction should return specific data. The client will use this data to update the information that is displayed in the GUI. Because of this, it is recommended that we take a look at the **Upgrades** GUI to see what information this GUI needs:

Figure 10.4 – Upgrades GUI

GUIs

The GUIs for this game were provided in the same file that the map is in. The GUIs are stored in the **StarterGui** service. Feel free to style them to your liking.

In *Figure 10.4*, we see a lot of data that needs to be displayed in the GUI. Here is a list of data that is required if we want to update our GUI accurately:

- Name of the upgrade
- Current progress number
- Maximum progress number
- Price to upgrade

We now know what the RemoteFunction could return. When we put this into a dictionary, it looks like this:

```
local data = {
    ["Speed Upgrade"] = {
        upgrade_name = "speed_upgrade",
        current_progress = 0,
        max_progress = 0,
        upgrade_cost = 0,
        multiplier = 0
    }
}
```

In the preceding code snippet, we see that this is a data dictionary containing all the data for the speed upgrade. The upgrade_name key contains the speed_upgrade value. This is because this is what the key in our DataManager is called. By doing this, we can tell the client which upgrade key to call when the player tries to upgrade without converting Speed Upgrade into speed_upgrade.

You might have noticed that the previous code snippet contains a multiplier key that was not required for our GUI. We added this because we could also use this dictionary on the server. After all, when players have to upgrade, all this data is also required.

Now that we know this, let us implement the RemoteFunction.

4. Listen to the GetUpgradeData RemoteFunction in the UpgradeService script. The parameter for this function is the player who is requesting their data. The result of this function should be a dictionary that contains the following data for each upgrade:

- Upgrade name
- Current progress number
- Maximum progress number
- Upgrade cost
- Multiplier

Tip for 4: First, get the current progress using the DataManager. Once you have this, figure out what the multiplier for this progress number is. Then, find out how much it costs to upgrade. Finally, calculate how many indexes there are in the table for the current upgrade. This will be your maximum progress number.

Now that we have implemented our GetUpgradeData RemoteFunction, let us continue with the Upgrade RemoteEvent. This is the RemoteEvent that the client will use to upgrade. However, before we can implement this, there is something we need to take a look at.

When a player upgrades, the information displayed in the GUI should change. Now, there are two options. We could either call our RemoteFunction directly after the RemoteEvent is fired, or create a new RemoteEvent that provides the exact same data as the RemoteFunction. However, the server fires this RemoteEvent to the client this time. This way, the server decides when the information in the GUI is updated.

We have decided to use the additional RemoteEvent. This RemoteEvent is called `UpgradeDataUpdated`. Follow the next step to implement our `Upgrade` RemoteEvent and our `UpgradeDataUpdated` RemoteEvent.

5.   Listen to the `Upgrade` RemoteEvent. When this RemoteEvent gets used, perform the following steps:

- Check whether the player has a cooldown or not.

- Check that if the player is on the final upgrade, they cannot exceed the upgrade limit. Current progress cannot be greater or equal to the maximum progress number.

- Check whether the player has enough money to upgrade. Use the DataManager to get the player's money.

- If all of the previous requirements are met, increment the upgrade number for the requested upgrade. In addition, lower the money with the price of this upgrade.

- Fire the `UpgradeDataUpdated` RemoteEvent for the same player that called this function. The second argument of this RemoteEvent should be the same data as the function we made in the previous step.

- Apply the new multiplier. Some upgrades have an instantaneous effect once players have upgraded. For instance, the speed after upgrading should be applied instantly. However, not all upgrades have an instantaneous effect.

Tip for 5: Use the function made in the previous step. This function contains a lot of the required data.

We have now implemented all the previously made RemoteEvents and RemoteFunction. If you got stuck somewhere in these steps, please look at the example answer you can find on the GitHub page for this chapter. This is the most complex system in the entire game. Therefore, it is understandable if you run into some issues.

In the following sections, we might need to use some of the multiplier data we made in this script. For instance, when claiming orbs, the amount of orbs the player gets is based on the orb multiplier upgrade that we made here. To transfer this multiplier between scripts, we use BindableFunctions. We learned about BindableFunctions in *Chapter 3, Event-Based Programming*.

Let's implement our BindableFunction.

6. Create a new `ServerEvents` folder in the **ServerStorage** service.

7. Create a new BindableFunction in the previously made `GetMultiplierUpgrade` folder.

8. In our `UpgradeService`, listen to the `GetMultiplierUpgrade` BindableFunction callback. Return the multiplier for the provided upgrade name. When this function gets called, you can use the following parameters:

    • The player whose multiplier is requested.

    • The name of the upgrade that is requested. The name of this upgrade matches the keys in the DataManager. An example upgrade name could be `speed_upgrade`.

    Tip for 8: To get the multiplier, use the function that we made two steps ago.

We have now finished implementing our upgrade system. Once again, this is the most complex system in our game. If you did not manage to implement this system, please take a look at the example answer, which can be found on the GitHub page for this chapter.

In the next section, we will implement the system that lets us claim the orbs that spawn inside the map.

Claiming orbs

Inside the map, there are many different circles. These are orbs. You can see an image of these orbs in *Figure 10.5*:

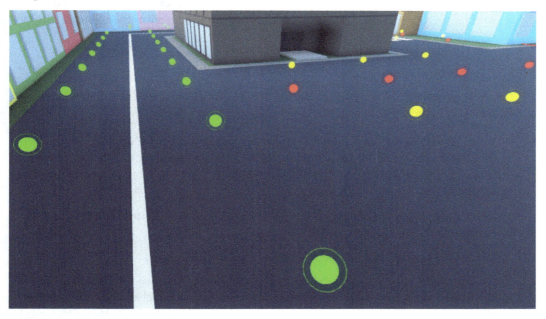

Figure 10.5 – Orbs on the map

All of these orbs are in a folder called `Orbs`. This folder is a direct descendant of the **Workspace** service.

When a player touches one of these orbs, the system should check whether this orb is claimable. An orb is considered claimable when players have not touched it for at least five seconds. When an orb is not claimable, it should be invisible. The challenge when implementing this is to ensure that each orb has its own five-second cooldown.

Luckily, we learned about **attributes**. We can create an attribute on these orbs that specifies the last time they were claimed. This way, we can read the attribute, check whether it was not touched for at least five seconds, reward the player, and reset the countdown.

When an orb is claimed, the `orbs` key in the DataManager should be incremented by 1. This is our base value. However, we must also check the orb multiplier upgrade. This upgrade multiplier must be multiplied against the base value 1.

Now that we know this, let us implement our system. Follow these steps:

1. Create a new `OrbsService` script in `ServerScriptService`.

2. Create a `setup()` function. This `setup()` function should do the following:

    -   Loop through all of the `BasePart` in the `Orbs` folder.

    -   Set the `ClaimTime` attribute on each `BasePart` to 0. We do this to initialize our attributes.

    -   Listen to the `.Touched` event on the `BasePart`. When this event fires, you should check whether the `hit` parameter that the `.Touched` event provides meets the following criteria:

        -   The parent of the `hit` instance must not be `nil`

        -   The parent of the `hit` instance should be a character

        -   When using the `:GetPlayerFromCharacter(hit.Parent)` function on the **Players** service, the result of this function should be a player

    -   When all of the previous requirements are met, check whether the orb that was touched does not have a cooldown. To do this, use the `ClaimTime` attribute and the `os.time()` function. The value of the `os.time()` function should be equal to or greater than the `ClaimTime` attribute plus 5 seconds.

    -   When the previous requirement is met, update the `ClaimTime` attribute and set it to the current `os.time()` value.

    -   Change the **Transparency** property of the orb and its children to 1.

    -   Calculate the number of orbs the player's data should be incremented with. The base value is 1 orb. However, this has to be multiplied against the upgrade multiplier of the orb multiplier. Once this is calculated, use the `:Increment()` function on the DataManager to increment the number of orbs this player has.

- Finally, use the `task.wait()` function and wait five seconds to change back the transparency of the orb and its children. The new transparency should be `0`.

We have now finished our orbs system. You can test whether it works by playing the game. Then, walk into the orbs on the map and watch them change transparency. Besides this, ensure the number of orbs in the leader stats increases. If this does not happen, check the **Developer Console** frame or the **Output** frame for possible errors. If, for whatever reason, you are unable to understand what is going on, look at the example answer, which can be found on the GitHub page for this chapter. The link for the GitHub page can be found in the *Technical requirements* section.

We can move on to the next section when you have tested your code. Next, we will create our rebirths system.

Implementing rebirths

While it is weird that we implement rebirths before selling orbs, we will need our rebirthing multiplier before implementing our selling system. We will implement this first to prevent us from having to change the orbs selling system after implementing the rebirthing system.

First, we will start by creating the required RemoteEvents and RemoteFunction for this system:

1. Create the following RemoteEvents and RemoteFunction in the `Events` folder in the `ReplicatedStorage` service:

   - A `Rebirth` RemoteEvent

   - An `OpenFrame` RemoteEvent

   - A `GetRebirthData` RemoteFunction

   - A `RebirthDataUpdated` RemoteEvent

   According to the requirements from the *Introduction to the game* section, the **Rebirthing** GUI should open when a player touches a `BasePart` in the `RebirthParts` folder in the **Workspace** service. We can implement this on both the server and the client. However, since our game must be compatible with **StreamingEnabled**, it is easier to implement it on the server. Therefore, when a player touches one of these `BasePart`, we should fire our `OpenFrame` RemoteEvent. That way, we can open the **Rebirthing** GUI based on this trigger.

   Now that we know this, let us implement the code related to opening the **Rebirthing** GUI.

2. Create a new `RebirthService` script in the `ServerScriptService` service.

3. Create a `setup()` function. This `setup()` function should do the following:

   - Loop through all of the `BasePart` inside the `RebirthsFolder` folder, which can be found in the **Workspace** service.

- Listen to the .Touched event on the BasePart. When this event fires, you should check whether the hit parameter that the .Touched event provides meets the following criteria:

  - The parent of the hit instance must not be nil

  - The parent of the hit instance should be a character

  - When using the :GetPlayerFromCharacter(hit.Parent) function on the **Players** service, the result of this function should be a player

4. When the previous requirements are met, fire the OpenFrame RemoteEvent for the player that touched the BasePart.

Next, we will implement the functions related to the **GetRebirthData** RemoteFunction. To figure out which data the client needs, let us take a look at the **Rebirthing** GUI:

Figure 10.6 – The Rebirthing GUI

In *Figure 10.6*, we need to display the price of the rebirth. The price of rebirthing should be displayed at **x**. However, because we can also use this function inside our own script, we might want to add a few keys to our dictionary. Instead of only including the price of rebirth, we also want to know how many times the player has been rebirthed already. In addition, it might be helpful to know the current rebirth multiplier. The dictionary could look like this:

```
local data = {
    current_rebirth = 0,
    rebirth_price = 0,
    rebirth_multiplier = 1
}
```

Even though the current GUIs do not need this data, it might be informative to let the players know this anyway. Feel free to change the GUI so that it displays all of the data that is provided in the preceding code snippet.

Besides this, the rebirth multiplier and price should increase every time the player decides to rebirth, according to the requirements in the *Introduction to the game* section.

Here are example formulae that you could use to do this. Feel free to use different formulae:

- For the rebirth multiplier: (currentRebirth ^ 2) / ((currentRebirth * .75) + 1) + 1

- For the rebirth price: (currentRebirth ^ 3) * 25 + 1_000

Both formulae increase exponentially. This means the multiplier and price increase significantly every time the player decides to rebirth. As previously mentioned, feel free to write a different formula.

Now that we know what this RemoteFunction should do, let us implement it.

5. Listen to the GetRebirthData RemoteFunction callback.

6. When this event is called, return the dictionary that was previously shown.

   Tip for 6: First, get the current_rebirth value using the DataManager. Based on this, use the previously mentioned formulae to calculate the rest.

   Next, we will make it so players can actually rebirth. All player data except for the rebirth multiplier should be reset when rebirthing, according to the requirements in the *Introduction to the game* section. Let us implement this.

7. Listen to the Rebirth RemoteEvent.

8. When this event gets called, check whether the player has sufficient money to perform this rebirth.

   Tip for 8: The function made two steps ago contains the rebirth price.

9. If this is the case, execute the following commands on the DataManager in just one pcall():

   - Set the money to 0

   - Set the orbs to 0

   - Set the speed_upgrade to 0

   - Set the orb_multiplier to 0

   - Increment the rebirths by 1

10. Fire the RebirthDataUpdated RemoteEvent for the same player that called this function. The second argument of this RemoteEvent should be the same data as the function we made in *Step 6*.

We have now implemented all the RemoteEvents and RemoteFunctions. However, as previously mentioned, we had to create our rebirths system before implementing the system allowing us to sell the orbs. This was because the selling orbs system requires the rebirths multiplier. For the selling orbs system to get this multiplier, we must implement a BindableFunction.

11. Create a new BindableFunction in the `ServerEvents` folder inside the `ServerStorage` service. Name this BindableFunction `GetRebirthMultiplier`.

12. Listen to the `GetRebirthMultiplier` BindableFunction callback. Return the multiplier for the current rebirth. When this function gets called, you can use the following parameter:

    - Player whose multiplier is requested

    Tip for 12: The function made in *Step 6* contains the multiplier for the current rebirth.

We have now finished our rebirthing system. This was a complex system. If your code does not work instantly, try to fix possible errors that show up in the **Developer Console** frame or the **Output** frame. If, for whatever reason, you are unable to understand what is going on, look at the example answer, which can be found on the GitHub page for this chapter.

You can move on to the next section when you have tested your code. Next, we will create a system that allows players to sell their orbs.

Selling orbs

Finally, we will implement our selling orbs system. When a player touches one of the `BasePart` inside the `SellParts` folder, the number of orbs should automatically be sold. Each orb is worth one dollar. Please remember that this has to be multiplied against the rebirth multiplier that we made in the previous section. In addition, there is a **2xMoney** game pass, which doubles this even more. But, before we worry about this, let us implement the `setup()` function. Follow these steps:

1. Create a new `SellService` script in `ServerScriptService`.

2. Next, create a `setup()` function. This `setup()` function should do the following:

   - Loop through all of the `BasePart` inside the `SellParts` folder, which can be found in the **Workspace** service.

   - Listen to the `.Touched` event on the `BasePart`. When this event fires, you should check whether the `hit` parameter that the `.Touched` event provides meets the following criteria:

     - The parent of the `hit` instance must not be `nil`

     - The parent of the `hit` instance should be a character

     - When using the `:GetPlayerFromCharacter(hit.Parent)` function on the **Players** service, the result of this function should be a player

3. Check whether the player has a cooldown or not. Players can only sell their orbs once every second.

We know that a player wants to sell their orbs. Now, we need to convert all of the orbs into money. First, we need to get the number of orbs. Back in the *DataManager functions* section, we decided to create a `:GetWithDefault()` function, instead of updating the `:Get()` function. This was because sometimes we do not want to continue our script when an error occurs. When selling orbs, we need to get the number of orbs the player has. When the DataManager fails to get this amount of orbs, we do not want to continue our script. After all, we cannot convert something if we get nothing.

Now that we know this, let us implement the system that implements the conversion of orbs into money.

4. Create a `pcall()` function that includes the following game logic:

   - Getting the number of orbs a player has using the `:Get()` function and storing this in a variable named `orbs`.

   - Setting the number of `orbs` to `0`.

   - Checking whether the player owns the 2xMoney game pass by checking the `2xMoney` attribute on the `Player` instance. When they own the game pass, double the `orbs` variable.

   - Invoking the `GetRebirthMultiplier` BindableFunction, which we made in the *Implementing rebirths* section. Then, multiply the `orbs` variable with the value that this BindableFunction returns.

   - Incrementing the amount of money that the player has with the value that is stored in the `orbs` variable.

We have now implemented the system that sells your orbs and converts them into money. While this is done, the requirements in the *Introduction to the game* section contain one more thing that we need to do. The requirements specify that players must be able to teleport to the nearest sell location.

Since our GUIs have a **Sell** button that allows players to do this, we must implement a RemoteEvent to teleport players in this direction. Since our game uses **StreamingEnabled**, we must call the `:RequestStreamAroundAsync()` function on the player before we can teleport them there. We learned about this function in *Chapter 5, Optimizing Your Game*.

Now that we know this, let us implement this into our game.

5. Create a new `TeleportClosestSellPoint` RemoteEvent in the `Events` folder.

6. When this event gets fired, check whether the player has a cooldown or not. Players may only use this RemoteEvent once every five seconds.

7. Loop through all of the BasePart in the SellParts folder. Use the .Magnitude property on two BasePart, your character's primary part and sell part, to calculate the distance between both parts. Use this data to figure out which BasePart has the least distance. This is the selling part that the player should be teleported to.

The following is an example code for the previous step:

```
local distance = ( sellPoint.Position - player.Character.
PrimaryPart.Position ).Magnitude
```

8. When you know which sell point is closest to the player, use the :RequestStreamAroundAsync() function to preload the area around this selling point.

9. Finally, teleport the player to this point using the :SetPrimaryPartCFrame() function on the player's character.

Tip for 9: To convert a Vector3 data type into a CFrame, use the following code:

```
CFrame.new(Vector3.new(0, 0, 0))
```

We have now finished our selling system. You can test whether the selling system works by walking up to a selling point. You should see the number of orbs and money changes in the leader stats. If this does not happen, check the **Developer Console** frame or the **Output** frame for possible errors. If, for whatever reason, you are unable to understand what is going on, look at the example answer, which can be found on the GitHub page for this chapter. The link for the GitHub page can be found in the *Technical requirements* section.

We have now finished all of our server scripts. Throughout the past sections, we made our leader stats, created scripts to reward game passes and developer products, and made it so that players can upgrade their character, rebirth, and claim and sell orbs. Most of these scripts use RemoteEvents and RemoteFunctions. We will need to use these when programming our GUIs. Now, let us continue programming our game's GUIs.

Programming GUIs

Now that we have finished all of the RemoteEvents and RemoteFunctions, we can start programming our GUIs. The primary thing that we need to do is use the RemoteEvents and RemoteFunctions at the correct times. This way, our GUIs will be updated correctly, and buttons will do what they are supposed to do.

Before we start implementing each GUI, we need to create a system that allows each GUI to open and close. In the *Exercise 6.1 – Creating a Shop GUI* section of *Chapter 6, Creating User Interfaces for All Devices*, we made this system already. At the time, there were two example answers for this exercise: a default and an advanced version. For our game, we will use the advanced version. Since it is not required to rescript these modules completely, we can copy and paste them into our new GUIs.

> **Tip**
>
> It is recommended that you read through all of the code for these modules. If you cannot figure out what specific modules do or how they work, redo *Exercise 6.1*.

When you copy the **UIHandler** module and the **FrameHandler** module from *Exercise 6.1*, your **StarterGui** should look like this:

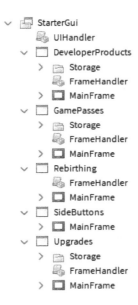

Figure 10.7 – Implemented UIHandler and FrameHandler modules

As shown in *Figure 10.7*, you should not paste the **FrameHandler** module in the **SideButtons** ScreenGui.

Now that we have implemented the modules that will help us change between frames, let us start programming each separate GUI. First, we will start with the **SideButtons** GUI.

Programming the SideButtons GUI

We will start by creating simple GUIs and slowly move on to the more difficult ones. Therefore, we will start with the **SideButtons** GUI. The **SideButtons** GUI are the buttons on the left side of your screen:

Figure 10.8 – Side buttons

Here is a list of what should happen when each button is pressed:

- When the **UPGRADE** button is pressed, the **Upgrade** GUI should open.

- When the **SELL** button is pressed, the `TeleportClosestSellPoint` RemoteEvent should be fired. We made this RemoteEvent in the *Selling orbs* section.

- When the **CURRENCY** button is pressed, the **DeveloperProducts** GUI should open.

When we need to open a GUI, we use the **UIHandler** module, which is a child of the **StarterGui** service. In this module, we can use the `:ToggleFrame()` function. The **UIHandler** module will ensure that frames do not overlap, as required by the requirements in the *Introduction to the game* section.

Follow these steps to program the **SideButtons** GUI:

1. Create a new **LocalScript** inside the **SideButtons** GUI.

2. Listen to the `.MouseButton1Click` event on the **Upgrading** button. When this event gets fired, open the **Upgrades** GUI.

3. Listen to the `.MouseButton1Click` event on the **PurchasingCurrency** button. When this event gets fired, open the **DeveloperProducts** GUI.

4. Listen to the `.MouseButton1Click` event on the **TeleportSell** button. When this event gets fired, fire the `TeleportClosestSellPoint` RemoteEvent.

   We have now implemented all the buttons that we previously discussed. However, there is one more thing we should do. In the *Implementing rebirths* section, we created an `OpenFrame` RemoteEvent. When this event on this RemoteEvent gets fired, we should open the **Rebirthing** GUI. Let us implement this into our current script.

5. Listen to the `.OnClientEvent` event on the `OpenFrame` RemoteEvent. When this event gets fired, open the **Rebirthing** GUI.

We have now implemented our **SideButtons** GUI. First, check whether all the buttons work and that they do what they should do. If it does not work instantly, try to fix possible errors that show up in the **Developer Console** frame or the **Output** frame. If, for whatever reason, you are unable to understand what is going on, look at the example answer, which can be found on the GitHub page for this chapter.

We can move on to the next section when you have tested that the buttons work. Next, we will program the **Rebirthing** GUI.

Programming the Rebirthing GUI

Next, we will move to a more complex GUI, the **Rebirthing** GUI. As displayed in *Figure 10.9*, we need to display the price for each rebirth in the GUI. Back in the *Implementing rebirths* section, we made a GetRebirthData RemoteFunction, which we could invoke to get a dictionary containing the rebirth price.

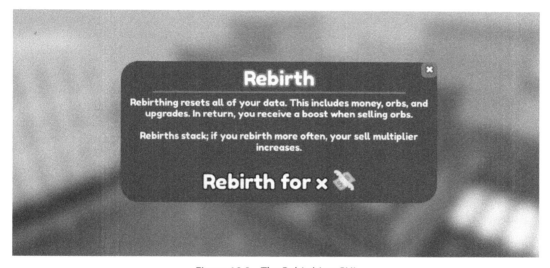

Figure 10.9 – The Rebirthing GUI

Besides this, we also made a RebirthDataUpdated RemoteEvent. When this RemoteEvent gets fired, the price in the GUI should be updated. Let us start by implementing the code related to updating the information displayed in the GUI. Follow these steps:

1. Create a new **LocalScript** inside the **Rebirthing** GUI.
2. Create a function named updateButton(). The parameter of this function should be named rebirthData. This parameter contains the dictionary made by our GetRebirthData RemoteFunction and our RebirthDataUpdated RemoteEvent.

3. Inside the updateButton() function, change the Text property of the RebirthButton, so it displays the new price to rebirth.

   Tip for 3: If you forgot what data is inside the rebirthData parameter, look at the dictionary we made inside the GetRebirthData RemoteFunction.

4. Listen to the .OnClientEvent event on the RebirthDataUpdated RemoteEvent. When this event gets fired, start the updateButton() function.

5. Create a setup() function. In the setup() function, do the following things:

   - Invoke the GetRebirthData RemoteFunction and store the result in a rebirthData variable

   - Check whether the rebirthData variable is nil or not

   - If the result is not nil, start the updateButton() function and provide the rebirthData variable as the argument

   The data in our GUI should now be updated. Try walking to the rebirth building and wait until the **Rebirthing** GUI shows up. When it does, ensure that the correct price is displayed.

   Next, we need to make our **RebirthButton** work. To do this, we must listen to the .MouseButton1Click event on the **RebirthButton**. When this happens, fire the Rebirth RemoteEvent. Besides being able to rebirth, we must also program the **Close** button. When a player presses this button, the frame should close. To do this, use the :CloseFrame() function on the **FrameHandler** module that you inserted into the **Rebirthing** GUI.

   Now that we know this, let us start programming the GUI.

6. Listen to the .MouseButton1Click event on the RebirthButton. When this event gets fired, fire the Rebirth RemoteEvent.

7. Listen to the .MouseButton1Click event on the **Close** button. When this event is fired, close the frame using the :CloseFrame() function.

Closing frames

All the GUIs we will program for this game will have a close button. To prevent repetition, we will not include a step to close each frame in the upcoming sections. However, this does not mean that you should not implement it.

We have now programmed our second GUI. In the next section, we will program our **DeveloperProducts** GUI.

Programming the DeveloperProducts GUI

In the previous sections, the complexity of the GUIs slowly built up. In this section, we will do something we have never done before. We will generate GUI Elements.

Inside the `Storage` folder, there is a **Template** TextButton. Each developer product gets its own template. Inside of each template, we must change the **Title**, the **Description**, and the **ImageLabel**, so it displays accurate information for the developer product.

Follow these steps to program our **DeveloperProducts** GUI:

1. Create a new **LocalScript** inside the **DeveloperProducts** GUI.

2. Create a table inside a `developerProducts` variable that contains all the developer product IDs.

3. Create a `setup()` function. The `setup()` function should do the following:

   - Loop through the `developerProducts` table.

   - Clone the **Template** TextButton for each developer product using the `:Clone()` function.

   - Change the **Name** property of the TextButton to the developer product ID.

   - Get the developer product info for the current developer product using the `MarketplaceService:GetProductInfo()` function and store the result in a `devProductInfo` variable.

   - Update the **Title** TextLabel inside the **Template** TextButton so that it displays the name of the developer product using the `Name` key from the `devProductInfo` variable.

   - Update the **Description** TextLabel inside the **Template** TextButton so that it displays the price of the developer product and a default text that informs the player that the product can be purchased multiple times. To get the price of the developer product, use the `PriceInRobux` key from the `devProductInfo` variable. See *Figure 10.10* for an example.

   - Update the **ImageLabel** inside the **Template** TextButton so that it displays the icon of the developer product. To get the icon image asset ID, use the `IconImageAssetId` key from the `devProductInfo` variable.

   Tip: Add `rbxassetid://` in front of the `IconImageAssetId` key.

   - Change the **Visible** property on the **Template** TextButton to `true`.

   - Parent the **Template** TextButton to the **Body** ScrollingFrame.

   - Listen to the `.MouseButton1Click` event on the **Template** TextButton. When this event gets fired, prompt the correct developer product.

Figure 10.10 – The Currency GUI

We now prompt and generate buttons for the developer products. However, there is one more button on our GUI. At the bottom of the GUI, as shown in *Figure 10.10*, there is a button allowing users to purchase game passes. This button will close the **DeveloperProducts** GUI and open the **GamePasses** GUI. To change to the **GamePasses** frame, use the `:ToggleFrame()` function in the **UIHandler** module inside the **StarterGui**. Follow these instructions:

4. Listen to the `.MouseButton1Click` event on the **SwitchGamePasses** TextButton. When this event gets fired, open the **GamePasses** GUI using the `:ToggleFrame()` function.

We have now implemented the **DeveloperProducts** GUI. First, open the **DeveloperProducts** GUI by pressing the **Currency** button on the left side of your screen. Once it is open, press any developer products for your game. When you purchase a developer product, your money should increase. You can check the leader stats to see whether this happens.

If it does not work, try to fix possible errors that show up in the **Developer Console** frame or the **Output** frame. If, for whatever reason, you are unable to understand what is going on, look at the example answer, which can be found on the GitHub page for this chapter.

We can move on to the next section when you have tested that the developer products work. Next, we will program our **Game Passes** GUI.

Programming the GamePasses GUI

Creating the **GamePasses** GUI will be very similar to how we created our **DeveloperProducts** GUI. However, there are a few slight changes. Follow these steps:

1. Create a new **LocalScript** inside the **GamePasses** GUI.
2. Create a table inside a `gamePasses` variable that contains all the game pass IDs.
3. Create a `setup()` function. The `setup()` function should do the following:

   - Loop through the `gamePasses` table.
   - Clone the **Template** TextButton for each game pass using the `:Clone()` function.
   - Change the **Name** property of the TextButton to the game pass ID.
   - Get the game pass info for the current game pass using the `MarketplaceService:GetProductInfo()` function and store the result in a `gamePassInfo` variable.
   - Update the **Title** TextLabel inside the **Template** TextButton so that it displays the name of the game pass using the `Name` key from the `gamePassInfo` variable.
   - Update the **Description** TextLabel inside the **Template** so that it displays the price and description of the game pass. To get the price of the game pass, use the `PriceInRobux` key from the `gamePassInfo`. To get the description of the game pass, use the `Description` key from the `gamePassInfo` variable.
   - Update the **ImageLabel** inside the **Template** so that it displays the icon of the game pass. To get the icon image asset ID, use the `IconImageAssetId` key from the `gamePassInfo` variable.

   Tip: Add `rbxassetid://` in front of the `IconImageAssetId` key.
   - Change the `Visible` property on the **Template** TextButton to `true`.
   - Parent the `Template` TextButton to the **Body** ScrollingFrame.
   - Listen to the `.MouseButton1Click` event on the **Template** TextButton. When this event gets fired, prompt the correct game pass.

We have now implemented the **GamePasses** GUI. Open the **GamePasses** GUI. Once it is open, press any created game pass buttons and confirm that a prompt appears. If it does not work, try to fix possible errors that show up in the **Developer Console** frame or the **Output** frame. If, for whatever reason, you are unable to understand what is going on, look at the example answer, which can be found on the GitHub page for this chapter.

You can move on to the next section when you have tested that the game pass buttons work. Next, we will program the **Upgrade** GUI.

Programming the Upgrade GUI

Finally, we must also program the **Upgrade** GUI. This will be the most complex GUI to script but do not worry, we will do this together. In the *Implementing character upgrades* section, we created a few RemoteEvents and RemoteFunctions. We will use these to make our GUI. But, first, we need to generate a TextButton for each upgrade, similar to how we did so in the previous chapters.

Before we can start generating TextButtons, we first need to figure out which upgrades are in our game. To get this information, we must invoke the GetUpgradeData RemoteFunction. If you forgot how this RemoteFunction works, view the code we made for the RemoteFunction.

Follow these steps to generate the TextButtons for each upgrade:

1. Create a new **LocalScript** inside the **Upgrades** GUI.

2. Create a setup() function. The setup() function should do the following:

   A. Invoke the GetUpgradeData RemoteFunction to get a dictionary with the upgrade data and save it in an upgradeData variable.

   B. Loop through the upgradeData dictionary. The dictionary's key is the upgrade name that should be displayed to players. The value of the dictionary is another dictionary that contains all the keys discussed in the *Implementing character upgrades* section.

Your loop code could look like this:

```
for upgradeName, upgradeInfo in pairs(upgradeData) do
```

   C. Clone the **Template** TextButton from the Storage folder using the :Clone() function.

   D. Change the Name property of the **Template** TextButton to the value of the upgrade_name key inside the upgradeInfo variable.

   E. Change the Text property of the **Title** TextLabel inside the **Template** TextButton to the value of the upgradeName variable.

   F. Parent the **Template** TextButton to the **Body** ScrollingFrame.

   G. Listen to the .MouseButton1Click event on the TextButton. When this event gets fired, fire the Upgrade RemoteEvent. The argument of the :FireServer() function should be upgradeInfo.upgrade_name.

So far, we have generated TextButtons that display the title of each upgrade. Besides this, we made it so that players are able to upgrade once they press the TextButton. However, the progress bar and **Progress** TextLabels do not receive updated information yet. Why not? Are we not supposed to show the latest data in the GUI instantly? Yes, we are. However, there is a RemoteEvent that will do this as well. This is the UpgradeDataUpdated event. We will create a new function that both the setup() function and the UpgradeDataUpdated RemoteEvent will use to prevent duplicate code.

Follow these next steps to make our `update` function.

3. Create a new `updateButtons()` function. This function has a parameter named `upgradeData`. This parameter contains the same data as the variable we made in *Step 2A*. This function should do the following:

   A. Loop through the `upgradeData` variable the same way we did in *Step 2B*.

   B. Look for the TextButton that matches the `upgradeInfo.upgrade_name`.

   C. If this TextButton can be found, change the `Text` property for the **UpgradeText** TextLabel so that it displays the correct price to upgrade. To get the price, use the `upgrade_cost` key in the `upgradeInfo` dictionary.

   D. Change the `Text` property for the **Progress** TextLabel. The TextLabel should display the current progress out of the maximum progress. For instance: **1/10**. To get the current progress, use the `current_progress` key in the `upgradeInfo` dictionary. To get the maximum progress, use the `max_progress` key in the `upgradeInfo` dictionary.

   E. Change the `Size` property of the **Bar** Frame so that it displays the correct progress length. If you want to take this to the next level, use the `:TweenSize()` function.

   Tip for 3E: To calculate the correct size, use the following code snippet:

   ```
   UDim2.new(upgradeInfo.current_progress / upgradeInfo.max_
   progress, 0, 1, 0)
   ```

4. In the `setup()` function, call the `updateButtons()` function once all the TextButtons have been generated.

5. Listen to the `.OnClientEvent` event on the `UpgradeDataUpdated` RemoteEvent. When this event gets called, start the `updateButtons()` function.

Now, we also update the TextButtons to display the most accurate information. To test whether it works, open the **Upgrading** GUI. If all the information is generated and updated correctly, test whether this is also the case when you try to upgrade. Make sure that all the information updates instantly. If it does not work, try to fix possible errors that show up in the **Developer Console** frame or the **Output** frame. Once again, this is the most complex GUI in the game. If you did not manage to implement this system, please take a look at the example answer, which can be found on the GitHub page for this chapter.

We have now programmed all the GUIs for the entire game. In the next section, we will take a look at the next steps you must take before releasing your game.

Updating your game

You have now finished your very own game. Congratulations! But, before you can release games, you must test them. How well you test your game can determine how many bugs end up in the final product. It is highly recommended that you play your game with a few friends and listen to their feedback. Once you have fixed all known bugs and implemented the feedback from your friends, you can release your game.

You might think your work is done now. However, this could not be further from the truth. The actual journey of your game starts now. Hopefully, many players will play and enjoy your game. At some point, these players will have finished their game. However, to prevent them from ever finishing your game, you must update your game with new content. Luckily, there are many things that you can include in your simulator.

Throughout the previous sections, we implemented many systems into our game, which we had previously learned about throughout the entire book. However, not everything we learned was used in this chapter but that does not mean that we cannot still implement it.

Here is a list of things that you could update your game with:

- A leaderboard of the richest players.
- A leaderboard for the most rebirths.
- Adding particles when collecting orbs.
- Different orb prices; currently, all orbs have a base value of 1. However, some orbs could be worth more.
- New regions for players to unlock.
- Daily rewards.
- Group rewards.
- Sounds when buttons are pressed.
- Sounds when orbs are collected.
- Sound when orbs are sold.
- Pets for an additional orb and sell multiplier.
- Badges.
- And much more.

Besides these features, there is still so much to explore in programming and the best part is that it's constantly evolving. Cool stuff is constantly added for you to explore and improve your games with.

Summary

Throughout this chapter, you learned how to make your very own simulator game. Together, we made a fully functioning game that uses data stores, server scripts, GUIs, developer products, and game passes based on a set of requirements.

Once we knew the requirements for our game, we started creating the data stores for our game. We saw how to analyze which keys we need to store in the data stores. In addition, we saw why it is a bad practice to store multipliers inside the data stores. Instead, we should save the amount of, for example, rebirths the players did. Then, we can convert the number of rebirths into a multiplier.

After implementing our data stores, we started creating the server scripts for our game. First, we analyzed what information should be displayed in the GUIs and which actions players can perform. Based on this, we created RemoteEvents and RemoteFunctions. These RemoteEvents and RemoteFunctions perform certain actions, such as converting orbs into money. While implementing these, we looked at server checks that we needed to implement to secure our game.

Because we implemented the RemoteEvents and RemoteFunctions before creating the GUIs, we could use these and directly display the correct information or perform the right actions. Furthermore, while creating these GUIs, we learned how to generate information that was displayed. This way, we have GUIs that automatically update to display the latest information without having to change anything for our GUIs.

Finally, we also looked at possible updates for our game. We have seen that we can still implement many cool features for our players to enjoy.

This wraps up the *Mastering Roblox Coding* book. In *Chapter 1*, *Getting Up To Speed with Roblox and Luau Basics*, we learned the first things to know about Roblox and Roblox Luau. Remember how we started with learning what data types are and how to do simple math operations with numbers? Look where you are now! We just finished our very first simulator game. You should be incredibly proud of yourself for achieving this. This proves that anything is possible if you invest enough time into it. Your future looks bright.

Roblox is constantly evolving and changing. It is important to stay up to date with what is going on. The following links are useful resources that every Roblox programmer uses:

- Stay up to date with the latest changes that are happening to Roblox by reading the **Announcements** channel on the **Developer Forum**:

  `https://devforum.roblox.com/`

- View the documentation and code examples for every function, event, and service on the documentation site:

  `https://create.roblox.com/docs`

- Hire a team to create other games on the Talent Hub:

  `https://talent.roblox.com/`

Index

Symbols

A

B

T

Packt.com

Subscribe to our online digital library for full access to over 7,000 books and videos, as well as industry leading tools to help you plan your personal development and advance your career. For more information, please visit our website.

Why subscribe?

- Spend less time learning and more time coding with practical eBooks and Videos from over 4,000 industry professionals

- Improve your learning with Skill Plans built especially for you

- Get a free eBook or video every month

- Fully searchable for easy access to vital information

- Copy and paste, print, and bookmark content

Did you know that Packt offers eBook versions of every book published, with PDF and ePub files available? You can upgrade to the eBook version at packt.com and as a print book customer, you are entitled to a discount on the eBook copy. Get in touch with us at customercare@packtpub.com for more details.

At www.packt.com, you can also read a collection of free technical articles, sign up for a range of free newsletters, and receive exclusive discounts and offers on Packt books and eBooks.

Other Books You May Enjoy

If you enjoyed this book, you may be interested in these other books by Packt:

Coding Roblox Games Made Easy - Second Edition

Zander Brumbaugh

ISBN: 978-1-80323-467-0

- Use Roblox Studio and other free resources
- Learn coding in Luau: basics, game systems, physics manipulation, etc
- Test, evaluate, and redesign to create bug-free and engaging games
- Use Roblox programming and rewards to make your first game
- Move from lobby to battleground, build avatars, locate weapons to fight

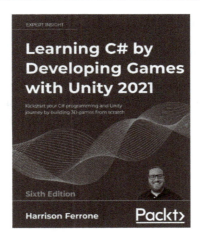

Learning C# by Developing Games with Unity 2021 - Sixth Edition

Harrison Ferrone

ISBN: 978-1-80181-394-5

- Follow simple steps and examples to create and implement C# scripts in Unity
- Develop a 3D mindset to build games that come to life
- Create basic game mechanics such as player controllers and shooting projectiles using C#
- Divide your code into pluggable building blocks using interfaces, abstract classes, and class extensions
- Become familiar with stacks, queues, exceptions, error handling, and other core C# concepts

Packt is searching for authors like you

If you're interested in becoming an author for Packt, please visit `authors.packtpub.com` and apply today. We have worked with thousands of developers and tech professionals, just like you, to help them share their insight with the global tech community. You can make a general application, apply for a specific hot topic that we are recruiting an author for, or submit your own idea.

Hi!

I am Mark Kiepe, author of *Mastering Roblox Coding*. I really hope you enjoyed reading this book and found it useful for building next-level Roblox games.

It would really help me (and other potential readers!) if you could leave a review on Amazon sharing your thoughts on *Mastering Roblox Coding*.

Go to the link below or scan the QR code to leave your review:

`https://packt.link/r/180181404X`

Your review will help me to understand what's worked well in this book, and what could be improved upon for future editions, so it really is appreciated.

Best Wishes,

Mark Kiepe

www.ingramcontent.com/pod-product-compliance
Lightning Source LLC
Chambersburg PA
CBHW081502050326
40690CB00015B/2891